BETWEEN RUIN AND RESTORATION

HISTORY OF THE URBAN ENVIRONMENT

Martin V. Melosi and Joel A. Tarr, Editors

BETWEEN RUIN AND RESTORATION

AN ENVIRONMENTAL HISTORY OF ISRAEL

Edited by Daniel E. Orenstein, Alon Tal, and Char Miller

UNIVERSITY OF PITTSBURGH PRESS

Published by the University of Pittsburgh Press, Pittsburgh, Pa., 15260

Copyright © 2013, University of Pittsburgh Press

All rights reserved

Manufactured in the United States of America

Printed on acid-free paper

10 9 8 7 6 5 4 3 2 1

Library of Congress Cataloging-in-Publication Data

Between ruin and restoration : an environmental history of Israel /
edited by Daniel E. Orenstein, Alon Tal, and Char Miller.

pages   cm — (History of the urban environment)

Includes bibliographical references and index.

ISBN 978-0-8229-6222-9 (pbk. : alk. paper)

1. Environmental policy—Israel—History. 2. Israel—Environmental conditions—
History. I. Orenstein, Daniel E. II. Tal, Alon, 1960– III. Miller, Char, 1951–

GE190.I75B48 2012

304.2095694—dc23   2012022367

Dedicated to Azariah Alon and Amotz Zahavi and the late Yosef Tamir: Among Israel's first environmental leaders, who saw that the road ahead could lead to ruin . . . or restoration.

CONTENTS

ACKNOWLEDGMENTS

We are deeply grateful to the authors of the chapters in this edited volume. In most cases, their scholarly contributions to Israel's environmental history are equally matched by their active participation and leadership in improving Israel's environment. We are honored to have them as colleagues and collaborators.

It is appropriate therefore that we dedicate this volume to three people who have also epitomized environmental activism on the one hand and environmental scholarship on the other. The first is the late former Knesset member Yosef Tamir (z"l), who was a pioneer of environmental legislation and a consistent advocate for Israel's environment throughout his long life, in and out of the Knesset. Azariah Alon and Amotz Zahavi, the founders of the Society for Protection of Nature in Israel, have probably done more than anyone on the planet to protect Israel's landscape and ecology. For sixty years they have been on the front lines fighting for, writing about, and often succeeding in saving Israel's unique natural world.

At the University of Pittsburgh Press we express our deep appreciation to Cynthia Miller, director of the press. She had originally contracted with the late Hal K. Rothman to edit a volume on Israel's environmental history; shortly after his untimely death, she spoke with Char Miller to relaunch the project and ever since has given it her steadfast support. Smoothing the way too were her assistant Kelley Johovic and former managing editor Deborah Meade.

No acknowledgment would complete without a thanks to our families. In particular, our children, Na'ama, Aviv, and Gil'ad; Mika, Hadas, and Zoe; and Benjamin and Rebecca who daily remind us of what sustainability is all about. This book is also for them.

INTRODUCTION

The December 2010 Mt. Carmel forest fire caught Israel off guard. The speed with which the flames moved, their ferocity and destructive force, was stunning: 44 people were killed and more than 17,000 had to be evacuated as the blaze swept into a nearby kibbutz and residential neighborhoods, destroying or damaging nearly 250 structures. The firestorm also damaged famed Hai-Bar Nature Preserve: some of its 600 hectares were among the 2,200 that were charred, constituting one-third of the forest cover along the Carmel range. The aftermath was stark, the *Jerusalem Post* observed: "Entire mountainsides that were once green are now black with the skeletons of burnt trees pointing into the sky" (Waldoks and Rabinovich 2010).

Nearly as unsettling was the firestorm of public opinion that erupted even before the inferno had been suppressed. Most commentators focused on the failure of Israel's firefighting operations and the resulting (and for some embarrassing) need to seek international help to extinguish the blaze; others blamed miniscule budgets and political factors for crippling firefighters' ability to respond quickly and effectively. No surprise, calls for the resignation of key cabinet officials followed suit. But largely absent from this anguished handwringing and contentious debate was an acknowledgment of the critical role of fire in the Mt. Carmel ecosystem. Although this particular conflagration was ignited by humans (though the culprits have never been conclusively identified) displaying gross negligence that led to a horrific loss of life, it is also true that these forests are fire adapted, a consequence of biology and history, of natural and anthropogenic sculpting across thousands of years (Naveh and Carmel 2003). That being so, these ecosystemic realities and historical forces must guide policy makers as they craft new fire-management practices in the aftermath of the tragic Mt. Carmel fire; if they do not, some of its key lessons will have been lost (Orenstein 2010).

Taking environmental history seriously is not simply a matter for policy wonks. This relatively new academic discipline can claim broader significance, a result of its multidisciplinary perspective: because it focuses on the reciprocal relationship between the natural environment and human development, and on how this ineluctable connection has changed over time, it offers unique insights into dynamic co-evolution of land and life. Fire, flood, and drought; grassland, forest, and soil; minerals, water, and animals—whether wild or domestic—are among those factors that have shaped, often definitively, the contours of human action. Put another way, environmental conditions influence the way human societies emerge—their economies, spatial organization, and carrying capacity depend in part on the sites in which they are located. Yet humans also have the capacity to manipulate the environmental conditions that confront them—agriculture, resource development, and lines of trade and transportation are but some of the ways that we have fundamentally changed the world around us.

This interplay, everywhere manifest in the Mt. Carmel fire, is yet another reason why it seems so imperative to study the environmental history of Israel. Although the nation is relatively young, its modern emergence has depended on a rich and conflicted past that has deeply influenced how contemporary Israelis live and imagine their connection to Eretz Israel. For more than a century, the associated zeal and visions of its Jewish settlers have complicated their struggle to reach an appropriate relationship with the natural world: To conquer or to respect? To exploit or to cherish? To pave or preserve? Israel moreover is home to people who have been informed by widely disparate sources, cultures, and ideologies. These include biblical narratives and cutting-edge science; Zionism and universalism, Judaism and Islam; ruralism and urbanization; socialism and capitalism; industrialism and deep ecology; altruism and greed. Such dialectics color the present environmental paradigms that jostle together in Israeli society and make the overall narrative all the more captivating, troubled, and complicated.

That said, there has been no sustained attempt to capture the environmental history of Israel, the dilemmas and difficulties that have shaped how its people, past and present, have tried to make their way in this oft-harsh land. Our goal for this volume has been to do exactly that: to offer a compendium that ranges from the biblical era to the twenty-first century, with a particular emphasis on the past 150 years or so, covering the geographic area of modern Israel.[1] For this ambitious task, we tapped a talented team of scholars whose chapters are designed to stand on their own. Among those contributing are emeritus and senior professors who have reflected on a lifetime of scholarly research. They have been joined by retired government policy makers who provide an inside perspective of how Israel's environmental regulations have evolved, as well as by younger scholars offering a fresh set of interpretative insights born of their differing life circumstances. Also contributing are activist professionals, here commenting on the challenges that face those seeking a more habitable, just, and sustainable landscape.

The chapters in this book are largely written by people who not only are qualified to write about Israel's environmental history but to a large extent have been involved in creating it. Rather than try to avoid such potential biases, we have embraced this familiarity, this subjectivity, as an advantage. Several of the chapters have been crafted to exploit their authors' personal experiences, supplementing objectivity with a human touch. These writers have synthesized their passion for the subject with scientific and historical data, which when combined with their learned reflections on policy conundrums, political debates, or public concerns, deepen our understanding of how complex it has been for Israel—and by extension for any country—to live more lightly on the land.

The book opens with two chapters covering the environmental conditions in Palestine under the Ottoman and the British colonial rulers, thereby establishing the terrain that greeted early Zionist immigrants to Israel at the beginning of the twentieth century. The next set of chapters surveys the rise of the Zionist movement to the present and are framed around individual resources and issues, from population, water, and open space to rangelands and biodiversity; from marine policy, desertification, and environmental politics to Israel's Arab community and environmental law. The final chapters address current environmental dilemmas and their deep historical roots, including examinations of the Israeli military's environmental impact, transboundary environmental issues, diplomatic implications of international environmental conferences, climate change, and national land-use planning. A final chapter reflects on some of the major challenges that are confronting the Israeli environmental community now and will continue to do so.

This broad coverage, illustrative of environmental history's multifaceted and interdisciplinary character, pushes beyond conventional and more narrowly scientific or sociological analyses to better explain the antecedents of Israel's environmental achievements and crises. And while it is true that the ideas that emerge from this collection to a great extent depend on the eye of the beholder, that perspective is also confounded by its contributors' conviction that no single vantage point can do justice to such a complicated set of histories. The implications of grazing in Palestine and Israel, for example, are interpreted quite differently in three separate chapters by Seligman, Kark and Levin, and Tal. Likewise, Tal and Yom-Tov provide differing reactions to the impact of forestry on Israel's ecosystems. Other instances of contrasting and complementary perspectives run throughout the volume: Schorr and Brachya on echoes of British policy in Israeli policy; Han and Orenstein and Silverman on the impact of Bedouin settlement in the Negev; Kerret and Adam on Mediterranean environmental conventions; and Schoenfeld, Michaels and Alpert, and Orenstein and Silverman who offer diverse interpretations of the historical sources and social, cultural, and intellectual significance of the modern Israeli environmental movement.

While environmental history as an academic discipline has had a profound impact on the historiographical analyses of European and North American studies, the same cannot be said for Israel; to date, its environmental history has received but modest attention. Part of the reason for this lacuna is that there is relatively little formal scholarly literature dedicated to the topic and few classes either at the undergraduate or graduate level. The only comprehensive coverage, by Tal (2002, 2006), poses a challenge and opportunity for this book's authors to set a new tone and focus for the writing of Israel's environmental history in the coming decades. We hope that by involving an eclectic group of writers whose interdisciplinary perspectives mirror the field's intellectual sweep, this anthology will contribute to introducing Israel's environmental history to a wider, even international audience. We recognize that its subject matter is so broad as to make any single text inherently incomplete, but we also believe that this book lays some of the groundwork for future interrogations of Israel's compelling and turbulent environmental history.

By almost any criterion, the State of Israel is not a normal country. The fact that much of its geography is familiar to the billions of people worldwide who know the Bible, or that it is deemed a "Holy Land" by four of the world's major religions,[2] conveys an unusual status. Over a century of ongoing political and territorial dispute is reflected in the disproportionate (and sometimes obsessive) news coverage that Israel receives. This long litany of religious, military, cultural, economic, and ecological encounters is packed into a landscape that encompasses a mere 22,000 square kilometers. Invariably, visitors are surprised at just how small and vulnerable the land of Israel is. Like longtime residents, they too are often amazed at just how far back one must go to comprehend the environmental pressures, historical factors, and social structures that have shaped—and have been shaped by—the landscape, its natural resources, and human communities. In Israel, the past matters—an argument this volume affirms anew by setting its tumultuous history into an evolving environmental narrative.

NOTES

1. The current edited volume deals primarily with Israel within the pre-1967 borders, unless ecological realities demanded a broader geographic context that includes those territories occupied in 1967.

2. To the oft-mentioned Islamic, Christian, and Jewish faiths, we add the Bahá'í faith; Israel is home to their international offices and most significant shrine (in Haifa) and tomb of the founder of the religion (in Acre). It is especially appropriate to mention the Bahá'í in an edited volume on Israeli environmental history, as their international center and shrine in Haifa, with its elaborate gardens, have become the signature landscape of the city.

REFERENCES

Naveh, Z., and Y. Carmel. 2003. "The Evolution of the Cultural Mediterranean Landscape in Israel as Affected by Fire, Grazing, and Human Activities." In *Evolutionary Theory and Processes: Modern Horizons. Papers in Honour of Eviatar Nevo*, edited by S. P. Wasser, 337–409. Amsterdam: Kluwer Academic Publishers.

Orenstein, D. 2010. "When Fire Is an Abnormal Event." *Ha'aretz.com*, December 12 http://www.haaretz.com/print-edition/opinion/when-fire-is-an-abnormal-event -1.329810.

Tal, A., 2002. *Pollution in a Promised Land: An Environmental History of Israel*. Berkeley: University of California Press.

———. 2006. *The Environment in Israel: Natural Resources, Crises, Campaigns and Policy from the Advent of Zionism until Twenty-First Century*. B'nei Brak, HaKibbutz: HaMeuhad Press. In Hebrew.

Waldoks, E. Z., and A. Rabinovich. 2010. "Carmel and Its People Prepare to Rise from the Ashes." *Jerusalem Post*, December 12. http://www.jpost.com/Features/InThe spotlight/Article.aspx?ID=198830&R=R1.

CHAPTER ONE

THE ENVIRONMENT IN PALESTINE IN THE LATE OTTOMAN PERIOD, 1798–1918

Ruth Kark and Noam Levin

THIS CHAPTER CONSIDERS stages in the process of environmental and spatial change in the landscape of Palestine in the nineteenth century and the beginning of the twentieth century and the determinants and catalysts. During this period, which began with Napoleon's invasion of Egypt, Palestine, and the Levant, Palestine was transformed from a neglected backwater of the Ottoman Empire to a focal point of world attention. Consideration is given to changes in the natural landscape of forests, wetlands, and other habitats, resulting from spatial change, including changes in land use, that were a consequence of political and legal reforms as well as immigration to Palestine. These processes influenced the nomadic and the settled populations, land ownership patterns, and agricultural practices.

It is surprising that Palestine's unique environmental history during this period has received only modest attention. Most studies have focused on its political-administrative and social history, ignoring the environmental aspects and processes of landscape change during the nineteenth century. Tal's (2006) book on the environmental history of Israel focused on the way it was shaped by the Zionist movement, especially since World War I. Reifenberg (1950) and Margalit (1955) reviewed Palestine's environmental history during the nineteenth century. This history was summarized also in maps in the *Atlas of Israel* (first edition [1955–1961] in Hebrew; 1970 edition in English). Here we consider these earlier contributions in light of the knowledge that has since accumulated. We make use of historical maps to further reconstruct aspects of the landscape as it was in the nineteenth century applying GIS (geographic information system).

GEOGRAPHICAL AND HISTORICAL BACKGROUND

One must keep in mind the basic physical structure of the country, which is divided into four longitudinal subregions paralleling the Mediterranean Sea (fig. 1.1), including:

- the coastal plains and the inner valleys (e.g., Jezreel Valley);
- the hilly region in the Negev to the south, Judea and Samaria in the center, and the Galilee in the north, the latter rising to an average height of 700 meters, and the highest peaks reaching 1,000–1,200 meters;
- the Jordan Valley (including the Dead Sea and Sea of Galilee) that is part of the Great Rift Valley;
- and the hills of Transjordan (Karmon 1971).

The years 1798–1799 will be our starting point. It was then that Napoleon's army invaded Egypt and Palestine, beginning a new era in the history of the Holy Land. From a forsaken province, it now became a focal point of contest between the European powers, Christian churches, and later Zionist efforts to establish a homeland for the Jews (Kark and Glass 1999).

From a political and administrative perspective, the history of Palestine in the last century of Ottoman rule (1798–1918) can be divided into four subperiods:

1. The period of the pashas (local strongmen, 1799–1831), in effect a continuation of the eighteenth century and the forms of government then prevailing.

2. The conquest of Syria and Palestine by the Egyptian ruler Muhammed 'Ali by means of his son, Ibrahim Pasha (1831–1840). In many respects this was a turning point, for despite the brevity of this period, the changes in government and other spheres were many. A catastrophic event during this subperiod was the lethal earthquake of 1837 that caused thousands of fatalities in Safed and Tiberias, the main centers of the Jewish population, and strongly influenced change of the Jewish center of gravity, from the Galilee to Jerusalem.

3. The period of reforms (1841–1876), when the Ottomans regained control of the region and, influenced by the Western nations, attempted to institute new patterns of government in the spheres of modernization of administration, improved municipal frameworks, legislation including

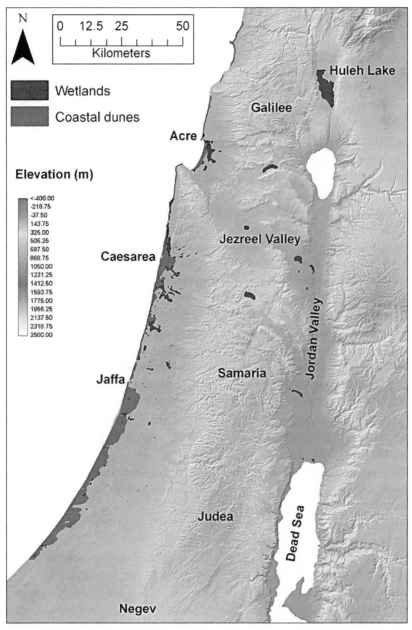

FIGURE 1.1. Topography of Palestine, overlaid by the nineteenth-century extent of coastal dunes and wetlands. Based on Palestine Exploration Fund (PEF) and British Mandate maps.

the Ottoman Land Laws of 1858 and 1867, educational reforms, and upgrading of the military.

4. The end of the Ottoman period (1877–1917). During the first part of this period (up to 1908), the region was under the centralized rule of Sultan Abdul Hamid II; the latter part was marked by the influence of the "Young Turks," from their revolution of 1908 until the British conquest in 1917–1918.

During the nineteenth century, the estimated total population of Palestine increased exponentially, from about 250,000 in 1800 to 450,000 in 1875 and 800,000 in 1914 (Kark 1984a; Glass and Kark 2007; fig. 1.2). From the point of view of settlement, the generalized process of spatial change in nineteenth-century Palestine can be divided into three subperiods: 1800–1830, 1831–1881, and 1882–1914 (Kark 1984a).

This classification into three periods is significant also in reference to the improved status and security of Jews, Christians, and foreign subjects. Foreigners and local minorities were granted greater freedoms between 1831 and 1881. In 1858 and more so post-1867, foreign nationals, predominantly Jews, were given rights under certain legal conditions to own land throughout the Ottoman Empire. However, particularly after 1897, the year in which the Zionist movement was formally established, laws and edicts were issued restricting Jewish immigration and land purchase in Palestine (Glass and Kark 2007).

The same periodization is also relevant when examining the available historical sources of scientific information for reconstructing the environmental history of nineteenth-century Palestine. Scientific exploration and the systematic mapping of Palestine by Westerners began in earnest with Napoleon's invasion. This also marks the starting point of informative sources with which one can reconstruct the environmental history of Palestine. In spite of the region's biblical importance, its natural characteristics were, prior to Napoleon's invasion, a terra incognita for the West.

This rediscovery of Palestine included surveys and mapping done by individuals such as Carel William Meredith Van de Velde (1854), Victor Guérin (1869, 1874, 1880), and Alois Musil (1907), as well as by organizations such as the Palestine Exploration Fund (PEF, founded in 1865; Moscrop 2000), and even by the Ottomans themselves (Kark 2004). Whereas maps of Palestine prior to the nineteenth century were mostly copies of earlier maps, following Napoleon's invasion explorers and surveyors produced new maps based on contemporary measurements, describing the topography and land cover of Palestine. These maps, and especially the celebrated 1:63,360 map of the PEF of western Palestine (1880) and its accompanying memoirs, form an important and reliable source for investigating the history of the landscape (Levin 2006; Levin, Elron, and Gasith 2009; Levin, Kark, and Galilee, 2010).

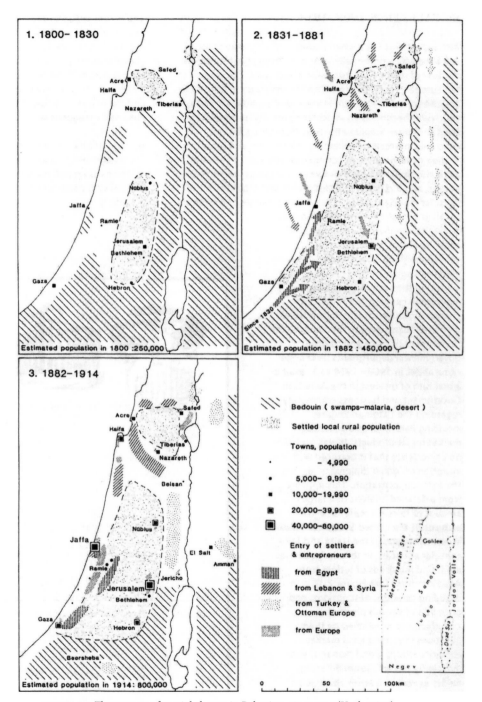

FIGURE 1.2. The process of spatial change in Palestine, 1800–1914 (Kark 1984a).

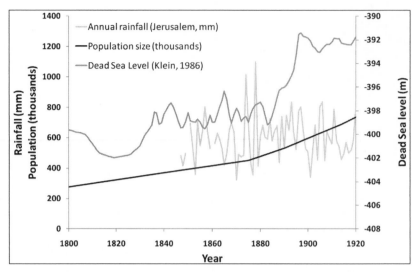

FIGURE 1.3. Annual rainfall in Jerusalem, population size in Palestine, and Dead Sea level (Klein 1986).

In addition, the nineteenth century also saw the beginning of scientific measurements of several variables, for example, rainfall (as of 1845, in Jerusalem; fig. 1.3). Based on the rainfall records and the reconstructed level of the Dead Sea, we can conclude that the climate during the nineteenth century was not significantly different from that of the twentieth century, at least with regard to rainfall.

Historical maps and explorers' memoirs were synthesized by the founding members of the Hebrew University of Jerusalem's Department of Geography—Hanah Margalit and Asher Schick. This was done in two maps (1:750,000), covering the entire western Palestine, prepared for the *Atlas of Israel* in 1955, and presenting the natural and cultural landscape of Palestine in the nineteenth century (*Atlas of Israel* 1955–1961, VIII/1; fig. 1.4). Schick based his map on the PEF's comprehensive Survey of Western Palestine maps and the seven-volume *Memoirs* (Conder and Kitchener 1883) to reconstruct the natural landscape of Palestine in the 1870s. From Schick we can learn about the distribution of forests and Mediterranean maquis, orchards, other vegetation, sands, swamps, wells, and main roads (*Atlas of Israel* 1955–1961, VIII/1; fig. 1.5).

When reconstructing past landscapes from historical maps, it must be remembered that a map cannot be thought of as an objective mirror of the land it portrays; rather, it is a text that must be read critically, through the lens of the people who created it, their motivations, the available technology, the time they had to conduct the mapping, and the scale on which the map was

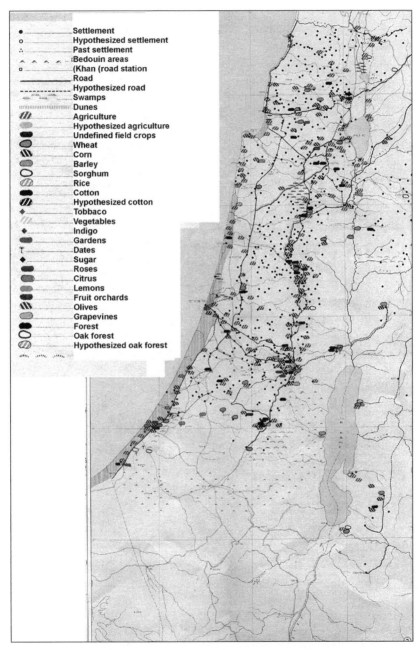

Settlement
Hypothesized settlement
Past settlement
Bedouin areas
(Khan (road station
Road
Hypothesized road
Swamps
Dunes
Agriculture
Hypothesized agriculture
Undefined field crops
Wheat
Corn
Barley
Sorghum
Rice
Cotton
Hypothesized cotton
Tobbaco
Vegetables
Indigo
Gardens
Dates
Sugar
Roses
Citrus
Lemons
Fruit orchards
Olives
Grapevines
Forest
Oak forest
Hypothesized oak forest

FIGURE 1.4. The cultural landscape of Palestine in the beginning of the nineteenth century based on explorers' descriptions (Margalit 1955). Courtesy of the Survey of Israel (*Atlas of Israel* 1956).

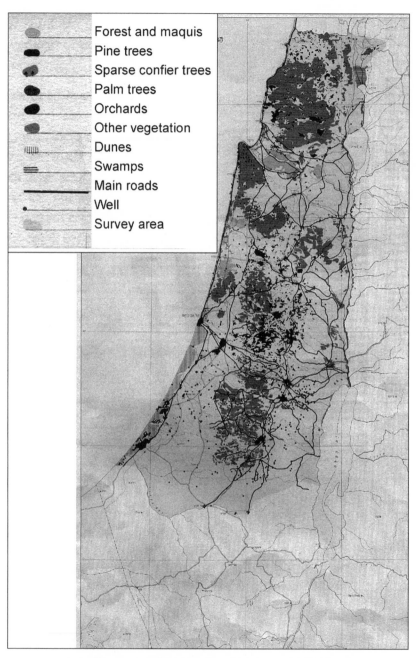

Forest and maquis
Pine trees
Sparse confier trees
Palm trees
Orchards
Other vegetation
Dunes
Swamps
Main roads
Well
Survey area

FIGURE 1.5. The landscape of Palestine in the 1870s, based on the PEF survey of western Palestine (Schick 1956). Courtesy of the Survey of Israel.

drawn. Nonetheless, in previous studies we have demonstrated that the past landscape can indeed be reconstructed from multiple historical maps, taking into account the differences between the various historical sources, using current state-of-the-art technologies (Levin 2006; Levin et al. 2009; Levin et al. 2010). During World War I, at the end of the Ottoman control of Palestine, aerial photographs taken by both the Germans and the British covered many regions of Palestine, objectively documenting the land cover and land use (Kedar 1999).

THE NATURAL LANDSCAPE

The end of the Ottoman rule over Palestine is considered to represent the end of an era, which had begun a few centuries after the Muslim occupation of Palestine in the seventh century, with ups and downs until the mid-nineteenth century. During most of this time there was a decline in the population size until the beginning of the nineteenth century.

Whatever the reasons for the decline of the Ottoman Empire as a whole may have been—once the central power had weakened, the existence of powerful nomadic tribes became the dominant factor in determining the stability of rural settlement areas. The raids could not be prevented and the villages near the frontier suffered first and foremost, until they were abandoned one after the other. Amiran (1953, 69) was right in giving the Bedouin raids as the main reason for the low settlement density in nineteenth-century Palestine, especially in the plains. This statement is confirmed by Imperial firmans of the sixteenth and early seventeenth century (Heyd 1960, 90–116) and proved by much new evidence given by Cohen (1973, 158–72; quoted in Hütteroth and Abdulfattah 1977). Changes in land use are thought to have led to land degradation and soil erosion through three main processes (Reifenberg 1950; Thirgood 1981):

- cutting down forests for building, heating and fuel, including use in lime kilns;
- overgrazing, especially by goats (as well as by sheep and camels), which prevented saplings from becoming established;
- and depopulation of once cultivated areas, leading to the neglect of agricultural terraces.

These processes, which were common throughout most of the Muslim rule over Palestine, culminated during the nineteenth century, with explorers and writers such as Mark Twain describing the barren landscape devoid of trees, in contrast with a "noble" past (Kark 1984a; Twain 1876). These trends in land usage, which are still prevalent in the countries surrounding Israel, are evident from satellite imagery, where much less vegetation cover is seen in Israel's neighbors, due to cutting, burning, trampling, and overgrazing (Tsoar and Karnieli 1996).

When the environmental history of Palestine was explored during the nineteenth century, it was seen as an example of the deterioration of lands in the Mediterranean region, from their peak condition during the Roman Empire to the poor situation under Ottoman rule (Marsh 1864). The question to be answered was whether this shift in the fertility of the land was due to climate change, or due to misuse of the land by its inhabitants. Marsh attributed the degradation to human misuse (369): "So long as the cisterns were in good order, and the terraces kept up, the fertility of Palestine was unsurpassed, but when misgovernment and foreign and intestine war occasioned the neglect or destruction of these works—traces of which still meet the traveler's eye at every step—when the reservoirs were broken and the terrace walls had fallen down, there was no longer water for irrigation in summer, the rains of winter soon washed away most of the thin layer of earth upon the rocks, and Palestine was reduced almost to the condition of a desert." An opposing view was voiced by Ellsworth Huntington in his book *Palestine and Its Transformation* (1911). He developed a geographic deterministic view (based on his own impressions and not on any hard evidence) that the degradation of Palestine since Roman times was due to climate and not due to changes in human land use. This debate continues to this day (Reifenberg 1950; Issar 2003; Issar and Zohar 2007).

Sometime after the Muslim occupation of Palestine in the first half of the seventh century, coastal dunes began to form. The decline of the coastal towns and settlements paved the way for Bedouins to spread into the coastal plain and valleys, with their livestock and customary land uses, a process similar to those taking place in the Sahara in North Africa. This change in land use along the coast was due not only to neglect and deterioration, but also to intentional ruin of the coastal towns and settlements of Palestine by the post-Crusade Mamluks from Egypt who ruled Palestine (1250–1517). The Mamluks intended to prevent the Christian West from cementing close ties with the Holy Land (Kark 1990b). It is possible that the encroachment of coastal dunes some 700–800 years ago was associated with this process, in which vegetation along the coast was removed, allowing sand grains to be carried inland by the wind. As the dunes migrated inland, they eventually buried villages, towns, and agricultural areas. By the end of the nineteenth century, coastal dunes were prevalent all along the coastal plain of Palestine covering about 360 square kilometers, except where there were coastal cliffs that prevented sand drift by the wind from the beach (Levin 2006).

The largest coastal dune fields were inland from Caesarea and south of Jaffa, where they extended up to five kilometers inland. The coastal dunes were utilized by the local population of Arab Fellaheen for *Mawassi* agriculture ("Mawassi" in Arabic means suction, referring to water that has been sucked out to the surface). In the Mawassi agricultural system the upper level of coastal underground water was used for growing grapes, palm trees, and other crops in the inter-dune areas, with the farmer actively protecting his crops from the encroaching sand dunes (Tsoar and Zohar 1985; see the coastal dunes in fig. 1.1).

In addition, Arabs and Bedouin living in the coastal plain destroyed the vegetation by cutting it and grazing their flocks on its remains, allowing the dunes to continue migrating inland (Levin and Ben-Dor 2004). This is evident because wind power in Palestine is quite low, and without human interference, the coastal dunes would have stabilized (Tsoar 2005). Based on an analysis of historical maps, Levin (2006) showed that the coastal dune fields advanced inland at a rate of between 4–6 meters a year between the 1870s–1930s. The PEF surveyors estimated that the progression was 1 yard per year around Gaza (Conder and Kitchener 1883). The burial of agricultural land under coastal dunes would be the catalyst for attempts at dune stabilization efforts initiated by the British after they acquired the Mandate for ruling Palestine in the wake of World War I.

The expansion of coastal dunes, however, had another important impact on the coastal landscape. It facilitated the formation of swamps and other temporary water bodies, as the sand dunes blocked the natural flow of some of the streams and rivers to the sea. On the eve of World War I (1914), wetlands and seasonal winter ponds were common in most of the plains and valleys of Palestine. These wetlands (whether seasonal or permanent) formed during the past millennia as part of land degradation processes in general and, more specifically, due to increased soil erosion and the formation of the coastal dunes, which blocked natural drainage patterns (Reifenberg 1950).

The prevalence of swamps and consequently malaria along the coastal plain and valleys in Palestine made it unfavorable for settlement during most of the Ottoman period, and the few lone, dispersed settlements in these areas were subject to recurrent raids by Bedouins. In 1915 Arthur Ruppin, Head of the Zionist Palestine Office in Palestine, summed up the health situation as follows: "In general the land may be considered healthy. The only diseases which are constant and epidemic in certain sections are malaria and trachoma. Malaria is prevalent in (a) the coastal zone, where swamps are formed by the rain water which is dammed up by sand dunes and rocks, (b) valleys with an impervious sub-stratum and imperfect drainage, (c) the banks of shallow streams, and (d) mountain districts where rain water is preserved in badly made cisterns for use in summer. Both these diseases could be [and subsequently were] successfully combated" (Ruppin 1918).

Another health indicator, the crude death rate, was calculated by Schmeltz, a demographer, for Palestine for the middle of the nineteenth century at the very high figure of 80 per 1,000 in the stable portion of the population of Palestine, with a birthrate of 40 per 1,000 resulting in a net population decrease. Overall mortality declined steeply to 17–19 per 1,000 at the beginning of the British Mandate period (1923–1925), compared with approximately 13 per 1,000 in the United States at that time. Following World War I the situation in Palestine improved with the introduction of better health services by the Mandatory authorities and NGOs and improved economic conditions. Among Muslims, infant mortality declined from 194 per 1,000 in 1928–1930 to 135 per 1,000 in 1940–1943 (Schmelz 1975; Kark and Glass 1999). These figures were certainly considerably higher in the nineteenth century.

A detailed study of the nineteenth-century extent of swamps and winter ponds in the central coastal plain of Palestine (between Hadera in the north and Ashkelon in the south) based on historical maps and aerial photographs estimated that there were between five hundred to eight hundred wetlands (greater than 0.1 hectares), covering an area of about 27 square kilometers in rainy winters, mostly north of Jaffa. Additional concentrations of swamps were in the northern coastal plain, the valleys of Jezreel, Bet She'an, Sanur, Netofa, and of course, the Huleh Valley (Karmon in *Atlas* 1970, VIII/2; see the wetlands in fig. 1.1).

Drainage of some of these swamps began already in the late nineteenth century by the Jewish immigrants as part of the Zionist ethos. An early example was drainage of the swamps of the Jewish settlement of Hadera that was established in 1891 in the Sharon, south of Caesarea (Avneri 1984; Kark 1984b). The 30,000-dunam area, purchased from the Christian Arab entrepreneur Salim Khouri, contained three large swamps—Birket Atta, Basat (swamp) el-Fukra, and Basat el-Cherkes—which were infested with malaria-transmitting anopheles mosquitoes. After the establishment of Hadera many of the settlers suffered from malaria with some deaths (Avneri 1984). Attempts to drain the swamps commenced in 1893 with the digging of an ineffective canal to the sea, and in 1896 with the planting of eucalyptus trees, in the false belief that their high water consumption would help in drying the swamps. This area has remained one of the largest eucalyptus forests in Israel up to the present.

The largest wetland in Palestine was in the Huleh basin north of the Huleh Lake in the Rift Valley. It was also subject to severe winter flooding, was one of the regions most plagued by malaria, and which suffered from Bedouin raids. A concession over the Huleh Lake lands in northern Israel, was granted by the Ottoman government in 1911 to Michel Sursuk and Muhammad Omar Beihum, Arab absentee landlords of Beirut, so that they could drain its swamps and develop the valley lands. The area of the Huleh concession was, accord-

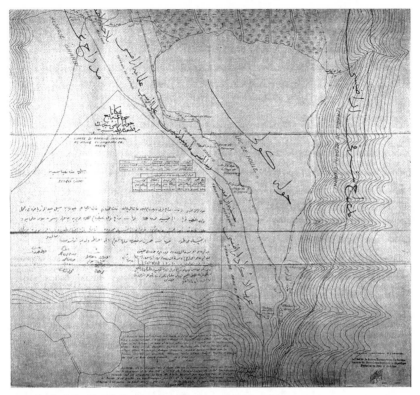

FIGURE 1.6. Lake Huleh Concession (Gavish and Kark 1993).

ing to Mandatory statistics, 57,000 dunams (1 dunam = 1,000 square meters; 1 acre = 4.047 dunams), of which 14,000–17,000 dunams were the lake itself, 21,000–31,000 dunams were swamp area, and 12,000–18,500 dunams were arable lands (Karmon 1956a). The Huleh Lake Concession Map, an authentic copy of one of the maps of Sultan Abdul Hamid II's private lands, shows the extent of the Huleh wetlands toward the end of the nineteenth century (fig. 1.6). Despite the malaria, we find in the swamp and its margins, even earlier than the nineteenth century, groups of seminomads, the Ghawarina, who raised jamus (water buffalo), and during the nineteenth century in the fringes of the swamp also the Arab Zubeid tribe and immigrants from Egypt, as well as a few seasonal settlements (Karmon 1956b). We also have information about Jews from Safed who cultivated sections of the Huleh Valley since the 1830s and Jews who settled in Rosh Pinna (1878) and in Shoshanat HaYarden and Yesud HaMaalah (1883) and cultivated lands in the Huleh Valley (Grossman 2004).

After World War I, the Huleh Valley was the subject of territorial negotiations between the British and French mandatory governments of Palestine and Lebanon, respectively. According to an agreement reached in 1923 regarding the demarcation of the border of the valley, which was included within the territory of Palestine, the concession to the Huleh lands that was transferred to the British Mandate Government of Palestine remained (from February 1924) in the hands of Arab landholders in Beirut, whose rights were guaranteed by the British High Commissioner. The original map, which had been drawn in April 1889, was copied by the French Topographic Service of Syria and Lebanon in 1922—one year prior to demarcation of the boundary—at the request of the Government of Palestine (Huleh Land Concession files 1925; Gavish and Kark 1993). In October 1934, Yehoshua Hankin purchased from Arab entrepreneurs the option for the Huleh Land Concession in the name of the Zionist PLDC (Palestine Land Development Company). The PLDC was obligated by the Mandatory authorities to transfer 16,000 dunams of the land after reclamation to the local Arab population. Due to the PLDC's economic problems, the Arab revolt of 1936–1939, and World War II, the drainage plan never materialized. Not until 1951–1958, after the concession was transferred to the Jewish National Fund (JNF), was the large-scale drainage of the Huleh Valley swamps finally completed by the JNF. This celebrated project, which became part of national ethos, was later recognized as a major ecological failure that is recently being redressed. The environmental and ecological value of the remaining wetlands in Israel is now recognized (Levin et al., 2009), and conservation efforts are being made to declare additional wetlands as nature reserves; and in some cases, wetlands have been rehabilitated (Rothschild and Perlman 2010).

THE CULTURAL LANDSCAPE

Hanah Margalit (1955) reconstructed the cultural landscape of Palestine at the beginning of the nineteenth century. Her excellent map was based on descriptions in the travel literature, the limitations of which she was aware. From it we can learn about the natural, agricultural, and built landscapes, the spatial distribution of forests, swamps and sand dunes, as well as settlements and nomads (Bedouins), roads and caravansaries (khans). Margalit also added to her map details about the distribution of agricultural areas and the cultivation of different crops such as grains, maize, cotton, tobacco, orchards and orange groves, forests, and more (*Atlas of Israel* 1955–1961, VIII/1; see fig. 1.4).

Margalit deduced from her sources that at the beginning of the nineteenth century, most of the settled area of Palestine was sited in the mountains. There were very few settlements in the coastal area, and almost none in the valleys. As previously stated, the main reasons for this were the swamps and coastal dunes, the political situation, and dangers due to the absence of security. In addition, the historical Via Maris, the great international highway along the coastal plain, was also the route over which large armies marched between Egypt and the Levant, another factor historically favoring settlement in the mountains (Karmon 1956b).

Kark discussed the stages in the process of spatial change of settlement distribution in Palestine in the nineteenth century and the beginning of the twentieth century along with its determinants and catalysts (Kark 1984a). The generalized process of spatial change of population and settlement in nineteenth-century Palestine can be divided into three subperiods as illustrated in figure 1.2. During the first three decades of the nineteenth century the situation in Palestine was characterized by a process of decline and stagnation, a stage which had affected the entire Ottoman Empire since the seventeenth century. The total population of the country did not exceed 250,000.

The settled rural, predominantly Arab, population was mainly confined to the mountainous areas of Judea and Samaria and the Galilee and was too small to cultivate all the available arable land. Bedouin tribes controlled most of the plains, valleys, and arid areas, including the coastal plain, the Jordan Valley, and the Negev in the south. Thus, only a fraction of the country was being utilized for agriculture (Finn 1878). The towns of Palestine at the beginning of the nineteenth century are best defined as large villages, each built on a small area and possessing a limited economic base and small populations of up to ten thousand (Kark 1984a).

The Ottoman government and its officials in Palestine were not strong enough to impose security and order in the mountainous rural areas and margins of the desert to the east and south. The rural areas were ruled de facto by independent local chieftains, fighting each other for supremacy, and the desert margins were controlled by Bedouin tribes. Incessant internal wars between the local chiefs and raids by the nomadic tribes damaged the economy, sometimes causing the destruction or total desertion of villages and even entire areas (Owen 1981). Some improvement in security and expansion of agriculture by the government took place during the Egyptian conquest (1831–1841) (Hoffman 1963).

The overall situation led to a large, fluid inventory of empty lands. There were great difficulties in land registration, which in turn prevented the obtaining of secure titles. It was possible at the time to settle in the unpopulated areas (which were nominally state lands) and cultivate them, without securing title or formal ownership. This expansion of settled areas began to take place only in the mid-nineteenth century (Granott, in Kark 1984a).

In the second subperiod (1840–1881), new patterns were beginning to emerge (see fig. 1.2, section 2). Their main characteristics were:

1. Expansion of the local rural population from the small core of mountainous areas to peripheral areas where settlement had not been possible
   earlier.

2. Penetration of settlers and entrepreneurs from outside Palestine to
   peripheral regions, areas close to the towns and to the towns themselves
   (Karpat 1974). This group included Muslims and native Christians from
   Syria and Lebanon, Egypt, North Africa, non-Arab Muslims from
   Turkey and other parts of the Ottoman Empire (comprising primarily
   Bosnians, Circassians and agents of the Sultan), representatives of
   Christian churches and orders, and private Christians and Jews who
   came independently mostly from Europe (although some also arrived
   from North America).

3. The partial retreat of the Bedouins to the east and south, which
   paralleled the aforementioned processes of settlement and which was
   connected with the changes in the Ottoman regime that began in the
   mid-nineteenth century (Finn 1878).

James Finn, the British consul in Jerusalem, provides a contemporary
description in 1851 of the state of the country, which indicates the progress
taking place in Palestine. He speaks of "the extension of agriculture . . . the
rebuilding of villages from utter heaps of desolation and the improvement of
others which have not ceased to be inhabited." He also noticed "the sudden
rise of the little town of Chiffa (Haifa) is very remarkable" (Finn 1851).

Other towns, especially Jerusalem and Jaffa, were also beginning to grow
at this time (Kark 1990a, 1990b). However, the situation of settlements in
southern Palestine remained unstable, as in the following example, which
relates to the Arab village of Edd-Dhahariyeh (the last village south of Hebron before the desert) that was given by Kitchener (1878, 11–12) and Conder
and Kitchener (1883; vol 3, sheet XIX under "orography," 233), respectively: "I
found out here that the next village I was going to, Dhoheriyeh, was entirely
deserted. Owing to the bad year, the inhabitants were not able to pay taxes,
and found it better to desert their homes." "This village," he continued, "contained some 300–400 persons in 1874; but in 1877 it was deserted, in consequence of the encroachment of the Arabs [i.e., Bedouin] into the country of
the fellahin." Consequently, the Arab villages south of Hebron were considerably larger than other villages, so as to offer further protection against Bedouin raids (Amiran 1953).

The end of the nineteenth century and the beginning of the twentieth century are characterized by a marked increase in the development of the country (see fig. 1.2, section 3). The population grew and the settled rural area expanded together with a major increase in the agricultural output. The rural

population descended in part from the hilly areas, and began to settle in the plains, valleys, and on the fringe of the desert. It became a common practice to establish new villages on old ruins (Grossman 1982; 2004). This boundary between the settled land and the wilderness inhabited by nomads is clearly seen in the maps produced by the German cartographer Hans Fischer, where he depicted the "current limit of permanent settlement" (Jetzige Grenze seBhaften Wohnens). Comparing Fischer's maps from 1890 and 1911, the growth of the settled land during this period is mainly seen in Transjordan and Syria; note especially the foundation of various permanent settlements beyond the settled land areas in Palestine, marked by small circles (e.g., Beer-Sheva; fig. 1.7) (Fischer and Guthe 1890, 1911).

After publication of the Ottoman Land Law of 1858, urban entrepreneurs (absentee landlords known as *effendis*) originating from Palestine, Syria, Lebanon, and other adjacent areas, concentrated huge tracts of lands in their hands and established agricultural estates (Kark, forthcoming). Those holdings sometimes amounted to hundreds of thousands of dunams. An outstanding example of this type of landlord is the Sursuk family, Greek Orthodox Lebanese from Beirut, who bought about 250,000 dunams in Palestine. By the end of the Ottoman period, 144 large landowners owned 3.1 million dunams (3,100 square kilometers). While their main motive was economic, the effendis also settled tenants and established new villages on their land and sometimes tried to reclaim, develop, and irrigate the land (Fawaz 1991; Avneri 1984).

This concentration of previously unsettled land in the hands of effendis made possible the purchase and settlement of part of this land by German Templers and Jewish immigrants from Europe in later years. As a consequence of the abundance of coastal dunes and swamps along the coastal plains and of wetlands in many of the inland valleys, these areas were more easily sold to German and Jewish immigrants. This later drove the N-shape settlement pattern of the Jews in Palestine until the late 1940s (Reichman 1979).

The pioneer foreign settlers in the 1850s and 1860s were American settlers from Philadelphia and Maine who, in spite of their short-lived existence, introduced modern farming methods: machines, tools, seeds, and animals, including the first threshing and harvesting combine (Kark 1995). They were followed from the late 1860s by the pietistic German Templers, who came from Germany, Russia, and the United States, and established six colonies between 1868 and 1917, when they numbered around 2,000 people. They instituted rational intensive farming, using irrigation and fertilizers (unknown to Arab Fellaheen), and regular crop rotation. They imported from Europe and America modern agricultural tools and machinery, such as steam-driven engines, for drill pumps and harvesters (Kark and Thalmann 2003).

The Jewish settlement effort succeeded despite Ottoman attempts begin-

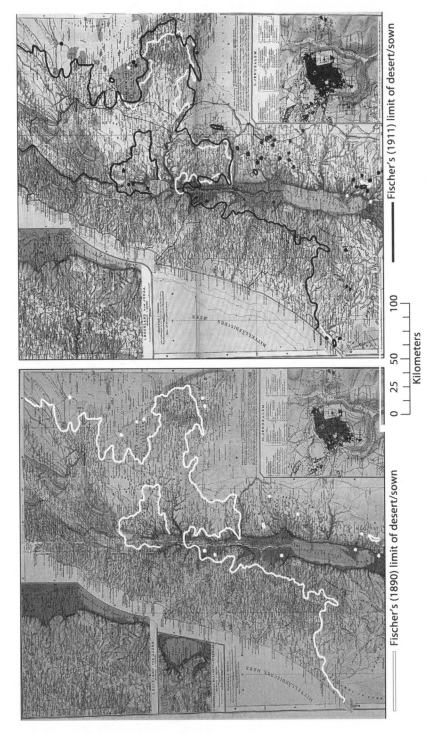

FIGURE 1.7. The boundary between the sown and the wilderness. Based on Fischer's maps from 1890 (*left*) and 1911 (*right*).

Fischer's (1890) limit of desert/sown

Fischer's (1911) limit of desert/sown

Kilometers

0   25   50   100

ning in 1882 to thwart the process. The regime issued regulations to prevent Jewish immigration and land purchase in Palestine, because the Ottomans feared the establishment of another national body in the empire following the loss of large territories in Greece and the Balkans (Oke 1982). Besides the Jews and Christians, other small ethnic groups settled in Palestine at the end of last century, such as the Bahá'ís, who had fled from Persia and settled in the area of Haifa and Acre and the Jordan Valley (Vilnay 1959).

This increase of immigration and settlement led to environmental, spatial, and physical change such as further cutting of forests, wetland drainage, and changes in settlement patterns including the descent of Arab villagers from the mountains to the piedmont and coastal areas and the development by Christians and Jews of modern rational agriculture (Kark 1995).

The Ottoman government and in particular Sultan Abdul Hamid II, who ruled between 1876 and 1908, were involved in an effort to restore large, deserted tracts of land to state control. The sultan demonstrated his intention to develop the state's land by building roads and other public works, founding new towns within this territory (such as Beisan and Beer-Sheva in 1900), and by fighting the Bedouin tribes or trying to settle them (Kark and Frantzman 2010). To generate income, part of the state land was sold to effendis, officials, or foreign settlers. The sultan privately purchased extensive tracts of land in different parts of the empire (northern Syria and Iraq and other regions), and in Palestine he bought over 800,000 metric dunams, making up approximately 3 percent of the total land area of the country.

The sultan initiated the establishment of new villages on his lands, as well as soil reclamation and irrigation projects. A good example of his intention to improve the soil, dry the swamps, and irrigate the land are the development plans in the Palestine section of the Rift Valley, from the Huleh (1894) and Beisan Valleys in the north to the *jiftlik* (private lands bequeathed to the sultan) area east of Nablus and surroundings of Jericho further south. In the latter, the sultan built an aqueduct above Wādī Qelt to bring water to his land near Jericho (Fischel and Kark 2008).

Compared to the rural areas, the towns developed at a faster pace; the urban population increased from an estimated 18 percent of the total in 1800 to 27 percent in 1882, rising to 38 percent in 1907. This population growth correlated with the expansion of the built-up area and the development of the urban economy (Kark 1977).

FORESTS AND AFFORESTATION

Human population increase and the development of agricultural and built-up areas usually resulted in the loss of forest cover. Vast forest areas once covered the Middle East, the majority of which disappeared as a result of damage by humans and animals (Zohary 1944). Lebanon, Jordan, and Iraq are good examples of the disappearance of forests due to human activity. A similar situation prevailed in Palestine until the beginning of the modern era. The main reasons for the destruction of forests in Palestine, as mentioned earlier, were Bedouin invasions and uncontrolled grazing, anthropogenic fires, and the cutting of trees for charcoal, timber, and lime kilns (Reifenberg 1950; Liphschitz and Biger 2004; Paz 2008). "The destruction of Syrian [including Lebanese and Palestinian] forests has been going on steadily, especially in the coastal regions, the vicinity of cities, and wherever good roads or railways permit the transportation of lumber . . . but the worst enemy of forests are the herds of sheep and goats" (Ruppin 1918).

Consequently, the region went through a degradation process that in marginal areas contributed to desertification. Walter Clay Lowdermilk, an expert sent by the U.S. Department of Agriculture, documented massive soil erosion during his visit to Palestine in 1939: "During our stay in Palestine, the elements also co-operated in our work. A fine demonstration of the 'latter rains' let us see how erosion had been carrying away the soils as a result of the neglect and breakdown of terraced agriculture. . . . Here before our eyes the remarkable red-earth soil of Palestine was being ripped from the slopes and swept down into the coastal plain and carried out to sea, where it turned the blue of the Mediterranean to a dirty brown as far as the eye could see" (Lowdermilk 1944).

Michael Zohary, one of the fathers of the field of botany in Israel attempted to reconstruct the ancient pre-agricultural flora landscape of Palestine. He concluded that a more developed and continuous vegetation ruled in the ancient landscape of Palestine (Zohary 1944). After centuries of human disturbance, however, forest continuity was affected, and many areas in Palestine in the first half of the twentieth century were covered by vegetation types that did not reflect the vegetation potential (climax), based on local soils and climate. These changes were brought about by human activities that damaged the natural landscape and introduced exotic plants (*Atlas of Israel* 1956–1961, VIII/1). Reifenberg, Naveh and Dan, and Thirgood strengthen this assumption, referencing historical sources that document the higher elevations in Palestine and Lebanon as covered with forests (see Reifenberg 1950; Naveh and Dan 1973; Thirgood 1981).

According to Liphschitz and Biger (2004), no systematic investigation of the forests in late Ottoman Palestine was undertaken by premodern researchers. They conclude that surviving reports reflect only impressions of travelers, based on their observations along the main routes by which they passed. However, the scholars Henry Baker Tristram (who visited Palestine in 1863–1864) and L. Anderlind (1880s and 1890s) made scientific contributions to the study of the fauna and flora of Palestine (Liphschitz and Biger 2004, 35–39). Furthermore, the careful surveyors of the PEF did in fact in the 1870s undertake a very orderly and systematic mapping of forests as evidenced from their maps and their seven-volume *Survey of Western Palestine Memoirs* (Conder and Kitchener 1883).

From Margalit's (1955) map, which was based on travel accounts, we can learn about the distribution of forest types at the beginning of the nineteenth century. We find small patches of undefined forests and oak forests in the Judean Hills (near Hebron and Jerusalem); in Samaria (near Nablus); near Nazareth, Mt. Tabor, and northwest of Safed in the Galilee. She also added "hypothesized" oak forests to the map, showing a relatively wide distribution in these areas as well as along the coastal plain (*Atlas of Israel* 1956–1961, VIII/1; see fig. 1.4).

A French traveler, the Count Constantine François Volney who visited Palestine in 1787, reported an oak forest near Caesarea (Volney in Reifenberg 1950). Karschon, who studied the Sharon oak forests, suggested that the massive destruction began as early as 1830s by the local Egyptian ruler Ibrahim Pasha, who cut down entire groves to supply his father, Mohammed Ali, the ruler of Egypt, with timber for constructing boats and for heating. Forest destruction continued as new settlements and agricultural activity expanded in the Sharon, increasing timber demand (Liphschitz and Biger 2004).

From Schick's map based on the PEF survey in the 1870s, we learn about the distribution of forests, Mediterranean maquis, coniferous trees, scattered coniferous trees, palm trees, orchards, and other types of vegetation. It details a large distribution of patches of forests in the Hebron and Judean Hills, the Piedmont (Shephelah), the Samarian Hills, the Lower and Upper Galilee, and the coast. Along the coastal plain we can identify two large forests in the Sharon, and forests in the Jaffa and Gaza areas (*Atlas of Israel* 1956–1961, VIII/1; see fig. 1.5).

Liphschitz and Biger write that during the 1870s natural oak forests appear to have grown on the coastal plain and in the lower Galilee, while mixed forests of conifers and oaks were present on the central mountain ranges. However, commencement of new settlement in Palestine, from the 1870s onward, brought with it a further decrease in forest distribution. This period also saw the beginning of afforestation in Palestine, associated with the German Templers who began in the 1870s to plant trees in their colonies at Haifa and Jerusalem. These plantings included cypress trees and various kinds of pines (e.g., *Pinus pinea* or Stone pine and *Pinus halepenisis* or Aleppo pine), as well as ornamental trees. In their colony of Sarona near Jaffa they preferred to plant *Eucalyptus* trees in an attempt to drain wetlands and combat malaria (Liphschitz and Biger 2004).

The Jewish founders of the first Zionist settlements, Baron Rothschild and the JCA and PICA organizations, also engaged in reforestation. They promoted the planting of groves and trees in almost all the new Jewish settlements in Judea and Samaria, and to a lesser extent in the upper Galilee (Liphschitz and Biger 2004). These new forestry efforts, intended to produce clean and healthy air, also involved ficus, mulberry, and melia trees, and the use of foreign species, for example, the Australian Eucalyptus. Following the common contemporary belief that eucalyptus trees can dry the swamps and prevent malaria, founders intensively planted them during the 1890s in the vicinity of the Jewish independent agricultural settlement of Hadera, founded in 1891, hoping to dry its swamps (Liphschitz and Biger 2004). Ruppin wrote in 1915: "In the Jewish colonies the eucalyptus tree, imported from Australia thirty years ago, has been used for the drainage of marshes, especially in Hudeirah (31 miles north of Jaffa)" (Ruppin 1918).

The new Forests Law enacted by the Ottomans in 1903 aimed to preserve and improve the forests, and plant new ones. The law was well intentioned, and some active attempts were made to plant trees in parks and boulevards in several towns in Palestine. These efforts increased during World War I, but on the whole, little was done to enforce the law in the few years remaining until the end of Ottoman rule in Palestine. The use of *bakshish* (graft) to get cutting permits or having the authorities overlook it, were not uncommon (Reifenberg 1950; Paz and Zahalka 1997; Biger and Liphshitz 1995).

In parallel, perhaps the most infamous cases of deforestation occurred at the very end of the Ottoman rule over Palestine. "The war has added to this destruction process, as wood has been used in the place of coal" (Ruppin 1918). During World War I (1914–1918) the Ottomans needed wood for constructing railways and driving the steam locomotives of those trains. To this end, several railways were constructed leading through forest stands that were then cut down (Weitz 1974). An example of this can be seen in the maps in figure 1.8, presenting an area east of Caesarea, where the town of Pardes-Hanah and the settlement of Karkur are now located (Paz 2008).

Forests represent the potential climax vegetation type in many areas, and as such, require longer periods of time to develop. Therefore, their recovery following destruction and disturbance by human activities may take decades of proper conservation and management activities.

The main determinants that led to processes of change in Palestine during the last 120 years of Ottoman rule were human. They were driven by political events and administrative and legal reforms. This led to an increase of personal and property security; the retreat of the Bedouin tribes and their periodic destructive influence on the settled areas; and the increase of immigration, rural settlement, and urbanization. One of the most important events

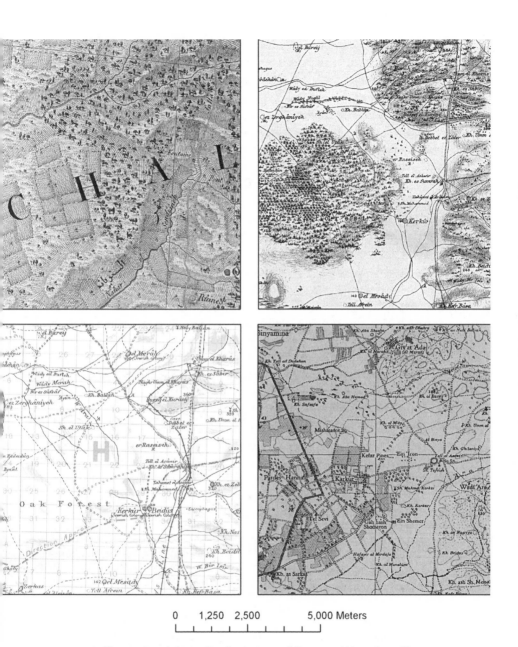

0   1,250   2,500   5,000 Meters

FIGURE 1.8. Changes in oak forest distribution east of Caesarea: (A) patches of forest as shown on Jacotin's map (1826), mapped during Napoleon's campaign in Palestine, 1799; (B) patches of forest as shown on the PEF (1880) map, based on mapping done between 1871–1877; (C) a railway track to the forests, constructed during World War I, as shown on a British map from September 1918–III; (D) a 1938 British map presenting the development of new Jewish settlements where the large patch of oak forest existed.

23

in the creation of new landscapes was the Ottoman Land Laws of 1858. The main purpose of the Land Code of 1858 was to precisely define landholdings and categories, abolish the system of tax farming, as well as consolidate and retrieve the state's rights to its *miri* (state) lands in order to increase agricultural production and the associated tax revenues. It was intended to extend and confirm the rights of land use, possession, and ownership. The law and other processes in nineteenth-century Palestine brought about the beginning of land survey and land settlement, land registration and systematic mapping, as well as new land ownership patterns and the modernization of agriculture. Privatization and estate formation led to spatial changes in land and settlement patterns, building and architecture, and in the landscape on the whole.

The land reform and processes of change in the Ottoman Empire included the modernization of its administration, strengthening of links with the West, and increased security for people and property. These led to economic development (entrepreneurship, rational economy, introduction of new technologies); population growth; and immigration of Arabs, Jews, Christians, and non-Arab Muslims; social change (classes, elites, stratification); and considerable new settlement (sixty-nine Arab hamlets and villages between 1871 to 1922 [Frantzman 2010], and forty-three Jewish agricultural settlements between 1870 to 1913 [Ruppin 1918]). These held considerable political implications, including sowing the seeds of the Arab-Jewish conflict.

Transformations in the human sphere and the introduction of new technologies (e.g., steam-operated trains) led to the destruction of the already threatened forest cover of Palestine (Kark 1995). In parallel Christian and Jewish settlers from Europe began, from the 1860s onward, a new process of afforestation, introducing new plant species into Palestine. Beyond this, most of the natural landscape of Palestine (e.g., distribution of wetlands and coastal dunes) did not change significantly during the last 120 years of Ottoman rule, reflecting the continuation of centuries-old land-use practices. However, the more modern cultural landscapes that developed in the plains and valleys, and around the growing cities, would subsequently bring about dramatic changes in land use and land cover that occurred during the British Mandate period (1918–1948).

REFERENCES

Amiran, D. H. K. 1953. "The Pattern of Settlement in Palestine." *Israel Exploration Journal* 3: 65–78, 192–209, 250–60.

Atlas of Israel. 1955–1961. Hebrew ed. Tel Aviv: Survey of Israel.

Atlas of Israel. 1970. English ed. Jerusalem: Survey of Israel and Ministry of Labour.

Avneri, Aryeh L. 1984. *The Claim of Dispossession: Jewish Land-Settlement and the Arabs, 1878–1948,* 53–63, 93–94. New Brunswick: Transaction Publishers.

Biger, G., and N. Liphschitz. 1995. "Australian Trees in the Land of Israel 1865–1950." *Journal of Israeli History* 16: 235–44.

Conder, C. R., and H. H. Kitchener. 1883. *The Survey of Western Palestine Memoirs.* vol. 3. London: Palestine Exploration Fund.

Fawaz, L., ed. 1991. *State and Society in Lebanon.* Oxford: Tufts University and the Centre for Lebanese Studies.

Finn, J. 1871. The British Consul in Jerusalem to Sir Stratford Canning, November 7 1851. London: Public Record Office, F.O. 78/874.

———. 1878. *Stirring Times.* London: C. K. Paul and Co.

Fischel, R. S., and R. Kark. 2008. "Sultan Abdülhamid II and Palestine: Private Lands and Imperial Policy." *New Perspectives on Turkey* 39: 129–66.

Fischer, H., and H. Guthe. 1890. *Palästina,* 1:700,000, Verlag der Geogr. Anstalt von Wagner & Debes, Leipzig, Jewish National and University Library, Laor Map Collection: Pal 1261-C8. From *Zeitschrift des Deutschen Palaestina Vereins.* vol. 13, 1890, T.2.

———. 1911. *Das Heutige Palästina,* No. 20, 1:700,000, Wagner & Debes, Leipzig. Ruth Kark private collection, Bibleatlas in 20 Haupt und 28 Nebenkarten von Hermann Guthe.

Frantzman, S. J. 2010. "The Arab Settlement of Late Ottoman and Mandatory Palestine New Village Formation and Settlement Fixation, 1871–1948." PhD thesis, Hebrew University of Jerusalem, June.

Gavish, D., and R. Kark. 1993. "The Cadastral Mapping of Palestine, 1858–1928." *Geographic Journal* 159 (1): 70–80.

Glass, J. B., and R. Kark. 2007. *Sephardi Entrepreneurs in Jerusalem: The Valero Family, 1800–1948.* Jerusalem and New York: Gefen Publishing House.

Guerin, V. 1868–1880. *Description Géographique, Historique et Archéologique de la Palestine, Accompagnée de Cartes Détaillées. Judee,* 1869; *Samarie,* 1874; *Galilee,* 1880. 3 vols. Paris: L'Imprimerie impériale.

Grossman, D. 1982. "The Expansion of the Settlement Frontier on Hebron's Western and Southern Fringes." *Geographical Research Forum* 5: 57–73.

———. 2004. *Expansion and Desertion: The Arab Village and Its Offshoots in Ottoman Palestine.* Jerusalem: Yad Izhak Ben-Zvi.

Huleh Land Concession files. August 1925. London: Public Record Office (PRO), CO 733/96/39606 and 41702.

Hoffman, I. 1963. "The Activity of Muhammad Ali in Syria." PhD thesis, Hebrew University of Jerusalem.

Hütteroth, W. D., and K. Abdulfattah. 1977. *Historical Geography of Palestine, Transjordan and Southern Syria.* Erlangen: Palm and Enke.

Issar, A. 2003. *Climate Changes during the Holocene and Their Impact on Hydrological Systems.* Cambridge: Cambridge University Press.

Issar, A., and M. Zohar. 2007. *Climate Change—Environment and History of the Near East.* 2nd ed. Berlin: Springer.

Kark, R. 1977. "Urban Development of Jerusalem and Jaffa at the End of the Ottoman Period." *Nofim* 9–10: 106–14. In Hebrew.

———. 1984a. "Landownership and Spatial Change in Nineteenth Century Palestine: An Overview." In *Transition from Spontaneous to Regulated Spatial Organization,* edited by M. Roscizewsky, 183–96. Warsaw: Polish Academy of Sciences.

———. 1984b. "Land Acquisition and New Agricultural Settlement in Palestine During the Tyomkin Period, 1890–1892." *Zionism* 9: 179–93. In Hebrew; English abstract.

———, ed. 1990a. *The Land That Became Israel: Studies in Historical Geography*. New Haven: Yale University Press.

———. 1990b. "The Decline and Rise of the Coastal Towns in Palestine 1800–1914." In *Ottoman Palestine 1800–1914, Studies in Economic and Social History*, edited by G. G. Gilbar, 69–90. Leiden: E. J. Brill.

———. 1995. "The Introduction of Modern Technology into the Holy Land (1800–1914CE)." In *The Archaeology of Society in the Holy Land*, edited by T. E Levi, 524–41. London: Leicester University Press.

———. Forthcoming. "Consequences of the Ottoman Land Law: Agrarian and Privatization Processes in Palestine, 1858–1918." In *Development Issues in Marginal Regions*, edited by R. Chand. Haifa: Haifa University.

———. Forthcoming. *Proceedings of the IGU Commission Conference, Marginalization, Globalization and Regional and Local Responses*. Nainital, India, May 1–9.

Kark, R., and S. Frantzman. 2010. "The Bedouin, Abdul Hamid II, British Land Settlement and Zionism: The Baysan Valley and Sub-District 1831–1948." *Israel Studies* 15: 49–79.

Kark, R., and J. B. Glass. 1999. "The Jews in Eretz-Israel/Palestine, from Traditional Peripherality to Modern Centrality." *Israel Affairs* 5/4: 73–107.

Kark R., and N. Thalmann. 2003. "Technological Innovation in Palestine: The Role of the German Templers." In *Germany and the Middle East—Past, Present and Future*, edited by H. Goren, 201–24. Jerusalem: Magnes Press.

———. 2004. "The Lands of the Sultan—Newly Discovered Ottoman Cadastral Maps in Palestine." In *Mediterranean Cartographies*, edited by G. Tolias and D. Loupis, 197–222. Athens: Institute for Neohellenic Research INR/NHRF.

Karmon, Y. 1956a. *The Northern Hulah Valley*. Jerusalem: Magnes Press.

———. 1956b. "Geographical Aspects in the History of the Coastal Plain of Israel." *Israel Exploration Journal* 6: 33–50.

———. 1971. *Israel, a Regional Geography*. London: Wiley.

Karpat, K. H. 1974. "Ottoman Immigration Policies and Settlement in Palestine." In *Settlers Regimes in Africa and the Arab World*, edited by I. Abu-Lughod and B. Abu-Laban Wilmett, 58–72. Medina: Medina University Press.

Kedar, B. Z. 1999. *The Changing Land: Between the Jordan and the Sea: Aerial Photographs from 1917 to the Present*. Jerusalem: Yad Yitzhak Ben Zvi.

Kitchener, Lieut. H. H. 1878. "Kitchener's Reports. VIII. Camp at Jerusalem, October 2nd, 1877." *Palestine Exploration Fund Quarterly Statement* for 1878. (January): 11–14.

Klein, C. 1986. "Fluctuations of the Level of the Dead Sea and Climatic Fluctuations in Israel during Historical Times." PhD thesis, Hebrew University. In Hebrew; English abstract.

Lowdermilk, W. C. 1944. *Palestine, Land of Promise*. London: V. Gollancz.

Levin, N. 2006. "The Palestine Exploration Fund Map (1871–1877) of the Holy Land as a Tool for Analyzing Landscape Changes: The Coastal Dunes of Israel as a Case Study." *Cartographic Journal* 43: 45–67.

Levin, N., and E. Ben-Dor. 2004. "Monitoring Sand Dune Stabilization along the Coastal Dunes of Ashdod-Nizanim, Israel, 1945–1999." *Journal of Arid Environments* 58: 335–55.

Levin, N., E. Elron, and A. Gasith. 2009. "Decline of Wetland Ecosystems in the Coastal Plain of Israel during the 20th Century: Implications for Wetland Conservation and Management." *Landscape and Urban Planning* 92: 220–32.

Levin, N., R. Kark, and E. Galilee. 2010. "Historical Maps and GIS: Mapping of Southern Palestine 1799–1948, Issues of Scale and Accuracy and Possible Applications." *Journal of Historical Geography* 36: 1–18.

Liphschitz, N., and G. Biger. 2004. *Green Dress for a Country, Afforestation in Eretz Israel: The First Hundred Years, 1850–1959.* Jerusalem: KKL and Ariel.

Margalit, H. 1955. "The Cultural Landscape of the Land of Israel." PhD thesis, Hebrew University of Jerusalem.

Marsh, G. P. 1864. *Man and Nature, or, Physical Geography as Modified by Human Action.* New York: C. Scribner.

Moscrop, J. J. 2000. *Measuring Jerusalem: The Palestine Exploration Fund and British Interests in the Holy Land.* London: Leicester University Press.

Musil, A. 1907–1908. *Arabia Petraea.* Wien: A. Hölder.

Naveh, Z., and J. Dan. 1973. "The Human Degradation of Mediterranean Landscapes in Israel." In *Mediterranean Type Ecosystems, Origin and Structure*, edited by F. di Castri and H. A. Mooney, 373–90. Berlin: Springer.

Oke, M. K. 1982. "The Ottoman Empire, Zionist and the Question of Palestine 1880–1908." *IJMES* 14 (1982): 329–41.

Owen, R. 1981. *The Middle East in World Economy 1800–1914.* London: Methuen.

Paz, U. 2008. *To Cultivate It and to Preserve It: Nature Conservation in Israel.* Jerusalem: Ariel. In Hebrew.

Paz, U., and M. Zahalka. 1997. "There Was a Forest: The Ramat Menashe Region." *Teva Hadvarim* 20: 86–107. In Hebrew.

Reichman, S. 1979. *From Foothold to Settled Territory.* Jerusalem: Yad Izhak Ben-Zvi. In Hebrew.

Reifenberg, A. A. 1950. *The War between the Sown and the Desert.* Jerusalem: Bialik Institute. In Hebrew.

Rothschild, A., and Y. Perlman. 2010. "Winter Ponds in Israel: Importance and the Challenge of Conservation—Information for Policy Makers and Managers, the Society for Protection of Nature in Israel." www.sviva.gov.il/Enviroment/Static/Binaries/index_pirsumim/P0545_1.pdf. In Hebrew.

Ruppin, A. 1918. *Syria: An Economic Survey.* New York: The Provisional Zionist Commission.

Schmelz, U. O. 1975. "Some Demographic Peculiarities of the Jews of Jerusalem in the 19th Century." In *Studies on Palestine during the Ottoman Period*, edited by Moshe Maoz, 119–41. Jerusalem: Magnes Press.

Shick, A. 1956. "The Landscape of Palestine in the Years 1870–1880." *Atlas of Israel*, map and text in Hebrew; sheet VIII/I. Jerusalem.

Tal, A. 2006. *The Environment in Israel: Resources, Crises, Campaigns and Policy from the Birth of Zionism until the 21st Century.* Tel Aviv: Hakibutz Hameuchad.

Thirgood, J. V. 1981. *Man and the Mediterranean Forest—A History of Resource Depletion.* London: Academic Press.

Tsoar, H. 2005. "Sand Dunes Mobility and Stability in Relation to Climate." *Physica A* 357: 50–56.

Tsoar, H., and A. Karnieli. 1996. "What Determines the Spectral Reflectance of the Negev-Sinai Sand Dunes." *International Journal of Remote Sensing* 17: 513–25.

Tsoar, H., and Y. Zohar. 1985. "Desert Dune Sand and Its Potential for Modern Agricultural Development." In *Desert Development,* edited by Y. Gradus, 184–200. Dordrecht: D. Reidel Publishing Company.

Twain, M. (1869) 1876. *The Innocents Abroad.* Hartford: American Publications.

Van de Velde, C. W. M. 1854. *Narrative of a Journey through Syria and Palestine in 1851 and 1852.* 2 vols. London: W. Blackwood and Sons.

Vilnay, Z. 1959. *Minorities in Israel, Jerusalem.* In Hebrew.

Weitz, J. 1974. *Forests and Afforestation in Israel.* Jerusalem: Massada.

Zohary, M. 1944. *Introduction to the Geobotany of Palestine.* Merhaviya: Ha-Kibutz ha'Artzi, Ha-Shomer Ha-Tsa'ir. In Hebrew.

CHAPTER TWO

THE ENVIRONMENTAL LEGACY OF THE FELLAHEEN AND THE BEDOUIN IN PALESTINE

No'am G. Seligman

THE DYNAMIC LANDSCAPE

HUMAN COMMUNITIES leave their imprint on the environment by erecting structures, changing topography, clearing forests or harvesting forest products, cultivating land, collecting desirable plants, hunting animals, and by the grazing of their domestic livestock. Over the past ten thousand years, agriculture has enabled the human population on our planet to grow but has also modified, damaged, or destroyed the ecosystems on which it is practiced. Even though the environment is at the receiving end of human actions, it is not a passive recipient of their impact. It is a dynamic system that interacts with the activities of people and with all the other components that constitute the environment. The organic elements—the plants, animals, and microorganisms—have complex responses to human disturbance. The inorganic elements—the geological substrate, the geomorphology, the soil, the water, the air—respond subject to the laws of physics and chemistry.

The intensity of human impact covers a continuum from the relatively mild effects of grazing, through the more severe effects of deforestation and cultivation, and culminates in the devastating effects of construction that totally replaces unique elements in an existing landscape. The ability of a landscape to recover from the less violent aspects of human disturbance generally requires time, sometimes much longer than a human lifespan as in the case of soil erosion, sometimes much less as in some cases of vegetation restoration after grazing.

This chapter reviews the role of traditional exploitation of the landscape resources on the quality of the environment in the region known for centuries as Palestine, the western extension of the Fertile Crescent. The main actors are the cultivators, the Fellaheen, and the pastoralists, the Bedouin who, over the course of history, have functioned within a changing cultural, political, and administrative context that has influenced their relationship with the environment. "Environmental quality" has an objective dimension—the state of the structures, the vegetation, the fauna, the soil, the water, the air—and a subjective dimension—the value judgment of the changes that have taken place at different times in the history of a region. The following discussion will concentrate on the objective dimension but will not be able to avoid some of its implications for current value judgments. For the purposes of this chapter, the working definition of "environment" will be limited to aspects of the rural landscape—the geomorphology, the soil, the vegetation, and the fauna.

PREVALENT IMPRESSIONS

Impressions of the environment in Palestine are influenced by the strongly seasonal nature of its Mediterranean climate, reflected in the dramatic contrast between the verdant, winter landscape often spangled with colorful flowers and the parched, yellow-brown landscape of summer. The vegetation on the hilly, rocky backbone of the region is particularly prone to the changes imposed by the alternating seasons. There the summer landscape can be stark, particularly when viewed by unsympathetic outsiders and especially before the twentieth century. Mark Twain's judgment was unfairly harsh: "Of all the lands there are for dismal scenery, I think Palestine must be the prince. . . . It is a hopeless, dreary, heart-broken land" (Twain 1869).

Even in the twentieth century Dr. W. C. Lowdermilk, who was once assistant chief of the American Soil Conservation Service and well versed in land lore, commented: "casual visitors consider as normal the rocky, semi-arid, run down condition of much of Palestine . . . erosion has wasted the neglected lands . . . over three feet of soil have been swept from the uplands of Palestine since the breakdown of terrace agriculture . . . neglect, ignorance, suicidal agriculture has created man-made deserts" (Lowdermilk 1944).

In line with this assessment is the review of agriculture in Palestine presented to the Anglo-American Committee of Inquiry (Shaw 1946):

> A large oak forest clothed the hills south and south-west of Hebron until
> destroyed by over-cutting and over-grazing. Most of the pine and oak
> forests on the Carmel have been lost over the past thirty years while
> the destruction of natural scrub forest in the Galilee is still progress-

ing. The scattered groves of Zizyphus in the Jordan valley have mostly disappeared in very recent times; one result of this process has been the disastrous flooding on the slopes above Tiberias. . . . Deforestation has resulted in wide-spread erosion. Some areas have been reduced to sheet rock and boulders; on others, the soil is so scanty that successful agriculture is impossible. . . . The vegetation of Palestine is rich in species and adaptable to changing conditions but it can be, and has been, destroyed by the combined processes of cutting, burning, uprooting and overgrazing. . . . While the soil [of Palestine] may be made highly productive by careful treatment, it may be easily ruined by ignorance and neglect. In fact, the second condition is the rule and a mature agricultural soil is the exception.

Adolph Reifenberg (1938), a professor of soil science, also regarded the relationship between traditional agriculture in Palestine and the landscape as a disaster: "For fifteen hundred years the land has steadily deteriorated. The abandonment of terraces, cultivation and the destruction of trees have left the soil bare and unprotected from the forces of erosion . . . the once fertile countryside is covered by sand dunes . . . the desert has crept over the country. . . . The destruction of the vegetation exposes the soil to wind erosion . . . most pronounced in the Beersheba area where dust storms are a frequent occurrence."

By contrast, the 1946 Shaw report noted: "The soils are very variable but are remarkably fertile even though they have been cultivated for millennia. The coastal plain, which is also the citrus belt, has large tracts of sandy or sandy loam soils interspersed with very fertile heavy soils. In the inland plains of Jezreel and Huleh there are rich alluvial soils. The hills of Judaea, Samaria and the Galilee hold pockets of red earths and are productive of olives, vines and fruit. . . . The soils of the Beersheba plateau are wind-blown loess and suitable for grain in years when rainfall is adequate."

There were also favorable impressions of the landscape in the nineteenth century. Bayard Taylor who traveled in Palestine during the spring of 1852 had the opportunity to see the landscape in its brighter colors: "the Plain of Esdraelon, a picture of summer luxuriance and bloom. The waves of wheat and barley rolled away from our path to the distant olive orchards; . . . we came upon the great plain of Sharon . . . people are ploughing now for their summer crops, and the wheat and barley which they sowed last winter are already in full head. On other parts of the plain, there were large flocks of sheep and goats, with their attendant shepherds. . . . The landscape had something of the green, pastoral beauty of England, except the mountains, which were wholly of Palestine. . . . The soil is a dark-brown loam, and, without manure, produces annually superb crops of wheat and barley."

Such different impressions of the landscape reflect the seasonality of the
Mediterranean climate, but also different approaches, beliefs, preconceptions,
prejudices, agenda and itinerary of the authors. A more objective evaluation
of the environment under the culture of the Fellah and the Bedouin depends
on reliable data. Even those are often ambiguous or incomplete and open to
interpretation. Still, the data allow for a more objective evaluation of the effect of the traditional agricultural practices on the landscape resources and
on the quality of the environment. Detailed numerical information on the
state of the landscape in Palestine and on the population and its activities
is available for the period of the British Mandate. Assuming that the overall
climatic conditions in previous centuries were not substantially different, the
data collected during the Mandate reflect the essential nature of traditional
agriculture and animal husbandry in the region (Biger and Grossman 1993).
Even though modern technologies started to influence life in Palestine from
the mid-nineteenth century, the agro-technology of the Fellaheen remained
mainly traditional, with virtually no intensification or development of an agricultural infrastructure (Kark 1995).

Consideration of grazing systems, soils, agricultural productivity, and
ecological indicators challenges the predominant paradigm that the land of
Palestine during the Ottoman period was run down by abusive grazing and
primitive, destructive agriculture.

THE REALITY

In 1936, the total area under cultivation, dry and irrigated, was 7,788 square
kilometers, 30 percent of the land area of the country. This was probably the
maximum area of cultivable land in Mandatory Palestine because "practically
every square yard of land . . . capable of producing a crop is ploughed (with indeed much land that should not be cultivated under strict conservation principles)" (Shaw 1946, 313). The irrigated area of citrus and vegetables totaled 412
square kilometers and was only about 5 percent of the total cultivated area. Of
the total area of cultivated crops (including citrus), 91 percent was in the Arab
sector of the country. This means that, except for citrus, cultivation in Palestine was largely traditional. On non-irrigated, cultivated land, the inputs were
only seeds and labor, human and animal.

Agricultural productivity, consequently, was a function of the natural fertility of the soil, the available labor, and the ecological context of the region.
The produce included grains, olives, citrus, grapes, almonds, legumes, more
than twenty different species of vegetables, melons, and tobacco (table 2.1).
Yields were not high but neither were the exogenous inputs: In 1944–1945, average wheat and barley yields over the whole country, including the semiarid
Negev, were between 500 and 700 kilograms per hectare all without fertilizer,

FIGURE 2.1. Landscape of traditional Fellaheen agriculture still current in present-day Palestine.

compared to current yields of 2,000 to 4,000 kilograms per well-fertilized hectare planted with improved varieties. If the range of crops reflects the productivity of the land after millennia of cultivation, then the traditional system of cultivation can only be described as a time-tested example of sustainable agriculture.

This scale of production, which continued well into the twentieth century, casts doubt on the validity of opinions regarding the degree of erosion that

TABLE 2.1. Area of principal crops in Palestine in 1936 (km²)

Grains and legumes		Vegetables		Plantations		Others	
Barley	2,723	Tomatoes	43	Olives	510	Melons	177
Wheat	2,320	Cucumbers	21	Citrus	250	Tobacco	30
Millet	772	Potatoes	10	Grapes	183		
Vicia ervilea	233	Cauliflower	6	Almonds	109		
Sesame	99	Cabbage	4	Figs	24		
Maize	67	Others	62	Apples	8		
Others	152			Plums	5		
				Bananas	1		
				Others	29		
Total	6,366		146		1,119		207

Lowdermilk so vividly described. Some terraces may have been neglected but on the whole, they were maintained as long as there were cultivators who depended on their efficacy to preserve the basis of their livelihood (Ron 1966). Their upkeep only required occasional labor. In the distant past, the bare hills may have been covered with a deep layer of soil but if it was eroded by the disturbance of cultivation, then that must have started soon after the introduction of agriculture into the region some ten thousand years ago. The terraces were a repository of some of the eroded soil.

Palestine over the centuries was not a wasteland. It maintained a modest population that lived off the land with the vagaries of its climate, resource limitations, and no modern inputs to agriculture. During the late 1930s and early 1940s, when most of the arable land was cultivated (Shaw 1946), grains (wheat, barley, pulses) were grown on 84 percent of the cultivated land, plantations (mainly olives, grapes, and figs) on 11 percent, and vegetables on 5 percent of the cultivated area. These were the same crops that were cultivated in biblical times (Vamosh 2009). The average production of grains was 234,000 tons. If we assume an annual food requirement of 250 kilograms of wheat equivalents per capita (Wilkinson 1999) then the local production should have maintained a population of 936,000 people. During the equivalent period, the rural population of Palestine averaged 988,000 people. This lends credence to the assumption that in a traditional society, productivity of agriculture and the size of the predominantly rural population are mutually dependent (Wilkinson 1999).

THE SOILS OF PALESTINE

The most basic resource of agriculture is soil. Its formation is the result of slow, ongoing pedological processes that depend on the properties of the substrate, on the geomorphology of the region, on the nature of the sediments deposited in floodplains and valleys, on the vegetation, the moisture regime and, in Palestine, on the eolian deposition of dust from the surrounding deserts and sand from the coast (Singer et al. 2003; Dan 1990). In the more humid areas within the region, the rainfall not only erodes the surface soil from the slopes but also leaches the soluble fractions out of the soil. Within a relatively small geographic area, the soils of Palestine are remarkably diverse in origin and characteristics (Ravikovitch 1981). Most of the hill soils are derived from calcareous rocks. They have good structure and are well drained, characteristics that allow for good water relations and provide a degree of resistance to dispersion and erosion. The human impact on soil formation is mediated mainly through the drastic changes wrought on the vegetation cover. Clearing the perennial vegetation cover to prepare land for cultivation at the beginning of agriculture conceivably accelerated the rate of erosion and it is possible that soil on the hills was lost already thousands of years ago. The landscape during the Ottoman period was probably similar in character to the biblical landscape.

Terra rossa soil that develops on the predominantly hard limestone and dolomite of the hills of the Galilee, Samaria, and Judea is partly derived from the weathering of desert dust that is deposited on them. The solution of the hard rock on the surface and deep within the rock creates the harsh karstic landscape. The deeper soil pockets on the hillsides that are cultivated are protected from severe erosion by the surrounding rock. On the soft limestone and chalks, relatively fertile rendzina soils are formed by the weathering of the basement rock. In the hills, a stepped landscape is formed by the alternation of hard limestone and soft chalk or marl layers. Such sites were terraced and cultivated. Soils in depressions and valleys and on the terraces were formed mainly from the sediments that were eroded from the adjacent slopes. On the margins of the floodplains of the coastal plain, fine-textured sediments form *nazaz*, tight soils with very poor drainage. Swamps occur on such areas. Along the coastal plain, sea currents deposited quartz sand during the last million years and wind carried the sand inland to create sand dunes. With the stabilization of the dunes and deposition of eolian dust, calcareous sandstone (*kurkar*) and sandy-loam (*hamra*) soils were eventually formed (Dan, Fine, and Lavee 2007).

The human contribution to soil formation was terracing in the hills and wadis (and accelerated erosion from cultivated slopes). Terracing was extensive already between 1000 BC and 600 BC and remained the best preserved of the ancient field systems in the country (Gibson 1995). Terraces created large areas of deep, fertile soil, most of it washed in by erosion of the slopes above them, but some of the fill was transported by hand. In the Judean Hills, about half the (total) area was terraced; more than 60 percent of the terraces were still cultivated by the end of the British Mandate (Ron 1966). Narrow wadis and valleys were often terraced to facilitate cultivation and to trap runoff. A small fraction was irrigated from springs, some of the installations going back to the first century (Ron 1966).

THE POPULATION

The supply of food, more than anything else, sets the parameters within which human societies, especially traditional societies, operate. The size of the population in such societies is not the only indicator of the productivity of the land. Yet there must be a connection between what the local environment can provide and what can be taken from it in the form of human or animal nutrition (Grigson 1995). Fertilizers, herbicides, pesticides, mechanization, fossil energy, and other adjuncts of the industrial revolution were introduced on a

TABLE 2.2. Population of Palestine, 1690–1947

Year	Total number of people (thousands)	Moslems (%)	Christians (%)	Jews (%)
1690	232	94	5	1
1800	275	89	8	3
1850	298	85	11	4
1890	532	81	11	8
1914	689	76	10	14
1922	752	78	9	11
1931	1,033	74	9	17
1947	1,970	60	7	32

Source: 1690–1947 data from DellaPergola (2001); 1850 data from Schölch (1993).

large scale into Palestinian agriculture in the twentieth century. Until then, as in antiquity, such exogenous inputs were minimal so that the natural fertility of the soil, the available labor, the technology of the time, and the ecology of the region limited agricultural output. This output also limits population and is probably a realistic indicator of Palestine's intrinsic human carrying capacity. Its population at the beginning of the twentieth century, when imported modern technologies and inputs had already begun to influence productivity, was less than three quarters of a million (table 2.2).

There is no consensus on population of Palestine at the beginning of the Christian Era. The numbers vary widely between less than a million and six million (DellaPergola 2001). As the potential productivity of the natural resources in the region sets a limit to population numbers, the lower estimate seems to be more realistic (Broshi 1979). In 1550, at the beginning of the Ottoman period, the total population was about three hundred thousand souls; between a fifth and a quarter lived in the six towns of Jerusalem, Gaza, Safed, Nablus, Ramle, and Hebron. The remainder consisted mainly of peasants engaged in agriculture, living in villages of varying size. Their main food-crops were wheat and barley, supplemented by leguminous pulses, olives, fruit, vegetables, and high-quality protein from livestock products. In and around most of the towns there were a considerable number of vineyards, orchards, and vegetable gardens (Lewis 1954). Over the next three hundred years, population numbers were around a quarter of a million, increasing to about half a million toward the end of the nineteenth century after which there was a dramatic increase in the twentieth century (see table 2.2 and table 2.3). During the 1930s when "practically every square yard of land . . . capable of producing a crop is ploughed" (Shaw 1946), the population was more than three times that of

TABLE 2.3. Rural and urban population of Palestine, 1850–1931 (in thousands)

	1850	1922	1931
Rural population	247	492.9	648.5
Urban population	103	264.3	387.3
Percentage rural (all)	71	65	63
Percentage rural (Moslem)	76	76	75

Source: 1850 data from Schölch (1993); 1922, 1931 data from Shaw (1946).

the Ottoman period. Even by the end of the nineteenth century, Ahad Ha'am (1891), a prominent Jewish personality of the period, found that "in the entire land, it is hard to find tillable land that is not already tilled."

In the past, disease, violence, and low life expectancy kept the population within the bounds of what could be produced. As elsewhere, population growth in Palestine was limited by high infant mortality and low life expectancy. Infectious disease rates were high and cholera, dysentery, malaria, and tuberculosis had a strong impact on daily life. Malaria and trachoma were also common ailments. Repeated cholera epidemics were transmitted by pilgrims returning from Mecca. Poverty and poor sanitary conditions facilitated an easy spread of diseases. Longevity vastly improved in the twentieth century: Whereas life expectancy at birth was 22–24 years in 1860, it subsequently rose to 32–34 years by 1914. Likewise, infant mortality dropped from 380 to 290 per thousand births during the same period (Davidovitch and Greenberg 2007).

During the early Ottoman period, most of the villages were in the hills, for health (malaria) but also for security reasons. They were generally no more than three kilometers apart. There were many Bedouin tribes, some located on the plains, including the coastal plain, and some in the Northern Negev and the Judean Desert (Hütteroth and Abdulfattah 1977). Fellaheen cultivated arable soils in the valleys and the terraces according to their needs and to their ability to provide the necessary manpower. Despite the depredations of disease, the rural population managed to cultivate much of the arable land and maintain most of the terraces (Ron 1966). Continuing, and even increasing, productivity of the land well into the twentieth century without substantially altering agricultural techniques would not have been possible if traditional Fellaheen cultivation had seriously degraded the land.

THE STATUS OF THE FELLAHEEN DURING OTTOMAN RULE

Prior to 1858, most of the cultivated land in Palestine was communally owned by the village and its allocation was arranged within the community (the traditional Musha' or Mesha'a system); some land was owned by local or urban individuals or families. The main classes of land according to Ottoman law were:

Miri: agricultural land that was leased from the government on condition of
  use. Individuals could purchase a deed to cultivate this land and pay a
  tithe to the government plus an additional tax.

Matruka: land set aside for public use.

Mulk: private property owned in complete freehold. Such ownership was
  rare.

Mawat: wasteland that was declared unsuitable for any purpose, generally
  desert or swamp.

Among the Tanzimat reforms that the sultan promulgated to modernize the
administration of the empire was the Ottoman Land Law of 1858 that required
the registration of land (Gerber 1986). In addition to increasing tax revenue,
its aim was to encourage the development of private property and agricultural
production. Peasants, however, saw no need to register claims that involved
greater taxes and registration fees (in addition to army service). Consequently,
land that previously was collectively owned by village residents was often registered in the name of the head of the village or members of the urban elite.
Merchants, local nobles, and Ottoman administrators took the opportunity to
register large areas of land in their own name. The result was that land became
the legal property of people who had never lived there, while the Fellaheen
who lived there for generations became tenants of absentee owners, many of
whom were of the affluent urban elite.

As in all traditional societies, agricultural produce was the main source
of income. All produce was taxed—often exorbitantly—sometimes more than
twenty percent of the produce was taken. Ownership of small livestock and
bees (sic!) was taxed, though oxen were not (Hütteroth and Abdulfattah 1977).
Even Bedouin residents were taxed. The heavy taxation and the lack of infrastructure kept the Fellah poor but he had no alternative livelihood but traditional agriculture (Singer 1994).

TRADITIONAL CULTIVATION

Growing crops was what the Fellaheen knew how to do. Traditional agricultural systems have emerged over centuries of cultural and biological evolution through the accumulation of the experiences of indigenous farmers interacting with the environment without access to external inputs. Farming
in Palestine was primarily rain-fed agriculture. Many of the crops the Fellaheen grew had been cultivated in the region for more than five thousand
years (Grigson 1995). They included wheat, barley, lentils, peas, chickpeas, and
bitter vetch (*Vicia ervilia*, kersanneh). Small areas were irrigated near springs
and streams, mainly for growing vegetables; well water in the coastal plain
was used to irrigate citrus. The grain crops, the olive and fruit plantations (al-

monds, grapes, stone fruits) were all rain fed. Consequently, rainfall patterns determined agricultural activities and the success or failure of the crop.

Crops were rotated, evidently as a measure to maintain fertility of the soil and to control weeds. Slopes were terraced in antiquity and maintained throughout the ages. Cultivation relied on a local version of the ancient plow, a wooden frame with a metal spike that furrowed the land without turning the soil, as is the case with the moldboard plow. It was held by the Fellah and pulled by two oxen or other animals (Dalman 1932). Traditional plows were adapted to different soils and were constructed of both curved and straight, sturdy branches—mainly of oak (*Quercus calliprinos, Quercus ithaburensis*)—which were items of value that were procured from the woodlands in the country. Toward the end of the nineteenth century, based on the design of the traditional plow, iron plows came into increasing use (Avitsur 1985).

After opening furrows, planters scattered seeds of wheat or barley by hand into the furrow and then covered them by another pass of the plow. When the soil was fallowed in winter and when there was sufficient moisture in the soil, summer crops (mainly *dura*, sorghum) were sown. Harvesting, threshing, and winnowing of grain crops occupied the months of June to August. Tools for harvesting included sickles of different sizes: small ones (*qalush*) for women and larger ones (*manjal*) for men (Crowfoot and Baldensperger 1932). Figs and stone fruits were picked in summer and the olives were harvested in October–November. Grain was milled by hand or in flourmills operated by animal power or by flowing water. Olive presses were also operated with animal power.

The scale of the agricultural operations required a heavy investment of labor and indeed, more than three-quarters of the population were engaged in agriculture and animal husbandry. The produce not only had to supply subsistence but a surplus, after tithes and taxes, for trading to obtain other necessities and for storage of reserves to be used in years of poor harvest. Artisans, including sickle sharpeners and blacksmiths, fashioned and maintained the metal spikes of the Fellaheens' plows. The traditional system was sustained with little change from ancient times until the beginning of the twentieth century. Among the salient features of such traditional systems are their sustainability and biodiversity (Grigg 1974). The simple cultivation technology of the Fellaheen and the opening up of dense woody thickets increased the diversity of microhabitats and with it the biodiversity of the flora and their dependent fauna (Paz 2008). Modern commercial agriculture with its much heavier impact on the ecosystem is bound to adversely affect environmental conservation more than most existing traditional systems (Altieri, Anderson, and Merrick 1987). Livestock were an integral part of the system. They not only provided food, hides, and skins but also manure—the only fertilizer available—that was often burned as fuel. Their nutrition was based overwhelmingly on natural pasture and crop residues.

GRAZING AND THE STATE OF THE PASTURE VEGETATION

The natural pastures of Palestine include swards of herbaceous, mostly annual species; land dominated by dwarf shrubs; scrub forest and oak woodlands; or Savannah-type parklands; and combinations of the different vegetation types (Seligman et al. 1959). Many species have developed ingenious defense mechanisms to herbivory that include plant toxins, thorns, hard leaves, rapid and staggered flowering, and reproduction from buds inaccessible to grazing animals (Perevolotsky and Pollak 2001). Bedouin maintained sheep and goat herds, but the Fellaheen kept some for domestic use; the villagers also had cattle, camels, and donkeys that served for work and transportation (table 2.4). Usually there were arrangements that determined when pastoralists could bring their herds to graze the crop residues (Hamel 1990) but there were also conflicts. A harvest song of the Bethlehem region sings: "O my corn, my tall one, / if it were not for God and myself, / the shepherds would have eaten you up, / pasturing on you their camels and sheep" (Crowfoot and Baldensperger 1932). Indeed, since the time of Cain and Abel, the antagonism between cultivators and herders was based on a fundamental conflict of interest.

Sheep, goats, cattle, horses, donkeys, and camels have different preferences for plant species but most of the dominant species are eaten to varying degrees

FIGURE 2.2. Goat grazing on a hillside alongside an olive grove continues today as in the past.

TABLE 2.4. Livestock numbers and animal units (AU) in the Arab sector
of Palestine in 1937 (in thousands)

Livestock class	Head	AU/head	AU
Goats	363	0.2	73
Sheep	209	0.2	42
Cattle	169	1	169
Donkeys	93	0.4	37
Camels	28	1.5	42
Horses	20	1.2	24
Mules	9	1.2	11
Buffaloes	6	1	6
Total	897		404

Note: Animal units (AU) are a normative unit that facilitates comparison of the nutritive demand of different classes of livestock. One AU is equivalent to the annual nutrient requirement of one head of cattle in the traditional animal husbandry context.

Source: Shaw (1946).

at some stage of their annual growth cycle. Even the shrubby vegetation with its anti-herbivory defenses, is forage for the animals, especially for goats (Kababya et al. 1998). Regenerating shoots of tree species that were cut for fuel, charcoal burning, implements, or building material were closely grazed by the livestock to fashion topiary-like plant shapes, often regarded as "overgrazing" from the landscape point of view but quite picturesque in their own right (Henkin, Hadar, and Nov-Meir 2004).

In traditional animal husbandry, supplementary feed—straw, tibben, barley grain—was fed mainly to work and draft animals and to a limited extent also to animals that were milked: cows, goats, and sheep and sometimes camels. The Bedouin, who at some stages in local history were rogue marauders who terrorized and robbed the settled communities (Ginat 1982) also made their living, legitimately, from the livestock both in the more arid south and east of the country and in the more settled humid north. They were sometimes regarded as "creators of the desert" who allowed their innocuous sheep and pernicious goats to destroy the vegetation by wanton overgrazing (Reifenberg 1955). Yet if the pasture vegetation was really destroyed, the Bedouin herds could not have persisted over the centuries. There were doubtless drought years, epidemics, and other catastrophes that devastated the stock and caused large fluctuations in animal population from time to time (table 2.5), but enough animals survived to allow the herd numbers to recover in better years.

The resilience of the herbaceous and woody vegetation, as well as the limits placed on grazing pressure by the defense mechanisms of plants, enabled the pasture to persist under such heavy grazing and to provide the main source of food for the domestic herbivores. Where animals depend on natural pasture

TABLE 2.5. Livestock numbers in the Arab sector of Palestine
between 1909 and 1943 (in thousands)

	1909	1920	1926	1934	1937	1943	Average	Coefficient of variation
Sheep	174	263	291	188	207	225	225	20%
Goats	239	272	341	381	361	315	318	17%
Camels	43	9	27	32	28	33	29	39%

Source: Data from Shaw (1946).

for survival, such long-term, co-evolutionary interactions between livestock and vegetation are common (McNaughton 1984; Ellis and Swift 1988; Sandford 1983). This "umbilical" connection between the grazing animal and the vegetation inspired the images inscribed on votive Philistine vessels of goats flanking a tree that "are a timeless, ever-renewing motif that originated around the 4th century B.C. . . . linking fauna and flora . . . denoting stability, well-being and regeneration" (Ziffer and Kletter 2007). The mutual co-evolutionary adjustments between plants and grazing animals explain many aspects of how the Mediterranean landscape developed (Perevolotsky 1999).

Estimates of the stocking rate of the pastures are difficult to define because of the varying numbers of animals during and between years, as well as the heterogeneity and dynamics of the pastures that are dependent on the vagaries of the climate, especially the rainfall (Perevolotsky and Pollak 2001). In addition, the mobility of herds complicates the relationship between animal numbers and area of pasture. However, where livestock nutrition is based on pasture throughout the year and where the animals are an essential source of high-quality protein for the local population and an integral adjunct to agricultural operations, both Fellaheen and Bedouin would tend to keep livestock numbers up to the limit that could be maintained on the available pasture resources, cultivated and uncultivated. The numbers vary from year to year with the fluctuations of the pasture productivity and following depredations from disease and violence (table 2.4). Nevertheless, the range of the number of animals that are kept in a region, the stocking rate, is an indicator of the order of magnitude of the livestock carrying capacity of the land, especially where the management system did not change for generations.

The census data of the British Mandate can be used to calculate the stocking rate of the pastures in Palestine. In 1937, the livestock population in the rural sector of Palestine was quite diverse. Grazing was not limited to the natural pastures. Part of the year, the crop residues and weeds were grazed, incidentally adding manure to the land and removing some weed growth. The area on which the livestock grazed was therefore the whole region except for the small areas occupied by the villages and towns. To calculate the stocking rate, the different classes of livestock have to be expressed in comparable units like the animal unit (AU) (see table 2.5). The stocking rate of the region is then the total number of AUs in each region divided by the area of the region. It ranged from 11 to 36 AUs per square kilometer, excluding the Beer-Sheva district.

To get some idea of the severity of the grazing pressure we can compare it to the stocking rates of the pastures administered by the Rangeland Authority of the Israeli Ministry Agriculture in contemporary times. In 2004, these ranged between 31 and 51 AUs per square kilometer (table 2.6). The cattle that graze on rangeland in Israel today are heavier than in the past, a fact that would suggest that the grazing pressure today is even higher than the calculated traditional stocking rate, if not for the fact that herds in Israel today are given supplementary feed that reduces their dependence on grazing. Differences in context and the scales of the comparison limit its validity, but they do not support the contention that the stocking rates of the traditional herds in Palestine were higher than current stocking rates in Israel, an argument often based on the unattractive appearance of the rocky, shrubby, often bare landscape rather than on the complex interactions between the herbivore and

TABLE 2.6. Stocking rate of livestock on the total grazed area in Palestine in 1937 and on the pasture area administered by the Rangeland Authority in Israel in 2004

MANDATORY CENSUS 1937			
Districts	Area (km²)	AU (in thousands)	AU/km²
Jaffa, Ramle, Gaza	1,819	66	36
Galilee, Haifa	4,347	154	35
Nablus, Tulkarm, Jenin	3,266	74	23
Hebron	2,076	38	18
Jerusalem, Bethlehem, Jericho, Ramallah	2,258	25	11
Beer-Sheva	12,576	47	4
Total	26,342	404	
RANGELAND AUTHORITY 2004			
Region	Area (km²)	AU (in thousands)	AU/km²
Golan	373	12	31
Galilee	527	27	51
Carmel, Megiddo	240	10	42
Jerusalem hills	130	5	38
Negev	208	4	22
Total	1,478	58	

Note: AU = animal unit.

Source: Shaw (1946); Rangeland Authority, Ministry of Agriculture, Tel Aviv.

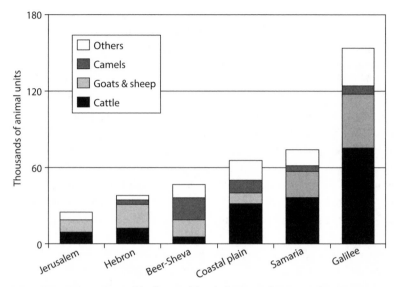

FIGURE 2.3. Composition of the livestock herds (in animal units, each unit a grazing equivalent to a head of livestock weighing 400 kilograms) in the different regions of Palestine in 1937. Jerusalem includes Jerusalem, Bethlehem, Ramallah, and Jericho subregions; Hebron includes southern Judea; Beer-Sheva includes the Negev and the Judean Desert; Coastal plain includes Jaffa, Ramleh, and Gaza subregions; Samaria includes the Nablus, Tulkarm, and Jenin subregions, Galilee includes Haifa, Nazareth, Tiberias, Safad, and Beisan subregions. Other livestock ("Others") include horses, mules, donkeys, and buffalo. Derived from Shaw (1946).

the pasture vegetation (Ellis and Swift 1988; Noy-Meir 1975; Perevolotsky and Seligman 1998; Perevolotsky and Pollak 2001).

Stocking rate on the land that was available for grazing varied over the different regions in Palestine. It was obviously very light in the Beer-Sheva subdistrict, which includes all of the Negev down to the Red Sea. Stocking was also not very heavy in the hilly subdistricts of Judea and Samaria, especially in those that included sections of the arid lower Jordan Valley. The heaviest stocking rate was on the coastal plain and in the Galilee and Haifa region, not only a large region but also the region with the most animals, a large proportion of which were cattle (fig. 2.3) primarily used for cultivating the large areas of arable land in these regions. The higher rainfall and the denser woodland vegetation on the Carmel and the Upper Galilee evidently provided ample pasture even when the stocking was relatively heavy. Stocking rate was clearly not arbitrary; it was related to the intrinsic carrying capacity of each specific region.

No doubt, when the pasture vegetation was fully exploited the grazed area looked dismally bare by the end of summer. Yet if the herds continued to graze the vegetation year after year during centuries till the present, it is unlikely that overgrazing destroyed the vegetation (Perevolotsky 1999). That still leaves open the question as to whether such intensive grazing was a major cause of accelerated erosion.

EROSION, RUNOFF, AND RAINFALL

Soil erosion depends of the reaction of soils to rainfall. Rainfall-runoff-erosion relationships on native pasture were studied in Israel, mainly in the Kinneret watershed, by Morin et al. (1979). They measured amounts of runoff and soil eroded in situ and in experimental plots. Some experiments were conducted under actual rainfall conditions; others employed a rainfall simulator that delivered drops of water with kinetic energy equivalent to that of raindrops falling at different rainfall intensities. A summary of their findings is presented in table 2.7. Its relevance is limited because the study did not cover the complexity of rainfall-runoff relations over the wide range of Israeli soils and climate but they are indicative of the ability of soils on moderate slopes to absorb rainfall even at rare, unusually heavy intensities. The study concludes that there is very little runoff and erosion from rangeland, even on sloping land. The good structure of most soils on calcareous and basaltic substrates ensures good drainage and contributes to the reduction of runoff even after fire (Kutiel et al. 1995).

Only small amounts of dry litter on the pasture soil (less than 50 grams per square meter) at the end of the dry season are necessary to attenuate the kinetic energy of the raindrops that otherwise would disperse the soil aggre-

TABLE 2.7. Rainfall-runoff relationships on basaltic and terra rossa soils

Soil type	Plant cover	Average slope (%)	Rainfall context	Rainfall intensity (mm/hr)	Probability of occurrence	Weight of eroded soil (kg/dunam)	Thickness of eroded layer (mm)
Basaltic	Range		Actual 1974–76			None	
Basaltic	Range	17	Simulated	100		Negligible	
Basaltic	Range		Simulated	26–32	Once in 10 yr	0.16–0.84	0.0001–0.0006
Basaltic	Range	2.6	Calculated	1968/69 intensities	Once in 40 to 200 yr	9–28	0.006–0.020
Basaltic	Cultivated	2.6	Calculated	1968/69 intensities	Once in 40 to 200 yr	113–302	0.075–0.200
Terra rossa	Range	2.6	Calculated	1968/69 intensities	Once in 40 to 200 yr	105–277	0.070–0.185
Terra rossa	Cultivated	2.6	Calculated	1968/69 intensities	Once in 40 to 200 yr	479–1,262	0.32–0.84

Source: Information extracted from Morin et al. (1979).

gates. Most eroded soil comes from bare cultivated soils pounded by occasional heavy rains. Soil erosion from sloping land is inevitable; and even the relatively small amounts of soil that are eroded, over time add up to substantial losses of fertile soil—some of which end up as the "fill" of the terraces, some as sediments in depressions and wadis, and some reaches the sea. Accelerated erosion from hillsides must have been initiated by the introduction of agriculture to the region and the clearing of forests many thousands of years ago.

THE PANTRY, HARDWARE STORE, AND PHARMACY OF THE FELLAHEEN

The native vegetation on the uncultivated and cultivated land provided the Fellaheen and the Bedouin not only with pasture for the domestic herds but also with a number of vital "ecological services": fuel, building material, culinary specialties, medicinal and spice plants, and even plants with "magical" properties like the Mandrake (*Mandragora officinarum*). Culinary and medicinal plants were not only collected for local use but were also sold in the urban markets (Crowfoot and Baldensperger 1932).

Where the regenerating oaks (mainly *Quercus calliprinos*) were available, the branches were cut to produce charcoal, to fire limekilns, and for construction. Dwarf shrubs (such as *Sarcopoterium spinosum, Retama roetam, Noea spinosissima, Ononis natrix*) served as tinder in the villages. Many species were used as salad or spice: "Early in March, bunches of leaves (*Salvia hierosolymitana, Brassica* sp., *Arum palaestinum*) from the countryside appear in the Jerusalem markets. *Salvia hierosolymitana* is wrapped around chopped meats etc. in little rolls like vine leaves (it is a wonder that the flowers are ever seen around Jerusalem so assiduously do the women gather the young plants). . . . Flower heads of *Gundelia Tournefortii* are a delicacy" (Crowfoot and Baldensperger 1932). They also write that bulbs of *Cyclamen* were used as soap; other bulbs, like those of *Erodium hirtum*, were dug up for food. *Majorana syriaca* (Hyssop, Za'atar, Ezov) has been used since ancient times both as condiment and as a medical plant. *Salvia triloba* and tens of other plants have been collected for their medicinal or aromatic properties. Some native trees, like the Carob (*Ceratonia siliqua*) and the Christ Thorn (*Zizyphus spina-christi*) were valued for their fruits.

Cutting, uprooting and picking of native plants or parts of them for diverse use was a common, ancient practice in both the Fellaheen and Bedouin cultures, a practice that has been discouraged in modern Israel with its far larger population. Yet this traditional harvesting of the more favored species did not threaten the existence of an unusually rich flora (more than nine species per square kilometer compared to less than four in California). Tristram (1885) listed a rich flora of Palestine consisting of more than 3,000 species that comprised "all Species hitherto recorded from Palestine" (on an area that evidently included the Lebanon). Over 2,600 species are listed in the *Analytical Flora of Eretz-Israel* (Feinbrun-Dothan and Danin 1998). The smaller number than in Tristram is probably related not to extinctions but to the exclusion of Lebanon from the *Analytical Flora* and differences in the definition of species. The flora evidently remained unchanged throughout history, except for changes in the proportion of plant species within populations (Danin 1995).

At the end of the nineteenth century and the beginning of the twentieth century, charcoal and even raw wood was used as fuel in the developing Turkish railway system. The spiraling demand for fuel during World War I led to the cutting down of many native forest stands, including extensive stands of Valonea Oak (*Quercus ithaburensis*) in the plain of Samaria (Paz 2008). At the end of the nineteenth century, the woodlands in the Galilee and other parts of the country must have been well developed to withstand the heavy exploitation of the early twentieth century. The vigorous recovery of large areas of these woodlands, following drastic reduction in exploitation after 1948, is a convincing indication of their resilience.

Tristram also compiled an impressive list of fauna in Palestine that included over a hundred species of mammals, 660 species of birds, 89 reptile and amphibious species, 60 species of fish, and over 1,100 species of insects and mollusks. With the introduction of firearms in the nineteenth century, many of the larger species (including crocodiles, the Syrian bear, foxes, Roe deer, and ostriches) were hunted to extinction (Paz 2008). In the twentieth century many vertebrates, insects, and other species have become endangered or extinct as a result of present-day habitat destruction following the draining of swamps and wetlands and by earth moving that precedes all major development projects (Dolev and Perevolotsky 2004). Thus, both in the case of floral and faunal extinctions, few if any are attributed to Fellaheen cultivation or Bedouin grazing. Rather, they are due to far more profound impacts of hunting, land-use change, and development.

THE ECOLOGICAL LEGACY

The establishment of the State of Israel changed the political, economic, and cultural context of the processes that influence the environment and determine the nature of the landscape. The rural landscape today provides an opportunity to evaluate the legacy of the past and in particular, the effect of Fellaheen and Bedouin husbandry on the integrity of the natural ecosystems.

The changes have been dramatic. Development of the water resources of the country has facilitated irrigation by fresh or recycled water of much of the arable land down to the Northern Negev; consequently, a wide range of crops and fruit plantations "green the summer." In accordance with worldwide technological developments in agriculture, the use of improved varieties, fertilizers, herbicides, pesticides, mechanization, and efficient irrigation techniques has increased yields many fold; "plastic agriculture" has increased the yields even more and added novel elements to the landscape; the woodland in the Galilee, the Carmel, and the hills of Judea has developed impressively in declared nature reserves and outside of them; the annual show of wild flowers all over the country in winter and spring brings thousands of urban visitors into the open; and more than a million dunam of planted forest provide countless opportunities for recreation.

These developments are a source of pride and pleasure for many people. They contrast vividly with the stark, "empty" landscape of traditional agriculture and animal husbandry that have elicited derisive comments, even from professional observers. But they also indicate that even after generations of villagers who lived off the land with few resources beyond their labor, the soil retained its potential fertility and the vegetation, its resilience (Perevolotsky and Seligman 1998). What has changed is the type and intensity of resource use.

Traditional agriculture and animal husbandry was based on the available natural resources—the intrinsic fertility of the soil, the diversity of the natural vegetation and its many uses, the products of the livestock, and the labor of the inhabitants and of their animals. As long as significant exogenous inputs were not available, there had to be a balance between the potential fruits of the resources and the livelihood of the dependent population (Grigson 1995). This is what was envisioned in the Torah as "a land of wheat and barley, of vines, fig-trees and pomegranates, a land of olive oil and honey . . . a land where you will never live in poverty" (Deut. 8:7–9).

The Fellaheen and the Bedouin, on the whole, lived lives of austerity, often under conditions of grinding poverty and with costly "exogenous inputs": marauders, disease epidemics, political upheavals, heavy taxation, wars, and revolutions. Periodic reductions in the size of the population meant reduction in the available labor required to cultivate the land. The area of land lying fallow would have to increase, a circumstance that favored land-fertility conservation rather than land degradation. Living off the local natural resources required peasant wisdom, "indigenous knowledge," to survive from generation to generation in a constantly changing but always unforgiving environment. Their practices of land use, like those of many indigenous cultures, when not disrupted by economic or political forces, tended to preserve the natural resources rather than destroy them (Altieri et al. 1987). The development of the Israeli landscape since the end of traditional agriculture, especially the regeneration of the vegetation, confirms this conclusion.

In accounting for the changes that have taken place in the environment since the termination of traditional land use, it is a sobering thought that the "new landscape" has forgone the use of the resources that maintained the Fellaheen and the Bedouin. The herbaceous vegetation on many uncultivated slopes is barely utilized and the products of the woody vegetation have little use today. In many cases, the woodland has developed into dense thickets that, with the plentiful tinder of dry grass, have become a fire hazard, dramatically illustrated by the conflagrations in Mount Meron (1975), Mount Carmel (1989), and the devastating Sha'ar Hagai forest fire in 1995.

All smaller patches of cultivated land have been abandoned. Terraces have fallen into disrepair, their soil increasingly eroded. Attempts at adapting hill country land to modern agriculture were generally futile. As a result, much of the previously intensely used landscape has "gone back to nature." Joseph Weitz, the "mythological" director of the Israeli forestry and land reclamation projects, after visiting the area south of Jerusalem in 1967, wrote in his diary: "as I look more deeply into the landscape, I'm filled with shame when I compare 'our' hills of Jerusalem with 'their' hills of Hebron. We, with the power of steel implements, extension services, enormous budgets, expensive water, have not achieved such success" (quoted in Segev 2007, 488–89; Hebrew edition).

That is not the whole story but should at least engender greater empathy for the traditional farmers and graziers who, from generation to generation and despite severe limitations, earned their livelihood from a difficult land.

NOTE

Thanks to Jon Seligman, Professor Avi Perevolotsky, and Mordechai Weitz who gave me access to useful information and reviewed an earlier draft of this chapter.

REFERENCES

Ahad Ha'am. 1891. "Truth from Eretz Israel." *Hamelitz.*

Altieri, M. A., M. K. Anderson, and L. C. Merrick. 1987. "Peasant Agriculture and the Conservation of Crop and Wild Plant Resources." *Journal of the Society of Conservation Biology* 1:49–58.

Avitsur, S. 1985. *Inventors and Adaptors: Agents of the Revolution in Production Methods in Eretz Israel.* Tel Aviv: Yad Ben-Zvi.

Biger, G., and D. Grossman. 1993. "The Village and Town Population in Palestine during the 1930's." In "Biblical Archeology Today," edited by A. Biran and J. Aviram, 19–30, in *Proceedings of the 2nd International Congress on Biblical Archeology,* Supplement, Jerusalem.

Broshi, M. 1979. "The Population of Western Palestine in the Roman-Byzantine Period." *Bulletin of the American Schools of Oriental Research* 236: 7.

Crowfoot, G. M., and L. Baldensperger. 1932. *From Cedar to Hyssop: A Study in the Folklore of Plants in Palestine.* London: Sheldon Press.

Dalman, G. 1932. *Arbeit und Sitte in Palästina. Der Ackerbau.* Band II, Schriften des Deutschen Palästina-Instituts. Gütersloh: Bertelsmann.

Dan, J. 1990. "The Effect of Dust Seposition on the Soils of the Land of Israel." *Quaternary International* 5: 107–13.

Dan, J., P. Fine, and H. Lavee. 2007. *The Soils of the Land of Israel.* Tel Aviv: Eretz-Geographic Research and Publications, Tel Aviv University. In Hebrew; English summary.

Danin, A. 1995. "Man and the Natural Environment." In *The Archeology of Society in the Holy Land*, edited by T. E. Levy, chap. 3. New York: Continuum International Publishing Group.

Davidovitch, N., and Z. Greenberg. 2007. "Public Health, Culture, and Colonial Medicine: Smallpox and Variolation in Palestine during the British Mandate." *Public Health Report* 122: 398–406.

DellaPergola, S. 2001. "Demography in Israel/Palestine: Trends, Prospects, Policy Implications." Paper presented at IUSSP XXIV General Population Conference, Salvador de Bahia, August 18–24.

Dolev, A., and A. Perevolotsky, eds. 2004. *The Red Book: Vertebrates in Israel.* Jerusalem: Israel Nature and Parks Authority. In Hebrew.

Ellis, J. E., and D. M. Swift. 1988. "Stability of African Pastoral Systems: Alternate Paradigms and Implications for Development." *Journal of Range Management* 41: 450–59.

Feinbrun-Dothan, N., and A. Danin. 1998. *Analytical Flora of Eretz-Israel.* Jerusalem: Cana Publishing House.

Gerber, H. 1986. "A New Look at the Tanzimat: The Case of the Province of Jerusalem." In *Palestine in the Late Ottoman Period*, edited by D. Kushner, 40–35. Jerusalem: Yad Izhak Ben-Zvi Press.

Gibson, S. 1995. "Landscape Ecology and Ancient Agricultural Field Systems in Palestine." PhD thesis, University College, London.

Ginat, J. 1982. *Women in Muslim Rural Society.* New Brunswick: Transaction Books, Rutgers University.

Grigg, D. B. 1974. *The Agricultural Systems of the World: An Evolutionary Approach.* Cambridge: Cambridge University Press.

Grigson, C. 1995. "Plough and Pasture in the Southern Levant." In *The Archeology of Society in the Holy Land*, edited by T. E. Levy, chap. 15. New York: Continuum International Publishing Group.

Hamel, G. 1990. "Poverty and Charity in Roman Palestine. Near Eastern Studies 23. Berkeley: University of California Press.

Henkin, Z., L. Hadar, and I. Noy-Meir. 2004. "Effect of Cattle and Goat Grazing on Landscape Features and Human Visual Qualities in Northern Israel." In *Proceedings of the 10th MEDECOS Conference, Rhodes Island, Greece*, edited by M. Arianoutsou and V. P. Papanastasis, 153–54. Rotterdam: Millpress.

Hütteroth, W-D., and K. Abdulfattah. 1977. *Historical Geography of Palestine, Transjordan and Southern Syria in the 16th Century.* Vol. 5. Erlangen: Geographische Arbeiten.

Kababya, D., A. Perevolotsky, I. Bruckental, and S. Landau. 1998. "Selection of Diets by Dual-Purpose Mamber Goats in Mediterranean Woodland." *Journal of Agricultural Science* 131: 221–28.

Kark, R. 1995. "The Introduction of Modern Technology into the Holy Land (1800–1914 CE)." In *The Archeology of Society in the Holy Land*, edited by T. E. Levy, chap. 31. New York: Continuum International Publishing Group.

Kutiel, P., H. Lavee, M. Segev, and Y. Benyamini. 1995. "The Effect of Fire-Induced Surface Heterogeneity on Rainfall-Runoff-Erosion Relationships in an Eastern Mediterranean Ecosystem, Israel." *Catena* 77–87.

Levy, T. E., ed. 1995. *The Archeology of Society in the Holy Land.* New York: Continuum International Publishing Group.

Lewis, B. 1954. "Studies in the Ottoman Archives." *Bulletin of the School of Oriental and African Studies* 16: 469–501.

Lowdermilk, W. C. 1944. *Palestine, Land of Promise.* New York: Harper and Brothers.

Morin, J., A. Michaeli, M. Agassi, B. Atzmon, and D. Rosenzweig. 1979. *Rainfall-Runoff-Erosion Relationships in the Kinneret Watershed.* Research Report No. 42. Hefer Valley: Soil Erosion Research Station, Agricultural Research Organization/Division of Soil Conservation and Drainage.

McNaughton, S. J. 1984. "Grazing Lawns: Animals in Herds, Plant Form, and Co-Evolution." *Amercan Naturalist* 124: 863–86.

Noy-Meir, I. 1975. "Stability of Grazing Systems: An Application of Predator-Prey Graphs." *Journal of Ecology* 63, 459–81.

Paz, U. 2008. *Le-avdah ule-shamrah : Shemirat Ṭeva be-Yiśrael* [To Till It and Conserve It: Nature Conservation in Israel]. Tel Aviv: Nature Conservation Authority.

Perevolotsky, A. 1999. "Conservation, Reclamation and Grazing in the Northern Negev: Contradictory or Complementary Concepts?" In *Arid Lands Management: Toward Ecological Sustainability,* edited by T. W. Hoekstra and M. Shachak, chap. 15. Champaign: University of Illinois Press.

Perevolotsky, A., and G. Pollak. 2001. *Ecology: Theory and the Israeli Experience.* Jerusalem: Karta. In Hebrew.

Perevolotsky, A., and N. G. Seligman. 1998. "Grazing in Mediterranean Ecosystems: Inversion of a Paradigm." *BioScience* 48: 1007–17.

Ravikovitch, S. 1981. *The Soils of Israel: Formation, Nature and Properties.* Tel Aviv: Hakibbutz Hameuchad Publishing House. In Hebrew; English summary.

Reifenberg, A. 1938. *The Soils of Palestine. Studies in Soil Formation and Land Utilisation in the Mediterranean.* London: Thomas Murby.

———. 1955. *The Struggle between the Desert and the Sown. Rise and Fall of Agriculture in the Levant.* Jerusalem: Jewish Agency.

Ron, Z. 1966. "Agricultural Terraces in the Judean Mountains." *Israel Exploration Journal* 16: 33–49, 111–22.

Sandford, S. 1983. *Management of Pastoral Development in the Third World.* New York: John Wiley and Sons.

Schölch, A. 1993. *Palestine in Transformation, 1856–1882.* Beirut: Institute for Palestine Studies.

Segev, T. 2007. *1967: Israel, the War, and the Year that Transformed the Middle East.* New York: Metropolitan Books.

Seligman, N. G., Z. Raz, N. H. Tadmor, J. Katznelson, and Z. Naveh. 1959. *Natural Pasture of Israel: Vegetation, Carrying Capacity and Improvement.* Merhavia: Sifriat Hapoalim. In Hebrew; English summary.

Shaw, J. V. W., ed. 1946. *Survey of Palestine Prepared in December 1945 and January 1946 for the Information of the Anglo-American Committee of Inquiry.* London: Her Majesty's Stationery Office.

Singer, A. 1994. *Palestinian Peasants and Ottoman Officials: Rural Administration around Sixteenth-Century Jerusalem.* Cambridge: Cambridge University Press.

Singer, A., E. Ganor, S. Dultz, and W. Fischer. 2003. "Dust Deposition over the Dead Sea." *Journal of Arid Environments* 53: 141–59.

Taylor, B. 1855. *The Lands of the Saracen*. New York: Putnam.

Tristram, H. B. 1885. *The Survey of Western Palestine: The Fauna and Flora of Palestine*. London: Palestine Exploration Fund.

Twain, M. 1869. *Innocents Abroad*. New York: Signet Classics.

Vamosh, M. F. 2009. *Food at the Time of the Bible*. Herzlia: Palphot.

Wilkinson, T. 1999. "Demographic Trends from Archeological Survey: Case Studies from the Levant and Near East." In *Reconstructing Past Population Trends in Mediterranean Europe*, edited by J. Bintliff and L. Sbonias, 45–64. Oxford: Oxbow Books.

Ziffer, I., and R. Kletter. 2007. *In the Field of the Philistines: Cult Furnishings from the Favissah of a Yavneh Temple*. Tel Aviv: Eretz Israel Museum.

CHAPTER THREE

HUMAN IMPACT ON WILDLIFE IN ISRAEL SINCE THE NINETEENTH CENTURY

Yoram Yom-Tov

D URING THE NINETEENTH CENTURY Palestine was a neglected part of the Ottoman Empire. Its human population had been decimated by wars and disease, and much of its area was deserted and uninhabited. Mark Twain visited the country during the mid-1880s, and was dismayed: "Palestine sits in sackcloth and ashes. . . . The noted Sea of Galilee, where Roman fleets once rode at anchor . . . was long ago deserted by the devotees of war and commerce, and its borders are a silent wilderness; Capernaum is a shapeless ruin; Magdala is the home of beggared Arabs; Bethsaida and Chorazin have vanished from the earth, and the 'desert places' round about them . . . sleep in the hush of solitude that is inhabited only by birds of prey and skulking foxes" (Twain 1869).

But while Twain reported a desolate and empty Palestine, Canon Henry Baker Tristram, reporting on the same birds of prey and foxes as Twain had noted, describes a Palestine rich in biodiversity. During his 1863–1864 tour of the region, Tristram provided a testament to the existence of animals that have since disappeared. In his description of a day in Wadi Hamam (now Nahal HaYonim, below Arbel near the Sea of Galilee), not far from where Mark Twain had despaired over what he saw, Tristram wrote: "We never met with so many wild animals as on one of these days. First of all, a wild boar got out of some scrub close to us. . . . Then a deer was startled below, ran up the cliff . . . passing close to us. Then a large ichneumon almost crossed my feet and run into a cleft; and, while endeavouring to trace him, I was amazed to see a Syrian bear clumsily but rapidly clamber down the rocks. . . . While working the ropes above, we could see the gazelles gripping lightly at the bottom of the valley. . . . L., who was below, also saw an otter, which came out of the water, and stood and looked at him for a minute with surprise. Five great griffons were shot by S. and U." (Tristram 1865).

Hence, the dismay of one traveler was the joy of another, and the neglect enabled wildlife to flourish where the human population had diminished. The land underwent profound changes in the century and a half that followed Twain and Tristam's visits to the region, and those changes have had an equally profound effect on the area's animal life. The aim of this chapter is to report on those changes that took place during the twentieth century in the former Palestine (Land of Israel). This historical overview of the fate of the region's biodiversity provides unique insight into human development patterns and our changing and intensifying impact not only on the region's animal life, but on the entire planet and its inhabitants.

During the course of the twentieth century many changes took place in the status, distribution, and abundance of vertebrates in the area that today encompasses Israel and the Palestinian Authority. In this area, comprising ca. 28,000 square kilometers, the human population grew from ca. 650,000 in-

FIGURE 3.1. A common Israeli approach to nature conservation: Acacia trees left to die after a contractor had excavated most of the soil around them. North of Eilat, 2004. Reproduced by permission from Eyal Bar-Tov.

habitants between 1900–1903 (Rupin 1920) to around 10 million in 2010 (of which 7.37 million are in Israel proper; Statistical Abstracts of Israel 2012); that is, a 16-fold increase in population. This population increase led to an increased use of land for human needs—construction of buildings, roads, and so forth. Many changes also took place in agricultural methods. The area of worked land (excluding pine tree planting) increased by about 50 percent to about 3,000 square kilometers (Avitsur 1977; Statistical Abstracts of Israel 2009); the irrigated area increased by ca. 135-fold, from 15 square kilometers at the beginning of the twentieth century (Avitsur 1977) to about 2,000 square kilometers approximately one hundred years later (Statistical Abstracts of Israel 2009). These changes (and many others) had a major, in many cases fatal, effect on the animal life in Israel.

THE EFFECT OF HUMAN ACTIVITIES ON ANIMAL LIFE

Hunting

Up until the World War I, when this region was still part of the Ottoman Empire, there were no legal restrictions on hunting. Although by 1924 the British Mandate government had enacted the "Conservation of Hunt Animals" law, this code was never enforced. The massive introduction of firearms into the Middle East at the end of the nineteenth century, together with the hunting tradition of the local Arab population and shooting excursions by European visitors (German, British, and others)—led to the disappearance of several vertebrate species by the end of the nineteenth century and the beginning of the twentieth century (Aharoni 1943, 1946; Talbot 1960; Dolev and Perevolotzky 2002). These were mostly mammals (four ungulates: the roe deer *Capreolus capreolus*, the fallow deer *Dama dama mesopotamica*, the Arabian oryx *Oryx leucoryx*, and the onager wild ass *Equus hemionus*; two predators: the Syrian bear *Ursus arctos syriacus* and the cheetah *Acinonyx jubatus*), but also one species of bird (the ostrich, *Strutio camelus*) and one reptile (the Nile crocodile, *Crocodilus niloticus*). Four of these species (roe and fallow deer, wild ass, and Arabian oryx) were returned to the wild in Israel by the Israel Nature and Parks Authority (INPA) in the 1980s and 1990s.

Hunting was also the main reason for the almost complete extinction of the green and the loggerhead sea turtles (*Chelonia mydas* and *Caretta caretta*, respectively), which had previously laid their eggs along the sandy shores of the Mediterranean in considerable numbers (Yom-Tov and Mendelssohn 1988). During 1920–1930 about thirty thousand turtles were killed along the sea shores: up to six hundred were caught daily (Sela 1979).

During the 1950s and 1960s illegal hunting was carried out by soldiers and civilians, from 4-wheel drive vehicles and using automatic weapons (Ilani 2004), which further worsened the situation and led to a drastic reduction in some mammal populations, such as the mountain and the dorcas gazelles (*Gazella gazella* and *G. dorcas*, respectively). This poaching was stopped during the late 1960s by the then chief of staff, Yitzhak Rabin (later Israel's prime minister) after a personal appeal by Professor Heinrich Mendelssohn.

Since the late 1970s, many of the wild animal populations have recovered, partly due to enactment of the "Protection of Wild Animals" law in 1955. According to this law, all wild mammals and birds in Israel are protected species, excluding a number of pest species and with the exception of species designated as legal hunting animals during the defined hunting season as determined by Israel Nature and Parks Authority. In 1990 the Protection of Wild Animals act was renewed to incorporate species of reptiles and amphibians. This far-sighted law provides effective means to provide protection to wild animals. Together with the fact that hunting is not a popular sport among the majority of Israelis (there are only a few thousand legal hunters, mostly Druze and Arab), hunting has not been a serious conservation problem until the 1990s.

Hunting resurfaced as a major conservation challenge in the early 1990s with the arrival of agricultural workers from Thailand. These workers have been brought into Israel to work in the agricultural sector and in 2008 their numbers stood at ca. thirty thousand. They are employed in every area of Israel on the agricultural settlements and private farms. These industrious workers bring with them hunting habits that were unfamiliar in Israel, such as snares and a variety of other traps deployed on the ground or hung on fences and branches, which trap the animals attempting to pass through the holes in the fence or beneath it. The traps are efficient at catching a variety of wildlife, including gazelles, wolves (*Canis lupus*), badgers (*Meles meles*), jackals (*Canis aureus*), porcupines (*Hystrix indica*), and wild boar (*Sus scrofa*). The Thai workers are also skilled at using slingshots to hunt small and medium-sized birds; they dig up rodent tunnels; and in the Arava Valley they also hunt reptiles, such as the Egyptian mastigure (*Uromastix aegyptius*). A survey carried out in 2000 (Yom-Tov 2003) indicates that the extent and cumulative impact of such trapping are extremely serious, and today it appears to constitute one of the greatest threats to wildlife in Israel.

Habitat Destruction

All Mediterranean and most desert wildlife habitats in Israel have been affected to some extent, or entirely destroyed, as a result of urban, industrial, and agricultural development, as well as by dense afforestation with mainly introduced trees. A detailed description follows of the changes that have taken place. A recent study found that habitat change is the most serious threat to the birds of Israel (Yom-Tov, Hatzofe, and Geffen 2012) and presumably also to other vertebrates.

Sand Dunes

Sand dunes cover about 920 square kilometers in Israel and form three distinct areas, geographically separated from each other. Of these areas, about half are seriously affected by human activity today. The coastal and western Negev dunes occur along the Mediterranean coastal plain and northwest Negev; the Arava Valley sand derived from the erosion of local Nubian sandstone occurs along the Rift Valley south of the Dead Sea; and the internal dunes form relatively small patches of sandy areas in the Negev and near the Sea of Galilee. The history of development of these areas differs, and they will be discussed separately below.

At the beginning of the twentieth century most sand dune areas were not inhabited—at the time considered worthless land, unfit for profitable agriculture, even along the Mediterranean coastal plain. The relatively low cost of coastal sand dune areas was one of the reasons that during the Ottoman and British Mandate period most Jewish immigrants settled along the Mediterranean coast. The establishment of Rishon Le'Zion (1882), Hadera (1891), and Tel Aviv (1909) was followed by other cities such as Netanya (1929) and Holon (1940) as well as many smaller settlements, including agricultural ones. The establishment of Ashdod (1956) further increased human impact, and presently most of Israel's population lives along the coastal plain. Today, almost the entire coastal sand dune area suffers from urban sprawl. In addition, until the late 1980s, coastal dunes were extensively mined for construction purposes (Sela 1979). This mining continues, albeit mostly illegally, even today.

Until the establishment of the State of Israel (1948), the dunes of the northwestern Negev were little affected by human activities. Since then, establishment of agricultural settlements along the Gaza Strip and the Egyptian border between 1949 and the 1970s eroded the natural value of these dunes. Further development occurred during the 2000s when new settlements were created in the western and northwestern sides of the dunes—development which continues to this day.

The sand dunes along the coastal plain and in the western Negev make up a unique habitat in Israel, as they constitute the easternmost reaches of the Sahara desert from the viewpoint of their flora and fauna. The relatively large grains of sand in these dunes are the main factor explaining the low capacity for water retention of the upper levels of sand, and the ability of the dunes to serve as a corridor for many species of Saharan wildlife into the Mediterranean climate region of Israel. Among vertebrates, the majority of Saharan species are reptiles, such as the Egyptian tortoise (*Testudo kleinmanni*), snakes (the horned viper *Aspis vipera*, false smooth snake *Macroprotodon cuculla-tus*, and crowned leafnose snake *Lytorhynchus diadema*), skinks (the sandfish *Scincus scincus* and wedge-snouted skink *Sphenops sepsoides*), geckos (Lich-tenstein's short-fingered gecko *Stenodactylus sthenodactylus* and Anderson's short-fingered gecko *S. petrii*), lizards (Nidua fringe-fingered lizard *Acantho-dactylus scutellatus*, Egyptian sand agama *Agama savignii* and Desert moni-tor *Varanus griseus*), and a distinctive subspecies of chameleon (*Chamaeleo chamaeleon musae*) (Werner 1987).

In addition, a number of mammals originating from the Sahara region can be found on these dunes, with the majority being rodent species (lesser Egyptian gerbil *Gerbillus gerbillus*, the greater Egyptian gerbil *G. pyramidum*, Anderson's gerbil *G. andersoni allenbyi*) and a subspecies of jerboa (*Jaculus jaculus schluteri*), but also a long-eared hedgehog (*Hemiechinus auritus*). The only endemic mammal in Israel, Buxton's jird (*Meriones sacramenti*), is re-stricted to these dunes (Werner 1988; Yom-Tov 1988).

Destruction of the sand dunes along the coastal plain, mainly in northern and central Israel but also in the western Negev, has led to a reduction in dis-tribution and survival of the majority of these species. Moreover, predation by feral cats and dogs has had an immense effect on the rodent species, on some of the reptiles (i.e., desert lizard *Varanus griseus*) (Perry and Dmiel 1995) and even on gazelles (Perry and Dmiel 1995, Manor and Saltz 2004).

Sand supply from the sea was greatly reduced after the construction of the Aswan Dam in Egypt. In addition, building along the coast prevented new sand from accumulating on the coastal dunes. A drastic reduction in grazing by domestic and wild ungulates was followed by sand stabilization. This pro-cess was documented by Perry and Dmiel (1995) in Holon, where plant cover increased ninefold between 1987–1990 (from 2.3 percent to 19.9 percent). At present almost all of this area is covered with buildings and roads.

Stabilization of the dunes and the resulting spread of invasive plants, such as the blue-leafed wattle (*Acacia cyanophila*), was followed by a dramatic change in rodent (Angelister 2006) and reptile communities. The process of stabilizing the dunes and isolating the remaining sandy areas in northern and central Israel has enabled the invasion of species from neighboring re-gions characterized by heavier soil. Examples include the Schreiber's fringe-fingered lizard (*Acanthodactylus schreiberi*), which outcompetes Nidua fringe-fingered lizard (*A. scutellatus*) in areas with denser vegetation, and Tristram's jird (*Meriones tristrami*), which invades stabilized and cultivated dunes that were formerly inhabited by Buxton's jird. Similarly, the European hedgehog (*Erinaceus europaeus*) and Anderson's gerbil have invaded cultivated areas formerly occupied by the long-eared hedgehog and the greater Egyptian gerbil. This phenomenon is particularly prominent in areas adjacent to urban and agricultural settlements.

The following anecdote illustrates the change in wildlife in the coastal dunes. In a course I teach at Tel Aviv University I take my students to the coastal dunes in order to show them *psammophilous* (sand dwelling) species. During the 1970s we went to Holon, less than 10 kilometers from the university; during the 1980s, in order to see the species, we had to move to Palmachim, a further 10 kilometers south; at present we go to Nizanim, 40 kilometers south of Tel Aviv, where we normally see fewer species and individuals than we formerly saw in Holon thirty years ago.

The sands of the Arava region cover an area much smaller than that of the coastal plain and the western Negev. Until the late 1950s these areas were seldom used by humans, and only then for sparse grazing. However, the establishment of about twenty, mostly agricultural, settlements between the Dead and Red Seas had a detrimental effect on the wildlife of the dunes. Sandy areas were and continue to be in increasing demand by farmers due to their low salinity relative to other desert areas. As a consequence, almost the entire sand area is now worked as agricultural land. In the past, these sands were populated by psammophilic animals. While some of these species are still found along the coastal plain, for others the Arava Valley is their only habitat in the country. These include the horned viper (*Aspis cerastes gasperettii*), the Middle Eastern short-fingered gecko (*Stenodactylus doriae*) (Werner 1987) and Wagner's gerbil *Gerbillus nanus*.

The near elimination of these sand dunes that took place during the 1980s–1990s was followed by a sharp decrease in the populations of Middle Eastern short-fingered gecko in the Arava. However, Wagner's gerbil populations persist elsewhere because this species also inhabits sandy marl soils and wide coarse sand wadis in the southern Negev.

The least affected sandy areas in Israel are the internal dunes. A large proportion of these, about 60 square kilometers or 30 percent are occupied by industry and by the Dimona nuclear reactor. Much of the latter area is fenced, so that the natural habitat is protected from overgrazing; for the time being plant and animal life there seems to be safe from these impacts.

Aquatic Landscapes

Israel lies at the edge of the Saharo-Arabian Desert, and wetlands of various types extended to less than 180 square kilometers in total. Until drained in the late 1950s, the Hula Lake, which spread over 13 square kilometers, and the adjacent swamp north of it, which extended over an area of 40 square kilometers, were the main wetland habitats in Israel (Weitz 1972). They were rich in flora and fauna, partially due to a rare convergence of the Palearctic and the Tropical worlds (Dimentman, Bromley, and Por 1992). Unfortunately, after the swamp and adjacent lake were drained for cultivation, only a small nature reserve (ca. 3 square kilometers) remained. Part of the original flora and fauna species, some of which were or are endemic, disappeared from the Hula, which was replaced by other habitat types, primarily agricultural. One of the most interesting species to disappear was the water vole (*Arvicola ter-restris*), whose southernmost world occurrence had been here (Dor 1947). Another species that disappeared after the drainage of the Hula was the endemic Israel painted frog (*Discoglossus nigriventer*). This species was discovered in 1940 and again in 1955, but none have been seen since then. However, during November–December 2011 seven specimens were found in the Hula Nature Reserve. Apparently a small population still strives there. Several birds that once bred in the Hula no longer do so (or elsewhere in Israel), including the grey heron (*Ardea cinerea*), great crested grebe (*Podiceps cristatus*), Baillon's crake (*Porzana pusilla*), black tern (*Chlidonias niger*), marsh harrier (*Circus aeruginosus*) and great reed-warbler (*Acrocephalus arundinaceus*). A pair of white-tailed sea eagles (*Haliaetus albicilla*) that bred near the reserve (one of the two pairs which bred in Israel) disappeared after the swamp was drained (Merom 1966; Shirihai 1996; Yom-Tov et al. 2012).

Several other wetlands existed in Israel during the nineteenth century, and many were infested with malaria-carrying mosquitoes. Hence, these areas were generally avoided by the local Arab population and were sold cheaply to Jewish immigrants. Several of the first Jewish settlements established in such areas which were then drained by the new inhabitants. Thus, the Hadera and Petach Tikva swamps were drained at the end of the nineteenth century, and most of the rest (Jezreel Valley, Kebaa'ra swamp near Ma'agan Michael, Emek Hefer, Zevulun Valley, and Bet Shean Valley) were drained between the 1920s and 1940s (Wietz 1972). Their aquatic wildlife has largely disappeared.

Riverine (Riparian) Habitats

The rivers, streams, and wadis in the temperate, relatively water-rich region of Israel flow west into the Mediterranean Sea or east into the Jordan River system. The western streams are generally longer and provide a larger area of riparian habitat than those flowing to the east. Eleven of the streams flowing westward and seven of those flowing eastward are perennial, possessing water throughout the year, at least along some stretches. The largest riparian system is the Jordan River, which flows into the Dead Sea.

Since the inception of the Israel Water Carrier in 1964, the flow to the Jordan River has been virtually eliminated and the waters diverted, primarily for agricultural use to the south of Israel. In most of the other streams the remaining water is polluted to some extent. Since the 1960s, in many of these ephemeral streams during drought years there are extended periods when no freshwater flows (Prushinski 1964).

As a consequence of these two factors most fish have disappeared from the west-flowing rivers. Among marine fish, at least three species—mullets (*Mugil cephalus* and *M. ramada*) and eel (*Anguila anguila*) fingerlings—used to spend their first years in these rivers (they reproduce in the sea) but have now disappeared from most of them. Eight species of freshwater fishes that inhabited the rivers were all seriously affected and today are very rare there. One of these, the Yarqon bleak (*Acanthobrama telavivensis*), is endemic to some of the west-flowing rivers and now faces extinction (Goren 1983; Goren and Ortal 1999).

The drying of the Hula Lake and diversion of adjacent streams resulted in the elimination of the endemic *Nun galilaeus* (*Cobitidae*) as well as an endemic subspecies of cichlid (*Tristramella simonis intermedia*). Another cobitid, fish, *Orthrias dori*, which is endemic to the Bet Shean Valley, is now threatened due to the draining of most springs in that area (Goren 1983). The soft-shelled turtle (*Trionyx triunguis*), which lived in many of the west-flowing rivers and nested on their shores until the 1970s, has disappeared from most of them. Only along the Alexander River does a breeding population persist, but many of the eggs fail to hatch and some hatchlings have various anomalies, presumably due to the poisonous and mutagenic effects of sundry pollutants. Currently, only large specimens and a few young turtles inhabit the Alexander River, with little apparent recruitment (Rozner 2007). During the 1970s Professor Mendelssohn transferred several dozens of soft-shelled turtles to the Hula reserve. The progeny of these specimens provide a stock from which the Israel Nature and Parks Authority (INPA) now takes specimens for experimental reintroduction into some coastal streams.

The river otter (*Lutra lutra*), a former inhabitant of all the west-flowing rivers, is now only occasionally encountered, mainly in three of the northernmost west-flowing rivers (Bezet, Keziv, Na'aman), although some scats were found in Nahal Alexander and Nahal Taninim during 2000 but not later. A small population, estimated at fifty to sixty specimens exists between the Hula and Bet Shean Valleys and the Golan.

Temporary Winter Ponds

In the Mediterranean, temperate region of Israel, low-lying areas were often flooded during winter, creating many hundreds of winter rain pools. The pools varied in size, in accordance with the topography and rainfall, from a few square meters to one square kilometer. Many of these pools were recent or ancient artifacts built as reservoirs by means of erecting a dam across a wadi, or were carved into rock on the slopes of foothills. In certain cases these pools constituted an important source of water for villages. But they were also a vital habitat for a rich variety of invertebrate species and amphibians.

The number of winter pools in Israel declined sharply during the second half of the twentieth century. A recent study (Levin, Elron, and Gasith 2009) has shown that at the beginning of the twentieth century, between Ashkelon and Hadera, there were up to six hundred temporary winter pools whose total area was 27.6 square kilometers. Only a few dozen of those exist today, and their total area is 2.4 square kilometers, a 90 percent reduction.

Spraying weed killers on the puddles along the roadside and railway tracks, and spraying with insecticides those pools adjacent to human settlements, destroyed this habitat and turned these water sources into habitats for species of insecticide-resistant mosquitoes. One result of these activities was that species of amphibians that had once been common are now endangered (Degani and Mendelssohn 1984). This is particularly true of the newt (*Triturus vittatus*), and even more so of the spadefoot toad (*Pelobates syriacus*) (Gafny 1986) which breeds exclusively in rainwater pools. These two species are now very rare along the coastal plain and their existence in the hill region is limited to a few places in the Golan, Galilee, and Samaria. The INPA has established a small number of new winter pools and rehabilitated old pools in a few locations in Israel.

Fishponds and Water Reservoirs

Since the 1930s, fish have been bred in fishponds in Israel and following establishment of the state, aquaculture has seen tremendous development. Fishponds can constitute an alternate habitat for some of those species whose natural habitats have disappeared. By 1998 such fishponds covered an area of ca. 32 square kilometers (Statistical Abstracts of Israel 1999), mostly in northern Israel and the coastal plain. They are encircled by banks 3–4 meters wide and accessed via dirt paths. Most of these ponds are surrounded by bulrushes and other aquatic plants, often creating a dense brush that serves as a habitat for riparian species.

In addition to the fishponds, in Israel in 1984 there were ca. 260 water reservoirs (Water Commission Office 1982; D. Rozenweig, pers. comm., 1984) constructed for collecting floodwater, wastewater, and spring water to provide irrigation in the summer. Since that time, the Jewish National Fund (JNF) has added over 200 reservoirs, primarily serving to store treated effluents during the winter for summer irrigation (Tal 2006). Both fishponds and water reservoirs create a favorable habitat for several species of animals. Among birds, herons, mainly the night heron (*Nycticorax nycticorax*), little egret (*Egretta garzetta*), and to a smaller extent the squacco heron (*Ardeola ralloides*), are the main beneficiaries; but the glossy ibis (*Plegadis falcinellus*) also breed near some reservoirs (Mendelssohn and Yom-Tov 1999a; Yom-Tov et al. 2012).

The availability of fish from aquaculture has affected not only breeding birds but also other piscivorous migrants. About seventy thousand white pelicans (*Pelecanus onocrotalus*) that migrate from East Europe to Africa used to stop over in Israel for a day or two during the 1980s (Leshem and Yom-Tov 1996). Since the 1990s several thousand pelicans began to spend longer periods of time, and several hundred of them even overwintered in Israel. They cause considerable damage to fisheries, eating large quantities of fish. The growth in the cormorant (*Phalacrocorax carbo*) populations in Europe led to a growth in the overwintering population in Israel, with fifteen to thirty thousand cormorants finding their food in the fishponds near the Mediterranean Sea and the Sea of Galilee (Shirihai 1996). The conflict between the farmers and the birds that feed on the fish from these ponds has yet to be resolved and there are still cases of direct injury to these birds and to the nesting colonies of species such as pygmy cormorant (*Phalacrocorax pygmaeus*).

Two species of mammals were also conspicuously affected by the fishponds, and to a lesser extent by reservoirs: the introduced coypu (*Myocastor coypu*) and the jungle cat (*Felis chaus*). The coypu, introduced during the 1950s for the fur industry, escaped from breeding farms in the Hula and Bet Shean Valleys. Other individuals were released after such fur breeding proved to be unprofitable. Today this species can be found in all wetland habitats in northern and central Israel and as far as the Gaza Strip in the south. They cause damage to native plants and agriculture, and their burrows damage the dams of fishponds. The jungle cat, which suffered heavily from the draining of wetland habitats and later from secondary poisoning during the 1960s, has now fully recovered and occurs in any suitable habitat, mainly near fishponds (Mendelssohn 1972a; Mendelssohn and Yom-Tov 1999a).

One species of amphibian, the frog (*Rana rhidibunda*) thrives in water reservoirs where it breeds during spring and even summer. This is the only Israeli amphibian species that has benefited from human activities.

Seashore

The Mediterranean coast of Israel covers an area stretching 190 kilometers long. Most of this is a narrow strip of sand, offering a suitable habitat for the Kentish plover (*Charadrius alexandrinus*) and the little ringed plover (*Charadrius dubius*), as well as for egg laying by the green and loggerhead sea turtles. Human recreational activities along the coast, mainly in spring and sum-

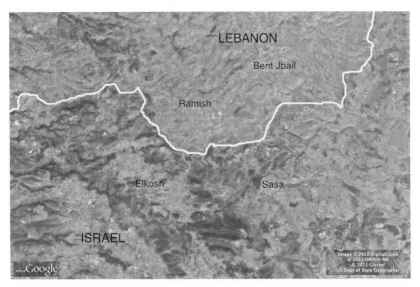

FIGURE 3.2. A satellite image of the middle section of Israel-Lebanon border, showing differences in land cover. Light areas denote vegetation cover; dark are areas of chaparral, garigue, and planted forest. Note that much of the Galilee in Israel has dense vegetation cover in comparison with areas north of the border. Before the establishment of the State of Israel in 1948 there was no difference in land cover between the two states. Image from Google Earth.

mer, which is the reproduction season of these animals, negatively affects the plover and turtle breeding activities. Presently these plovers do not nest there anymore.

Although hunting was the main factor in reducing the number of turtles laying eggs along the Israeli shore (see Hunting above), the mining of sand for construction from these shores and shore development has contributed significantly to the destruction of egg-laying areas (Sela 1979). Large quantities of sand were dug annually; for example, about one million cubic meters of shore sand were removed in 1963 (Sela 1979). The shores near Atlit (about 20 kilometers south of Haifa) exemplify the destruction caused by this mining; 80 meters of the coast were eroded along an 8-kilometer stretch of beach. In the 2000s less than one hundred turtle nests were found each year along these shores, rather than the many hundreds that had existed until midcentury.

Afforestation and Gardening

By the beginning of the twentieth century most of the natural thickets in Israel had disappeared as a result of logging for firewood, construction, joinery, charcoal production, and overgrazing by goats (Weitz 1970). The last major damage occurred during World War I, when the Turkish army destroyed the forest of the Sharon and other areas, mainly to build the railway track to Sinai and feed the steam engines. Despite this, in 1920 the Forestry Commission of the British Mandate government and later the Jewish National Fund (JNF) began to collaborate in rehabilitating and conserving the natural forests and in reforestation. Currently, natural forests cover about 350 square kilometers (Orni 1978; Statistical Abstracts of Israel 1985) and afforested areas an additional 980 square kilometers (Statistical Abstracts of Israel 2009).

During the first half of the twentieth century, most of the forests were planted in the wetter areas of central and northern Israel. They comprised ca. 51 percent pine forest, ca. 8 percent eucalyptus, and ca. 27 percent variegated forest (Statistical Abstracts of Israel 2009). The majority of these planted areas had in the past been subjected to deep plowing and spraying with herbicides, which seriously harmed the local flora and apparently also the wildlife in the treated area. Since the early 1980s the JNF gradually changed its afforestation policy: planting density decreased and native trees were planted together with pines; and native trees that grew in the forests were preferred over pines (see Alon Tal, chapter 5 in this volume). During the last decade there was only a minute increase in the planted area, and in 2008 only 8.3 percent of the trees were younger than ten years (Statistical Abstracts of Israel 2009).

Although recovery of the natural woodland (as well as gardening) enabled rehabilitation of a number of animal species (e.g., the Syrian woodpecker *Dryobates syriacus*, blackbird *Turdus merula*, great tit *Parus major,* and jay *Garrulus glandarius*), the dense pine forests constitute an ecologically impoverished system with a diminished ability to support wildlife. These forests, which replaced natural open areas, offer poor habitats inhabited by a meager fauna, alongside natural areas hosting a much richer variety of species. Several studies demonstrate this observation. Lehman and Perevolotsky (1992) reported that in the southern Mount Carmel rodent species richness and abundance was significantly lower in coniferous plantations in comparison with adjacent native habitats. Manor and Saltz (2008) found that general habitat structural diversity, vegetative structural diversity, and abundance of native small mammals were higher in the natural maqui in comparison to planted tree stands of pine (*Pinus halepensis*) and carob (*Ceratonia siliqua*) stands, and the commensal house mouse was more abundant in the plantations. Levanony (2005) found that species richness and abundance of beetles and spiders was significantly higher in maqui compared to afforested areas. In addition to afforestation, the area dedicated to fruit orchards greatly increased during the twentieth century at the expense of open areas more suitable for wildlife.

Planted forests replaced open habitats, thus affecting raptor populations that forage in such habitats (e.g., the griffon vulture *Gyps fulvus,* long-legged buzzard *Buteo ferox*, lanner falcon *Falco biarmicus*, and Egyptian vulture *Neophron percnopterus*; Sela 1977; Friedemann et al. 2011). Because ca. 17 percent of land in central and northern Israel is covered in forest, much of it pine planted by humans, this is an important factor affecting the composition and abundance of wildlife in the Mediterranean region of Israel. However, at present about 70 percent of the planted trees are older than ten years (Statistical Abstracts of Israel 2009) and the forest has become more open. The above change in planting policy enabled the regeneration of broadleaf trees and bushes, thus creating a more diverse habitat. This trend should be encouraged, and it seems that the JNF foresters favor it. The above-mentioned change in afforestation policy in which native trees are planted in combination with pines, as well as the natural reduction in tree density, in time was followed by an increased use of these forests by wildlife. One already observed positive result is the inhabitation of some forests by the sparrowhawk (*Accipiter nisus*) that prefers to build its nests there (Shirihai 1996).

Since the 1960s, afforestation has been initiated in the semiarid northern Negev, on low hills and loess soil plains, and at present occupies about 50 square kilometers (Yitzhak Moshe, JNF, pers. comm., 2000). In order to succeed in this water-deprived environment, a series of contour catchments are constructed to accumulate runoff to support planted trees (Sachs and Moshe 1999). These activities fundamentally affected the structure of the lizard assemblage in the planted areas, with Mediterranean lizards replacing desert species. In addition, avian predators use the planted trees as observation spots for hunting lizards, and they have seriously reduced the lizard density in tree plots compared to the natural plots. As a consequence, the populations of two local lizard species (the Beer-Sheva fringe-fingered lizard *Acanthodactylus pardalis* and the Egyptian sand agama *Agama pallida*) have been seriously diminished (Hawlena and Bouskila 2006).

Veterinary Care

Until the establishment of a veterinary service by the British Mandate in the 1920s, no veterinary care existed; past animal husbandry practices resulted in the availability of many domestic herd carcasses for scavenging raptors as well as for jackals, wolves, and striped hyenas (*Hyaena hyaena*). No doubt, the sight of thousands of vultures and other raptors reported by Tristram (1865) was a result of this food availability. Three main factors contributed to this situation: death from infectious diseases (e.g., anthrax and rinderpest) (Dafni 1972; Shimshony 1983), offal from slaughtered animals (estimated at 30–40 percent of the whole animal's body weight), and the discarding of stillborn animals. This waste matter once provided a significant source of food for raptors and other predators and enabled the existence of a large population of scavenging animals.

Modern veterinary care has reduced this food source considerably, and consequently there has been a reduction in the number of carcasses of domesticated animals that had once been available to the carrion eaters. Nevertheless and in practice, many of present-day farmers do not remove cattle carcasses from the field and even carelessly throw dead poultry in the field. All these dead carcasses constitute a significant source of food and have a notable effect on population size of red foxes, jackals, wolves, and to some extent also striped hyenas, particularly in the Golan and the Galilee. Some of these scavengers prey on cattle, thus raising tensions between farmers and nature conservation (Yom-Tov, Ashkenazi, and Viner 1995).

While carrion-eating mammals can find substitute sources of food at rubbish dumps, most scavenging birds are selective in their food and cannot exploit this alternative. For example, vultures are entirely dependent on carrion. In order to support the diminished vulture population, the INPA has established feeding stations, which receive a steady supply of carcasses. In addition, the INPA designated areas in the Negev and Judean Desert in which a regular supply of carcasses is ensured (O. Hatzofe, pers. comm., 2000). In certain cases the breeding success of colonies of vultures improved when food was regularly supplied and deteriorated when it was not (Nadav Levy, pers. comm., 2000).

Poisoning

Over four hundred permitted chemical compounds are listed in Israel for agricultural use, and offered in more than a thousand forms. They include pesticides such as insecticides, acaricides, nematocides, fungicides, herbicides, bactericides, molluscicides, rodenticides, insect attractants, bird and mammal repellents, fumigants, plant growth regulators, defoliants, and so forth (Lichtanier 2009).

The effects of pesticide residues on wildlife began to be observed shortly after DDT came into use at the end of World War II. The most dramatic effect in Israel took place in the 1950s, when wheat grain coated in thallium sulfate was widely applied against rodents. In retrospect it is clear that the use of thallium sulfate was unnecessary. The main damage caused by these rodents took place before 1950, when most agricultural areas had been shallow-plowed, leaving the rodents' burrows unharmed. With the change in land management and the introduction of deep plowing, the burrows were destroyed, the animals were exposed to predation and the weather, and the damage caused by rodents was considerably reduced.

The use of thallium sulfate had grave consequences, harming almost all thirty-nine raptor species that had existed in Israel prior to the use of this pesticide (Mendelssohn 1962, 1972b; Mendelssohn and Paz 1977; Mendelssohn, Schluter, and Aderet 1979; Mendelssohn and Leshem 1983). Only the short-toed eagle (*Circaetus gallicus*) remained unaffected, probably due to its specialized reptilian diet and to its absence in winter when most of the poison grain was applied.

Following a ban on the use of DDT, as well as on other chlorinated hydrocarbons and thallium sulfate during the 1960s, some of the raptor populations have been restored, such as the kestrel (*Falco tinnunculus*), which has recovered well. For most of the other raptor species, however, the present nesting populations are only a fraction of their original size. The observed increase in numbers of the blackbird, bulbul (*Pycnonotus xanthoprymnos*), palm dove (*Streptopelia* [*Stigmatopelia*] *senegalensis*), Syrian woodpecker, and jay may be partly attributed to the decreased numbers of their predators, mainly the sparrowhawk (Mendelssohn 1975b).

Secondary poisoning by insecticides also affected the insectivorous birds, mainly species inhabiting areas near fields, human settlements, and areas of shrubbery where their populations were significantly reduced. The population size of the swallow (*Hirundo rustica*), red-rumped swallow (*Hirundo daurica*), white-throat (*Sylvia communis*), rufous bushchat (*Cercotrichas galactotes*), Nubian shrike (*Lanius nubicus*), spotted flycatcher (*Muscicapa striata*), roller (*Coracias garrulus*), bee-eater (*Merops apiaster*), and Egyptian nightjar (*Caprimulgus aegyptius*) were consequently reduced (Yom-Tov and Mendelssohn 1988). This reduction was in the main not caused by any one factor but by a combination of a number of factors (i.e., habitat change), some of which are still not sufficiently understood.

The population size of certain species rose during this period (e.g., the cattle egret) due to the proximity of the habitat to human settlements, which ensured a constant supply of food. This, along with their resistance to pesticides, reduced competition with those species decimated by the pesticides, and there was a reduction in predation threat. One example is that of the blackbird, which was found in woodlands in the Galilee and Carmel mountain areas. During the 1950s and 1960s the population of sparrowhawk (a predator of the blackbird) was affected by secondary poisoning, while in parallel there were increasing sources of food available from gardens and settlement areas. The relative resistance of the blackbird to the various pesticides enabled an unnatural growth in its population, with the species spreading as far as the desert region.

The group of mammals most affected by pesticides has been insectivorous bats (*Microchiroptera*), mainly in the Mediterranean region. Israel features thirty-two known species of such bats, and in the past many caves were populated with thousands of bats. Since the 1950s there has been a severe decline in the number of individuals occupying the caves. Most of the species have become rare, mainly in the Mediterranean region. The reduction is exemplified by the following example: a cave on Mount Carmel was visited by three different researchers during the 1930s, 1974, and 1994. The number of bat species (and estimated number of individuals) observed there was six (thousands), three (less than a thousand) and one (fewer than ten), respectively. This reduction is related to two main factors. One factor is the fumigating of caves with Ethylen-Dibromide and later with Lindane (Gammexan) by the Plant Protection Department of the Ministry of Agriculture (Mendelssohn 1974a). This fumigation was intended to eradicate the fruit bat (*Rousettus aegyptiacus*), which was considered a pest to farmers of certain fruits. These bats frequently inhabited the same caves as the insectivorous bats. It was discovered later that the damage caused by the fruit bats to agriculture was minimal and had been exaggerated by certain pest-control inspectors. Notwithstanding the eradication of thousands of fruit bats through cave fumigations, it still remains the most populous Israeli bat species (Mendelssohn and Yom-Tov 1999b).

A second factor that affected the insectivorous bats was that of secondary poisoning. Most species of bats are found in the agricultural areas in northern and central Israel. They tend to be particularly vulnerable to secondary poisoning as a result of insecticide use against certain moths of the Noctuidae family, which constitute an important component of their diet. The Noctuidae larvae, such as the prodenia (*Spodoptera littoralis*), are severe agricultural pests and fields are regularly sprayed with pesticides against them. Pesticides are also in increasing use among the agricultural settlements in the desert, but caves were not fumigated there. In those places insectivorous bats are still common, indicating that it is cave fumigation and not pesticide spraying per se that is the main factor responsible for the reduction in the insectivorous bat populations in the Mediterranean region of Israel. The remaining bat populations today face another danger: hikers and visitors to the caves who disturb the bats in their hibernation and sleep, causing depletion of body fat stores and desiccation of the hibernating individuals.

Predatory mammals, too, have been affected by poisoning. In 1964, the Veterinary Services decided that jackals constituted a significant pest as a vector for rabies. As part of the eradication strategy a wide campaign was begun to destroy the jackal, a result of which other predatory mammals suffered from both direct and secondary poisoning, including the wolf, red fox, Egyptian mongoose (*Herpestes ichneumon*), jungle cat (*Felis chaus*), and African wild cat (*F. sylvestris*). The farmers also poisoned jackals due to the damage they caused to plastic pipelines and plastic cover of vegetable plants (Mendelssohn 1972a). Most of the species recovered in the 1970s and 1980s, and their numbers in 2000 resembled those before the poisoning campaign, or were even higher (Mendelssohn and Yom-Tov 1999b).

Nonetheless, farmers (primarily cattle and sheep ranchers) continue to use poison to destroy predators. This illegal poisoning harms populations (that are in any case small) by disrupting breeding units. The activities also severely affect species not intended to be harmed, such as the griffon vulture and other avian predators (Leader et al. 2009).

A recent survey by the Israel Nature and Parks Authority indicated that between 2005 and 2007 the Authority dealt with an average of 116 poisoning cases each year. These poisoning affected at least forty-five species of birds, mainly raptors, and twenty-one species of mammals. Most poisoning occurred in areas with poor sanitation and increased populations of scavenging carnivores.

A very recent threat to scavengers comes from infighting among ranchers, who compete for grazing areas and attempt to poison one another's herds. Dozens of cattle are killed this way and secondary poisoning has caused considerable damage to the griffon vulture population in northern Israel. Occasional poisoning of wolves by ranchers harms this species as well as other carnivores (Leader et al. 2009).

Garbage

Growth of the human population, accompanied by a rise in living standards, has also led to a significant increase in the amount of solid waste produced—more than one million tons in 2000 (Statistical Abstracts of Israel 2007). Many small settlements and military bases created their own (illegal) garbage dumps, where their waste remained largely untreated. Garbage in Israel includes about 41 percent organic material and until recently this percentage was as high as 75 percent, providing a readily available source of food for birds and mammals (Ostrovsky, Kozer, and Garfinkel 2009).

In the Golan, for example, in 1993 only two official waste dumps existed, side by side with seventy "unofficial" ones (Yom-Tov et al. 1995). An estimated amount of 1,200 tons of meat (42 percent turkey, 36 percent chicken) were dumped at these sites, with 70 percent of it available to predators (Yom-Tov et al. 1995). The availability of garbage as a food source has led to a rise in the populations of red fox, golden jackal, and the hooded crow (*Corvus corone*) in the Mediterranean zone of Israel and the brown-necked raven (*C. ruficollis*) in the Negev. Accordingly, the large populations of these species may have led to the observed decrease in the numbers of their prey species, such as ground-breeding birds, reptiles, rodents, and even the sand fox (*Vulpes ruppelli*) in the Arava.

The availability of organic garbage enabled range expansion of the golden jackal and the hooded crow from the Mediterranean region into desert areas. Until the 1960s the hooded crow bred in the Mediterranean region as far south as twenty kilometers north of Beer-Sheva. Presently it breeds in Mitze Ramon, 50 kilometers south of Beer-Sheva, and several other settlements in the northern Negev. Responding to the stepping-stone of human settlements scattered along the Negev, the golden jackal expanded its range south, down the Rift Valley, and during the early 2000s reached Eilat at the southern tip of Israel.

Changes in Agricultural Practices

Agricultural practices common in Israel today differ greatly from those in the recent past. About half of all agricultural land is irrigated, and areas that were once left untouched in the summer are today worked even in the dry season, constituting an attraction to wildlife. Summer crops are more exposed to pest insects, which leads to an increased use of pesticides on cotton and other crops (see above). Current agricultural practice combines use of a variety of mechanical tools, heavy tractors, and deep plowing. Although deep plowing destroys burrows of rodent pests thus saving the need to use rodenticides, the modern practices also have negative effects on a number of terrestrial animals. Among reptiles, those mainly affected are several lizards (Schreiber's fringe-fingered lizard, Beer-Sheva's fringe-fingered lizard, Olivier's sand lizard *Eremias olivieri*, and snake-eyed lizard *Ophisops elegans*) and the Caucasian sand boa (*Eryx jaculus*); among birds the calandra lark (*Melanocorypha calandra*) and the collared pratincole (*Glareola pratincola*); and among mammals the greater Egyptian jerboa (*Jaculus orientalis*) appear to suffer due to agriculturally altered habitats.

Roads and Other Barriers

In 2008 Israel had ca. 18,096 kilometers of paved roads, serving ca. 2.39 million vehicles, a 2.75-fold increase since 1951 (Statistical Abstracts of Israel 2009). Many of these roads have several lanes divided by a central concrete barrier with the occasional opening, enabling the passage of small animals. Mammals, reptiles, amphibians, and even many birds are injured by passing cars and die on the roads.

The increasing number of major roads, especially those with central barriers, has led to habitat fragmentation, the effects of which on Israeli wildlife are still unknown. The most affected habitats are those densely populated (by humans) along the coastal plain, that is, the remaining sand dunes along the shore and other areas of light soil, as well as the forested areas in the Galilee. The roads in these developed areas hinder the free movement of medium and large-size animals, such as gazelles, wild boar, and many species of predators. Those trying to cross the roads are often run over by cars and trucks.

The problem is further exacerbated by the recently built "security fence" that stretches hundreds of kilometers along the "Green Line" on the former border between Israel and the West Bank. In fact, the fence is much longer than it otherwise would be, because intense lobbying by Israeli West Bank settlers managed to extend the fence into the West Bank to include their communities. For example, in the Qalqilya-Alfei Menashe area the length of the fence is four times that of the former border (the "Green Line") in that region. This barrier prevents the free movement of medium and large-size animals, but objections by environmentalists were not considered during its planning and construction.

To date, few data have been collected on the extent of animal roadkill in Israel. One study carried out in the Hula valley (Kenigstein 1994) showed a clear link between traffic volume and number of animal predators killed on the roads. More than half of these carcasses were of jackals, and the rest comprised red foxes, badgers, mongooses, wild and jungle cats, otters, and hyenas. In another study the number of snakes run over by vehicles was counted along the 83-kilometer road from Jerusalem to Ein Gedi over a period of four years (Greenberg 1978), and was shown to be 158 specimens of 15 species, the most common of which were the Arabian tiger snake (*Telescopus dhara*) and the Palestine saw-scaled viper (*Echis colorata*). Road traffic is a serious threat to populations of some rare species, such as the otters. Proposals to reduce this mortality by means of creating additional and larger openings in the road divisions were blocked by the Ministry of Transport. At present the INPA is working with Israel National Road Company to create safe passages for animals in new roads.

Excursions in all-terrain vehicles, introduced commercially in Israel during the late 1980s, grew increasingly popular over the following decade. These cause various types of damage, including leaving deep tracks on the sensitive desert ground. They have become a major problem to nature conservation in various areas, but especially in the Negev desert. Efforts by rangers of the INPA to curb the problem have been only partially successful.

Interactions between Wild Animals and Domestic Pets

Interbreeding with domestic conspecifics is a conservation problem for the rock pigeon (*Columba livia*) and the African wild cat, and to smaller extent for the wolf. Until about forty years ago flocks of rock pigeons in Israel were purebred. But with increased human settlement across the country, domestic pigeons were brought into close contact with their wild relatives, and interbreeding became intensive. Today most flocks of rock pigeons are mixed with feral pigeons. Only in the Negev desert can one still observe seemingly pure wild flocks.

The African wild cat faces a similar problem. Feral cats are common all over the country, particularly in the densely inhabited northern and central Israel. Today most wild cats in the Mediterranean region are mixed with domestic cats. The establishment of agricultural settlements in the Arava Valley and of army camps in the Negev desert created a similar problem there. Inbreeding between wolves and dogs is known mainly in the Golan. Some of this inbreeding occurs between sheep dogs, introduced for guarding cattle against predation by jackals and wolves.

The domestication of dogs and cats did not affect their predatory instincts, and feral cats and dogs continue to prey on wildlife. Studies on predation of wildlife by domestic and feral cats in Israel revealed that many domestic cats enrich the diet provided by their owners and scavenge on garbage and prey on many species of wild animals, including twelve species of mammals, twenty-six of birds, eighteen of reptiles, and one amphibian species (Brickner-Braun, Geffen, and Yom-Tov 2008). In a densely populated country like Israel, particularly in the northern and central Mediterranean region, there are hardly any settlements that are farther than five kilometers from one another. Feral dogs can easily walk this distance in one night, as do some feral cats. Hence, no area in the Mediterranean region is likely to be free from their impact that may be considerable, especially for endangered species.

Current regulations (in fact, the nearly sacred status of cats) do not allow eradication of feral or street cats except in special cases such as a danger to public health (e.g., spread of diseases like rabies). Thus, the legal protection of feral and stray cats threatens wild animals that would otherwise be protected by conservation laws.

Feral dogs and domestic dogs released for several hours a day by their owners often form packs that hunt and disturb wild animals, such as the hare, the mountain gazelle, and Nubian ibex. Dogs had detrimental effect on mountain gazelles and desert monitors in the sand dunes near Holon, where these wild animals have since been exterminated (Perry and Dmiel 1995). Their effect on wildlife was demonstrated in a study carried out in the sand dunes south of Ashdod. The study revealed that dog packs hunt the fawns and harass the adults of mountain gazelles, thus significantly decreasing gazelle breeding success (Manor and Saltz 2004). Similar phenomena have been reported from many other parts of the country (reviewed in Gingold et al. 2009), where feral dogs prey on mountain gazelles and fallow deer, a globally endangered species. It seems that political correctness overcame common sense.

Invading Species

A few species of animals have been introduced into Israel from other countries, deliberately and accidentally. The most well known of these is the nutria (or coypu), discussed above. Another successful mammalian introduction is the Indian palm squirrel (*Funambulus pennati*) that was deliberately released into nature near Mitzpe Ramon in the Negev and spread several kilometers from the release site. Half-hearted operations by the INPA failed to eliminate this introduced population in nature, but during the 2010s their number decreased considerably, apparently due to a series of drought years in the Negev.

About twenty species of alien birds have settled in Israel since its establishment and are now resident in the country (Yom-Tov et al. 2012). Some of these species appear to have arrived independently, while others appear to have been introduced, either intentionally or unintentionally, by humans. Some of these species (e.g., the ring-necked parakeet *Psittacula krameri* and the common mynah *Acridotheres tristis*) are now widespread and compete with hole-nesting birds for nesting cavities. The ring-necked parakeet also causes considerable damage to pecan plantations and sorghum fields. The Indian house crow (*Corvus splendens*) first appeared in Eilat in 1976 (Paz 1986); today it is a common breeder in this town and in settlements north of it in the Arava. It is known to feed on bird eggs and nestlings, and is thus a potential threat to local passerines, among them the rare hoopoe-lark (*Alaemon alaudipes*).

Most of the newly established bird species are of tropical origin, and this has been explained as a possible consequence of two factors: the recent increase in ambient temperature and the extensive irrigated agriculture in the Arava Valley. Both factors create a semblance of tropical environment that enables the introduced tropical species to settle and breed (Hatzofe and Yom-Tov 2002).

The rough-tail gecko (*Cyrtopodion scabrum*) was apparently introduced accidentally via the port of Eilat and is now established in Eilat (Bouskila and Amitai 2003). The red-necked turtle (*Chrysemys picta*) was apparently released into water courses by amateur collectors and is now found in the Yarkon and Nahal Taninim. However, it is not clear if it breeds there.

Various kinds of introduced fish were found in streams and in the Sea of Galilee. The trout *Salmo gairdneri* escaped from fishponds in Kibbutz Dan and now breeds in the Dan River (Goren 1983) and some other introduced species of fish are occasionally found in various streams, apparently after being released there by amateur breeders. The introduced mosquito fish (*Gambusia affinis*) found its way to various natural pools in which the endangered fire salamander breeds, and preys on metamorphs, causing considerable damage (Segev, Mangel, and Blaustein 2008).

CURRENT STATUS OF THE ENVIRONMENT

Ecosystems in Israel have undergone radical transformation over the past century. Many species—mainly the large herbivores and secondary consumers such as raptors, insectivorous birds, bats, and predators—have been harmed by humanity's various activities. A smaller number of species in these same groups have nonetheless succeeded in adapting to the new conditions, reproducing and, in certain cases, even becoming pest species. This situation has led to a conflict with the agricultural community and to the emergence of new threats to species that were not previously considered as harmful and dwelt in balance with nature.

The continuing growth of the human population in Israel, urban sprawl, and the accompanying rise in the standard of living will lead to continued harm to regional animal populations. Conventional agricultural practices will increasingly harm and diminish natural habitats. Consequently, the areas available to those species of wildlife unable to adapt to human-created habitats will continue to diminish. Although some of the natural ecosystems may survive within nature reserves, given the limited area of these sanctuaries, frequently, they are ecologically unstable.

Most of the wildlife in Israel can still be found in the open spaces beyond the nature reserves, but the reduction of these areas will make the nature reserves the final sanctuary for many species. Construction of new settlements (contradicting government decisions to the avoid such development), and the trend of single-story houses spread over wide areas, constitutes a meaningful threat to the open countryside.

Moreover, an examination of the status of nature reserves in Israel is not encouraging: 63 percent of the existing and proposed reserves are smaller than 1 square kilometer, 25 percent are smaller than 10 square kilometers, and only 4 percent are larger than 100 square kilometers. The small size of the majority of reserves, their relatively long borders, and lack of buffer areas around them make them vulnerable to every negative factor in the surroundings, so that the very future of the ecological systems in the nature reserves, the flora, and the fauna that inhabit them is in question. Even relatively large reserves suffer from human pressures. On Mount Meron, for example, the largest reserve in northern and central Israel (originally ca. 100 square kilometers), around 30 square kilometers have been legally given over to agriculture for use by the local Druze farmers. Additional areas are exploited by the Israel Defense Forces. It is reasonable to expect that within a decade only half of this reserve will remain relatively free of continuous disturbance by humans, and even this part suffers from occasional logging and uncontrolled sheep and goat herding. The largest reserves are in the Negev and overlap with training grounds for the military.

"Nature tourism" also increases pressure on certain nature reserves even as it raises public awareness about these protected places. For example, the sport of rock climbing which began with encouragement from the Society for the Protection of Nature quickly became a severely disturbing factor to nesting raptors in some places. Similarly, all-terrain vehicles have become very popular, and many of them are driven through the desert, scoring deep tracks in the desert sand off the existing paths. To date, in Israel, very little has been done to put a halt to this phenomenon or actively enforce control of the damage.

Although small in size, Israel has a very diverse landscape, soils, and climate, reflected by its rich animal and plant diversity (Tchernov and Yom-Tov 1988). The aim of nature conservation in Israel is to preserve this great habitat and species diversity. For example, in the Galilee all stages of the plant succession—batha, garigue, closed and open forests, should be present with their typical fauna (Yom-Tov 1985). Instead, we witness a trend of impoverishment and simplification of Israel's fauna.

These trends do not permit an optimistic vision of the future of wildlife in Israel. If they continue, Israeli wildlife will greatly diminish in number and variety of species and will be far from representing the wide variety of wildlife that once made Israel so unique from the ecological and zoogeographical perspectives.

The above pessimistic prospect is partly moderated by the fact that Israel has advanced nature conservation laws, by the relatively large proportion of land allocated to nature reserves (although, as mentioned, mostly small reserve size) and by an advanced public awareness of nature. With time, uniformly planted forests incorporate more native trees and enable wildlife to settle. Many nature conservation projects are being carried out to conserve the habitats and flora and fauna of Israel.

There is a growing understanding among the agricultural community and nature conservationists that they share a common interest to preserve open areas and avoid further "development." Farmers have an interest to keep their fields, orchards, grazing areas, and fishponds, while conservationists realize that open areas are essential for wildlife conservation. Future cooperation between these partners may well benefit both farmers and wildlife.

Multiple laws, if properly enforced, will also help contain the damage. The "Wildlife Protection Law" (since 1955) protects in principle all mammals and wild birds and was extended in 1990 to include species of reptiles and amphibians. "The National Parks and Nature Reserves Law" (enacted in 1963) also protects those animals that are not included in the "Wildlife Protection Law," as well as plants and habitats defined as being a "natural asset." The government Israel Nature and Parks Authority is in charge of enforcing these laws, managing the nature reserves, and supervising hunting.

Civil society is also attempting to rise to the conservation challenge. The public nongovernmental organization The Society for the Protection of Nature (SPNI; established in 1954) functions to educate the public and disseminate the nature conservation message. Another very positive development was the establishment (by the SPNI) of Deshe, an organization that works for conserving open areas not declared as nature reserves. As mentioned above, most Israeli wildlife lives outside nature reserves, and conserving open spaces is of utmost importance for wildlife conservation. In recent years additional organizations have come into being (e.g., the Israel Union for Environmental Defense), which engage with various problems of nature and landscape conservation, to no small success.

This historic review of Israel's wildlife suggests that the rise in human population in Israel has come at the expense of the other creatures of the land. Modern conservation biology policies if implemented and enforced faithfully can prevent much of this damage. We can only hope that the race between nature lovers and developers will be won by the former.

NOTE

This chapter is dedicated to the memory of Professor Heinrich Mendelssohn, father of nature conservation in Israel. This chapter is an updated, revised, and extended version of an article I wrote with him in 1986–1987. I wish to acknowledge Professor Mendelssohn's guidance, mentorship, and friendship.

The following persons provided us with information and allowed us to quote unpublished information: Professor Shmuel Avitzur, Dr. Eliezer Frankenberg, Mr. Eitan Gluzman, Dr. Menachem Goren, Mr. Ohad Hatzofe, Mr. Offer Hochberg, Mr. Avinoam Lurie, Mr. Yitzchak Moshe, Dr. Uzi Paz, Dr. Aviva Rabinovitz, Mr. Dan Rozenzweig, and Professor Arnon Shimshony. Professor Char Miller, Dr. Daniel Orenstein, and Professor Alon Tal made numerous helpful comments. Shlomith Yom-Tov commented on the manuscript. Uri Roll produced the Galilee map and Eyal Bar-Tov kindly allowed me to use his photo of Acacias in the Negev. I thank them all. Special thanks are due to Ms. Naomi Paz for her careful editing.

REFERENCES

Aharoni, I. 1943. *Memories of a Hebrew Zoologist*. vol. 1. Tel Aviv: Am Oved. In Hebrew.
———. 1946. *Memories of a Hebrew Zoologist*. vol. 2. Tel Aviv: Am Oved. In Hebrew.
Angelister, N. 2006. "The Effect of Human Disturbance on Rodents Community in the Southern Coastal Plain." MSc thesis, Zoology Department, Tel Aviv University. In Hebrew.

Avitsur, S. 1977. *Changes in Agricultural Practices in Eretz Israel. 1875–1975.* Tel Aviv: Milo. In Hebrew.

Brickner-Braun, I., E. Geffen, and Y. Yom-Tov. 2008. "The Impact of Domestic Cats (*Felis catus*) on Israeli Wildlife." *Israel Journal of Ecology and Evolution* 53: 129–42.

Bouskila, A., and P. Amitai. 2003. *Handbook of Amphibians and Reptiles of Israel.* Jerusalem: Keter. In Hebrew.

Dafni, I. 1972. "A Brief History of the Government Veterinary Services." In special Jubilee issue, edited by A. Shimshony, 17–38. Tel Aviv: Israel Veterinary Medical Association. In Hebrew.

Degani, G., and H. Mendelssohn. 1984. "Amphibians." In *Plants and Animals of the Land of Israel,* vol. 5, edited by A. Alon, 190–221. Tel Aviv: Publishing House, Ministry of Defense, and the Society for Protection of Nature. In Hebrew.

Dimentman, C., H. J. Bromley, and D. F. Por. 1992. *Lake Hula: Reconstruction of the Fauna and Hydrobiology of a Lost Lake.* Jerusalem: Israel Academy of Sciences and Humanities.

Dolev, A., and A. Perevolotsky. 2002. *Endangered Species in Israel: Red List of Threatened Animals.* Jerusalem and Tel Aviv: Nature and Parks Authority and the Society for the Protection of Nature. In Hebrew.

Dor, M. 1947. "Observation sur les micromammiferestrouves dans les pelotes de la Chouette Effraye (Tyto alba) en Palestine." *Mammalia* 11: 49–54.

Friedemann, G., Y. Yom-Tov, U. Motro, and Y. Leshem. 2011. "Shift in Nesting Ground of the Long-Legged Buzzard (*Buteo rufinus*) in Judea, Israel—An Effect of Change in Land Cover?" *Biological Conservation* 144: 402–6.

Gafny, S. 1986. "Biology and Ecology of the Syrian Spadefoot Toad, *Pelobates syriacus syriacus* in Israel." MSc thesis, Department of Zoology, Tel Aviv University. In Hebrew.

Gingold, G., Y. Yom-Tov, N. Kronfeld-Shor, and E. Geffen. 2009. "The Effect of Guard Dogs on the Behavior of Gazelles *Gazella gazella* in Cattle Enclosures in the Golan Heights." *Animal Conservation* 12: 155–62.

Goren, M. 1983. *Freshwater Fishes of Israel: Biology and Taxonomy.* Tel Aviv: Hakibbutz Hameuchad. In Hebrew.

Goren, M., and R. Ortal. 1999. "Biogeography, Diversity and Conservation of the Inland Water Fish Communities in Israel." *Biological Conservation* 89: 1–9.

Greenberg, Z. 1978. "Snakes on the Road." *Teva VeAaretz* 20: 20–22. In Hebrew.

Hatzofe, O., and Y. Yom-Tov. 2002. "Global Warming and Recent Changes in Israel's Avifauna." *Israel Journal of Zoology* 48: 351–57.

Hawlena, D., and A. Bouskila. 2006. "Land Management Practices for Combating Desertification Cause Species Replacement of Desert Lizards." *Journal of Applied Ecology* 43: 701–9.

Ilani, G. 2004. *Ma'ale Namer—Memories of an Israeli Zoologist.* Tel Aviv: Sifriat Poalim. In Hebrew.

Kenigstein, M. 1994. *Carnivore Kills on Roads in the Hula Valley.* A Study Submitted to the Joint High School of the Hula Valley. In Hebrew.

Leader, N., E. Dror, R. King, and Y. Shkedi. 2009. *Animal Poisoning in Israel during 2005–2007: The Problem and Ways of Solving It.* Jerusalem: Science Section, Israel Nature and Park Authority. In Hebrew.

Lehman, T., and A. Perevolotsky. 1992. "Small Mammals in the Conifer Plantations and Native Environment in Southern Mt. Carmel, Israel." *Mammalia* 56: 575–85.

Leshem, Y., and Y. Yom-Tov. 1996. "The Magnitude and Timing of Migration by Soaring Raptors, Pelicans and Storks over Israel." *Ibis* 138: 188–203.

Levanony, T. 2005. "Species Diversity in Pine Plantations and Natural Maquis in the Judean Foothills." MSc thesis, George S. Wise Faculty of Life Sciences, Tel Aviv University, Israel.

Levin, N., E. Elron, and A. Gasith. 2009. "Decline of Wetland Ecosystems in the Coastal Plain of Israel during the 20th Century: Implications for Wetland Conservation and Management." *Landscape and Urban Planning* 92: 220–32.

Lichtanier, L., ed. 2009. "Pesticides for Plant Protection Registered for Use and Sale in Israel." Jerusalem: Ministry of Agriculture, Department of Plant Protection and Inspection. In Hebrew.

Manor, R., O. Cohen, and D. Saltz. 2008. "Community Homogenization and the Invasiveness of Commensal Species in Mediterranean Afforested Landscapes." *Biological Invasions* 10: 507–15.

Manor, R., and D. Saltz. 2004. "The Impact of Free-Roaming Dogs on Gazelle Kid/Female Ratio in a Fragmented Area." *Biological Conservation* 119: 231–36.

———. 2008. "Conservation Implications of Competition between Generalist and Specialist Rodents in Mediterranean Afforested Landscape." *Biodiversity and Conservation* 10: 2513–23.

Mendelssohn, H. 1962. "Mass Destruction of Bird-Life Owing to Secondary Poisoning from Insecticides and Rodenticides." *Atlantic Naturalist* 17: 247–48.

———. 1972a. "Ecological Effects of Chemical Control of Rodents and Jackals in Israel." In *The Careless Technology: Ecology and International Development*, edited by M. T. Farvar and J. P. Milton, 527–44. New York: Natural History Press.

———. 1972b. "The Impact of Pesticides on Bird Life in Israel." *Bulletin of the International Council for Bird Preservation* 11: 75–104.

———. 1974a. "On the Extermination of Bats in Israel." *Teva Va'aretz* 16: 51–53. In Hebrew.

———. 1975b. "Report on the Status of Some Bird Species in Israel in 1974." *Bulletin of the International Council for Bird Preservation* 12: 265–70.

Mendelssohn, H., and Y. Leshem. 1983. "The Status and Conservation of Vultures in Israel." In *Vulture Biology and Management*, edited by S. R. Wilbur and J. A. Jackson, 86–98. Berkeley: University of California Press.

Mendelssohn, H., and U. Paz. 1977. "Mass Mortality of Birds of Prey Caused by Azodrin, an Organophosphorus Insecticide." *Biological Conservation* 11: 163–70.

Mendelssohn, H., P. Schluter, and Y. Aderet. 1979. "Report on Azodrin Poisoning of Birds of Prey in the Huleh Valley in Israel." *Bulletin of the International Council of Bird Preservation* 13: 124–27.

Mendelssohn, H., and Y. Yom-Tov. 1999a. "Birds and Mammals Which Increased Their Distribution and Abundance in Israel Due to Human Activity." *Israel Journal of Zoology* 45: 35–47.

———. 1999b. *Mammalia of Israel*. Jerusalem: The Israel Academy of Sciences and Humanities.

Merom, C. 1966. *Birds of Israel*. Tel Aviv: Hakibbutz Hameuchad. In Hebrew.

Ostrovsky, G., R. Kozer, and M. Garfinkel. 2009. *Garbage and Recycling in Israel: A Report and Recommendations*. Tel Aviv: Adam Teva V'Din. In Hebrew.

Paz, U. 1986. "Birds." In *Plants and Animals of the Land of Israel*, vol. 6, edited by

A. Alon, 1–486. Tel Aviv: The Publishing House, Ministry of Defense and Society for Protection of Nature, Israel. In Hebrew.

Perry, G., and R. Dmiel. 1995. "Urbanization and Sand Dunes in Israel: Direct and Indirect Effects." *Israel Journal of Zoology* 41: 33–41.

Prushinsky, Y. 1964. *The Water in Israel*. Tel Aviv: Ministry of Agriculture, Israel.

Rozner, O. 2007. "Aspects of the Ecology of Nile Softshell Turtle (*Trionyx triunguis*) in the Alexander River." MSc thesis, Department of Biology, Haifa University.

Rupin, A. 1920. *Syrien als Wirtschaftsgebiet*. Berlin: B. Harz.

Sachs, M., and I. Moshe. 1999. "Savannization: An Ecologically Viable Management Approach to Desertified Regions." In *Arid Lands Management—Towards Ecological Sustainability,* edited by T. W. Hoekstra and M. Shachak, 248–53. Urbana: University of Illinois Press.

Segev, O., M. Mangel, and L. Blaustein. 2009. "Deleterious Effects by Mosquitofish (*Gambusia affinis*) on the Endangered Fire Salamander (*Salamandra infraimmaculata*)." *Animal Conservation* 12: 29–37.

Sela, Y. 1977. "The Recovery of the Forest—A Problem for the Preservation of Wildlife." *Teva Va'aretz* 11: 81–84. In Hebrew.

———. 1979. "The Victory in the Struggle over the Digging of Sand Came Too Late for the Sea Turtles." *Teva Va'aretz* 21 (2): 58–63. In Hebrew.

Shimshony, A. 1983. "Activities of the Israeli Veterinary Services, 1973–1983." *Refuah Veterinarith* 40: 143–203.

Shirihai, H. 1996. *The Birds of Israel*. London: Academic Press.

Statistical Abstracts of Israel. 1999. No. 50. Jerusalem: Central Bureau of Statistics.

———. 2007. No. 58. Jerusalem: Central Bureau of Statistics.

———. 2008. No. 59. Jerusalem: Central Bureau of Statistics.

———. 2009. No. 60. Jerusalem: Central Bureau of Statistics.

Tal, A. 2006. "Seeking Sustainability: Israel's Evolving Water Management Strategy." *Science* 313: 1081–84.

Talbot, L. M. 1960. "A Look at Threatened Species." *Oryx* 4-5: 153–293.

Tchernov, E., and Y. Yom-Tov. 1988. "Zoogeography of Israel." In *The Zoogeography of Israel: The Distribution and Abundance at the Zoogeographical Crossroad,* edited by Y. Yom-Tov and E. Tchernov, 1–6. Dordrecht: Dr. W. Junk.

Tristram, H. B. 1865. *The Land of Israel*. London: Society for Promoting Christian Knowledge.

Twain, M. 1869. *The Innocents Abroad*. London: Collins' Clear Type Press.

Water Commission Office, Ministry of Agriculture. 1982. *Survey of Water and Sewage Collection and Use*. Jerusalem. In Hebrew.

Weitz, Y. 1970. *Forests and Afforestation in Israel*. Ramat Gan: Massada. In Hebrew.

———. 1972. *Migamda leravcha*. Ramat Gan: Massada. In Hebrew.

Werner, Y. L. 1987. "Ecological Zoogeography of the Saharo-Arabian, Saharan and Arabian Reptiles in the Sand Deserts of Southern Israel." In *Proceedings of the Symposium on the Fauna and Zoogeography of the Middle East, Mainz 1985,* edited by F. Krupp, W. Schneider, and R. Kinzelback. *Beihefte zum TAVOLA* 28: 272–95. Wiesbaden: L. Reichert Verlag.

———. 1988. "Herpetofaunal Survey of Israel (1950–1985), with Comments on Sinai and Jordan and on Zoogeographical Herpetogeneity. The Zoogeography of the Birds and Mammals in Israel." In *The Zoogeography of Israel,* edited by Y. Yom-Tov and E. Tchernov, 355–87. Dordrecht: Dr. J. Junk.

Yom-Tov, Y. 1985. "Nature Conservation in Israel." *Teva Va'aretz* 27 (4): 19–26. In Hebrew.

———. 1988. "The Zoogeography of the Birds and Mammals in Israel." In *The Zoogeography of Israel,* edited by Y. Yom-Tov and E. Tchernov, 389–409. Dordrecht: Dr. J. Junk.

———. 2003. "Poaching of Israeli Wildlife by Guest Workers." *Biological Conservation* 110: 11–20.

Yom-Tov, Y., S. Ashkenazi, and O. Viner. 1995. "Cattle Predation by the Golden Jackal *Canis aureus* on Cattle in the Golan Heights, Israel." *Biological Conservation* 73: 19–27.

Yom-Tov, Y., O. Hatzofe, and E. Geffen. 2012. "Israel's Breeding Avifauna: A Century of Dramatic Change." *Biological Conservation* 147 (1): 13–21.

Yom-Tov, Y., and H. Mendelssohn. 1988. "Changes of the Distribution and Abundance of Vertebrates during the 20th Century in Israel." In *The Zoogeography of Israel,* edited by Y. Yom-Tov and E. Tchernov, 515–48. Dordrecht: Dr. J. Junk.

CHAPTER FOUR

ZIONIST AND ISRAELI PERSPECTIVES ON POPULATION GROWTH AND ENVIRONMENTAL IMPACT IN PALESTINE AND ISRAEL

Daniel E. Orenstein

The key to immigration is the people, not the land, not the
lifeless crust of earth but the dynamics and creation of farmer
and factory-hand.

—BEN-GURION 1954a, 44

DEMOGRAPHY HAS a profound impact on politics (Bookman 2002; Teitel-baum 2005). This is all the more so in a country like Israel: a political hotspot where population statistics are wielded as weapons to prop up one's ideology, to justify a proposed policy or to support a historical theory. From scholarly debate on the biblical period to contemporary election campaign speeches, demography colors political discourse. It is imperative, then, to study population-environment (P-E) interactions in not only an ecological context, but in a sociohistorical context as well.

Intuitively, Israel should be a good laboratory for studying the impact of population growth on selected environmental indicators. Its population growth rates are similar to those of developing nations, but its economic well-being and equivalent consumption rates are similar to the developed world. Several natural resources—in particular, water and open land—are discussed in terms of scarcity. Technological progress struggles to mitigate increased per capita pollution production. There is constant pressure, due to population growth and increase in per capita consumption, to increase electricity produc-tion capacity and water supply.

Indeed, there seems to be a consensus among Israeli scholars and activists that population growth places pressure on scarce national resources and on the ability of ecosystems to absorb the waste products of human society (Ayalon 2003; Ministry of Environment 1999). And yet, most environmental scholars and even the hard-core environmental activists do not place population growth on their short list of environmental challenges.[1] The explanation is fourfold: (1) procreation is viewed as sacrosanct in the Jewish community for religious, historical, and political reasons; (2) the most popular Zionist vision for the future of Israel is a Jewish, democratic state, and this rests on the foundation of a solid secular Jewish majority in Israel; (3) there is not a consensus among scholars regarding the exact role of population growth on environmental quality in Israel or whether it is useful to consider policy intervention in demographic processes (Orenstein 2004), and (4) Israelis are particularly enamored with the potential of technology (rather than population control) to solve the country's most pressing environmental challenges (Tal 2008).

In light of these characteristics of P-E discourse, it is evident that a sociohistorical perspective is crucial for understanding the nature of today's popular and academic discourse about the topic. This chapter considers Israel's ancient and modern history, as both have particular relevance to modern P-E discourse. The chapter begins by assessing scholarship on the period prior to the destruction of the Second Temple and subsequent exile of the Jews from Eretz Israel, and then jumps to the beginning of the twentieth century and the rise of the modern Zionist movement and continues through the present. The overarching goal is to show the extent to which P-E discourse is inseparable from contemporary ideological and political debate. This is not to say that assessment of environmental impact of population growth cannot be performed in a sober and objective manner. But it does suggest that a proper analysis of the relationship in the Israeli context, and especially the development of policy-relevant conclusions, requires an a priori understanding and explicit recognition of the ideological context in which the assessment is taking place.

NUMBERS FROM THE PAST: POPULATION, ENVIRONMENT, AND ANCIENT ISRAEL

A consideration of the biblical period is a good starting point for understanding today's P-E discourse. The Jewish and Zionist communities draw direct lessons from biblical teachings that help guide their behavior and even policy making. Further, the biblical period was a time of real "carrying capacities," when local natural resource availability (water, grazing lands, agricultural productivity) had a direct impact on the number of people who could live in the land. Finally, several biblical scholars and archeologists attach important political meaning to population estimates of the period, using them in a debate about the veracity of the historical existence of an Israelite Kingdom. Since the Zionist narrative is based in part on a Jewish "return" to the Land of Israel, debate around the existence of an Israelite nation has important ideological and symbolic implications in the Israeli-Palestinian conflict.

Two types of literature deal with P-E relationships during the biblical period. The first uses the Bible itself as a starting point toward exploring questions ranging from how the environmental conditions on the land affected the size and location of the human population to how the Bible (and subsequent commentary) deals with the issue of population growth. A second body of literature, written by biblical historians and archeologists, also studies how environmental conditions may have affected population size and vice versa, but this literature derives its support from the physical remains of ancient civilizations and, to a lesser extent, from written text.

Soil scientist Daniel Hillel, reading the Bible through the lens of a natural scientist, exemplifies this first type of scholarship with his book *The Natural History of the Bible* (Hillel 2006). One commonly recurring biblical P-E theme in Hillel's analysis is that of carrying capacities for grazing animals, or how many herders could populate a given area based on the land's vegetative productivity. This theme surfaces, for example, when Abraham arrives in Canaan: "the land could not support them [Abraham and Lot] staying together, for their possessions were so great" (Gen. 13:6), and is repeated with Jacob and Esau who, too, could not live together because "the land where they sojourned could not support them because of their livestock" (Gen. 36:7). A second limiting resource, water, was the subject of negotiations between Abraham and Abimelech, king of Gerar, in what would become Beer-Sheva. Following the negotiation, Isaac digs another well in Rehoboth, avoiding further conflict with Abimelech by effectively raising the environmental carrying capacity of the land; "Now at last the Lord has granted us ample space to increase in the land" (Gen. 26:22).

Population pressures on environmental resources may have also, according to Hillel, contributed to political tension between the Egyptians and the Israelites during their period of enslavement there. The Israelites, he suggests, were originally nomadic pastoralists who traditionally had high fertility rates to cope with high infant and maternal mortality rates. The Egyptians, on the other hand, may have kept birthrates deliberately low "in order to avoid excessive disputes over the inheritance of such limited resources as land and water rights" (Hillel 2006, 106). Tensions mounted between the Egyptians and their Israelite slaves, prompting Pharaoh to order infanticide against the Israelites. Likewise, Hillel interprets the rivalry between the Israelites, upon their return from Egypt, and the Amalekites as illustrative of the "grim fight-to-the-death rivalry between nomadic tribes over territorial rights in the desert domain, the rights to sparse pastures and meager water supplies" (131).

Environmental anthropologist Jeremy Benstein finds contemporary advice regarding P-E interactions in his reading of the Bible. For example, when facing famine in Egypt, Joseph (who came from a family with eight children) had only two sons (Gen. 41:50), prompting Benstein to suggest that Joseph had foreseen the coming famine in Egypt and deliberately limited his childbearing (Benstein 2001). He supports his argument referring to the Talmud tractate Ta'anit, writing, "it is forbidden to engage in marital relations in time of famine," and the Jerusalem Talmud's "When you see great deprivation entering the world, keep your wife childless." This contrasts with the commandment "Be fruitful and multiply, and fill up the earth" (Gen. 1:28), often employed in popular discourse to support and encourage high rates of fertility among religious Jews. In contrast to the latter quote, Benstein's sources suggest that Jews assess the availability of resources before making decisions regarding procreation.[2]

Biblical historians and archeologists use environmental parameters (alongside and interacting with economic and political conditions) to estimate the size of the population in Israel in the biblical period (Faust 2003; Finkelstein 1990; Hopkins 1987). Magen Broshi and colleagues offered a series of estimates of the population of biblical Palestine using various methods, including minimum per capita water requirements and grain-growing capacity (Broshi 1979) and size of inhabited areas multiplied by a density coefficient (Broshi and Finkelstein 1992; Broshi and Gophna 1984, 1986). They estimate relatively low numbers of 150,000 (Early Bronze, 2500 BCE), 100,000 to 140,000 (Middle Bronze, 2000 to 1500 BCE), and 400,000 (Iron Age II, 800 BCE), and the peak population size of 1,000,000 during the Late Byzantine Era (600 CE; fig. 4.1).

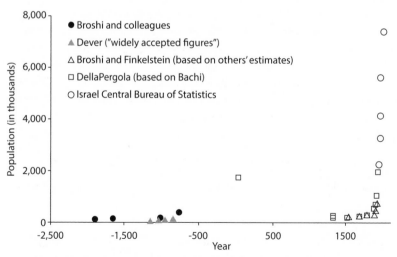

FIGURE 4.1. Population estimates for Israel from biblical times to the present (Broshi 1979; Broshi and Finkelstein 1992; Broshi and Gophna 1984, 1986; CBS 2009; DellaPergola 2003; Dever 2004).

For some scholars, these population numbers (and other estimates) have become a vibrant point of political contention. Demographic estimates are used to provide evidence for major historical processes, in particular the rise of the Israelite kingdoms (e.g., when did they arise and from what population groups?). Dever (2004) describes a fierce ideological battle in which revisionists (those who doubt the existence of a United Monarchy of Israel) suggest that low population numbers in tenth-century BCE Judah, for example, rule out the possibility of a significant Israelite monarchy.[3] Antagonists to Zionist goals extend this debate into modern times, arguing that the strength of ancient Israelite settlement and governance has direct bearing on modern Zionist-Israeli claims to Palestine (e.g., Whitelam 1996). While it is beyond the scope of this chapter to assess the debate in full, what is relevant is that population numbers have important contemporary meaning, even if they are more than 2,000 years old.

WHEN IS THE LAND FULL? BRITISH AND ZIONISTS DEBATE CARRYING CAPACITY

Following the destruction of the Second Temple in 70 CE and subsequent rise of the Jewish Diaspora and until the rise of the modern Zionist movement, the minority Jewish presence in the land was numerically small, though symbolically significant (Sachar 1985). The total population of western Palestine, after reaching a peak of one to two and a half million during the late Byzantine period, did not surpass 300,000 until the mid-nineteenth century. Population growth—Jewish and Arab—began in earnest during the rise of the Zionist movement at the turn of the twentieth century (see fig. 4.1).

Following the British conquest of Palestine from the Ottoman colonial rulers, the Zionist drive to establish a Jewish state was dominated by a fundamental and recurring question: How to move as many Jews to Palestine as possible, thereby garnering the political and demographic support needed to establish an independent Jewish political entity. The Zionist leadership and institutions set out to prove that the arid land of Palestine was ready for the absorption of millions of Jewish immigrants. In 1918, David Ben-Gurion explained:

> The true aim and real capacity of Zionism are not to conquer what has already been conquered (e.g., land cultivated by Arabs), but to settle in those places where the present inhabitants of the land have not established themselves and are unable to do so. The preponderant part of the country's land is unoccupied and uncultivated. According to the figures of the Turkish Ministry of Agriculture, only 5.28 percent of the land in the Jerusalem district is under cultivation. . . . According to an estimate of Prof. Karl Ballod, the country's irrigable plains are capable of support-

ing a population of six million. . . . The demand of the Jewish people is based on the reality of unexploited economic potentials, and of unbuilt-up stretches of land that require the productive force of a progressive, cultured people. (Ben-Gurion 1973, 7; written in 1918 and first published in *Der Yiddisher Kempfer*)[4]

These words exemplify what would become signature Zionist optimism about the technological possibilities for increasing water availability and agricultural output in Palestine, which were crucial for enlarging the Jewish population. Modern irrigation and hydroelectric power would help to realize the utopian vision described in Herzl's 1902 fiction *Altneuland*, where the efficient application of existing technologies turn a dirty and decaying region into a blossoming, peaceful, and multicultural success story. Such ideas both echoed and foreshadowed an enduring Zionist trust in the ability of technology to resolve any of Palestine and Israel's diverse environmental problems, and in particular limitations on water and agricultural productivity (Tal 2008).

The major goal of the Zionist movement was thus to increase the size of the Jewish population in Palestine. The leaders of the nascent Palestinian Arab national movement, on the other hand, believed that increased Jewish immigration would inevitably lead to Arab dispossession, and were increasingly and actively opposed to it (Fargues 2000; Sachar 1985). The British colonial authorities were caught in the middle and faced with the dilemma of deciding to either allow or prevent Jewish immigration, and to what degree.

In 1922, the British, under pressure to limit Jewish immigration, formally adopted the concept of population carrying capacity of Palestine, in the form of an estimate of the land's "absorptive capacity," to set quotas for new immigrants. According to science historian Samer Alatout, by adopting a scientific-technical determinant for allowing or preventing immigration, the British set the tone for the next two decades of debate about the future of Palestine. For the Palestinians, it "rendered insignificant Palestinian objections based on moral-historic logic" (369). Yet for the Zionists, who were skeptical of the concept, it presented a tremendous opportunity. Rather than debate the need for a Jewish state as such, the debate became centered on the question of how many Jews should be allowed to immigrate; in this way "the Zionist movement found that it could exploit the *seemingly depoliticized* nature of Jewish immigration for its own purposes" (Alatout 2009, 369).

Over the next two decades, following major events of Arab unrest (the riots of 1929, the Arab revolt of 1936–1939), the British sent commissions of inquiry to Palestine to explore the reasons behind the unrest. Their reports, including the Hope Simpson report of 1930 and the 1937 Peel Commission Report, as well as policy statements such as the 1930 Passfield White Paper, each returned to the theme of economic capacity of Palestine to absorb (Jewish) immigrants. Economic capacity was interpreted, in these cases, as primarily resource limitations including cultivatable land and water for agricultural production.

The recurring British assessment was that the amount of land in Palestine available for cultivation was too small to support massive Jewish immigration (agriculture being considered the major economic activity for the region). The British further considered limited prospects for irrigation. Not surprisingly, British estimates for cultivable land were consistently lower than Jewish estimates. The Hope Simpson report (named after its author, British envoy Sir John Hope Simpson), for example, cites Jewish sources estimating 16 to 27 million dunam of cultivable land as compared with 8 to 12 million estimated by British experts (Hope Simpson 1930). Hope Simpson himself concluded that 6.5 million dunam were appropriate for cultivation, supporting his final assessment that "it has emerged quite definitely that there is at the present time and with the present methods of Arab cultivation no margin of land available for agricultural settlement by new immigrants, with the exception of such undeveloped land as the various Jewish Agencies hold in reserve" (Hope Simpson 1930, chap. XI).

Hope Simpson's caveat regarding the Jewish Agencies' undeveloped land reserves actually left much room for Zionists to argue that through technological advance and better exploitation of the land's existing water and land resources many more immigrants could be brought to the region. They could, after all, summon more of the "capital, science and organization . . . and . . . energy of the settlers" to which Hope Simpson attributed the "remarkable progress" of the Jews to further increase agricultural productivity (chap. XI).

Ben-Gurion dealt with the question of absorptive capacity in many of his writings, attesting to the centrality of this ostensibly scientific question in the political debates over future Jewish self-determination in Palestine. In his 1932 book *Rebirth and Destiny of Israel* he dedicates considerable print to the question of whether Palestine can absorb all of the Jews. Here he asks rhetorically, "how are we to interpret the principle of absorptive capacity?" and "is Palestine a land of absorption at all?" (42). In a publication ten years later, his answers to these questions, as were typical of his writings, were a rich mixture of unflinching political convictions, technological optimism (often vague, though sometimes specific), and reference to earlier Zionist successes:

> It is useless to survey only the country, as British "experts" like Hope Simpson and French did—we must also take account of Jewish capacity and potential. Twenty-six years ago, what expert could have predicted that some thousands of dunams of sand-dunes near Jaffa would absorb

the population of Tel Aviv? What expert could have foreseen how varied in their intense production the new agricultural villages of Jezreel and the Jordan Valley would become, if he had seen only the wasteland and knew not at all the pioneer passion that came to fertilize it? (Ben-Gurion 1954a, 44, first published as a pamphlet in 1942)

But while the Zionists continued to inflate the potential for population growth, the British stuck to the theme of limited absorptive capacity throughout the Mandate period. A direct response to Zionist technological optimism came in the form of the 1937 Peel Commission Report on Palestine. The report was defined by one prominent British geographer as a "masterly review" of the problem of subsistence areas in Palestine (Willatts 1946) and it dealt comprehensively with, among other subjects, the issues of economic carrying capacity as defined by cultivable land and water availability. The report, like its predecessor the Hope Simpson report, presented estimates of the amount of cultivatable land that were consistently lower (7 million dunam) than those offered by the Jewish Agency (9 million dunam).[5]

The British, for their part, found Jewish reliance on potential economic and physical investment to be unrealistic. The report concludes dryly that "we consider that, until the contrary is proved by experience and practical experiment, the Administration will be wise in adhering to their own definition in so far as it relates to an increase of immigrants on the land" (Palestine Royal Commission [PRC] 1937, 175).

Interestingly, later in the Peel report, having noted Jewish agricultural achievements in communities near Jerusalem, the authors write: "Our impression . . . was that they were in every way a remarkable testimony to the enthusiastic energy not only of the immigrants but of those who financed and advised them. Land which under ordinary methods of cultivation would have given a precarious crop of cereals has been turned over to mixed farming; and, although these farms cannot be judged on any ordinary economic basis, they are a valuable feature in the Jewish colonization as affording a livelihood for settlers and training centres for young immigrants" (267).

After recommending a partition of Palestine into a Jewish and an Arab state, the Peel report recommended severe restrictions on Jewish immigration. Further, "the volume of Jewish immigration should be determined by the economic absorptive capacity of Palestine less the Arab Area" (294). The Zionist response to the Peel report was predictably negative as its recommendations were the antithesis of their goals in Palestine (goals which were captured graphically in dozens of posters produced by the Zionist movement; fig. 4.2). By severely curtailing Jewish immigration it essentially froze demographic conditions that ensured an Arab majority (Muhsam 1983). Nonetheless, the

FIGURE 4.2. Poster announcing a 1949 conference of the youth of the Workers' Party of Eretz Israel (Mapai, under the leadership of David Ben-Gurion) and emphasizing key elements of the predominant Zionist ideology at the time: immigration and agricultural development. Note the existing agriculture in the Jezreel Valley and coastal plain, with tree roots spreading into the Negev. Poster by the artist Moshe Raviv (Vorobeichik; Moi Ver), reprinted with permission of the artist's son.

indefatigable Ben-Gurion used the opportunity to put forward an argument against the entire concept of "absorptive capacities." To Ben-Gurion, there was no limit to Jewish ingenuity and willpower:

> No square inch of land shall we neglect; not one source of water shall we fail to tap; not a swamp that we shall not drain; not a sand dune that we shall not fructify; not a barren hill that we shall not cover with trees; nothing shall we leave untouched. An intensive agriculture, planned in accordance with a scientific and practical scheme worked out by the Government, operated by pioneering labour, and maintained by the full

strength of the State and of supporters from abroad, with an assured home market, and with access on a reciprocal basis to foreign markets, will be the fundamental basis of a national economy created by the State through the energy of citizens no longer dependent on the favours of a foreign Administration. Set free from the Mandate which enchains our trade, under a Jewish Government whose first consideration will be the increase of the absorptive capacity of the country, assisted by its position of vantage at the cornerstone of three continents and on the sea coast, there will develop a Jewish industry to whose growth we can set no limits. (Ben-Gurion 1938, 63)

During this period, Ben-Gurion sensed that British immigration policy was becoming more a political question, concluding that the British had forfeited the scientific debate on absorptive capacity. He quotes British High Commissioner in Palestine Herbert Samuel: "They [Jews] must consent to a limitation of immigration other than on the principle of absorptive capacity. They must accept the principle proposed by the Commission that political considerations must be brought in" (Ben-Gurion 1938). Ben-Gurion concludes, in his speech to the Extraordinary Zionist Conference in New York in 1942, that "there is no conflict of economic interests between Jews and Arabs in Palestine, none between present population and new arrivals. The very fact that the Mufti and his friends, and the Chamberlain-MacDonald Government which tried to appease them, insisted on abolishing the principle of economic absorptive capacity as the only yardstick of Jewish immigration implies that the Arabs as well as the authors of the White Paper realized that on purely economic grounds there is room for a very large influx, which may turn Palestine into a Jewish country" (Ben-Gurion 1954b, 120).

Zionist optimism regarding potential for agricultural cultivation was also reflected in their perceptions of water availability. The Zionists latched on to the influential study in 1944 by American soil conservationist Walter Lowdermilk, later supported by American engineers James Hayes and John Cotton, which claimed that through proper utilization of the Jordan River water and groundwater, Palestine could support a population of five million. According to historian Howard Sachar (1985), the Lowdermilk plan "laid the basis for all subsequent water planning in Israel."

The British regarded such numbers as pure speculation. In response to Jewish estimates provided to the Peel Commission, they write "We are not in a position to pronounce upon these estimates nor do we consider it in any way necessary for us to attempt to do so" (PRC 1937, 255). British geographer Willatts concluded that "in spite of the claims of propagandists, Palestine is very badly placed for irrigation" (Willatts 1946). Regarding the Lowdermilk plan, he added: "In general it seems that the project, which has a strong political flavour, is over ambitious in proposing to use more water than is available" (169). He concludes his analysis more definitively than the Peel Commission: "In considering the much discussed 'economic absorptive capacity' of the country it is difficult to avoid the conclusion that agriculturally the country is already saturated," and suggests that Palestine should "temper [its] zeal and energy with economic caution" (173).

American demographers Notestein and Jurkat also broached the issue of carrying capacity in Palestine as affected by resources, capital, and political conditions (Notestein and Jurkat 1945). They describe the area in terms of high population density at 108 persons per square kilometer (without the sparsely populated Beer-Sheva subdistrict), higher than many European countries prior to World War II. They speculated that the local demographic trends demanded rapid and sustained economic growth, and in its absence the result would be a highly congested, desperately poor population. Such economic progress, they suggested, was likely to be stymied by the ongoing political clash between the two population groups. However, they also note that "in a trading world, there are no simple relations between density of settlement and living conditions" (349), so the combination of a nonagricultural economy and trade could allow the region to retain economic viability and a high standard of living.

In measured academic fashion, Notestein and Jurkat both raised and lowered the expectations of the Jews in Palestine. They observed that the demographic situation "leads to the conclusion that all parties concerned would benefit by the continuation of Jewish interest as a source of capital and skill for the region and of Jewish immigrants on a limited scale." They then qualify this assertion: "On the basis of the growth prospect it appears that a catastrophe of major proportions is not outside the bounds of possibility if enthusiasm for a Jewish state should result in the really heavy immigration sometimes talked of. There are almost no limits to the population that could be supported, given someone to bear the cost" (350). While crediting the Jews for raising the carrying capacity of the area, Notestein and Jurkat were skeptical that the Jews would ever obtain a majority in Palestine based on demographic trends. Notestein testified as such to the Anglo-American Commission of Inquiry on Palestine, and this testimony, according to Notestein's colleague Ansley Coale, "helped the Jewish leaders decide in favor of the partition of Palestine" (Coale 1983, 5).

Perhaps, as Coale suggested, it was this sobering demographic message, coupled with the new demographic reality created by the Holocaust that caused the Zionists to take an increasingly practical approach with regard to partitioning Palestine into a Jewish and an Arab state. If before the Holocaust Zionist leaders argued that the suggestion of an absorptive capacity of

Palestine was, for the British and Arabs, a political question wrapped in economic packaging, then after the destruction of Europe's Jewish community, the question became purely political for the Zionist leaders as well. There was now no moral justification, in their eyes, for limiting Jewish immigration to Palestine. They seemed to have eschewed the concept of carrying capacity for the moral urgency of bringing as many Jews as possible, and at the same time internalized the demographic message that they would not be able to achieve a demographic majority in all of Palestine west of the Jordan River.

The impact of the Holocaust on demographic thinking cannot be underestimated, as one-third of the global Jewish population was destroyed (Schmelz 1991). Not only did it add a new sense of Zionist urgency toward establishing a Jewish state in Palestine, but it is woven into any discussion on Jewish demographics, and inevitably has surfaced in contemporary environmental-based discussions about potentially limiting population growth in Israel (Benstein 2006; Schwartz 2002).

ISRAEL KNOWS NO LIMITS: A ZIONIST DISCOURSE ON POPULATION IN THE NEW STATE

The establishment of Israel in 1948 allowed Zionist leaders to realize their demographic ideology without interference from a colonial government. The ingathering of the exiles became a shining example of the Israel's new demographic policy, with the Law of Return, which grants any Jew automatic Israeli citizenship, exemplifying the country's enduring raison d'etat.[6]

A window into postindependence Zionist thinking is provided by a social studies textbook authored by Itzhak Kanev, *Population and Society in Israel and in the World* (1957). Kanev, a longtime Mapai member and activist, was one of the architects of the early Israeli social welfare state. He was a founder of the Kupat Holim health care system and among its directors for thirty-eight years, a member of the first Knesset, head of the committee that established Israel's National Insurance program, and 1962 Israel Prize laureate for the Social Sciences. He had a profound influence on the structuring of Israel's health care and social welfare system.

Kanev's textbook features a chapter on population that begins by disparaging Thomas Malthus and his theories. The problem with Malthus's 1798 theory that overpopulation generally outstrips food production leading to poverty and misery was, according to Kanev, that humans had not yet developed proper social programs to organize society and encourage technological development to deal with population growth. He believed that in mid-twentieth century, technological advances created abundant food production, but the problem with faulty social systems remained, and thus, some places of the world continued to suffer from overpopulation and undernourishment. A great irony exists, wrote Kanev, where millions suffer in the presence of rich natural resources. Despite the rationalism of science and technology that should assure well-being, this irony could be attributed to the concurrent lack of social security (Kanev 1957). Kanev then waxed ideological: "man doesn't organize his life in a socially intelligent way—correctly and purposefully—and therefore millions of people suffer from want and poverty, rather than living a comfortable life" (176). His insights were clearly nested in the broader Marxist critique of Malthusian theory, which viewed population growth as an irrelevant factor in human well-being. Rather, an economy governed by social equity and technology could support a growing population with no detrimental side effects (Weeks 1999).

Kanev, representative of other early state leaders, found the keys to the state's success lay in increasing its Jewish population and its agricultural technology ("the solution to the problem of food is the key to the solution to the problem of population" [133]), all accompanied by good social welfare planning. The former goal would be met through Aliyah (immigration of Jews) and raising fertility. Meeting the latter goal depended on investment in state-of-the-art technologies on the one hand, and state-of-the-art social policy on the other. With regard to agricultural technology, Kanev enthusiastically advocated biological engineering, increasing the area of cultivation, use of advanced fertilizers, control of plant diseases and destruction of agricultural pests, returning neglected land to production, and settling areas empty of human settlement. He also encouraged pro-natal social policy, including caring for families, education, health, housing, and rational nutrition. He pointed to the importance of health care for mothers and children, social insurance, preferential housing policies for families, and other policies that would lighten the burden on parents of large families.

Kanev looked to Holland and Denmark to provide national models that combined just economic policies, pro-natal population policies, an assiduous work ethic, a lack of natural resources, but a complete exploitation of existing land resources. He observed that in Denmark, rarely was a plot of ground not under cultivation. So, Israel too must find its development path in "conquering nature." For Kanev, there were no environmental limitations on population growth. Technology, ingenuity, and determination—when combined with pro-natal health and social programs—and the establishment of socioeconomic equity would allow the young nation to overcome any potential barriers.

Indeed, technology, ingenuity, and pro-natal health and social programs were to follow in Israel. Regarding the latter, the country saw the implementation of a variety of pro-natal policies, including monthly child allowances, one-time birth grants, tax assistance for large families, rent subsidies, laws protecting pregnant women and new mothers in the workplace, paid maternity leaves, and subsidized daycare. Other policies related to fertility included investment in fertility technologies and programs encouraging establishment of families and childbearing (Portugese 1998). In 1962, a government-sanctioned "Committee for Natility Problems," chaired by Hebrew University demographer and Ben-Gurion adviser Roberto Bachi was charged with creating policy to encourage Jewish demographic growth (Fargues 2000; Portugese 1998).

There is a diversity of thought regarding the nature of fertility policy in Israel during its first decades. Schiff (1981), for example, suggests that although there was clear pro-natalist sympathy in Israeli society, the eclectic mix of ostensibly pro-natal measures had not produced an effective, concrete pro-natal policy. For one, many of the laws were enacted with equal, if not more, concern for social welfare as for pro-natalism. Thus, while some laws may seem pro-natal, they were initiated with other goals in mind. Second, other laws had effectively stymied any potential effect of the pro-natal legislation (e.g., universal conscription and liberal abortion laws). Portugese (1998), on the other hand, believes that the aggregation of all of Israel's pro-natal measures, whether stated explicitly or not, reflect a clear and consistent desire to increase Jewish fertility.

Child allowances have been among the more visible (and often controversial) of these policies. Child allowances began to be distributed to families with four or more children in 1959 by the National Insurance Institute. Over time, the policy came to include all children, and, in 2000, the amount of the per-child payment became steeply progressive with increasing amounts of payment going to each successive child in a family (Winckler 2008). Historically, the intent of child allowances was twofold: as a social policy to provide aid to families living below the poverty line (many of whom are large families), and to encourage fertility, in particular among Israel's Jewish population, by providing financial incentives for large families (Portugese 1998; Schiff 1981; Winckler 2008). Ironically, the child allowances primarily benefited those sectors of the population that did not share in the democratic, Zionist vision of the policy makers—namely Moslem Arabs and Ultra-Orthodox Jews. As of 2002, the child allowances were drastically reduced during a recession by an economically conservative government led by Benjamin Netanyahu.

Aside from pro-natal policy, the Israeli government implemented a generous package of policies to encourage Jewish immigration to the state. The cornerstone policy was, and remains, The Law of Return, enacted in 1950, which grants Jews anywhere the legal right to immigrate (Sachar 1985). Jews are also offered a generous package of incentives to entice them to move to Israel, and the governmental and quasi-governmental offices are maintained around

TABLE 4.1. Population growth in Israel and the contribution of immigration
to total growth

Period	Population, beginning of period	Population, end of period	Percent of total growth contributed by migration balance
1948–1960	805.6	2,150.4	64.6
1961–1971	2,150.4	3,120.7	37.7
1972–1982	3,115.6	4,063.6	19.6
1983–1989	4,033.7	4,559.6	5.9
1990–1995	4,559.6	5,619.0	56.0
1996–2000	5,612.3	6,369.3	39.1
2001–2008	6,369.3	7,374.0	14.7
1948–2008	805.6	7,374.0	37.5

Source: CBS (2009).

the world to assist Jews who consider immigration. In part due to this policy, immigration has historically accounted for a large proportion of population growth in Israel, particularly during the 1950s and 1990s. Over the sixty-year history of the state, immigration has accounted for 37 percent of population growth in Israel (Central Bureau of Statistics [CBS] 2009; table 4.1).

"THEY ARE THE POPULATION PROBLEM": THE INSEPARABILITY OF POPULATION, ENVIRONMENT, AND POLITICS

The attitudes set out by the early Zionist and Israeli leaders are similar in many ways to those that dominate population-environment discourse today (Orenstein 2004). The democratic and Jewish nature of the state continues to be predicated on the maintenance of a solid secular Jewish majority. Yet, in Israel at the start of the twenty-first century, fertility patterns are sharply disparate among various sectors of the population. Presuming that high fertility groups have a distinctly different sociopolitical vision of the state's future, these differences in fertility among different population sectors have caused consternation within the country's Jewish-Zionist majority (e.g., Blum 2004; Khoury 2008; Leibowitz 2007). Discourse on the implications of population growth (on the environment, for example), should be considered with caution as a subset of the larger political-demographic debate.

In Israel, there are roughly three discernable schools of thought regarding P-E interactions that regularly appear in the academic literature and mass media. The primary disagreement among the various schools is regarding the mechanisms by which population growth places stresses on environmental systems. There are those who reflect a neo-Malthusian approach that population growth has a direct and negative impact on Israel's environment (Tal 2002; Warburg 1997). Second are those who suggest that overconsumption of natural resources and resultant production of waste are the primary stressors of Israel's environment (de-Shalit 2004; Garb 2002) and that pressure resulting from population size could be relaxed with lowered consumption. Overconsumption is attributed to the more affluent, low-fertility sectors of Israel's population. Finally, there are those who suggest that population growth need not be a major environmental stressor and that proper economic and social policies, planning, or technological innovation can relieve actual or potential environmental stress (Feitelson 1994).

Most academic and policy documents dealing with P-E interactions seem to endorse a neo-Malthusian perspective, arguing that population growth is a stressor for any number of resource or environmental pollution challenges (Ayalon 2003; Israel Ministry of Environment 1999; Khenin et al. 2000). However, the viewpoint that population growth is crucial to the well-being of the state is so ingrained in Israeli thinking that the policy discussion of P-E generally turns toward how best to facilitate for the growing population (as with the reports cited above). Thus facilitation of population growth, and not confrontation, seems to be the norm (Orenstein 2004). Tal, who writes that "population pressure promises to undermine even the most optimistic [environmental] scenarios" in Israel, is one of the few exceptions. He states bluntly that "the land of Israel no longer needs more people" (Tal 2002, 420–23).

In Israel, the ostensibly objective question about the environmental impact of population growth is exceedingly difficult, if not impossible, to separate from questions of political demography (Orenstein 2004; Rabinowitz 2004). University of Jerusalem demographer H. V. Muhsam (1983) explained the Zionist demographic dilemma succinctly that (Zionist) Israelis desire (but cannot have) a big country, a Jewish country, a democratic country, *and* a long-lasting country. At best, Muhsam considered, Israel could have three of the four alternatives.

Among the Jewish-Zionist majority, an Arab population that is growing proportionally relative to the Jewish majority is frequently perceived as a "demographic threat" (Blum 2004; Sheleg 2001; Soffer and Bystrov 2007; fig. 4.3). Historian Onn Winckler has termed the Arab demographic as "the paranoia object" among the Jewish majority (Winckler 2008). Along the same lines, Ultra-Orthodox Jews are considered, among some, a second component of the "demographic threat" because they are perceived as advocating a theocratic, rather than secular, state.

Geographer Arnon Soffer and his colleague and coauthor Evgenia Bystrov

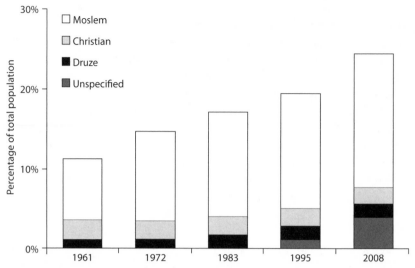

FIGURE 4.3. Proportional contribution of non-Jewish population to the total population in Israel (CBS 2011).

provide an explicit and uncompromising narrative about how Arab Muslim and Ultra-Orthodox Jewish population growth threaten the environment and the democratic, Jewish character of the state (Bystrov and Soffer 2008; Soffer 1988, 2003; Soffer and Bystrov 2005, 2007). A quote from their polemic *Israel: Demography and Density 2007–2020* sums up this perspective:

> The decline is advancing at a dizzying pace because of the unique
> combination of two conflicting trends: population growth rates typical
> of the third world against demands for land at rates typical of the West-
> ern world, where the living standard is rising. . . . The result is Israel's
> nearing the limit of its carrying capacity. . . . Proximity to the carrying-
> capacity limit causes collapse of the water regime, the transport system,
> garbage disposal, sewage treatment, and non-prevention of flooding
> in the major cities, destruction of the sea shore, disappearance of the
> sand dunes, destruction of agriculture, disappearance of open spaces,
> collapse of the physical planning system on the national and municipal
> levels, non-enforcement of the law, deterioration in relations between
> people, and yawning social gulfs between the Tel Aviv population and
> the populations of country's centre and periphery. (Bystrov and Soffer
> 2008, 62)

Among the many problems (security, politics, economy, education, envi-ronment) the authors cite, "All are associated with demography, that is, to the high natural increase of the different populations, which are becoming increasingly impoverished, hence increasingly violent" (Bystrov and Soffer 2008, 69). Note that the authors are influenced by any number of theories on the connection between population and environment, including population growth as driver of environmental degradation (Ehrlich 1970), increased consumption as driver of environmental degradation (Commoner, Corr, and Stamler 1971), and political-demographic conflict driven by competition over scarce resources (Homer-Dixon 1994; Homer-Dixon, Boutwell, and Rathjens 1993). Yet, the writing does not reflect academic inquiry into the drivers of environmental degradation, but rather a strong endorsement, in the cited cases, of a political opinion.

CARRYING CAPACITY DEFERRED

Two to three thousand years ago, according to biblical accounts and the assumptions of archeologists, environmental carrying capacities were real. Carrying capacities proposed by British and other scientists during the British Mandate, however, were met with obstinate resistance and optimistic counterarguments by Zionists for whom such limitations were a direct threat to achieving a Jewish majority in Palestine. History largely vindicated the Zionists—the land could indeed support a population several times larger than scientific experts had suggested. Israel seemingly eluded natural carrying capacity though planning, technology, and (especially) import of goods. In biblical times too, planning, trade, and technologies may have raised local carrying capacities (Finkelstein 1990; Hopkins 1987). Thus, it may not be surprising that many Israelis greet similar claims today with denial, indifference, or unfettered technological optimism.

Israel now supports a population of 7.4 million and, not including the sparsely settled Negev, has a population density slightly less than twice that of Holland and six times that of Denmark (Population Reference Bureau [PRB] 2009).[7] While its Gross National Product is lower than that in those countries, it is similar to that of Ireland, Hong Kong, and Portugal (World Bank 2010). With a population growth rate of 1.6 percent (far more than the developed world's 0.2 percent and similar to the less developed world's 1.7 percent) (PRB 2009), Israel is crowded, relatively rich, and growing fast demographically.

The policies so enthusiastically promoted by Ben-Gurion, Kanev, and their contemporaries have produced loss as well as abundance. Population growth, coupled with growing demand for resources, has had a measurable impact on resources (water, energy, biodiversity, living space, and recreational area) and environmental quality. Israel carries a large negative agricultural trade balance and a negative trade balance in general (Food and Agricultural Organization 2009), suggesting that local land and water resources do not suffice for supporting such a large population and that the country is transferring its ecological footprint elsewhere (Wackernagel et al. 2002). Numerous species extinctions in Israel are attributed to intensive agriculture and draining and pollution of Israel's streams and wetlands (Dolev and Perevolotsky 2004; Sapir and Shmida 2006; Yom-Tov in this volume). Public health has been severely compromised through the accumulation of pesticides in the local environment (Tal 2002). Decline of biodiversity, chronic water shortages, persistent rise in energy demand, and the shrinking amount of open space all suggest unsustainable levels of growth.

Policy makers and the public already have no choice but to confront population growth, if not directly, then via its results. Land-use planners, particularly since the 1990s, are acutely aware of population pressures as they devise ways to provide residential alternatives for a growing population while attempting to assure crucial open-space preservation. But with the exception of expensive and ecologically questionable artificial islands, land cannot be created in the same way that water can be desalinated. Despite the planners' best efforts, under a regime of perpetual population growth, an increasingly crowded country with dwindling agricultural and natural open space will result. Competition over this scarce resource will intensify—between nations, population sectors, economic classes, and vested interest groups.

The myriad ways in which population growth is interwoven into politics, economics, ideology, and religion make a dispassionate discussion in the policy arena difficult. Nonetheless, a candid and honest discussion about the environmental cost of population growth must commence—among policy makers, researchers, and the public—in order to either direct the country's investments and planning to best prepare and adapt to a more crowded country or to consider eliminating policies that encourage immigration and high fertility.

NOTES

I would like to thank Char Miller, Alon Tal, and Benjamin Langer for their careful and constructive suggestions and criticisms of earlier versions of this chapter.

1. There are exceptions, prominent among which is work done within the land-use planning community on population growth, land availability for development, and environmental implications (Feitelson 1994; Frenkel 2004, unpublished manuscript; Mazor 1993; Orenstein and Hamburg 2009; Shoshany and Goldshleger 2002), as well as some exceptions in the activist community (Arguman 2010; Reshef 2010).

2. These two examples provide an ideological and intellectual bridge between ancient and modern Israel. Hillel grew up in Palestine as a youngster and was among the first generation of Israeli scientists—a generation that eagerly studied every aspect of the region's environment, motivated by scientific inquisitiveness on the one hand and by Zionist zeal on the other. The Hebrew Bible, for Hillel, is "a subjective record of the formative experiences, memories, perceptions, and evolving faith of numerous generations of the people called the Hebrews or the Israelites." As such, biblical accounts of

P-E interactions have direct relevance to the modern Jewish-Zionist narrative. Benstein, in his capacity of deputy director of Israel's Heschel Center for Environmental Learning and Leadership, is considered one of the Israeli environmental movement's leading thinkers. The lessons he draws from Judaic sources regarding P-E relationships (e.g., Benstein 2001, 2006) may have broad influence on this movement.

3. Dever himself believes that population size need not be a factor in defining states, but they are, rather, defined by degree of centralization.

4. Note that Ben-Gurion affirms the presence of a local population in contrast the slogan so often attributed to the Zionist movement: "A land without a people for a people without a land." According to historian Amos Elon (1971), that slogan had some influence among Zionists abroad around the turn of the century, but not much usage among Zionists after that period. Elon suggests that the Zionists in Palestine under the Ottomans felt they were operating in a political void rather than a demographic one, as they were well aware of the local population. Later claims suggest that the importance of the slogan among Zionists has been greatly inflated by opponents of Zionism and Israel (Muir 2008).

5. The Jewish Agency estimate included forested land that was not included in the British estimate, but even taking this into account, the Jewish Agency still estimated 1.2 million dunums more cultivatable land than the British. As of 2007, there were approximately 2.8 million dunam of land under agricultural cultivation in Israel and another 1.8 million dunam of natural and planted forest land (CBS, 2009). The amount of cultivated land has remained fairly constant over the years, with the only sizable change being a drop in the early 2000s due to a change in data collection methods. Since 2004, the amount has been fairly constant around 2.9 million dunam. The amount of land covered in planted forests rose consistently between 1948 and 2000. Over the following decade, the area of planted forest remained approximately 985,000 dunam. While these estimates do not include the West Bank (that were included in the various estimates of the 1930s), the actual amount of cultivated land is much closer to the British estimates than those of the Jewish Agency. Of course, as discussed later, much of this argument is merely academic in light of higher obtainable yields and reliance on food imports.

6. Yet, even as Israel's Jewish and Arab population began its rapid half century rise from 1949, the Palestinian Arab population had fallen rapidly as an outcome of the 1948 war. This event represents not only a major demographic shift in Palestine and Israel, but has wide-ranging implications for the discussion on population size and resource availability. In particular, if we are to consider changes in carrying capacity in Israel according to agricultural production, we must consider that the outmigration of hundreds of thousands of Palestinian Arabs facilitated for the transfer of large amounts of agricultural land from Arab to Jewish-National hands (Forman and Kedar 2004).

7. According to CBS data in 2008 there were 330 persons per square kilometer in Israel, including the Negev, and 745 persons per square kilometer if considering only the northern 40 percent of Israel (Central Bureau of Statistics of Israel 2009).

REFERENCES

Alatout, S. 2009. "Bringing Abundance into Environmental Politics: Constructing a Zionist Network of Water Abundance, Immigration, and Colonization." *Social Studies of Science* 39 (3): 363–94.

Arguman, T. 2010. A Letter to Rabbis on the Subject of Fertility. http://www.beofen-tv.
co.il/cgi-bin/chiq.pl?%EE%EB%FA%E1_%EC%F8%E1%F0%E9%ED_%E1%F0%E5%F
9%E0_%E9%EC%E5%E3%E4. In Hebrew.

Ayalon, O., ed. 2003. *National Priorities for Environment in Israel*. Haifa: Economic
Forum for the Environment in Israel, Samuel Ne'eman Institute.

Ben-Gurion, D. 1938. *The Peel Report and the Jewish State*. vol. 10. London: Palestine
Labour Studies Group.

———. 1954a. "The Key to Immigration (1932)." In *Rebirth and Destiny of Israel*, edited
by M. Nurock, 41–44. New York: Philosophical Library.

———. 1954b. "Test of Fulfillment." In *Rebirth and Destiny of Israel*, edited by M. Nurock, 113–32. New York: Philosophical Library.

———. 1973. *My Talks with Arab Leaders*. New York: Third Press.

Benstein, J. 2001. "Bedroom Politics." *Jerusalem Report*, December 17.

———. 2006. *The Way into Judaism and the Environment*. Woodstock: Jewish Lights
Publishing.

Blum, R. 2004. "It's the Demography, Stupid: Interview with Professor Arnon Sofer."
Jerusalem Post online edition, May 21. http://www.jpost.com.

Bookman, M. Z. 2002. "Demographic Engineering and the Struggle for Power." *Journal of International Affairs* 56 (1): 25.

Broshi, M. 1979. "The Population of Western Palestine in the Roman-Byzantine Period." *Bulletin of the American Schools of Oriental Research* 236: 1–10.

Broshi, M., and I. Finkelstein. 1992. "The Population of Palestine in Iron Age-II." *Bulletin of the American Schools of Oriental Research* 287: 47–60.

Broshi, M., and R. Gophna. 1984. "The Settlements and Population of Palestine during
the Early Bronze Age II–III." *Bulletin of the American Schools of Oriental Research*
253: 41–53.

———. 1986. "Middle-Bronze-Age-Ii Palestine, Its Settlements and Population." *Bulletin of the American Schools of Oriental Research* 261: 73–90.

Bystrov, E., and A. Soffer. 2008. *Israel: Demography and Density 2007–2020*. Haifa:
Chaikin Chair in Geostrategy.

Central Bureau of Statistics of Israel (CBS). 2009. *Statistical Abstract of Israel*. Jerusalem: Central Bureau of Statistics of Israel.

———. 2011. *Statistical Abstract of Israel*. Jerusalem: Central Bureau of Statistics of
Israel.

Coale, A. J. 1983. "Frank W. Notestein, 1902–1983." *Population Index* 49 (1): 3–12.

Commoner, B., M. Corr, and P. J. Stamler. 1971. "The Causes of Pollution." *Environment* 13 (3): 2–19.

de-Shalit, A. 2004. "From Malthus to Six Billion—and Back." *Environmental Politics* 13
(4): 781–85.

DellaPergola, S. 2003. "Demographic Trends in Israel and Palestine: Prospects and
Policy Implications." In *American Jewish Yearbook 2003* (Serial publications ed.).
New York: American Jewish Committee.

Dever, W. G. 2004. "Histories and Non-Histories of Ancient Israel: The Question of the
United Monarchy." In *In Search of Pre-Exilic Israel*, edited by J. Day, 65–94. London: Continuum International Publishing Group.

Dolev, A., and A. Perevolotsky, eds. 2004. *The Red Book: Vertebrates in Israel*. Jerusalem: Israel Nature and Parks Authority and the Society for the Protection of Nature
in Israel.

Ehrlich, P. R. 1970. *The Population Bomb*. New York: Ballantine Books.

Elon, A. 1971. *The Israelis: Founders and Sons*. London: Sphere Books Limited.

Fargues, P. 2000. "Protracted National Conflict and Fertility Change: Palestinians and Israelis in the Twentieth Century." *Population and Development Review* 26 (3): 441–82.

Faust, A. 2003. "Abandonment, Urbanization, Resettlement and the Formation of the Israelite State." *Near Eastern Archeology* 66 (4): 147–61.

Feitelson, E. 1994. "Allowing for Sustainable Growth under Drastic Immigration Stress in Israel." *Journal of Environmental Planning and Management* 37 (4): 379–94.

Finkelstein, I. 1990. "Review: The Emergence of Early Israel: Anthropology, Environment and Archaeology." *Journal of the American Oriental Society* 110 (4): 677–86.

Food and Agricultural Organization. 2009. *FAO Statistical Yearbook 2007–2008*. Statistics Division FAO. http://www.fao.org/economic/ess/ess-publications/ess-yearbook/fao-statistical-yearbook-2007-2008/en/.

Forman, G., and A. S. Kedar. 2004. "From Arab Land to 'Israel Lands': The Legal Dispossession of the Palestinians Displaced by Israel in the Wake of 1948." *Environment and Planning D-Society & Space* 22 (6): 809–30.

Frenkel, A. 2004. "The Potential Effect of National Growth-Management Policy on Urban Sprawl and the Depletion of Open Spaces and Farmland." *Land Use Policy* 21: 357–69.

———. "Spatial Population Distribution: From Dispersed to Concentrated." Unpublished manuscript. In Hebrew.

Garb, Y. 2002. "Population Dynamics and Sustainability in the Israeli Context." In *Paths to Sustainability: Shadow Report to the Government of Israel's Assessment of Progress in Implementing Agenda 21*, 204–31.

Hillel, D. 2006. *The Natural History of the Bible*. New York: Columbia University Press.

Homer-Dixon, T. F. 1994. "Environmental Scarcities and Violent Conflict: Evidence from Cases." *International Security* 19 (1): 5–40.

Homer-Dixon, T. F., J. H. Boutwell, and G. W. Rathjens. 1993. "Environmental Change and Violent Conflict." *Scientific American* 268 (2): 38–45.

Hope Simpson, J. 1930. *Palestine. Report on Immigration, Land Settlement and Development*. http://unispal.un.org/UNISPAL.NSF/0/E3ED8720F8707C9385256 D19004F057C.

Hopkins, D. C. 1987. "Life on the Land: The Subsistence Struggles of Early Israel." *Biblical Archeologist* 50 (3): 178–91.

Israel Ministry of Environment. 1999. *Towards Sustainable Development*. Jerusalem: Ministry of Environment.

Kanev, I. 1957. *Population and Society in Israel and in the World*. Jerusalem: Bialik Institute.

Khenin, D., A. Ettinger, M. Epstein, and M. Hanson. 2000. *Vital Signs 2000 Israel*. Tel Aviv: Heschel Center for Environmental Education and Leadership and the Worldwatch Institute.

Khoury, J. 2008. "Danny Ayalon: Galilee Arabs Are Secessionist Threat." *Haaretz.com*, September 2. http://www.haaretz.com/print-edition/news/danny-ayalon-galilee-arabs-are-secessionist-threat-1.253040.

Leibowitz, R. B. 2007. "I Didn't Suggest We Kill Palestinians." *Jerusalem Post*, October 11. http://www.jpost.com/servlet/Satellite?cid=1191257273616&pagename=JPArticle/ShowFull.

Mazor, A. 1993. *Israel 2020: Master Plan for Israel during the 21st Century.* Haifa: Technion.

Ministry of Environment. 1999. *Towards Sustainable Development.* Jerusalem: Israel Ministry of Environment.

Muhsam, H. V. 1983. "Zionism and Population." In *Jewish Population Studies: Papers in Jewish Demography 1981*, vol. 16, edited by U. O. Schmelz, P. Glikson, and S. DellaPergola, 33–41. Jerusalem: Hebrew University of Jerusalem.

Muir, D. 2008. "A Land without a People for a People without a Land." *Middle East Quarterly* 15 (2): 55–62.

Notestein, F. W., and E. Jurkat. 1945. "Population Problems of Palestine." *Milbank Memorial Fund Quarterly* 23 (4): 307–52.

Orenstein, D. E. 2004. "Population Growth and Environmental Impact: Ideology and Academic Discourse in Israel." *Population and Environment* 26 (1): 41–60.

Orenstein, D. E., and S. P. Hamburg. 2009. "To Populate or Preserve? Evolving Political-Demographic and Environmental Paradigms in Israeli Land-Use Policy." *Land Use Policy* 26 (4): 984–1000.

Palestine Royal Commission. 1937. *Palestine Royal Commission Report.* http://unispal .un.org/pdfs/Cmd5479.pdf.

Population Reference Bureau. PRB. 2009. *World Population Data Sheet.* http://www .prb.org/pdf09/09wpds_eng.pdf.

Portugese, J. 1998. *Fertility Policy in Israel: The Politics of Religion, Gender and Nation.* Westport: Praeger Publishers.

Rabinowitz, D. 2004. "Disentangling Nationalizing Projects and Sustainable Development: Can the Case of Israel and Palestine Provide a Model." Paper presented at the Conference on Palestinian and Israeli Environmental Narratives, York University, Toronto, Ontario, December 5–8.

Reshef, D. 2010. "Population Growth." http://www.greenchange.co.il/group/ population. In Hebrew.

Sachar, H. M. 1985. *A History of Israel: From the Rise of Zionism to Our Time.* New York: Knopf.

Sapir, Y., and A. Shmida. 2006. "Mispar Adom" L'Kviat Kdimoioot L'Shimoor Shel Minai Tzmakhim B'Sakanat Hakkhada ["Red Number" for Assigning Protected Status to Plant Species under Threat of Extinction]. http://rotem.huji.ac.il/red%20 number_H.htm.

Schiff, G. S. 1981. "The Politics of Fertility Policy in Israel." In *Modern Jewish Fertility*, edited by P. Ritterband, 255–78. Leiden, Netherlands: E. J. Brill.

Schmelz, U. O. 1991. *The Demographic Impact of the Holocaust on the Jewish People.* Jerusalem: Division of Jewish Demography and Statistics, the Institute of Contemporary Jewry, Hebrew University of Jerusalem.

Schwartz, R. H. 2002. *Judaism and Global Survival.* New York: Lantern Books.

Sheleg, Y. 2001. "The Demographic Problem." *Ha'aretz*, English edition, April 12.

Shoshany, M., and N. Goldshleger. 2002. "Land-Use and Population Density Changes in Israel—1950 to 1990: Analysis of Regional and Local Trends." *Land-Use Policy* 19: 123–33.

Soffer, A. 1988. *On the Demographic and Geographic Situation in the Land of Israel: The End of the Zionist Vision?* Haifa: Gestalit.

———. 2003. B'tachon Leumi, Hebetim Demographim V'Adiphoot Svivatit [National Security, Demographic Aspects and Environmental Priorities]. In *Sedrei Adiphoot*

Leumit B'Tchum Eichoot HaSviva B'Israel [National Environmental Priorities in Israel], edited by O. Ayalon, 9–24. Haifa: Samuel Ne'eman Institute.

Soffer, A., and E. Bystrov. 2005. *Israel Demography 2004–2020; In Light of the Process of Disengagement.* Haifa: University of Haifa.

———. 2007. *Israel: Demography and Density 2007–2020.* Haifa: Chaiken Chair in Geostrategy, University of Haifa.

Tal, A. 2002. *Pollution in a Promised Land.* Berkeley: University of California Press.

———. 2008. "Enduring Technological Optimism: Zionism's Environmental Ethic and Its Influence on Israel's Environmental History." *Environmental History* 13 (April): 275–305.

Teitelbaum, M. S. 2005. "Political Demography." In *Handbook of Population,* edited by D. L. Poston and M. Micklin, 719–30. New York: Kluwer Academic/Plenum Publisher.

Wackernagel, M., N. B. Schulz, D. Deumling, A. C. Linares, M. Jenkins, V. Kapos, C. Monfreda, J. Loh, N. Myers, R. Norgassrd, and J. Randers. 2002. "Tracking the Ecological Overshoot of the Human Economy." *PNAS* 99 (14): 9266–71.

Warburg, P. 1997. "Taboo That Needs Breaking." *Jerusalem Post,* January 1.

Weeks, J. R. 1999. *Population: An Introduction to Concepts and Issues.* London: Wadsworth.

Whitelam, K. W. 1996. *The Invention of Ancient Israel.* London: Routledge.

Willatts, E. C. 1946. "Some Geographical Factors in the Palestine Problem." *Geographical Journal* 108 (4/6): 146–73.

Winckler, O. 2008. "The Failure of Pronatalism in Developed States 'with Cultural-Ethnic Hegemony.'" *Israeli Lesson* 14 (2): 119–34.

World Bank. 2010. *Gross Domestic Product 2009.* http://siteresources.worldbank.org/DATASTATISTICS/Resources/GDP.pdf.

CHAPTER FIVE

COMBATING DESERTIFICATION
Evolving Perceptions and Strategies

Alon Tal

We stand today on lands which show deep scars and damages
of the rise and fall of nations and civilizations. These arid lands
have been afflicted by the course of the conflict of Cain and Abel,
the conflict between farmer and nomadic shepherd along the
borderland of the "sown" and the "unsown." The conflict still
hangs over these lands and similar lands of eastern Asia, as a
sword of Damocles. "Conquest of the Desert" involves not only
the sciences, but social organization and a square deal for all
segments of a population.

—WALTER CLAY LOWDERMILK, JERUSALEM, 1952

WHEN DAVID BEN-GURION stunned the nation in 1953 and moved to Sede
Boqer, a newly formed, remote southern kibbutz, it was a radical statement
from a radical leader reflecting the depth of his personal commitment to conquering the Negev desert. Ben-Gurion was obsessed with what he perceived
to be the neglected state of Israel's southlands—an area that included some 60
percent of the country's area, but only a tiny fraction of its people. After leading his nation through a war of independence, it was as if he had decided to
personally wage war against his country's hot and desolate desert: "If the state
does not exterminate the desert . . . the desert will exterminate the state" was
his grim battle cry.

Thirty years later, the world would acknowledge that desertification posed
a crisis of global dimensions. But the diagnosis and the cure to this global
challenge, as defined by the United Nations Convention to Combat Desertification (UNCCD) (UNCCD 1994) and elsewhere, have emerged as fundamentally different from the human-environment conflict paradigm that Ben-
Gurion trumpeted and epitomized. Rather, the problem termed "desertification" is largely characterized as one of carrying capacity exceeded, requiring

greater human humility, restraint, and resourcefulness in settling and developing the drylands.

Whereas Ben-Gurion saw the desert itself as a threat to human progress, today it is human activities that are perceived as threatening the long-term health of desert ecosystems. Accordingly, desertification is understood not so much as the ineluctable expansion of the world's deserts with unstoppable sand dunes overrunning civilization, but rather, as dispassionately defined by the United Nations: "land degradation in arid, semi-arid and dry sub-humid areas resulting from various factors, including climatic variations and human activities" (UNCCD 1994). By this definition, some of the measures inspired by Ben-Gurion for "conquering the recalcitrant Negev" actually have the potential to accelerate desertification processes, degrading the vulnerable soil. For example, transforming traditional rangelands to intensely cultivated farmlands frequently triggers natural erosional processes (Schlesinger et al. 1990). Today's anti-desertification policies around the world seek to stop and even reverse such negative impact through *sustainable* agriculture and forestation, regulation of erosive activities, and economic development that does not exacerbate pressures on the soil.

Although the Israeli government has never articulated a comprehensive program to combat desertification per se, almost a century of sundry efforts to increase dryland productivity constitutes a proxy for such a strategy. Aggregated, the strategy includes aggressive water management and extensive irrigation, intensive desert agriculture, afforestation, and erosion control as well as regulation of rangelands and grazing. For the most part, management strategies that have emerged over the years produce net gains for the health and productivity of Israel's lands.

Israel's experience provides a unique case study in desertification for at least three reasons. First, unique, local climatic features contribute to the country serving as a real-world laboratory. Israel has an extremely steep precipitation gradient. Over only a couple hundred kilometers, Israel's "drylands" run the full spectrum of climatic zones: beginning with hyper-arid and arid areas in the south, semiarid lands in the central and northern Negev, and dry subhumid zones up through the Galilee. Indeed, only some 3% of Israel has sufficient precipitation to avoid classification as drylands (CLEMDES 2004). Naturally, influenced by the country's myriad climatic conditions, activities to combat desertification are diverse, and can be contrasted and evaluated.

Technically, the hyperarid and arid zones, which constitute almost half of the country's territory, are not given to desertification processes. Development can certainly damage land conditions in these parched, low-rainfall areas. For example poorly executed irrigation can exacerbate salinization. But generally, soil erosion per se is nonexistent. Quite simply there is not a natural, organic base to be lost or degraded. While defining and pursuing sustainable economic development in these desiccated regions has come to be a part of broad desertification strategies, initiatives to combat desertification typically focus on preventive and restoration measures for soils in semiarid areas with annual rainfall of at least several hundred millimeters. This chapter, therefore focuses on policies affecting Israel's semiarid and dry subhumid drylands— from the greater Beer-Sheva region to the north, except for small, relatively wet areas of the Galilee.

Second, any Israeli success in combating desertification took place through aggressive development. It is worth noting that desertification is fundamentally different from other conventional environmental media because of the human context. To a large extent, problems of air pollution, biodiversity, toxic waste, or marine pollution are best solved by limiting damaging activities. Completely stopping the activities that cause desertification, however, is usually not an option. Land degradation in drylands is often caused by communities whose subsistence activities barely allow them to eke out a living. But the more their numbers increase, the greater the toll their farming or shepherding take on the soil (Dregne 2002). Part of the battle against desertification involves providing alternative livelihoods that will offer a modicum of prosperity. Progress lies in sustainable development—not strict preservation of the drylands. Accordingly, Israel's relative "success" in overcoming desertification in the Negev is also the story of innovative agricultural, industrial, and tourism ventures uniquely suited to the hot and dry climate that, together, form a new economic infrastructure.

Third, Israel's idiosyncratic ideological context promoted anti-desertification policies, even before the term "desertification" was coined internationally. Prior to Israel's establishment, Zionists set out to "make the desert bloom." Admittedly land managers and planners were not particularly concerned about climatic nuances or ecological integrity. Rather, Zionist ideology, demography, and geopolitics often drove their thinking. And yet, the resulting trial-and-error process in arid agriculture, water management, and dryland forestry led to remarkable advancements in these fields. Many of these uniquely Israeli innovations today can make valuable contributions to international efforts to combat desertification. While desertification remains a challenge that Israel still needs to address, some sixty years of ongoing policies in the country's southlands and dry subhumid soils offer a relatively long history of intervention that is often held up internationally as an example of how development in the drylands can be sustainable and how desertification can be contained and even reversed (Tal 2007a).

THE STATE OF THE LAND IN PALESTINE

The degraded condition of soils in Palestine was a common theme in travelers' testimonials from the French philosopher-traveler Constantine Francois Volney (1805) to Mark Twain's well-documented 1867 visit (Twain 1996). Descriptions of the land repeatedly emphasized massive soil loss and deforestation. Later aerial photographs and soil scientists would validate these impressions (see No'am G. Seligman, chapter 2, this volume, for an alternative perspective).

Walter Clay Lowdermilk was a prominent witness in this regard. Not only was he a key figure in crafting Israel's approach to soil conservation in its dryland, but was a highly influential soil scientist in the United States ("Man Who Cared," 1976). In 1938, after the trauma of the "dustbowl" and the massive erosion that took place across America, the U.S. Department of Agriculture began to question its land management strategy. It sought answers in the Middle East—a dryland area with a far longer history of human, agrarian settlement than America. The Department of Agriculture sent Lowdermilk, its deputy chief, to head its fact-finding delegation to the region to learn about the state of the soils. Touring lands from Tunisia to Iraq, Lowdermilk came away appalled at the scope and the magnitude of erosion caused by the imprudent cultivation, grazing, and irrigation practices in the countries he visited, including those of indigenous Arab Fellaheen (peasants) in Palestine.

In his subsequent book, *Palestine: Land of Promise*, he describes the pathology of ecological devastation: "Here before our eyes the remarkable red earth soil of Palestine was being ripped from the slopes and swept into the blue of the Mediterranean to a dirty brown as far as the eye could see. We could well understand how many centuries this type of erosion had wasted the neglected lands. It is estimated that over three feet of soil has been swept from the uplands of Palestine after the breakdown of terrace agriculture" (Lowdermilk 1944, 5).

The new, and rather idiosyncratic, Jewish agricultural activities in Palestine were a notable enough exception to attract the soil scientist's attention and praise (Lowdermilk 1944). Indeed, Lowdermilk, a devout Christian, was so impressed by the commitment to soil conservation practices and land reclamation in the Jewish Yishuv, that in 1951 he would return to the nascent Jewish state to take part in the new national rebirth. Upon arrival, he helped found the Department of Agricultural Engineering at the Technion, the Israel Institute of Technology.

And so it was that when Israel's foreign ministry convened an international conference along with UNESCO in 1952 with the goal of considering different strategies for life in deserts, Lowdermilk's keynote address about the origins of Israel's degraded soils was among the more compelling presentations:

> Under certain conditions, the natural landscape has been so much damaged by such acceleration of erosion as to create man-made deserts. These man-made deserts stand as one of the great indictments of man's failure in the stewardship of the good earth. Science and technology have come late to the assistance of the farmer and the shepherd in the use of these delicate mechanisms of nature. Such misuse of land throughout the ages has been brought about by a complex of causes among which is ignorance of natural processes, exploiting of farms by civil and military powers and by lack of public policy and assistance in conservation of land under use.

Similar findings emerged in Adolph Reifenberg's tome *The Struggle between the Desert and the Sown.* In it, the Hebrew University soil scientist systematically documented the advanced state of erosion in the drylands:

> The Israel we see today is but the ruin of a once flourishing country. The change to desert conditions in many parts of the country has to be ascribed to ecological causes. It is human mismanagement, which has brought a continuing deterioration in the natural conditions. Man has wantonly destroyed the original vegetation. Overgrazing, lime and charcoal-burning as well as ruthless exploitation of forests has caused the denudation of the country, thus exposing the soil to every form of erosion. The skillful exploitation of water resources carried out in ancient times has been forgotten and the old irrigation installations were in ruins when Jewish colonization started again after a lapse of nearly two thousand years. (Reifenberg 1955, 378)

Fortunately, soil is a renewable resource and land degradation can be abated. The new Jewish state would soon prove that when faced with acute desertification, a combination of ideological fervor and basic soil-management practices could change degradation patterns that had taken hold for hundreds of years. Indeed, even before Israel's independence, a national program of soil conservation had begun.

SOIL CONSERVATION UNDER THE BRITISH MANDATE

The Zionist perspective about erosion was not entirely different from that of the British colonial administration, which began overseeing Palestine under the League of Nation's Mandate in 1919. The Mandate's Department of Agriculture was keenly aware that the soils of the Negev, central Palestine, and the Galilee had suffered greatly from the cumulative effect of deforestation, overgrazing, and ill-considered plowing. Policies imposed by the long litany of conquerors—such as the tax placed by the Ottoman colonial governor on tree ownership—had only made the devastation worse.

While the British Mandate's legislative efforts in most environmental media were generally unimpressive, in the realm of soil conservation, they were relatively energetic. Soon after assuming control, the first High Commissioner passed a Sand Erosion Ordinance and a Forestry Ordinance and years later, in 1941, a Soil Erosion (Prevention) Ordinance. These soil conservation statutes were sufficiently advanced to remain in force as law in Israel to this very day (Soil Erosion [Prevention] Ordinance. Official Gazette 1944). Hence, legislatively, for the duration of the history of the State of Israel, the Mandate has continued to provide a somewhat archaic, but passable normative basis for government efforts to combat desertification—even as newer and more comprehensive statutory models have emerged (Tal 2007a).

Institutionally, most activities related to soil conservation were based in the Agriculture and Forestry Department of the British Mandate until an independent Department of Forests was established in 1936 (Forestry Ordinance 1936). Among the department's responsibilities was to take action to prevent erosion when agriculture was threatened. This operational objective was reflected in a colonial official's report: "The main purpose of forestry is the collection, retention and improvement of the soil on the wide stretches, mountain slopes and other lands which have been damaged or even ruined by wind or water erosion" (Government of Palestine 1946).

During its thirty years in power, the British Mandate declared 830,000 dunams of land as 430 separate forest reserves. This constitutes roughly 4 percent of modern Israel, but most of the reserves were concentrated in lands north of the country's arid regions. At least in theory, human activities were greatly restricted inside the reserves. Proscriptions included:

- taking of any wood products,
- uprooting of any tree by its roots,
- burning or otherwise removing bark from trees,
- burning of weeds without taking precautions to prevent the spread of fires,
- allowing for cattle grazing in or near reserves,
- cultivating lands inside protected woodlands,
- damming any waterways, and
- taking up actual residence inside a reserve.

Violators of the law faced penalties of up to twelve months incarceration in addition to monetary fines. While the law had all the tough insouciance that one would expect from a colonial administration, it attempted to make a modest accommodation for the local Fellaheen community whose reliance on the woodlands for firewood was a major component in the deforestation of Palestine. Accordingly, the law held that fallen trees could be removed by villagers who lived nearby, provided that they received a permit to remove timber from the forests. The government by law was committed to helping in the fighting of forest fires.

Another important legacy of the British Mandate was the strong aversion to the overgrazing that had characterized pastoral activities for centuries. They were especially concerned about the Bedouin community's nomadic lifestyle. During the first half of the twentieth century, the Negev desert region was largely unsettled and Bedouin herders reportedly numbered about 65,000. These pastoral tribes wandered, as they had for generations, across a 10,000-square-kilometer desert region to find seasonal pastures for their goats and sheep. When rains were early and plentiful, in some areas Bedouin would grow barley and wheat as early spring crops, though crop failures and drought were often the rule. On a few isolated sites, stone dams could trap sufficient water to allow for floodwater collection and small stands of pomegranates, almonds, and even grapes. But these efforts were marginal; like the ancient Israelites of old, the Bedouin primarily lived off of their herds and this was to bring them in conflict with the colonial government policies in Jerusalem.

Jews and Arabs may look back with resentment at what they perceive as the favoritism that the British Mandate government harbored toward their adversaries. But it can be argued that the only real enemy targeted by the Mandate officials was Palestine's grazing livestock. With almost half a million goats in Palestine in 1930, 80 percent of which were held by the Fellaheen (Hirsch 1933), the British were convinced that grazing was the real reason behind the pitiful condition of soils in Palestine (Wachs and Tal 2009). Colonel E. R. Sawer, director of Agriculture and Forests in the British Mandate government, exemplified the British aversion to local livestock in his 1928 lecture to the Palestine Economic Society: "There remains the outstanding and distasteful problem of the goat—the alleged evil genius of the Mediterranean, against whom has been directed a larger body of legislation than has honoured, or otherwise, any domestic animal" (Sawer 1928).

While acknowledging the possible contribution of grazing to reducing forest fire risks, Sawer recommended restricting access to regenerating forests for grazing. In general, public policy in Palestine was to encourage goat owners to replace them with sheep and require licenses for animals grazing in Palestine's rangelands.

After World War II, a British fact-finding mission was commissioned to consider the condition of the disputed land. J. W. Shaw, a soil science expert, placed responsibility for Palestine's erosion problem directly on black goats and implicitly on the pastoral Bedouin and Fellaheen communities that relied on them:

> The practice of extensive grazing, a tolerable and even sound practice in temperate regions, is in the Palestine climate and conditions the greatest single barrier to rural prosperity. In the time of Abraham a few pastoral nomads roamed through great areas of forests and scrub and found an easy livelihood. Since then the population has vastly increased, the area and volume of vegetation has correspondingly dwindled, and it is now an inescapable fact that the destruction of vegetation by the grazing of animals is severely damaging the economy of the plains and bringing ruin to the hill country. . . . The remedy lies in the curtailment of the numbers of animals to be grazed and in radical change of the present regime, familiar to scores of past generations. The instinctive and traditional methods of a peasant population are not easily altered and persistent attempts to give practical instruction in this matter by precept, demonstration and persuasion must be continued for a considerable period. (Shaw 1946, 428–29)

While implementation of soil conservation policies and enforcement during the tumultuous days of the Mandate were often hardly worthy of note, these rules did establish a normative infrastructure that was to be pursued with far greater alacrity once the State of Israel was established (El-Eini 1999).

THE MANDATE'S LEGISLATIVE LEGACY AND ISRAEL'S NORMATIVE PROGRAM TO COMBAT DESERTIFICATION

A review of Mandate policies is important because they continue to inform the Israeli government's efforts to address desertification. Indeed, there is probably no area of environmental management where British policies remained influential for so long. This is particularly manifested in the legislative realm. Sixty years after declaring independence, in most areas of life, Israel's Knesset has largely replaced the legislation ratified during the Mandate. This has *not* been the case for many laws addressing desertification. Most critical statutes in Israel regulating the drivers of desertification (e.g., overgrazing, deforestation, poor land management) remain Hebrew translations of British regulations with minimal amendments.

For instance, Israel's basic penal code promulgated in 1977 left intact a 1936 law which makes it a misdemeanor crime for persons or their animals to enter a planted field or a protected grazing area without an acceptable explanation. Even original Israeli, "modern" regulations or "secondary legislation" designed to support activities to combat desertification that are relatively modern have been promulgated pursuant to British Mandate statutes. Under the original Sand Erosion Ordinance, wherever the Forest Conservator concludes that eroded sands pose potentially negative consequences for agriculture or prospective cultivated lands, he is authorized to specify those measures necessary to save the lands from being degraded. This includes the enacting of:

1. regulations to impose soil testing on lands and to declare them to be "special regions"

2. regulations that prohibit grazing of any sort on sensitive lands or even passage rights through them

3. regulations to prohibit land cultivation in a special region

4. regulations that limit land clearing activities in a special region

5. regulations that prescribe soil conservation activities in a special region (Sand Erosion Ordinance 1922)

The law focused on the financial ramifications of implementing these activities and expediting the participation of landowners in the restoration work. At the same time it exempts the government from any liability or civil fines for any activities conducted pursuant to the law.

Similarly, the 1922 Forestry Ordinance has only been amended, with minor technical changes, and remains the law of the land in Israel. (While the Minister of Agriculture technically can still declare any lands that are not privately owned to be a forest reserve, in practice forests are now established under a National Master Plan approved by the country's National Planning and Building Council.) Ultimately, it has been British ordinances, albeit extremely basic by modern standards, that provided the statutory foundation for Israel's strategy to combat desertification.

ISRAEL'S ANTI-DESERTIFICATION STRATEGY

In retrospect, the strategy employed by Israel to combat desertification can be divided into four primary areas of activity, each of which will be briefly described:

- a water management strategy that allowed for cultivation of arid and semiarid regions;

- agricultural development in the drylands and promotion of soil conservation practices within the farming sector;

- an aggressive program of afforestation, starting in the north and reaching as far south as the 250 millimeters of rain per year rain line—roughly around the Beer-Sheva region;

- and continued controlled regulation of grazing.

While there often was no formal synchronization among these disparate initiatives, or even monitoring for their cumulative impact, each can be deemed a relatively successful policy with the collective results being a uniquely successful national effort.

Zionist and Israeli efforts to increase agricultural productivity in the desert are intricately linked with the geopolitical desire to increase a Jewish presence in the Negev. At the same time, sustainable farming is one of the key mechanisms for combating desertification. Hence, nationalistic and ecological impulses pushed together in the same general direction. With passion and optimism, the Jewish Yishuv steadily expanded its territorial claim during the first half of the twentieth century through the establishment of agricultural outposts that ultimately established the geographic dimensions of a future state (Blass 1973). The dry southlands, however, initially fell outside the perimeter of the Zionist agricultural revolution. This failure was frustrating enough to leave Ben-Gurion with his metaphor of waging "war" on the desert. While British White Papers and settlement policy posed obstacles to more aggressive expansion, a far more daunting factor was water availability.

With no water import available to the early settlers, they turned to searching for groundwater. During those years, technologies for drilling deep wells and reaching the aquifers in the Negev desert were simply unavailable in Palestine. In a 1952 presentation, Leo Picard, the leading geohydrologist before and after the establishment of the state offered a succinct review of the technological drivers of local water resource development:

> In the history of technical groundwater exploration we thus have three periods:
>
> 1. the well-shaft and hand-bore period, from Roman to post-World War I;
>
> 2. the genuine percussion-drill phase, starting with the 1929 riots up to the end of World War II;
>
> 3. the rise in the last years of the rotary system, alongside percussion, which is still prevalent.
>
> It was not before the end of 1946 that rotary machines reappeared in the country, this time in connection with the oil exploration program. The rotary phase started, though it was immediately interrupted by the hostilities. Thus it is only in the last three years after more and bigger machines arrived that the sight of a rotary rig became a more familiar picture in our drive through the country. With the introduction of "rotaries," the reluctance against deep-boring decreased, and the growing number of deep bores of an average depth of 400 meters is well documented. (Picard 1953, 584)

Some modest, shallow wells allowed for establishment of a dozen agricultural settlements in the northern Negev. In retrospect, the incipient kibbutzim constituted an impressive stop during the 1947 visit of the UN Special Commission on Palestine (UNSCOP), influencing the commission's subsequent recommendation to grant a considerable portion of the Negev region to a future Jewish state. Deeper well-drilling capacity was now available—and once the state was established, the institutional capacity and political will to create massive water carriers also suddenly existed (Shoham and Sarig 1955). It would not take long for a nascent nation's vision of a blossoming desert to find an outlet in an aggressive national water policy. The investment in water infrastructure was prodigious as new agricultural settlements were established across the drylands of the country, relying largely on the newly delivered water. While far less intensively developed, even the hyperarid regions were targeted for settlement and in 1956, Kibbutz Yotvata was the first of some two dozen agricultural communities established in the Arava—all relying on the now accessible groundwater. Agricultural production itself increased by 700 percent—growing even faster than the burgeoning population, with Negev farmers fueling much of the growth.

The centerpiece of Israel's water infrastructure were two pipelines that by 1964 had created a national water-delivery grid from the Kinneret Lake in the north, that to this day reaches as far south as the desert town of Mitspeh Ramon (Galnorr 1980). The result was the availability of 500 million cubic meters of moderately saline water, which for many years provided most of the country's irrigation supply. In recent years, a growing proportion of the freshwater delivered via the national carriers goes to domestic needs. As the Galilee's rainfall began flowing through the carrier's pipe network, "making the desert bloom" suddenly moved from being a rhetorical, ideological "slogan" to a new, on-the-ground reality, especially in Israel's semiarid lands

This impressive engineering achievement is tempered by the ecological hazards that have emerged since as a result of its construction. In reviving the country's drylands, water resources were critically wounded. For instance, the Yarkon–Negev pipeline carrier left only poorly treated sewage flowing in the Yarkon River and the Jordan's natural flow to the Dead Sea almost ceased completely, contributing to the steady disappearance of the world's lowest and saltiest lake.

Soon thereafter, Israel began to recycle its wastewater, and agriculture received an additional source of water. Today some 75 percent of Israel's sewage effluent is recycled, providing more than half of present agricultural irrigation needs. Most of it is transported to the southlands (Shani 2009). A national network of reservoirs, built by the Keren Kayemeth L'Yisrael allows farmers to store the effluents during the rainy season and irrigate during the dry summer months. This ostensible hydrological triumph is hardly trouble free. Here too, there have been serious environmental consequences (Zaslavsky, Guhteh, and Sahar 2004), including the systematic dissemination of hazardous industrial chemicals (Muszkot et al. 1990), and endocrine disruption and antibiotics (Avisar, Lester, and Ronen 2009; Avisar, Levin, and Gozlan 2009), as well as exacerbation of soil and water salinization (Avnimelech 1993). To make wastewater reuse sustainable will require a substantial upgrading in advanced sewage treatment. On April 14, 2005, the government approved broader and tougher wastewater reuse standards, along with a ten-year funding commitment to finance the 220-million-dollar infrastructure investment associated with the upgrade (Lawhon and Schwartz 2006).

But the substantial quantities of water provided to Israel's southlands constituted a resource that was immediately exploited by the remarkable innovation of Israel's agricultural researchers and by the even greater resourcefulness of the young farmers in the drylands. New strains of "salt resistant crops" moved from the experimental stage to the fields to markets around the world (Ben-Gal, Tel-Tsur, and Tal 2006). The area north of Beer-Sheva that had long been considered a wasteland, became a virtual "bread basket." Much of Israel's citrus orchard production moved south. Vegetation cover increased and degraded soils began to revive, providing food for domestic consumption and for export.

Rapidly expanding farming on traditional rangelands in other countries and contexts is often associated with desertification. In Israel this has not been the case and not by coincidence. While several agencies are formally involved in activities associated with combating desertification, the battle is largely overseen by Israel's Ministry of Agriculture. A Department of Soil and Drainage has been in operation for over fifty years (and presently is based at the ministry headquarters at Beit Dagan). In its heyday, the department had six field offices, with agents working across the country. Through the department, the gospel of soil conservation could be promoted and delivered to the nation's farmers by the virtual army of Ministry's extension "counselors." In recent years, the department's resources have been cut in half, with much of its work and projects farmed out to the Drainage Authorities that are active across Israel's sundry watersheds. But the general program continues.

In 1960, the Minister of Agriculture promulgated the Soil Conservation Regulations. Special regions were established in which specific directives were issued to control livestock grazing (including outright bans) by the Soil Conservation Branch at the Agricultural Ministry. Soil conservation programs can be required in vulnerable areas. Anyone with an "interest in the lands" can file objections to the program, but once approved, any land-moving activities or cultivation must be consistent with program provisions. "Soil Conservation Authorities" can also be established in the regions, with authority to initiate soil conservation activities. These go beyond limitations on farming or grazing to include reclamation initiatives and broader soil conservation plans. Local Conservation Authorities can take administrative actions to ensure compliance with the individual plans, or simply implement the changes themselves and pass the costs on to the recalcitrant landholder. Generally, however, land improvements have been initiated in a "cooperative" spirit.

As early as 1953—at Lowdermilk's recommendation—a research and monitoring program was established to study local runoff dynamics. While its activities have been scaled down somewhat, the Soil Erosion Research Station continues to operate a national program from its offices at the Rupin Agricultural College near the coastal city of Netanya. The station serves as a professional facility for applied research and monitoring on behalf of the Ministry of Agriculture, with a mandate to support erosion-control programs.

It is worth noting that the Ministry of Agriculture has never perceived itself as a regulatory agency. Nor do its field agents see themselves as inspectors. The soil erosion–control strategy was promoted by appealing to farm operators' hearts and minds and offering subsidies, even as these have dropped dramatically in recent years. Crop selection is an important part of its promotional work. This can include encouraging a shift from more erosive field crops (that require constant plowing) to fruit orchards, with the attendant promises of reduced soil loss.

Promotional work appears to be easier among the communal kibbutzim than the private farmers living on Israeli moshavim. The former typically appointed a representative to take responsibility for soil conservation. In recent years, extension agents find that economic exigencies may have reduced the commitment among many kibbutzim to make the long-term investment in soil conservation. When persuasion falls short, subsidies and other economic incentives are sometimes available to sweeten the recommendations. Indeed, should farmers stand to lose money because of adoption of erosion-control measures, the government provides financial compensation—albeit funds that are not sufficient to cover full expenses nor reach every "deserving operation" (Tal 2006).

The basic strategy for reducing erosion promoted by the agents involved reducing the quantities and the velocity of runoff following rainfall events. Water is slowed by building terraces and impounding water during its flow downstream and dramatically decreasing the amounts of soil carried away (Sachs and Itshack 1999). In addition, extension agents promoted a standard package of "best management practices" for controlling soil erosion (conservation tillage, terracing, contour plowing, etc.). These measures were encouraged on lands whose slope or soil types made them especially vulnerable to erosion.

Water and soil management are always linked and the management practices were promoted with the potential contribution to groundwater recharge in mind. The goal was to reduce drainage to a minimum even on lands with considerable slopes. Rather than running off, rainfall not taken up by crops should percolate into groundwater. One obstacle to the soil transmissivity necessary for this recharge strategy is the soil crusts that develop on lands that lack vegetative cover. The crust seal not only prevents recharge but accelerates runoff.

These practices have not always been successfully conveyed to local agricultural units. For example, for many years while vegetation was reduced on the farms surrounding Ramot Menashe, velocity of runoff increased and with it erosion. Historic soil testing suggests that there has been a net loss of as much as 50 millimeters of soil since the 1950s. But soil conservation remains an important component of farming culture in Israel and is still supported by government extension services.

Following the establishment of the state, the Jewish National Fund (Keren Kayemeth L'Yisrael, hereinafter KKL), a corporation owned by the World Zionist Organization, expanded its afforestation work (Amir and Rechtman 2006). The KKL was already heavily involved in land acquisition and agricultural development in Palestine prior to the creation of the state. While not a major institutional priority, the KKL forestry department also planted on steep and marginal lands.

After the country gained independence, rather than a new government agency being created, the KKL retained de facto responsibility for tree planting in 1949. In 1961, based on a formal written covenant with the government, it became the de jure Israeli forestry agency. It has remained so ever since (Tal 2010). After a major land acquisition deal with Israel's government in the early 1950s, the KKL became the owner of 13 percent of Israel's lands, much of which it leases at considerable profit. It also operates a strong international fundraising network in over twenty countries. Consequently, since the country's independence, Israeli forest programs have enjoyed a relatively sizable, stable, and independent source of funding.

Trees have always had a special place in Zionist heritage. Founding Zionist visionary Theodore Herzl's frequently confided his enthusiasm for afforestation in Palestine to his diary. No sooner had he planted a symbolic tree outside Jerusalem during his 1900 visit, than afforestation came to be perceived as an expression of the new Jewish ideological aspiration to "redeem the promised land" (Tal 2002). This has undoubtedly affected the economic perspective of

KKL's senior management and the motivation behind Israel's forestry programs. The reasons for the country's passion for tree planting have evolved over time. But nationalism and ensuring Jewish sovereignty over lands it purchased prior to independence (Cohen 1995) remains a salient motivation. Subsequently, afforestation provided employment for the immigrants arriving to the young nation (Segev 1986). Recently, KKL's tree-planting program has largely focused on creating recreational opportunities and ecological restoration (Kaplan 2009). Given the modest precipitation, establishing a "timber industry" was never a major factor in afforestation policy. Local forests have never really exceeded 10 percent of domestic demand for lumber (Tal 2010).

But Israel's forests continue to expand. After sixty years of steady afforestation efforts, some 260 million trees have been planted on lands which are almost all classified as drylands. In the south, successful stands are located in semiarid areas with as little as 250 millimeters of rain per year—a precipitation level generally considered too modest for dense forests (Schiller and Atzmon 2009). In fact, Israel has successfully created conifer forests in these regions with full canopy cover doubling the carbon present in underlying soils within thirty-five years (Safriel et al. 2010).

Trees typically have been planted in rocky areas, with steep and erosive topographies. Accordingly, forests have not come at the expense of agricultural development. With ample funding, subsidized "cheap labor," and enthusiastic political support from the most senior of Israel's leaders, the country's dryland forestry was able to move forward expeditiously. For instance, in 1951, soon after independence, Prime Minister David Ben-Gurion boldly announced in a Knesset speech that he envisioned: "many hundreds of thousands of trees on an area of 500,000 hectares, a quarter of the area of the state. . . . We are a state at the beginning of repairing the distortion of generations, distortion that was done to the nation and distortion that was done to the land" (Weitz 1970). This is in fact a far higher percentage of the country's available semiarid and dry, subhumid lands that have sufficient rainfall to sustain trees. Ultimately, the National Master Plan 22 for forests, which was adopted in 1996, designates that forests fill only 10 percent of Israel's territory. It is also worth noting that the woodlands do not include the 25 percent of the lands allocated under Master Plan 8 for nature reserves and national parks, even as the forests often provide excellent buffers or even ecological corridors to supplement biodiversity conservation efforts (Kaplan 2009).

Initially, most of the trees planted in Israel were tall and hardy Australian eucalyptus, which first arrived in Palestine during the 1880s. But by the 1920s, the Aleppo or Jerusalem pine became the Mandate's tree of choice as well as the KKL forestry department, comprising some 98 percent of overall plantings by 1938. The *Pinus halepensis* offered four advantages that remain particularly compelling for land reclamation in the dry southlands: (1) climatic versatility, (2) ability to thrive in a variety of soils, including rocky lands, (3) ease of planting and cultivation, and (4) rapid growth rate (Tal 2010).

Given the need of the Zionist foresters to establish legal sovereignty and quickly create a presumption of control over land purchased in Palestine, forests soon became Jerusalem pine monocultures. This inclination remained particularly strong during the 1950s when afforestation was perhaps the country's leading public works program. As much as 5,600 hectares of land was planted with seedlings during the year 1951–1952, more than four times present rates.

The conflict that raged during the ensuing decades between the KKL foresters and Israel's incipient—but vociferous—environmental movement continues to inform the public discourse about Israeli forestry. The Society for Protection of Nature (SPNI), which by the end of the 1950s had become Israel's largest NGO of any type, found the crowded conifer plantations unwelcoming, ecologically anomalous, and just plain ugly. Leading academics, including zoologists Yoram Yom-Tov and Heinrich Mendelsohn supported the ecological critique. Also assailed was the aggressive, almost militaristic approach to planting that invoked the ire of the ecological advocates. Opponents argued that the KKL had declared war on open space by burning all indigenous flora, bulldozing steep terrain, spraying heavily with chemicals to constrain weeds and potential pests, and then planting in tight rows a tree species that they deemed invasive. In fact, the Aleppo pine is indigenous to Israel, although the Brutia pine commonly planted today, was probably more prevalent in terrain just to the north of Israel (Lipshitz and Biger 2004).

Eventually, it was not a green ideological conversion that convinced KKL foresters to diversify plantings and phase out dependence on the Jerusalem pine. Rather, it was accepting one of the period's inconvenient ecological truths. This came in the form of a tiny but highly persistent aphid (*Matsucoccus josephi* or Israel pine bast scale) that happily devastated entire Jerusalem pine stands. The decimation of large swaths of woodlands forced the KKL forestry department to realize that such monocultures were simply not sustainable. It would take considerable adjustment, but by the 1990s, other "broadleaf" indigenous species would replace the conifers as the default trees that received preferential treatment. In particular oak, pistachio, carob, tamarisk Syrian pear, storax, hawthorn, madrone, and even olive trees were introduced and ultimately formally adopted in new national forestry policies (Jewish National Fund 2005).

While KKL foresters acknowledge that their predecessors got it "wrong" ecologically, they are quick to add that the state's initial forestry program got it "right" politically (Tal 2002). Without the rapid-growing pines to establish botanical facts, a far smaller area in modern Israel would be designated as forests today. Notwithstanding these lessons learned, in the driest of KKL's forests in the Negev desert, Jerusalem pines remain the most effective and best surviving tree, even while in the wetter valleys, broader leaf species are introduced. The reduced density of newly planted stands and the unforgiving climate itself appear to be enough to avoid past infestations (Noy-Meir 1998).

For many years there was a spirited public debate about the optimal extent of afforestation in Israel's Negev desert. Even as late as the 1990s the press reported JNF chairman Moshe Rivlin's call for a million more dunams of forest in the Negev and the SPNI's outraged retort that the desert constituted a unique and rich ecosystem that would be best left alone (Zacharia 1997). But by then the argument was largely moot, as the neutral national planning bureaucracy had already resolved the dispute, setting borders for the forests of the future in the drylands

Today, all afforestation activities in Israel are done according to detailed landscape plans that have to be approved by Israel's planning commissions after notice and comment. The detailed plans specify the kinds of trees and attendant physical preparation as stipulated under National Master Plan 22 for Forestry (Kaplan 2009). For example, some areas are zoned as natural woodlands where any afforestation activities are proscribed. Other areas take the form of "savannazation": woodlands where diverse salt- and drought-resistant species are planted at low densities on semiarid lands, where drainage has been reconfigured to allow for water enrichment during the sporadic rains. The Master Plan, approved by the government of Yitzhak Rabin but two weeks before his assassination, was the culmination of almost twenty years of planning. While it expanded the area under KKL's supervision, at the same time it limited the organization's botanical discretion.

Today, there are some 30,000 hectares of lands under the National Master Plan that remain to be forested—all of which are in drylands, with the majority in the northern Negev desert region. The cost of planting a tree in the southlands is roughly 2.5 times more expensive than planting in the rainier north. This is due to both the considerable earth moving required to ensure adequate diversion of water and the massive terrace and dike system that slows runoff so trees can soak in the very intermittent rains and prevent soil from being washed away.

There is a faction within Israel's environmental community that remains unhappy with the dryland afforestation policy that ultimately emerged in Israel. Members point out that, with a few exceptions, the trees will not regenerate naturally—by definition making these arid woodlands "unsustainable." Natural biodiversity is impoverished or usurped by nonnative, migrating species. But their real objection appears to be that these open spaces, which have been rangelands from time immemorial, should be left untouched because they are more beautiful, authentic, and inspiring without tree cover. From surveys, however, it would seem that most Israelis are very happy with the new forest stands. Whether authentic or not, the plantings surely look and act like trees.

A prevailing assumption among international forestry experts, until very recently, was that even if trees could be grown in semiarid and arid conditions, their ability to sequester carbon from the atmosphere was inferior and their relative contribution to global carbon sequestration trivial. Yet, the findings of research conducted by Weitzman Institute professor Dan Yakir's team at the Yatir forest surprised even the most enthusiastic dryland forestry advocates. Planted in the mid-1960s, Yatir is Israel's southernmost conifer forest—and also its driest. Average precipitation is 280 millimeters per year here—but in recent years has been far lower. It was assumed that in such a jejune climate, conventional forestry was an impossibility. But forty years of afforestation efforts have created a lush, green 3,000-hectare canopy that provides innumerable shaded picnic sites, comely archaeological corners, playgrounds, and even a scenic reservoir. Most importantly, the trees have also brought considerable quantities of carbon from the atmosphere into their trees and branches as well as into the soil. Roughly 2.6 tons of carbon are sequestered per hectare, which is more or less comparable to the European average of 2.7 tons (Grunzweig et al. 2007). During rainy years, sequestration levels have gotten as high as 3.5 tons per hectare. While recent data suggest that due to other factors, such as the albedo effect, forests may absorb and retain more heat than was initially anticipated (Rotenberg and Yakir 2010), the overall balance still suggests that dryland forests constitute important carbon sinks.

Given the hundreds of thousands of Israelis who enjoy the recreational respite from the often bleak, desert landscape, Israel's dryland woodlands are generally perceived as making a significant contribution to the quality of life in a landscape that for many remains foreboding. And the profound reduction and even elimination of runoff makes these forests' contribution to soil conservation unquestioned.

The importance of grazing regulation in Israel's overall strategy to combat desertification is significant, especially because overgrazing was a principal driver in land degradation during the centuries prior to Israel's establishment. Demography teamed up with aggressive public policy to lead to a dramatic change in these dynamics. Some 90 percent of Palestine's Arab population left Israel during the country's war of independence and, with them, a sizable amount of the country's grazing livestock. The Bedouin population of the Negev plummeted from 60,000 to 12,500 as most of the indigenous pastoralists quickly understood the meaning of the new geopolitical reality and led their flocks to friendlier pastures (Tal 2002). This exit immediately eased pressure on rangelands and allowed Israel's agricultural ministry to establish new norms that soon brought the Palestinian tradition of unregulated overgrazing to an end.

It is difficult to think of a British Mandate proclivity that was more seamlessly passed on to Israeli successors than the antipathy to unregulated grazing, especially by goats (Wachs and Tal 2009). The very first environmentally motivated law in the new state was the Plant Protection (Damage from Goats) Law passed in 1950. Grazing by goats on public rangelands was absolutely banned, and private lands faced a burden of proof to prove that reasonable carrying capacity from grazing would not be exceeded. Stock limits for other grazing animals were soon established, based on a two-tiered standard for different soil conditions (Tal 2009). Sixty years later, these standards still only allow one goat for every four hectares of rain-fed lands. If lands are irrigated, the standard is relaxed, allowing a hectare of land for each grazing goat.

This meant that grazing became a regulated activity and was no longer deemed the God-given right of pastoralists. Israel's Minister of Agriculture was granted authority to ban grazing of goats altogether based on considerations of soil conservation. Grazing, the rules stipulated, must be done pursuant to permit conditions set by this ministry. And shepherds pay a symbolic fee for the privilege of grazing on public lands. Accordingly, grazing rules are part of Israel's criminal law. And while the maximum six months' imprisonment is rarely if ever evoked, other penalties, such as confiscation of livestock can and do take place. The most common and effective regulatory response to illegal grazing is simply not renewing grazing permits, which is done only after a warning process that is intended to lead to a reduced and sustainable level of grazing.

The establishment of a Grazing Authority at the end of the 1970s, a small agency run under the auspices of the Ministry of Agriculture, was an important institutional step to this end. While the authority had no formal statutory powers, it brought together all relevant land-management agencies including Israel Lands Authority and the KKL (65 percent of Bedouin grazing takes place in KKL forests) on its overseeing board. Its modest staff of planners and field agents work with the forty-seven rangers and staff at the "Green Patrol," monitoring some three hundred thousand animals with the goal of protecting 200,000 hectares of public rangelands. (This constitutes 10 percent of all of the country's land.) The authority continues to perceive its role primarily as providing assistance to seminomadic and static agricultural communities. This takes the form of land seeding and fertilizing, pruning to reduce fire hazards, and fencing.

The transformation in attitudes toward grazing (see Seligman, chapter 2, this volume) was soon manifested in Israel's public policies (Pervolotsky and

Seligman 1998). No longer are goats considered "Public Enemy Number One" by land managers, but rather a critical partner in land management and fire prevention (Gutman et al. 2001). Grazing is probably the most cost-effective fire-prevention strategy for forests around Jerusalem. Ironically, KKL now subsidizes Bedouin herders to bring their flocks into certain woodlands and graze down the biomass. Consistent with ecology's intermediate disturbance theory, researchers also confirm that moderate grazing actually increases biodiversity (Pervolotsky 2006). At the same time, the unlimited use of commons that led to the massive soil loss prior to the state is not forgotten and the return in productivity in many previously degraded rangelands underscores the importance of continued vigilance in preventing overgrazing. For example, with the closing of several Israeli military training grounds and the reduction (or cessation) of grazing therein, erosion rates dropped precipitously (Moshe, pers. comm., May 2010).

One of the major obstacles to meaningful progress in combating desertification internationally is the inability of the scientific community to define a single set of benchmarks and indicators of land degradation. Israel also has never delineated a clear standard for when land is "desertified" or when soil conditions are stable or even recovering. Nonetheless, decades of agricultural productivity and the growing biomass and carbon stocks of Israel's dryland forests suggest that national efforts to combat desertification are on the whole a success story. The thousands of African participants in Israeli training programs, run through the foreign ministry's "Mashav" foreign aid division or who flock to classes and conferences at Ben-Gurion University's internationally renowned Blaustein Institutes of Desert Research, confirm the relevance of Israel's experience for developing dryland countries (BGU 2012). This success is particularly impressive in light of the general sense of failure surrounding global efforts to address the phenomenon (Zafar and Safriel 2005).

The ultimate public-policy challenge for ensuring long-term progress in preventing land degradation involves alternative livelihoods for local residents. New ventures that seek to live "with the desert" rather than conquer it will allow Israel's southern denizens to reach reasonable levels of prosperity without pressuring soils beyond recovery levels. To some extent, Israel's development strategy in the Negev has begun to achieve this. An ecotourism industry has blossomed and for many communities, such as Eilat and Mitspeh Ramon, it eclipses agrarian ventures as the primary, local income source. The fact that Israel's petrochemical industry has moved many of its major facilities to the Negev causes a plethora of pollution problems, but has surely provided jobs that enable residents of the Negev to make a living without exceeding the land's carrying capacity.

Conquering the desert and land redemption have given way to the discourse of sustainability that seeks greater harmony with the unique arid environment by turning its "curses" into "blessings." Combating desertification remains an ongoing challenge, and Israel would do well to continue its commitment to restoring its degraded soils and sharing its experience internationally (Tal 2007b). Perhaps most important to Israel's overall historic environmental narrative, the national experience in combating desertification and overcoming a long, discouraging history of soil degradation gives reason for hope that trend need not be destiny.

REFERENCES

Amir, S., and O. Rechtman. 2006. "The Development of Forest Policy in Israel in the 20th Century: Implications for the Future." *Forest Policy and Economics* 8: 35–51.

Avisar, D., Y. Lester, and D. Ronen. 2009. "Sulfamethoxazole Contamination of a Deep Phreatic Aquifer." *Science of the Total Environment* 407: 4278–82.

Avisar, D., G. Levin, and G. Gozlan. 2009. "The Processes Affecting Oxytetracycline Contamination of Groundwater in a Phreatic Aquifer Underlying Industrial Fish Ponds in Israel." *Environmental Earth Science* 59 (4): 939–94.

Avnimelech, Y. 1993. "Irrigation with Sewage Effluents: The Israeli Experience." *Environmental Science and Technology* 27 (7): 1279.

Ben-Gal, A., N. Tel-Tsur, and A. Tal. 2006. "The Sustainability of Arid Agriculture: Trends and Challenges." *Annals of the Arid Zone* 45 (2): 1–31.

BGU. 2012. "The Jacob Blaustein Institutes for Desert Research." Ben-Gurion University website. http://cmsprod.bgu.ac.il/Eng/Units/bidr/About/.

Blass, S. 1973. *Water in Strife and Action*. Givataim: Masada. In Hebrew.

CLEMDES. 2004. "National Background of Israel." *Clearing House Mechanism on Desertification for the Northern Mediterranean Region*. www.clemdes.org.

Dregne, H. E. 2002. "Land Degradation in the Drylands." *Arid Land Research and Management* 16: 99–132.

El-Eini, R. I. M. 1999. "British Forestry Policy in Mandate Palestine, 1929–48: Aims and Realities." *Middle Eastern Studies* 35 (3): 72–155.

Galnorr, I. 1980. "Water Policy Making in Israel." In *Water Quality Management under Conditions of Scarcity, Israel as a Case Study*, edited by H. Shuval, 296. New York: Academic Press.

Government of Palestine. 1946. *Survey of Palestine*. Prepared for the Anglo-American Committee, Jerusalem.

Grunzweig, J. M., I. Gelfand, Y. Fried, and D. Yakir. 2007. "Biogeochemical Factors Contributing to Enhanced Carbon Storage Following Afforestation of a Semi-Arid Shrubland." *Biogeosciences* 4: 891–904.

Gutman, M., A. Perevolotsky, R. Yonatan, and R. Gutman. 2001. "Grazing As a Management Tool for Prevention of Fire in Open Areas: Ramat Hanadiv Park (1990–1999)." *Ecology and Environment* 6: 239–48. In Hebrew.

Hirsch, S. 1933. *Sheep and Goats in Palestine*. Tel Aviv: Palestine Economic Society.

Forestry Ordinance. 1936. *Laws of Palestine 1937*. vol. 2: 1314.

Jacob Blaustein Institutes for Desert Research (BIDR). 2006. Ben-Gurion University website. http://www.bgu.ac.il.

Jewish National Fund. 2005. *KKL Afforestation Objectives: The Preservation of Diverse and Sustainable Forest That Offers Services to the Public.* http://www.kkl.org.il/kkl/english/main_subject/about_kkl/organization/afforestation%20.x.

Kaplan, M. 2009. National Masterplan 22, Afforestation Policy. Jeruaslem: KKL.

Lawhon, P., and M. Schwartz. 2006. "Linking Environmental and Economic Sustainability in Establishing Standards for Wastewater Re-Use in Israel." *Water Science and Technology* 53 (9): 203–12.

Lipshitz, N., and G. Biger. 2004. *Green Dress for a Country: Afforestation in Eretz Israel, the First Hundred Years, 1850–1950.* Jerusalem: Ariel.

Lowedermilk, W. C. 1944. *Palestine—Land of Promise.* New York: Harper and Brothers.

———. 1953. "Desert Research, Proceedings, International Symposium Held in Jerusalem May 1–4, 1952 by the Research Council of Israel, in Cooperation with the United Nations Educational, Scientific and Cultural Organization." Jerusalem: Jerusalem Post Press.

"A Man Who Cared for the Earth." 1976. *Jerusalem Post,* July 5.

Muszkot, L., D. Raucher, M. Magaritz, D. Ronen, and A. J. Amiel. 1990. "Large Scale Contamination of Deep Groundwaters by Organic Pollutants." *Advances in Mass Spectrometry* 11B: 1628.

Noy-Meir, I. 1989. "An Ecological Viewpoint on Afforestation in Israel: Past and Future." *Algemeine Forst Zeitschrift* 24–26: 616.

OECD. 2009. "The Environmental Performance of Agriculture: Key Trends and Policies." Draft document reviewing agriculture in Israel. Paris: OECD.

Perevolotsky, A., N. and Seligman. 1998. "Role of Grazing in Mediterranean Rangeland Ecosystems." *Bioscience* 48 (12): 1007–17.

———. 2006. "Livestock Grazing and Biodiversity Conservation in Mediterranean Environments: The Israel Experience." *Options Mediterraneaneennes Series A* 67: 51–56.

Picard, L. 1953. "The History of Groundwater Exploration in Israel." In "Desert Research, Proceedings, International Symposium Held in Jerusalem May 1–4, 1952 by the Research Council of Israel, in Cooperation with the United Nations Educational, Scientific and Cultural Organization." Jerusalem: Jerusalem Post Press.

Plant Protection (Damage from Goats) Law. 1950. Sefer HaChokim, 311.

Portnov, B., and U. Safriel. 2004. "Combating Desertification in the Negev: Dryland Agriculture versus Dryland Urbanization." *Journal of Arid Environments* 56: 659–80.

Reifenberg, A. 1955. *The Struggle between the "Desert and the Sown."* Jerusalem: Hebrew University.

Rotenberg, E., and D. Yakir. 2010. "Contribution of Semi-Arid Forests to the Climate System." *Science* 327: 451–54.

Sachs, M., and M. Itshack. 1999. "Savannization: An Ecologically Viable Management Approach to Desertified Regions." In *Arid Lands Management,* edited by T. W. Hoekstra and M. Shachak, 248–53. Champaign: University of Illinois Press.

Safriel, U., et al. 2010. "Soil Erosion-Desertification and the Middle Eastern Antroscapes." In *Sustainable Land Management,* edited by S. Kapur, W. Blum, and H. Eswaran. Heidelberg: Springer.

Sand Erosion Ordinance. 1922. *Laws of Palestine.* Vol. 2: 1314.

Sawer, E. R. 1928. *The Restoration of Palestine's Hill Country: An Address to the Palestine Economic Society on 25th October, 1928.* Government of Palestine. Jerusalem: Central Zionist Archives (CZA) Box 94, 3630.

Schiller, G., and N. Atzmon. 2009. "Performance of Aleppo Pine (*Pinus halepensis*) Provenances Grown at the Edge of the Negev Desert: A Review." *Journal of Arid Environments* 73 (12): 1051–57.

Schlesinger, B., W. H. Reynolds, J. F. Cunningham, G. L. Huenneke, L. F. Wesley, R. Jarrell, V. Whitford, and W. G. Whitford. 1990. "Biological Feedbacks in Global Desertification." *Science* 247: 1043–48.

Soil Erosion (Prevention) Ordinance. Official Gazette. 1944, 37. Sefer HaChokim, 1958, p 13.

Shani, U. 2009. "Israel's Water Crisis." Lecture, Israel, Palestine Water Workshop, Tucson, September 1.

Shaw, J. V. W. 1946. *A Survey of Palestine, Prepared in December 1945 and January 1946 for the Information of the Anglo-American Committee of Inquiry.* Jerusalem: Government Printers.

Shoham, Y., and O. Sarig. 1955. *The National Water Carrier.* Sapir: Mekrot. In Hebrew.

Tal, A. 2002. *Pollution in a Promised Land—An Environmental History of Israel.* Berkeley: University of California Press.

———. 2006. *National Report of Israel, 2003–2005.* Submitted to the United Nations Convention to Combat Desertification (UNCCD). http://www.unccd.int/cop/reports/northmed/national/2006/israel-eng.pdf.

———. 2007a. "Adding 'Top Down' to 'Bottom Up': A New Role for Environmental Legislation in Combating Desertification." *Harvard Journal of Environmental Law* 31 (1): 163–219.

———. 2007b. "Losing Diplomatic Ground: Israel's Declining International Commitment to Combat Desertification." *Israel Journal of Foreign Affairs* 1 (3): 121–30.

———. 2009. "The Logic and Logistics of Grazing Regulations." *Journal of Land Degradation and Development* 20: 455–67.

Tal, A., and J. Gordon. 2010. "Carbon Cautious: Israel's Afforestation Experience and Approach to Sequestration." *Small-Scale Forestry* 9(4): 409–20.

Twain, M. 1996. *The Innocents Abroad.* New York: Oxford Press.

UNCCD. 2004. United Nations Convention to Combat Desertification in Those Countries Experiencing Serious Drought and/or Desertification, Particularly in Africa. June 17, 1994, art. 9, 33 I. L. M1328.

Volney, C-F. 1805. *Travels through Syria and Egypt in the Years 1783, 1784, and 1785.* London: G. and J. Robinson.

Wachs, L., and A. Tal. 2009. "Herd No More: Livestock Husbandry Policies and the Environment in Israel." *Journal of Agricultural and Environmental Ethics* 22: (5): 401–22.

Zacharia, J. 1997. "The Final Frontier." *Jerusalem Report,* May 1.

Zafar A., and U. Safriel. 2005. *Millennium Ecosystem Assessment, Ecosystems and Human Well-Being, Desertification Synthesis.* Washington, DC: World Resource Institute. http://www.millenniumassessment.org/proxy/document.355.aspx

Zaslavsky, D., R. Guhteh, and A. Sahar. 2004. *Policies for Utilizing Sewage in Israel—Sewage Treatment for Effluent Irrigation or Desalinating Effluents to Drinking Water Quality.* Haifa: Technion.

CHAPTER SIX

THE AGRICULTURAL ROOTS OF ISRAEL'S WATER CRISIS

Hillel Shuval

THE WATER CRISIS IS NOT ONLY AN ACT OF GOD

BETWEEN 2006 AND 2009 Israel faced one of the most severe droughts in the preceding eighty years. Rainfall was 15–20 percent less than the average, resulting in severe cutbacks in water allocations to agriculture, which for some farmers resulted in cuts of up to 40–50 percent or more to their annual allocations. There was a national wave of concern and anxiety about the implications of the water crisis, which was exacerbated by the media and to a great extent by the farmers and the agricultural lobby. Aside from the lower amounts of precipitation, however, the water crisis is arguably no less the result of a chronic problem of mismanagement and overutilization of Israel's limited natural water resources.

This mismanagement resulted mainly from perpetual demands from the agricultural sector for increasing the already heavy allocations of subsidized water, even after the country's natural water resources were fully developed and exploited to their limit in the 1980s. To meet these growing demands, Israel's agricultural and water authorities, dominated by the agricultural sector, embarked on a conscious program of overpumping of groundwater and surface water resources beyond the limits of the mean annual safe yield, resulting in serious degradation of the country's natural water resources: intrusion of seawater many kilometers from the coastline, the irreversible salination of numerous coastal sweetwater wells, and the lowering of groundwater and Lake Kinneret levels below the red line of pollution danger (Plaut 2000; Siton 2003; State Controller 1991; GICMIWR 2010). All of these factors are the central and real precursors of Israel's water crisis.

While many of Israel's top water scientists and engineers were fully aware of the potential dangers involved in its water policy, few were prepared to oppose it actively within the official circles of the water establishment and even less so publicly. This lack of opposition was mainly due to the atmosphere of almost total and unconditional support for prioritizing the needs and interests of agriculture that prevailed within Israel society in general and within the water establishment in particular.

Why has Israel, a modern nation with a well-organized and apparently rational water administration, some of the world's top water engineers and scientists, and a modern high-tech economy, developed such an illogical and environmentally destructive water resources policy? We will examine the relationship between on the one hand Israel's water management perceptions, concepts, ideology, and problems and its deep historic and cultural commitments to agriculture and on the other hand a romantic vision of a pastoral Israel, which is part of Israel's collective memory that to this day still influences water policy in conscious and subconscious ways.

Israel has two main natural water sources of good-quality drinking water, surface water and groundwater, and two main supplemental, nonconventional water sources—recycled wastewater and desalinated brackish and seawater. There are varying estimates of the natural water resources of Israel ranging from an annual total of 1,400 million cubic meters a year to 1,800 million cubic meters a year depending on the source. Estimates are based on a number of sources, including the Israel Water Authority (2008); and presented here are my estimate of the range of annual mean safe yields of Israel's natural water sources (expressed in millions of cubic meters per year) prior to the severe 2006–2009 drought (Israel Water Authority 2008; IMFA-Israel Ministry of Foreign Affairs 2002; Siton 2003; Kislev 2001; GICMIWR 2010) and the lower estimates, based on a personal communication from Professor Uri Shamir-Technion 2010:

Jordan River/Lake Kinneret System	500–700
Floodwaters	200
Groundwater	700–900
Coastal Aquifer	320
Mountain Aquifer-Yarkon-Tananim	370
Total estimate of natural water sources:	1,400–1,800

The seasonal and geographic distribution of the rainfall in Israel presented a serious problem for the agricultural development of the country. The rainfall in Israel is seasonal, with 90 percent falling during the period of September to April, the nonirrigation season. The summer agricultural season is basically dry. The geographic distribution is such that the rainfall is heaviest in the north—the Galilee and Golan with about 800–1000 millimeters per year, tapering off to the south with a mean of 500–600 millimeters in the center of the country, and dropping to 10–100 millimeters per year in the Negev and South. It is estimated that 20 percent of the usable agricultural land is in the north, 30 percent in the center of the country, and 50 percent in the south. Thus, it can be seen that 80 percent of the water resources of Israel are derived from the north while 80 percent of the arable land is in the center and south (Siton 2003).

Israel's natural water resources are distributed seasonally, in such a way that they are not generally available during the spring and summer agricultural irrigation season when they are needed most; and distributed geographically, with more in the north, far from the main central and southern areas which have good, available agriculture land. During the debate in the National Water Council on building the National Water Carrier in 1955, which some economists considered too expensive, Israel's first prime minister David Ben-Gurion insisted that it was essential for the development of the country to "correct the faults of nature—regardless of costs." Thus, the initial national water resources engineering and management planning concepts called for a major water transport facility pumping water to the center, south, and Negev from the Jordan River and Lake Kinneret system and from other northern water sources. This was mainly accomplished by the National Water Carrier and other regional systems.

The second conceptual element of Israel's national water planning concept was interseasonal storage of water in Lake Kinneret and in the coastal and mountain aquifers. Here, water was to be stored during the winter rainy months to supply water for summer irrigation. These concepts basically assumed in those early years that the major role of water resources transport, storage, and redistribution was for agricultural use. This was basically true for Israel's first fifty years or so.

However, by 2010, a majority of the water of the National Water Carrier was utilized year round for drinking water and domestic, urban, commercial, and industrial use. With the increased desalination of seawater from sites along the central coastal areas of Israel supplying almost as much water as the north, the dominant role of Lake Kinneret as a source and as an interseasonal storage basin is no longer as clear as it was in the earlier days.

UNCONVENTIONAL WATER SOURCES

Israel has pioneered water recycling and reuse and by 2009 had the highest recycling rate of any country in the world. Some 75 percent of the urban wastewater flow is recycled, mainly for agricultural irrigation. It should be noted that recycling highly treated wastewater is one of the most cost-effective alternative water sources for agriculture and nature. In addition to its value as water, it contributes important nutrients to the soil and crops. The amounts of recycled wastewater will increase in the future as urban populations grow and require more water, some of which will come from the reallocation of good quality agricultural water and some from desalinated seawater.

In light of Israel's growing population and increased demands for potable water, a massive program for the desalination of seawater was initiated with the first major plant, the largest "reverse osmosis" desalination facility in the world, coming online in 2005 (Tal 2006). According to the Israel Water Authority, Israel plans to produce 700 million cubic meters per year of desalinated seawater in the next twenty years at a reasonable low cost of about $0.60 per cubic meter. This will be enough to meet all of the growing urban, domestic, and industrial demands. It will also make it economically and politically feasible to meet Israel's potential obligations for water sharing—without doubt Israel will find it necessary to increase the Palestinian allocation of the shared water resources in the framework of a peace agreement. with the Palestinians and Syria. With unlimited access to the sea for the production of desalinated water, Israel will never be short of water to meet all domestic and urban needs, even with the most pessimistic scenarios of global warming. However, to reduce the contribution to global warming from such a massive energy-intensive desalination program, Israel will need to make major strides in the production of alternative non-global-warming energy such as solar and wind energy.

WATER MANAGEMENT

Under the initial water management scheme as established by the Israel Water Law of 1959, all natural water sources—surface and groundwater, including recycled wastewater—are the exclusive property of the public and should be managed centrally under the authority of the Office of the Water Commissioner and the National Water Council. Such central management of water resources is very beneficial particularly under conditions of scarcity. From the advent of Israeli independence, these offices were placed under the Ministry of Agriculture. The post of Water Commissioner, particularly in the early days during 1950–1990, was generally filled by an official drawn from the agricultural sector. In the early years of the state, the post most often alternated between someone from the kibbutz movement and someone from the moshav sector. This rotation more or less ended in the 2000s.

The membership of the National Water Council was dominated by representatives of the various agricultural movements, branches, and allied organizations. Mekorot—*the* National Water Company—was officially owned by the government and the Jewish Agency but in practice was controlled informally by the agricultural sector. Thus, until relatively recently agricultural interests dominated water management in Israel. This changed to a certain degree with the establishment of the Israel Water Authority in 2007. The government appoints the head of the Israel Water Authority, although the body is associated with the Ministry of National Infrastructure, which is considered neutral. However, the first minister was himself a farmer and an outspoken advocate of the agricultural sector. It is worth noting that despite its organizational independence and formal separation from the agriculture establishment, the first head of the Israel Water Authority was a highly respected agricultural expert from the faculty of Agriculture of the Hebrew University and a former member and farm manager of Kibbutz Yotvata. Thus despite reorganization, the dominant role of agricultural interests in water management and policy remained to some extent.

DIVISION OF WATER BETWEEN THE AGRICULTURAL AND URBAN SECTORS

Historically, Israel's water management policies did not accord sufficient respect for the rapidly growing water demands of the urban, commercial, and industrial sectors, nor for the rapidly approaching total exploitation of Israel's limited natural water resources. The allocations of water to agriculture remained relatively high despite agriculture's diminishing role in the national economy and the rapidly increasing demand for water in the urban sector. The country's population, 96 percent urban in 2008, had grown almost tenfold, from 800,000 in 1948 to 7,500,0000 (Central Bureau of Statistics 2008). The country's long-term safe yield of fresh potable water had been fully developed and by 2009 reached a fixed maximum upper limit of about 1,400–1,800 million cubic meters per year. The domestic demand for drinking water and water for urban, commercial, tourism, and industrial use grew from a modest 100 million cubic meters per year in 1948 to about 900 million cubic meters per year—or some 65 percent of the total available natural sweetwater potential—prior to the 2006–2009 drought (Central Bureau of Statistic 2008; Israel Water Authority 2008). Agriculture had over the years, up to the drought of 2006–2009, used some 60 percent–70 percent of Israel's good-quality drinking water, while representing 2–3 percent of the country's GDP and 3–4 percent of the population.

TABLE 6.1. Estimated distribution of natural fresh water between the
agricultural and domestic, urban, and industrial sectors, 1960–2010, and in
the future (excludes desalinated water and recycled wastewater)

Year	Agriculture (%)	Domestic/Urban/Industrial (%)
1960	80	20
1970	78	22
1980	76	24
1990	62	38
2000	56	44
2010	35	65
2020 est.	20	80

Source: Israel Central Bureau of Statistics (2008), the Israel Water Authority (2008),
and estimates by author.

Table 6.1 presents the estimated distribution of natural freshwater between
the agricultural sector and the domestic, urban, and industrial sectors in the
period from 1960 to 2010, based on reports from the Israel Water Authority
and the Central Bureau of Statistics, with an estimate for the year 2020 made
by the author. As pointed out above, the urban population grew in this period
from under one million to over seven million in 2010 with a major increase in
water supply requirements of the urban sector. Since the total amount of the
country's natural water resources were fully exploited by the 1980s, the only
source for increased water supply to the urban sector was the reallocation of
water from agriculture; thus the need for a reduction in that sector's water
allocations. However, during much of that period the reduction in the water
allocations to agriculture did not cover the increased water allocations to the
urban sector, resulting in dangerous overutilization and overpumping of the
groundwater and surface water sources.

ROOTS OF AN AGRICULTURAL NATION

Why did Israel's highly advanced water and agricultural management establishment initiate this dangerous water management policy? To understand
Israel's deep commitment to agriculture and its overcommitment, as far as
allocation of water resources and the substantial subsidy of water for agricultural use is concerned, it is necessary to understand the unique historic evolution of the role of agriculture in Israel society and culture and its place in the
nation's collective memory.

The first period, which established the initial deep roots of Israel as an
agricultural nation, goes back as early as 1000–2000 BCE when, according to
the Bible, the Twelve Tribes of Israel, the Jewish nation, lived mainly as farmers in their own land in areas such as Jerusalem, the Mountains of Judea, and
the Galilee. This area was later called Palestine in reference to the Phoenicians

or Philistines, a non-Semitic people who settled along the coastal areas of the country around Ashkelon and Gaza in the south and Acco in the north.

The Bible is replete with passages about Israel's agricultural heritage and issues of water. On the one hand, there are biblical passages that extol the availability of water and the fertility of the land such as the following passage from Deuteronomy 8:7–9: "For the Lord your God is bringing you into a good land, a land with flowing streams, with springs and underground waters welling up in valleys and hills, a land of wheat and barley, of vines and fig trees and pomegranates, a land of olive trees and honey, a land where you may eat bread without scarcity, where you will lack nothing."

However, in another contradictory, and more realistic, biblical passage the people of Israel are warned that they will face shortages of water and difficult rocky soil in the Land of Israel and will not have a land as fertile as they had in Egypt. "For the land which you are going in to take possession of is not like the land of Egypt where you came from, where you sowed your seed and watered your garden easily with your foot like a vegetable garden. But the land which you are going over to, is a land of hills and valleys which drink up the water by the rain of heaven" (Deut. 11:8–11). These conflicting biblical passages apparently represented the reality of the unstable, unpredictable, and varying water and agricultural conditions of the Land of Israel.

During the two thousand or so years of the Diaspora, which began when the Romans expelled the Jews from Jerusalem in 70 CE, the image of Israel as an agricultural nation was continually maintained and reinforced in the Jewish collective memory by religious rituals, extensive Talmudic law, which was continuously studied, and Jewish holidays, largely based on the agricultural seasons in Palestine.

The Succoth holiday (Feast of the Tabernacles) in the fall has its roots in the harvest festival, and the Passover holiday in the spring has its roots in the new agricultural season. Jews all over the world pray for dew or rain at Rosh Hashanah (the Jewish New Year) and Succoth, which occurs in the fall prior to the beginning of the rainy season in Palestine, even if they live in countries with different seasonal patterns of rainfall and no shortages of water or rain. Celebrating the Jewish holidays, all having major agricultural components and symbolism, was more or less universal in the Jewish communities throughout the world. Even during modern times, with the secularization of the Jewish world, the celebration of the holidays has flourished, particularly for children, with even greater emphasis on their agricultural and national symbolism as an important part of the folklore of the nation.

Some Jewish communities, such as Pk'in and Safad, which were mainly based on religious study and scholarship, survived and even thrived in Palestine during the past 2,000 years. Yet, the Israeli nation only began to reestablish its national roots in the land and soil with the establishment of the first new Jewish agricultural settlements in Palestine, such as Petach Tikva, Zichron Yaakov, Qiriyat Ekron, and Rosh Pina. These settlements were established in what is called the first wave of immigration or the First Aliyah 1880–1905. This was followed by a more ideologically motivated period of settlement of the land termed the second wave or Second Aliyah led by such thinkers as A. D. Gordon, who in 1910–1920 preached the "Religion of Labor" and the mystic need for the nation to reestablish its roots by working the soil in its native land (Hertzberg 1982).

It must be noted here that throughout most of the history of Jewish life in the Diaspora, Jews frequently were not allowed to own land or be farmers and thus were forced to make their living through commerce, crafts, trade, and the professions. In the pre-state period, the ideology, dream and vision of a re-born pastoral agricultural nation with roots in the land was promoted in the popular culture by poems, press, books, youth movements, folk dances, popular songs, and children's stories. Every child studied agriculture and worked in gardens in school. Thus, through the centuries the agricultural dream and agrarian vision have became deeply imbedded in the collective memory of the nation (Almog 1997). The deep seated, subconscious residual, surprisingly, still affects water and agricultural policy to some extent till this day in the modern high-tech society of Israel.

SETTLING THE LAND, "DUNAM HERE, DUNAM THERE"

The issue of the limitations of land and water became a serious existential political threat to the Yishuv—the Jewish community in Palestine—when there were attempts by the British to cancel the Balfour Declaration. That critical document committed the League of Nations and the British Mandate, which was established in 1918, to assure the creation of a "National Jewish Home in Palestine." The Hope Simpson White Paper in 1930, the MacDonald White Paper of 1939, and other official British reports undermined the basic tenets of the Balfour Declaration and recommended to end Jewish immigration to Palestine due to "lack of economic absorptive capacity . . . specifically lack of water and land" (Mendes-Flohr and Reinharz 1980). This led to a valiant massive renewed impetus and national drive to settle the land by establishing agricultural settlements with the "dunam after duman" policy (or one-fourth acre after one-fourth acre) by the Jewish Agency and the organized settlement movements.

The national commitment for urgent agriculture and water development deepened. In 1936, in one dramatic major settlement thrust, some thirty-five new Jewish agricultural settlements—"Stockade and Tower" (Choma v' Migdal)—were built, some on the same day, in all corners of the country (Siton 2003). The U.S. Department of Agriculture sponsored the important study by Dr. Walter Clay Lowdermilk, one of the world's leading soil conservationists and water experts who published the 1944 popular work *Palestine Land of Promise.* The book provided an important and persuasive geopolitical and engineering study showing that the land and water available in Palestine could support a Jewish population of up to four million and an Arab population of some two million (Lowdermilk 1944); it also negated the politically motivated British estimates of the Hope Simpson White Paper in 1930 and later British white papers that would have required the ending of Jewish immigration to Palestine (Siton 2003).

In 1918, at the beginning of the British Mandate there were only forty-three Jewish agricultural settlements and villages. However, by the time the State of Israel was established in 1948, under the international legitimacy and authority of the UN Partition Plan and Resolution Number 181 of November 29, 1947, three hundred Jewish agricultural settlements had been established (Siton 2003). Parallel with the establishment of the new settlements major efforts were made to develop water supplies for agriculture, which included the pioneering six-inch, 150-kilometer-long water pipeline to the new Negev settlements in 1947. Although modest in its diameter it was critical in the survival of those settlements (Siton 2003). Effective modern water prospecting methods succeeded in the development of many new deep wells, and Mekorot and other Jewish water companies were organized that supplied water to the new settlements (Blass 1960; Naor 1987). Leading Jewish hydrogeologists, such as Professor L. Picard who immigrated from Germany in 1924 (Siton 2003) and Dr. Y. Goldsmith, led the way in modern water prospecting methods and identified sites for numerous successful deep wells in areas the British had overlooked or ignored, possibly for political reasons. These Jewish settlements, with limited startup water supplies, without doubt played a critical role in determining the borders of the new State of Israel under the UN-sponsored and approved Partition Plan of 1947.

OVERDEVELOPED AGRICULTURE

With the 1948 founding of the State of Israel the drive to establish hundreds of new settlements, moshavim and kibbutzim, became top priority. The government sought to settle the land and assure the borders of the new state, as well as to provide jobs for new immigrants and to provide food security. During those early years some seven hundred new agricultural settlements were valiantly established (Siton 2003). The planners of this massive agricultural settlement development program were not fully cognizant or preferred to overlook the limited water supplies of the country. Some, such as Simcha Blass, the leading pre-state Mekorot water engineer and later the first founding director of Tahal Water Planning for Israel, were vastly overoptimistic and unrealistic in their estimates. Blass, for example, made a statement at a meeting of the Israel Water Council that I attended, that the "Hydrological Service had seriously under-estimated the country's water resources," which in his opinion were twice that of their estimate and that they were "not doing their job." Blass's optimistic beliefs and estimates were never validated.

Yet, even the water establishment would come to question this optimism. In the view of Meir Ben Meir, a former Israel water commissioner and other water and agricultural experts, Israel overdeveloped agriculture in those early years and could never have met the full water allocations promised to many of the new settlements. Actual water allocations were often only 50 percent or less than originally promised. It is not unreasonable to estimate that the available water resources might support only some 50 percent of the agricultural settlements established in the early years of the state.

Simultaneously, soon after Israel's independence, major efforts were made to develop the nation's water resources. The National Water Carrier was built in the inspirational spirit of Israel's first prime minister, David Ben-Gurion, who held that it should be done regardless of costs and economic implications to correct the faults of nature. Hundreds of new wells, some very deep and expensive, were also drilled. Very high costs were involved in extracting and transporting water produced by these heroic national projects, to a great extent due to the extensive pumping of water from very deep wells and, in addition, due to the pumping required in transporting the water from the north to the south (Plaut 2000; Siton 2003). The cost of the water became greater than most farmers could afford. To overcome this barrier to agricultural development the concept of a subsidy of water for agriculture was initiated by the water and agricultural establishment and became a basic undisputed axiom of national water and agricultural policy. The subsidy of water for agriculture became an untouchable "holy cow."

Table 6.2 demonstrates that as of the late 1990s, the price for household water charged by municipalities was some four times greater than the average price paid for water by agriculture. Plaut (2000) pointed out that the fiscal budget for the year 2000 allotted approximately 300 million NIS (at that time $73 million) for direct water subsidization, or 27 percent of the entire water system governmental budget. He concluded his analysis of the subsidy of water to agriculture by saying that "water subsidization has been one of the most expensive forms of subsidization in Israel's budget. The general pattern of subsidized prices of water for agriculture has changed little over the decades since Israel was created. Agriculture benefits from the lowest prices and urban residential users pay the highest prices." However, since the establish-

TABLE 6.2. Water prices per cubic meter 1999 (in NIS)

Agricultural use	NIS
Up to 50 percent of the users' 1989 allotment	0.691
Average price of water to agriculture	0.818
Household use	
Average domestic water price by Mekorot	1.374
Household use charged by municipalities	3.460

Source: Israel Ministry of Finance and Plaut (2000).

ment of the Israel Water Authority in 2007 there is a definite trend of reduced water subsidies for agriculture.

While Israeli agriculture became highly efficient in water utilization and world famous for its productivity, the heavy subsidy of water has incentivized farmers to grow many crops that would otherwise not be economically feasible and to use more water than is economically or hydrologically justified. As an example, in the 1980s and 90s the intensive growth of cotton, with heavily subsidized water, resulted, in effect, in massive exports of Israel's limited freshwater reserves. This was very profitable for the farmers but not advantageous to the national economy and drew heavily on the overdraft of the country's limited water resources. It is generally accepted by economists that when a subsidy is provided to a vital element of production that is in short supply, it leads to irrational and uneconomical utilization of the resource (Siton 2003; Kislev 2001; GICMIWR 2010). That is what Israel had been practicing by subsidizing water to agriculture for its first forty to fifty years.

Israel's water managers are now finally realizing that they are functioning in a system of severe water scarcity and must do everything possible to rationalize the use of this scarce resource for the maximum social benefit, even if it involves fundamental changes in historic policies and preconceived notions. Israel is now in a process of ending wasteful water subsidies to agriculture and to any other sector now benefiting from water subsidies including industry, gardens, and others. Under current conditions, from an economic point of view, the rational pricing of water for all consumers in all sectors—to assure its rational use—should be based on the marginal cost of an additional aliquot of water added to the system, which is currently desalinated seawater at about $0.60 per cubic meter. That should be the basis of the price of water to all consumers.

ISRAEL'S DILEMMA

When the natural water resources development reached its limit in about 1980, Israel faced a dilemma—there simply was not enough water to meet both the growing domestic, urban, and industrial needs of the rapidly growing population and maintain historic allocations for agriculture. The agriculture-dominated water establishment objected to cutbacks in allocations of water to agriculture and developed a new strategy of "temporary" overpumping and "one-time drawdown" of aquifers to justify maintaining the high levels of water allocations for agriculture. The State Controller report on the water crisis of 1991 points out that "irresponsible management of the water supply for the past 25 years has caused destruction of Israel's water reserves and . . . as a result of over pumping and over utilization, underground water levels were lowered to dangerous levels below the red line; water reserves held for emergency use in case of droughts have dwindled and seawater pollution has intruded to contaminate ground water." The 2010 report of the Government Investigating Committee on Water Resources basically came to the same conclusion (GIC-MIWR 2010). One authoritative study estimated that the cumulative deficit of Israel's renewable water resources as a result of overpumping amounted to 2,000 million cubic meters by the year 2002, which is equal to Israel's total annual water consumption (IMFA 2002).

Water planners even promised that eventually these dangerous overdrafts would be repaid with cheap desalinated water, which might be produced at a price as low as five to ten U.S. cents per cubic meter. This scenario was totally unrealistic and never came about. Thus, based on Israel's deep overcommitment to agriculture, the seeds of Israel's water crisis due to gross and dangerous overpumping and overdraft of the natural water reserves were planted, leading to the near collapse of rational water management.

As early as 1980, the consequences of the joint policy of the Office of the Water Commissioner and Ministry of Agriculture in favoring increased subsidized water allocations to agriculture became clear. Hydrologists warned about irreversible salination that would be caused by the dangerous overpumping of limited groundwater resources. In our book *Water Management under Conditions of Scarcity—Israel as a Case Study* (Shuval 1980) a team of scientists warned of the impending water crisis resulting from overutilization of Israel's water resources and urged authorities to "act swiftly and clearly to assure the future of our vital water resources." The first attempt to mobilize the support of academic and professional colleagues in the water profession to join an organized campaign to save the country's water resources began at that time. Yet, many of the leading water scientists and engineers also worked as consultants and advisers to the Office of the Water Commissioner or the other official and unofficial water and agricultural organizations and companies such as Mekorot and Tahal. They were disinclined to take a public stand that involved overt criticism of public policy.

However, with time, the author mobilized a group of eighteen top water scientists into the Committee of Concerned Water Scientists. It led to an effective advocacy campaign with the help of the media to save the country's water resources. Here is an example of one headline of an item published in the Hebrew daily *Yidiot Achronot*: "Professor Shuval Warns: Israel Will Remain Without Water If the Over Exploitation Is Not Stopped" (May 20, 1989). One of the committee members, Professor Yaakov Baar of the Technion, worked closely with the State Comptroller's Office to assist in preparing a report on Israel's water resources mismanagement (State Comptroller 1991).

As a result of the media campaign and citizen pressure, the public mobilized in support of instituting changes in the national water policy. The harsh report of the State Comptroller of 1991 criticizing the water management policy of the Israel Water Commission and the results of the recommendation of the Knesset committees that studied the report finally led to the resignation of Mr. Zemach Yishai who was then the Water Commissioner and was one of a series of Water Commissioners who shared the responsibility over the years for the serious mismanagement of the country's water resources. Professor Dan Zaslavsky a highly qualified water scientist, was then appointed as Water Commissioner and initiated a policy of ending the reckless and irresponsible policy of overpumping. Another promising result of this active campaign to save the country's water resources was the transfer of the Office of the Water Commissioner out of the vested interest hands of Ministry of Agriculture and into the supposedly more neutral Ministry of National Infrastructure. However, the first minister, Mr. Ariel Sharon, later to become prime minister, was a devoted and articulate private farmer.

Notwithstanding the success of the campaign mounted by the Committee of Concerned Water Scientists, it turned out to be limited and short lived. Within a few years, despite the change in the administrative location of the Office of the Water Commission within the Ministry of National Infrastructure, the agricultural lobby remained powerful and regained control over water policy and management and the policy of overpumping of the groundwater and surface water resources was resumed. By the time the drought of 2006–2009 got under way the groundwater reserves were once again seriously exhausted.

REEVALUATING THE ROLE OF AGRICULTURE IN ISRAEL

One of the fundamental lessons from Israel's water management history involves the importance of reevaluating the perception of the role of agriculture in Israeli culture and society. Painful as it may be, it can be argued that Israel can survive only as a high-tech urban-industrial society and will have to reallocate most of its high-quality drinking water from agriculture to the domestic, urban, tourist, and industrial sectors. Agriculture can no longer be viewed as a high-priority food production branch when it comes to the allocation of freshwater. At the same time, agriculture will benefit from the growing amounts of high-quality recycled purified wastewater and will be able to maintain a level comparable to its current one. It can be estimated that about 65 percent of the urban water supply can be treated and recycled for reuse in agriculture and in parks, gardens, and nature.

Given historic trends, estimated domestic and urban water supply requirements will reach over 1,000 million cubic meters per year in a few years' time—with 650 million cubic meters per year of treated recycled water available. The limited high-quality freshwater resources should be used to maximize social benefit and human welfare. Studies have shown that the economic return on a cubic meter of water used in agriculture is about $2 while the return on a cubic meter of water used in commerce, industry, and tourism is roughly $100–$500 (Beaumont 2000).

WHERE WILL ISRAEL'S FOOD COME FROM?

The historic question raised by Israel's need to reduce its freshwater allocations to agriculture is, how will it be able to manage to provide food for its population? The notion that Israel's food supply is dependent on local agriculture is a mistaken one. For many years now, the vast majority of the caloric value of Israel's food supply has been based on imports. Research (Buchwald and Shuval 2003) has shown that some 80 percent of Israel's caloric intake is imported. This includes almost 100 percent of the wheat, grain, rice, animal feed, edible oils, soybeans, fish, and sugar. This means that the caloric content of almost all of the so-called local products are imported calories not grown by Israeli agriculture. For example, most of the calories of the local milk and dairy products come from imported animal feed. Similarly, almost all of the calories from chickens and eggs are from imported chicken feed. This has been called by Professor Tony Allen of England the import of "virtual water"—the water required to produce food and food products with water that is "imbedded" in those imported products from other countries that are rich in water and land (Allen 1995). For example it takes 1,300 cubic meters of water to grow one ton of wheat and 16,000 cubic meters of water to produce one ton of meat.

A study by Gleick (2000) based on Food and Agriculture Organization (FAO) data (1989) has found that the amount of water required by a country to produce the full "food basket" from local agriculture varies from about 1,000 to 2,000 cubic meters per person per year. It is obvious that countries like Israel with a total water resources potential of significantly less than 1,000 cubic meters per person year can never approach total food self-sufficiency based solely on locally grown food: Israel, with a total available amount of water per person per year in 2010 of less than 200 cubic meters (half of which, at least, is required for domestic, urban, commercial, and industrial use), can at best meet only 10–20 percent of its food needs locally. It is thus like many other countries with serious water shortages that solve their food security problem by importing staple food products from the world market; or, in the words of Professor Allen, doing so in the form of virtual water.

CAN ISRAEL RETAIN ITS AGRICULTURAL HERITAGE IN THE REALITY OF SEVERE WATER SHORTAGES?

Israel will have to face a historic challenge of finding ways to retain at least some of its dream and the vision of its agricultural heritage which is embedded to some degree in the national historic collective memory. Israeli society apparently agrees that assuring the survival of as many agricultural communities as possible is an important national goal and a legitimate and worthwhile aspiration of the nation's national culture, self-image, and ideology. Such a goal also fulfills an important environmental and ecological function of preventing the conversion of open agricultural spaces to built-up areas. Assuring the survival of agricultural communities fulfills, in some areas of the country, the important national mission of maintaining control of the land. The question is whether subsidies of agricultural water are the optimum way or even an effective way of ensuring the survival of agricultural communities as well as ensuring that those communities do survive fulfill their new role to "Keep Israel Green." This should be carefully studied and evaluated. New ways must be found to retain and preserve not only as many agricultural communities as possible but also their way of rural life.

The author has proposed one possible way of supporting agricultural communities and assisting them to survive: to consider subsidizing green farm areas as the Swiss do—the Swiss Option. In 1989 the Swiss people in a national referendum decided to maintain their agricultural heritage and green countryside by putting an end to agriculture as a crop-for-profit producing industry and to subsidize "green agriculture areas" by "direct payments" for the "common good" (Swiss-Bundesamt fur Landwirthschaft BWL www.admin .ch/blw). The Swiss concept is to maintain green areas for recreation, camping, tourism, and general environmental sustainability as well as to protect against landslides and snowslides.

This national decision was made to save the Swiss green agricultural heritage based on hundreds of years of national, cultural, and farming traditions. What this might mean for Israel is that farmers would be paid an additional premium for keeping agricultural land in crops or in the words of the Swiss "in Green." The subsidy would have to be set at a level high enough to enable hard-working farmers to continue to make a livelihood in working the land.

If the Swiss Option were adopted in Israel this would partially help farmers to maintain the economical basis of continuing to work the land and grow crops on agricultural land despite the higher price of water and other economic problems facing them. This subsidy would help many agricultural communities to survive and maintain their rural way of life, while keeping the country as green as possible within the constraints of limited water resources. Such a new role for agriculture could be among the main driving forces to "Keep Israel Green" as well.

NOTE

The author has been involved in the national policy discourse over sustainable water policy for over sixty years and bases many of this chapter's anecdotes and assertions on his personal experience and direct impressions.

REFERENCES

Allen, J. A. 1995. "The Political Economy of Water: Reasons for Optimism." In *Water in the Jordan Catchment Countries—A Critical Evaluation of the Role of Water and Environment in Evolving Relations in the Region*, edited by J. A. Allen and J. H. O. Court, 35–59. London: School of Oriental and Asian Studies (SOAS), University of London.

Almog, O. 1997. *The Sabra–A Profile*. Tel Aviv: Am Oved. In Hebrew.

Beaumont, P. 2000. "The Quest for Water Efficiency-Restructuring of Water Use in the Middle East." *Water, Air and Soil Pollution. Proceedings of the IWRA Conference in Jerusalem, 2000*, edited by S. Belkin, 123: 551–64. Netherlands: Kluwer Academic Publishers.

Blass, S. 1960. *Mai-Miriva v'Maas* [Waters of Conflict and Water Development]. Tel Aviv: Massada. In Hebrew.

Buchwald, S., and H. Shuval. 2003. *The Role of the Import of Virtual Water in the Israel Food Supply*. Unpublished study. Israel: Division of Environmental Sciences, Hebrew University of Jerusalem. In Hebrew.

Central Bureau of Statistics. 2008. *Annual Report 2008*. Jerusalem: Israel Central Bureau of Statistics.

FAO. 1989. *Food and Agriculture Organization Production Yearbook*. vol. 43. Rome: FAO.

GICMIWR. Governmental Investigation Committee on the Management of Israel's Water Resources. 2010. *Report of Committee*. Haifa, March. In Hebrew.

Gleick, P. H. 2000. "Water for Food." In *The World's Water 2000–2001*, 6–93. New York: Oxford University Press.

Hertzberg, A. 1982. *The Zionist Idea—A Historical Analysis and Reader*. New York: Atheneum.

IMFA Israel Ministry of Foreign Affairs. 2002. *Israel's Chronic Water Problem*. Facts About Israel Series. Jerusalem: Ministry of Foreign Affairs.

Israel Water Authority. 2008. *Israel Water Authority Annual Report 2008*. Tel Aviv: Israel Water Authority.

Jewish Virtual Library. 2010. *Israel's Chronic Water Problem*. The American-Israel Cooperative Enterprises.

Kislev, Y. 2001. *The Water Economy of Israel-Discussion Paper 11.01.* Center for Agricultural Economic Research, Department of Agricultural Economics and Management, The Hebrew University of Jerusalem–Rehovot. http://departments.agri.huji.ac.il/econmics/indexh.html.

Lowdermilk, W. C. 1944. *Palestine Land of Promise.* New York: Harper.

Mendes-Flohr, P. R., and Y. Reinharz, eds. 1980. *The Jew in the Modern World.* "Malcolm MacDonald White Paper—1939." 613–15. Oxford: Oxford University Press.

Naor, M. 1987. *Pinchas Sapir and the Founding of the Mekorot National Water Company.* Tel Aviv: Massada.

Plaut, S. 2000. "Water Policy in Israel." *Policy Studies No. 47.* Jerusalem and Washington, DC: Institute for Advanced Strategic and Political Studies.

Shuval, H. 1980. *Water Quality Management under Conditions of Scarcity—Israel as a Case Study.* New York: Academic Press.

Siton, D. 2003. *Focus on Israel: Development of Limited Water Resources—Historical and Technological Aspects.* Jerusalem: Israel Ministry of Foreign Affairs.

Swiss-Bundesamt fur Landwirthschaft BWL [Federal Office for Agriculture]. www.admin.ch/blw.

Tal, A. 2006. "Seeking Sustainability: Israel's Evolving Water Management Strategy." *Science* 313 (August 25): 1081–84.

CHAPTER SEVEN

OPEN SPACE IN AN URBAN SOCIETY

Iris Han

L AND RESOURCES AND open space in Israel are of greatest importance: these resources are finite and hardly can be reproduced. As one of the most densely populated and most rapidly growing countries in the developed world—scarcity of open space in Israel is much more severe than in other countries around the globe, and the effort to protect them is much more challenging (Kaplan and Dayan 1996; Tal 2008).

Despite its small area, only 22,000 square kilometers, Israel is blessed with a variety of landscapes, unique natural assets, a rich diversity of species, historic and cultural landscapes, and sacred sites for all faiths. All these assets, as well as other benefits, are provided by Israel's open space. Protecting open space in Israel is important for a variety of reasons:

- Provision of crucial ecosystem services. Humankind is supported by services produced by the biosphere and its ecosystems, and benefits from the various resources supplied by natural ecosystems. These "ecosystem services" include provisioning services (food, water, wood, fiber, and fuel), regulating services (climate regulation, flood regulation, and disease control), cultural services (aesthetic, spiritual, educational, and recreational benefits), and supporting services (nutrient recycling, soil formation) (Millennium Ecosystem Assessment 2005). Israel is blessed with enormous biodiversity in various ecosystems: The country is home to approximately 2,400 species of vascular plants, 100 species of mammals, 530 species of birds, 90 species of reptiles, and 15,000 known species of insects. All of these are located in an area equivalent to a major national park in the United States. In comparison, Great Britain, which is ten times the size of Israel, has only 1,500 species of plants.[1] Since conversion of natural and semi-natural habitats to urban, suburban, and exurban land uses is one of the main threats to biodiversity, protecting open spaces is a main key to all benefits provided by biodiversity and ecological services (Meffe and Carroll 1997).

- Provision of important cultural landscapes. As the cradle of three of the world's major religions, Israel's landscapes have been the arena in which many significant historic and spiritual events took place (Sar Shalom et al. 2010). Like an open book, the open space tells the stories of the Bible, the New Testament, and the Koran. For example, the last battle between David and Goliath took place in Ha'ela valley, near Beit-Shemesh; the open landscape of the Galilee between Nazareth and the Sea of Galilee was the backdrop to the interaction between Jesus and his apostles.

- Ensuring space for leisure and recreation. Open space has become an attractive and popular destination for leisure and recreation activities, especially during holidays. In Passover 2010, about 400,000 visitors visited the nature reserves and the national parks during a single day.[2] During Succoth 2010, more than 1.5 million people choose to visit Israel's forests and Jewish National Fund (JNF) parks.[3] A detailed survey conducted in the Judean mountains found that open space in the investigated area is of crucial importance with regard to regional planning, because of the high demand for recreation in natural settings (Zalutzki 2002). As long as population density in Israel continues to rise, the demand for recreation in open spaces will continue to grow.

Protecting open space in Israel, with the appropriate amount, quality, and spatial continuity to support the many roles that open spaces serve, has been called a mission impossible. There are, in fact, specific characteristics of Israeli society that make this laudable goal challenging, including high population density, rapid population growth, and inefficient use of land resources. We expand on each of these challenges below.

The population density in Israel in 2008 was 320.9 people per square kilometer,[4] making it ten times denser than the average of the Organization for Economic Cooperation and Development (OECD) countries. While this alone constitutes a very high density, a much more complicated situation hides behind this figure—namely the low density in the southern, more arid, areas of Israel.[5] In the Beer-Sheva subdistrict (including Beer-Sheva and the Negev south of the city to Eilat), population density is only 45.2 people per square kilometer, while in the central and northern areas of the country it is 710. By 2020, assuming moderate growth projection (1.3 percent–1.6 percent growth every year), density in the central and northern areas will climb to 900 persons per square kilometer, close to the average density in Bangladesh (2007). This exerts extremely powerful pressures on the remaining open spaces in the Mediterranean area of the country. Population growth rate in Israel in 2008 was 1.8 percent per year.[6] This value, comparatively high by developed country standards, was actually the lowest rate since the country was founded. Following the establishment of the state, the population in Israel at the end of 1948 was about 800,000 people.[7] As a result of 3.7 percent annual average growth, sixty years later more than 7,000,000 persons lived in the country. The sources of rapid growth include high birthrates along with immigration (*aliya*) from all over the world. Assuming the population continues to grow at the present rate, the population size will double in forty years. Even with the present density, very strong competition exists for every piece of land.

Despite the rapid population growth and limited land reserves, population density in Israeli communities varies widely, from 0.5 to 28.5 inhabitants per built dunam. Thus, the distribution of land resources is highly dichotomous: half of the population uses 70 percent of the built-up land for residences, while the second half uses only 30 percent. Population density in 75 percent of the settled area (including 768 communities) was less than four inhabitants per dunam (Kaplan et al. 2007). These characteristics can be explained by two phenomena. First, development (particularly in the past thirty years) has become increasingly low-density, suburban-type development. About 40 percent of construction begun during 2008 involved single-story dwellings (12,507 out of a total 31,507),[8] and only half of the total dwellings were buildings with three stories or more (16,224 dwellings). The Israeli dream of private homeownership has led to inefficient development.

Secondly, historic policy of dispersed development has also led to wasteful land-use patterns. During the first decades of the country, national development policy prioritized dispersal of the population into the periphery to demonstrate an Israeli presence throughout the new country and to strengthen the borders. As a result of the dispersal policy, there are now around one thousand communities scattered across the country, many of which are small rural settlements. The current development policy is to build within or contiguous to existing built areas (see later discussion about National Outline Plan 35). Indeed, since the last decade of the twentieth century only a few new settlements have been established, though several of these are located in ecologically sensitive areas.

As a result of the dispersed model of development in Israel, massive frag-

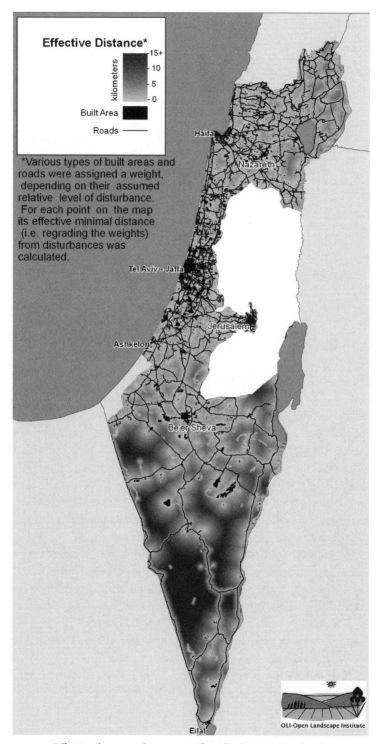

FIGURE 7.1. Effective distance of open space from built areas. Map by Eitan Romem.

mentation of open space has occurred. From northern Israel to Beer-Sheva, most patches of open space are not more than three miles from the closest built area (Levin et al. 2007). This development pattern exposed natural areas to harmful side effects such as light and noise pollution, while expediting the introduction and proliferation of invasive species.

While every country must cope with competing demands for land uses (housing, commercial uses, transportation, etc.), the Israeli case is somewhat unique. The military, for example, has a very high demand for land relative to the country's total land area. Some 46 percent of the country's land area is designated military zones, including 30 percent for military training or firing zones (mostly in the south of the country, which often overlap with nature reserves), 5 percent for military camps and other security bases, and 11 percent not occupied by the army but restricted because of military activity (e.g., buffer zones around bases) (Oren and Regev 2008).

Open space that comprises military zones can be considered as highly threatened ecologically, but there are also positive aspects to this situation. Areas held by the army are protected from other harmful land uses. For example, some of the most protected areas along Israel's coasts are military zones. The fact that the public cannot walk in freely (or cannot visit at all) gives a level of protection to natural ecologic systems. Dunes within military zones are protected from a variety of destructive activities common to publicly accessible dunes, including illegal sand mining and off-road vehicle use.

The military is also very cooperative with the Nature and Parks Authority. During the last decades, several agreements were signed between these two authorities that aimed to provide maximum protection to nature in military zones.[9] The cooperation has generally been a success at all levels. Such cooperation includes detailed coordination before every military activity that utilizes open space—defining exact vehicle routes, camp locations, and so on.

Yet, the military does not always abide by regulations. In 2004, the state Comptroller and Ombudsman published a report assessing the Israeli's army environmental record. It found severe defects on military bases, including inadequate sewage treatment and severe pollution of soil and water, including groundwater contamination from jet fuels and solvents.[10] Nonetheless, ironically, looking to the future, military zones may offer the primary future reserves of natural open space for the coming generations (Oren and Regev 2008; Gordon in this volume).

Another feature that makes Israel unique among developed nations facing loss of scarce open space is the country's commitment to the continuing absorption of immigrants. In addition to high natural growth rates, immigration is also a substantial contributor to growing population size. The first wave of immigration following the establishment of the state occurred during the

1950s, and in a very few years the young country doubled its population.[11] This propelled massive development of new settlements all over the country, first in peripheral areas, and later in more central locations. Between 1989–1999 Israel absorbed approximately one million new immigrants,[12] most from the former Soviet Union and approximately 5 percent from Ethiopia. During those years, Israel population grew from 4,500,000 to 6,200,000, an abrupt shift that came with an urgent demand for housing and other related forms of development.

The massive immigration of the 1990s was not the first such episode in Israel history during which the planning system had little time to cope with an urgent demand for land. The first decades of the country's life were also characterized as an ongoing emergency to which the planning and building system had to provide solutions. Similarly, in 2005, during Israel's withdrawal from Gaza Strip, housing solutions had to be developed for up to two thousand families, a process that was complicated by social considerations, such as keeping communities together and trying to find landscapes similar to the Gaza Strip for settlement.[13]

Each of these moments presented planners with a considerable challenge: protecting open space during national emergencies is difficult when short-term goals tend to trump any desire to pursue long-term environmental aspirations. In some cases, however, long-term goals win out. During and following the withdrawal from Gaza Strip, for instance, conflict arose around the plan to build number of new settlements for evacuees in the Nitzanim dunes, the largest sand dune area remaining on Israel's coasts—lying between Ashdod and Ashkelon. The conflict concluded with a government decision that established the sand dunes as a nature reserve and directing development to nearby, less environmentally sensitive areas.[14] The declaration was in part a result of many years of educational and public activities in support of dune protection by the Society for the Protection of Nature in Israel (SPNI) through its Nitzanim Field School.[15] In this case, long-term ecological considerations, rather than emergency-driven exigencies prevailed.

Such outcomes, however, have not always been the case. In 2008, another plan for settlement of the Gaza evacuees was suggested for the Lachish area, a region that had been planned as a biosphere reserve because of its very high ecological value. It is a very rare piece of land: one of the only areas in the central part of Israel, just one hour's drive from Tel Aviv and Jerusalem, where a person can stand on a hill and see no development. This conflict did not have a happy end from an environmental point of view. The government planning committees decided to build three new settlements for only a few dozen families, fragmenting open space and changing forever the unique landscape of Lachish.[16]

As a result of all of these circumstances, the open space in Israel is under perpetual threat of development. By 2003, the built land cover of the country for all uses reached 1,094 square kilometers, which is approximately 5 percent of the country's total land area. Excluding the sparsely populated area south of Beer-Sheva, built land cover is 11 percent of the total area. Roads alone comprise 130 square kilometers of the built area (Kaplan et al. 2007).

From an environmental perspective, the quality of development is as important as the magnitude. Because of the dispersed pattern of development, remaining open space in Israel is quite fragmented. North of Beer-Sheva, there are very few stretches of open space that are more than three miles from a built-up area. Even in the south, such moderately isolated open space is becoming rare. There is very little wilderness left in Israel, with biodiversity indicators suggesting that nature has paid a steep price for expanded human presence (see Yom-Tov in this volume).

The law that gives full and direct protection to open spaces in Israel is the National Parks and Nature Reserves Law. When the law was enacted in August 1963, it established two separate government bodies, the National Parks Authority and the Nature Reserves Authority. These were merged in 1998, under the rubric of the Nature and Parks Authority (NPA). The law authorizes the Ministry of Interior to declare a specific area as a nature reserve or a national park on the basis of a detailed plan that the NPA prepares and that public planning and building committees approve.

As of 2010, 230 nature reserves, comprising over 4,000 square kilometers and 66 national parks with 191 square kilometers, had been officially declared, covering approximately 20 percent of Israel's landmass. More than 200 additional proposed nature reserves and national parks are in various stages of the declaration process.[17]

Although the proportion of land set aside for natural reserves in Israel suggests success in creating an extensive network of such protected areas, the process of approving and declaring nature reserves pursuant to the law is not without its problems. First, declaring a nature reserve requires a detailed plan. Then, approval of the plan requires the consent of the local municipal government in which the reserve area is located. Negotiating with municipalities to obtain their consent for declaration of a nature reserve is not always easy. In many cases discussion leads to important achievements, but it also sometimes requires compromise regarding ecological protection. A telling example was the plan for a new settlement Michal in the Gilboa mountains. To obtain the municipality's agreement for a sizable nature reserve (20,000 dunams), during the years 2004–2006, the NPA agreed to decrease the planned nature reserve by 200 dunams to allow for the creation of the new settlement, part of which provided habitat to a rare Iris (*Iris haynei*). This compromise generated considerable criticism, so much, in fact, that Michal was ultimately not approved.[18]

Nature reserves alone are not enough to assure the preservation of Israel's ecological resources. Protected sanctuaries that cover some 20 percent of the country's total area may seem adequate, but most of them are located in the south (e.g., the Negev desert), and most of these function as military training zones as well. In the Mediterranean areas of Israel, only 2.5 percent of the land is protected by law, which is far from sufficient. Moreover, many of the nature reserves in the central part of Israel are small and isolated, making nature conservation much more difficult to achieve.

These realities led the NPA, as well as nongovernmental environmental organizations, to conclude that national protection of individual nature reserves, forests (see below), and national parks was not enough to ensure long-term preservation of Israeli landscapes and ecosystems, and that areas linking protected and other open areas also needed to be preserved. Thus, the protection of "ecological corridors" has gradually become a central factor in Israeli nature preservation (Shkedy and Sadot, n.d.). These corridors are mainly intended to guarantee movement and distribution of flora and fauna, but also provide open landscape areas. Corridors do not enjoy nature reserve status. At present, there is no official land-use designation for these eco-corridors, and they are protected mainly indirectly by zoning restrictions that limit development nearby. In a few pioneer plans, eco-corridors are recognized. For instance, in the proposed regional master plan for metro Jerusalem and the regional plan for Hanadiv Valley, land in corridors is not delineated for development per se. Rather, it is highlighted for special consideration by the planning committee. This may prove to be a better approach for establishing eco-corridors in Israel's planning system, since regulations that are too restrictive (e.g., forbidding development from the outset) can cause antagonism. At the same time, plans that allow for cooperative decision making within local communities can lead to better results for local residents and nature preservationists.

In addition to nature reserves and parks, Israel also has an extensive network of forested land that significantly augments the amount of open space. There are around 500,000 dunams in Israel protected by the British Mandate's 1926 Forest Act, which provide a core for current, formal afforestation policy in Israel. Although the act is still in force, afforestation policy actually takes place largely through the guidelines set forth in the 1995 National Outline Plan for Forests and Afforestation (NOP 22). NOP 22 protects about 1.6 million dunams in Israel as both existing and proposed forestland. The plan defines five main types of forests, each with its individual regulations, including existing and proposed planted forests, existing and proposed park forests, natural woodlands for preservation (mainly scrub) or cultivation, coastal park forests, and plantings along streams and rivers.

Planning committees can convert up to 25 percent of any forest plot for various development purposes, depending on the sensitivity of the forest type. But the Jewish National Fund, responsible for implementing the plan, has begun to implement a "no net loss" policy for development of woodlands where cities and developers must provide alternative lands for forestry if they wish to develop existing woodlands. Such forestry policies have proven to be an effective tool for preserving open spaces. Since 1995, loss of forests protected by the plan has been minimal: only 17,333 dunams or 1.08 percent of the planned forested area have been lost, but this includes land whose status was changed to nature reserves (Kaplan 2009).

In 2004, the Knesset also enacted a law for the protection of the coastal environment, declaring these natural assets to be public property. The law established a special planning committee that assesses every development project proposed in the coastal zone. The law was expanded in 2007 to include the Red Sea coast, and again in 2008, to include the Kinneret coast. In its first five years, it reviewed approximately 340 plans. It also conducted twenty-four sessions, which considered issues of principle, such as guidelines for holding public and private events on the coasts.[19]

In light of the links between protecting open spaces and planning, the history of efforts to protect open spaces in Israeli's urban society is best considered in the context of the country's National Outline Plans. These plans determine the direction of development and the balance between development and protection on a national scale. The suitability of the land-development practices that have emerged is evaluated in light of explicit policy principles (as stated in the plans themselves), identifying disparities between declared policy and actual practices.

A famous phrase from an old Israeli folksong declares, "We shall clothe you in a robe of cement and concrete."[20] It expressed the spirit popular during the first decades of the country, when massive development took place to create the physical infrastructure for the new society. During these years, open space was often considered an enemy of progress, a symbol of weakness, and a wasteland.

This development impulse was mirrored in the country's first national outline plan, the 1951 Sharon Plan, named after its creator, architect, and planner, Aryeh Sharon (Sharon 1951). This conceptual blueprint built upon three priorities for planning in Israel: land, population, and time. With regard to land, planning was to consider that the country serves as a bridge between continents in a very limited area, including regions that vary widely in terms of their natural characteristics. The population of the country at the time, which started at around eight hundred thousand people in 1949, was growing rapidly, doubling within three years, as a result of the absorption of immigrants from all over the world. Social factors became a main focus of the plan, which aimed to integrate "the exiles" from all over the world. Lastly, the plan focused on significant development within a very short timeframe; an urgent necessity expressed in the plan was to provide for a tripling of the population within a few years, which also meant tripling the agricultural and urban settlements, providing a sufficient supply of dwellings, public buildings, and so on.

The plan established five main sectors for planning: agriculture; industry; communications network; parks, afforestation, and landscape preservation; and residential development. In its open space provisions, the plan called for "afforestation areas on the mountain and hill slopes, which are at present desolate on account of the neglect and soil erosion prevailing for many generations" (Sharon 1951, 6). In addition to special areas that were earmarked for preservation because of their environmental qualities, the Sharon Plan included a system of national parks.

Among the national parks included in the Sharon Plan were: Jermak Park near Safed, in the Galilee (95,000 dunams for a national recreation center); Carmel Park near Haifa (over 105,000 dunams); Falik-Shfaim–Yarkon Park along the sands of the seashore (intended for weekend recreation for the densely populated Tel Aviv area); and Nahal Sorek Park west of Jerusalem.

Observations from sixty years later show that the main components of the plan remained intact over the years. The system that the Sharon Plan created was an essential start, but certainly not enough to ensure the country's ecological and landscape integrity. The fate of each of the four national parks proposed in the Sharon Plan noted above provides insight into the successes and challenges of the principles set out in the plan. The Jermak–Meron Mountain nature reserve was officially declared in 1964, including 84,000 dunams. During the years, small sections of the nature reserve were narrowed to allow for development of a few residential settlements. But it remains the largest natural reserve in the northern part of Israel. The Carmel Park was officially declared in 1971, with 64,000 dunams as a national park and 37,600 dunams as nature reserve. The present sanctuary is very close to the parameters (size and location) set by the Sharon Plan. Both the Carmel Park and Meron Mountain nature reserve have Druze settlements located in or near the parks, leading to acute land-use conflicts with these communities and challenging the ability to preserve these areas as undeveloped. While there is a consensus about the need to protect these two important and unique areas, property-rights conflicts have not yet been resolved and the ongoing land-use conflict sometimes reflects deeper conflicts between the Druze minority in Israel and national preservation policies.

The name of Falik Park was changed to Poleg Park. As of 2009, both governmental (e.g., Ministry of Environment) and nongovernmental organizations (e.g., SPNI) are making great efforts to convert the Poleg area into a park for the population that lives in the central district of Israel. The planned park is located in an area of high real estate value and is thus threatened by plans for new roads, commercial centers, extension of residential areas, and so on.

The Nahal Sorek sanctuary was planned more recently. The main park and nature reserve lie to the east of the Sorek stream (west of Jerusalem) and include large areas in the Jerusalem hills. In recent years, the Nahal Sorek area has been planned as a metropolitan park for Jerusalem and its environs. This idea goes back to Sharon Plan, which envisioned Nahal Sorek as just such a recreation area. One difference, however, is that the Sharon Plan placed the park well to the west of Jerusalem, in the heart of the open spaces of the Judean Hills, while today's Nahal Sorek is planned as a metropolitan park that forms a green ring within and around the city, from Arazim Valley to Nahal Refa'im. It seems that while in the Sharon Plan the park was envisioned as a refuge outside the city, today the park is integrated into the very fabric of the metropolitan area.[21]

The formal state-planning system has been and remains the main arena for national decision making concerning the designation of open spaces. Among the actors that influence planning and building committees are the nongovernmental organizations. The first environmental NGO, the Society for the Protection of Nature in Israel (SPNI), was founded in 1953 as a response to the massive and rapid development in the first years of the country. Its origins date back to the protests of a group of scientists and concerned citizens who organized against the draining of the Huleh Lake and wetlands in northern Israel. These activists claimed that the loss of the swamp would destroy the valley's rich natural resources. When their efforts failed, it became evident that a more formal organization would be necessary for conservation efforts to be effective. Today, the SPNI is the largest independent membership organization in Israel with over fifty thousand members. It was only a decade later that the first governmental agency for the protection of nature, the Nature Reserves Authority, was founded.[22]

Since the founding of the SPNI, the environmental movement in Israel has grown significantly. In 1974, Life and Environment, the umbrella body of environmental NGOs, was founded. One of its first achievements was a small but significant amendment to the planning and building law: a representative of the environmental NGOs was added to the National Council for Planning and Building. Greater growth in the environmental movement occurred during the 1990s, including the growing involvement of Adam Teva V'din (Israel Union for Environmental Defense, established in 1990) and student activists from Green Course (established in 1997), and another 150 NGOs that operated on the local level. Environmental NGOs are involved in decision-making processes and are members of the planning and building committees. Thus, these NGOs have begun to influence open-space protection efforts in Israel, both inside and outside of the cities. Coastal protection is the best evidence of their success: NGOs have been instrumental in reducing the spatial extent and impact of development plans approved along the coasts and catalyzed the establishment of the National Committee for the Protection of the Coastal Zone.[23]

The first forty years of Israel's history can be summarized as a time in which the central developmental model was to disperse the population as part of the effort to shape and to control the nation's borders. Protection of open spaces was part of the planning strategy as well, as reflected in the 1951 Sharon Plan and the 1981 National Master Plan for nature reserves and national parks. But for all their virtues, the original plans concentrated on specific protected areas and did not consider the need for open space as a whole. Nor did they consider the value of continuous corridors of open space. These latter concepts represent a new and more holistic way of thinking about open-space policy.

The first steps toward adopting this new way of thinking took place during the 1990s. Due to the large-scale absorption of immigrants and the resulting massive and urgent development needs, Israelis became acutely aware of the shortage of open space and the need to plan carefully and protect the little that remained. In response to this awareness, between 1990 and 1997, teams of experts prepared a nonstatutory master plan for the twenty-first century, known as "Israel 2020." The twelve volumes of the plan demonstrated the harmful results of a "business as usual" policy for Israel's public spaces (Mazor 1996). The 2020 plan placed the issue of depletion of open spaces at the heart of a future national agenda. Its orientation was adopted as the basis for two statutory national master plans that the government subsequently approved: National Outline Plan 31 (1993) and NOP 35 (2005).

At the same time, the Open Landscape Institute (OLI) was established as an independent unit in the SPNI in 1992 to cope with the severe shortage of open space in Israel and to promote sustainable development. OLI began collecting and analyzing data on the status of and need for protecting more open space and developed policy principles and tools to safeguard that space. The institute emerged as a driving force in the fight for preservation of open space.

In 1993, the government approved the National Outline Plan for Building, Development and Immigrant Absorption (NOP 31), the first integrated master plan since the Sharon Plan, forty years earlier. NOP 31 facilitated the absorption of one million new immigrants while simultaneously providing for open-space protection. The plan made an important distinction between open space and built areas and established a crucial guideline, innovative at the time, to avoid building new residential communities and instead to expand existing ones. Although only sanctioned until 1998, it remained in force until 2005, when the Israel government approved the Comprehensive National Outline Plan for Construction, Development and Conservation (NOP 35).

NOP 35 was enacted to address Israel's development needs until the year 2020.[24] The plan divides Israel's land area into five main typologies: two of which are development oriented (an urban and a rural typology) and three of which are preservation oriented (coastal, mixed preserve, and national preserve typologies).[25] Each typology has different "rules of the game" regarding allowable development. The boundaries of the urban typology constitute "red lines" that constrain urban development and direct current and future development demands into those urban areas. The urban typology includes around 9 percent of the land area of the country and the goal for this typology is to provide residential needs for 85 percent of the nation's population. Rural and preservation typologies take up the remaining 91 percent of the country's area and are to serve as home to 15 percent of the expected population. The plan's overarching goal is clear: "Most future development of Israel will have a distinct urban character. It will be characterized by the consolidation of large urban blocs, by medium to high building density, and by the significant strengthening of the urban lifestyle" (Assif, n.d.).

The spatial structuring of NOP 35 is informed by three principles, which are:

1. Deconcentrated concentration: The population will be dispersed at the national level, and concentrated at the regional levels. The spatial expression of this principle is intensive urban development within and contiguous to the existing urbanized areas. The plan discourages the establishment of new settlements.

2. Metropolitan structure: Most of Israel's urban, industrial, and commercial development will be organized within metropolitan frameworks. There are four metropolitan regions, Tel Aviv, Haifa, Jerusalem, and Beer-Sheva metropolitan regions, which are in different stages of development. Green buffers are to separate the metropolitan regions and provide "green lungs" between and within the urbanized areas.

3. National green backbone of open space: A national green backbone, from north to south, serves as the main framework for the protection of open spaces. The green spine includes the majority of the most valuable and sensitive open and rural areas. The green spine is aimed to assure the continuity of open spaces, and to serve as the main ecological corridor through the country. Green buffers complete the green backbone, including metropolitan parks and protected streams (which run primarily in

the east-to-west direction). The green buffers create a ladderlike pattern, whose rungs sprout out of the vertical, north-south national green spine.[26]

NOP 35 also introduced new innovations regarding the protection of open spaces. It was the first time, for example, that a national eco-corridor was included in a statutory master plan. It also protects an additional one million dunams of open space beyond those previously noted as scenic open areas.

It is difficult to judge how effective NOP 35 has been since its 2005 launch. An intermediate assessment, prepared by the Ministry of Interior, has shown that some of its goals were achieved. Frankel and Orenstein (2012) also identify characteristics of NOP that suggest preliminary successes (e.g., encouraging high density development and maintaining development within red lines), as well as areas in which the plan has been less successful (e.g., slowing development in rural areas and increasing socioeconomic equity between communities). The plan identified a few areas especially worthy of preservation, which require the preparation of detailed plans including Bikaat Hanadiv and its vicinity (near Zichron Yaakov); the Shiqma river basin in the south; and the Ayalon and the Poleg streams in the central district. The Ministry of Interior, with the intensive involvement of green agencies such as the Ministry of Environmental Protection, Nature and Parks Authority, and environmental NGOs—is working to approve those plans. Preparation is ongoing, but intermediate results suggest that these types of detailed plans constitute a promising tool to protect open spaces.[27] Moreover, because of the provisions of NOP 35, relatively few plans for new settlements or the extension of existing settlement into ecologically sensitive areas have been approved (e.g., Michal in the Gilboa mountains and Ramat Arbel in the Galilee mountains).

At the same time, because of governmental pressure, as of 2010 a few new settlements have been approved including Mirsham in the Lachish area, Mitzpe Ilan in Wadi Ara area, and Nimrod in the Golan Heights. The guidelines of the plan point out that these new settlements are not the preferred type of development, especially not in sensitive areas. Yet it seems that the approach of the national master plan is not yet strong enough to deter developers or stop government or private-sector initiatives that have the political support of strong interest groups. Another type of development not fully prevented by the national plan, is single-family homesteads. This kind of development stands in direct opposition to almost all the national plan principles. The family farms are located in the middle of the open spaces, disrupting their continuity and granting a single family large areas of land. Additionally, many of the farms are sited in ecologically sensitive areas. Despite this, the Israeli government has continued to encourage such farms, especially in the Negev.

In 2010 a new law was enacted, aimed at supporting single-family homesteads (also see Orenstein and Silverman in this volume).

The primary goal of NOP 35—to direct the main portion of development to urban areas, while significantly strengthening urban lifestyle—has been only partly achieved. About half of new approved housing in Israel since 2005 is in a single-story, suburban style. What this suggests is that even a well-intentioned national master plan is powerless to improve quality of life in urban areas in Israel without significant governmental intervention; absent such support, Israel's cities will not be able to compete with the suburbs, and open spaces will continue to be threatened.

Several other national master plans directly address open spaces, the most important of which (aside from NOP 35) are the aforementioned Outline Plan for National Parks and Nature Reserves (NOP 8), and for Forests and Afforestation (NOP 22). NOP 8 was approved in 1981, and as its name suggests, it designated large areas across the country to be set aside as national parks and nature reserves.[28] Many changes to this plan have been made since then—nature reserves were occasionally reduced in size due to the flexibility mechanism in the plan (reduction of up to 30 percent of the total area is permitted in each nature reserve). At the same time, many new reserves were approved. As described earlier, the land lost from NOP 22 in the past decade was found to be minimal—only 17,333 dunams, or 1.08 percent of the plan area, including land converted to nature reserves in which protection will be even more vigorous (Kaplan 2009).

The aggregate effect of NOP 8, 22, 35, and regional plans is that there is a substantial base for the protection of open spaces in Israel. However, this base does not sufficiently guarantee the long-term future of open spaces—and in particular the ecological assets they contain. The present flaws are significant: First, flexibility mechanisms built into the plans sometimes leave open spaces vulnerable to pressure from developers (public or private); second, significant gaps exist between policies "on paper" and reality (Ben David 2010); and finally, there still exists a lack of operational tools for use in implementing the master plans, as will be explained later.

The last few years witnessed great changes in Israel's planning for open spaces. The first generation of master plans made strict distinctions between areas aimed for development and areas designated for preservation. Today, we can see a new set of land uses that introduce innovative combinations and interfacing between development and preservation. This phenomenon reflects Israel's attempts to find new solutions for protecting open spaces in a highly urbanized country. One such example is plans to establish biosphere reserves around the country, for instance in the Megiddo region or in the Carmel mountains outside Haifa. The Ministry of Interior is conducting research to determine the criteria for the establishment of additional biosphere reserves in Israel.

Since the 1990s, surveying and evaluating open land and its natural and cultural resources has become a routine part of the planning process. Several plans address farmland from an environmental perspective, restricting some agricultural activities because of ecological or scenic considerations. These only represent first steps since Israel does not yet subsidize farming for meeting environmental goals, as is commonly done in Europe.

The next step for establishing open-space protection planning principles in Israel involves the development of policies that are not merely "on paper." The great challenge for the coming years will be the implementation of such tools and regulations. Operational tools are needed to translate the policy planning into reality, among them the capacity to purchase land rights to preserve open spaces (Gothelf 2008); the transfer of development rights; and the creation of budgetary incentives for the maintenance of open spaces. Such tools will offer new modalities for protection and incentives and may help resolve some of the difficulties that the planning system alone cannot solve.

Among these difficulties is the fate of high-value open areas that are privately owned. Although most of the land in Israel is publicly owned (93 percent), some valuable open space remains in the hands of private owners. Those areas cannot be protected without addressing complicated property-rights issues.

Even within publicly owned lands, challenges abound. For example, there is a desire to protect farmlands that are leased by the state to agricultural settlements. This is complicated by the fact that there are no incentives for farmland holders to maintain open spaces. There is also the issue of how to protect open space that has already been zoned for development but that has not yet been developed (Orenstein 2008). Using a policy instrument, such as the transfer of development rights, can help to create better zoning conditions. In July 2010, for instance, the Israeli government decided, as a result of a successful public campaign led by local activists, to cancel an approved plan for a holiday village on the Palmachim coast south of Rishon Le'Zion. This, however, was an unusual decision, and many sensitive spaces in Israel are still threatened by legally valid, yet environmentally destructive, plans that are as yet unrealized. These offer reminders of an era when environmental protection was not sufficiently emphasized during the planning process.

A new and important tool for protecting open spaces was included in the August 2009 Land Reform Act. Although the act was very controversial because it was aimed at privatizing public land, the final version included a proposal for a governmental land fund that would be established with the aim of providing better funding for efforts to protect for open spaces. The budget for the fund is derived from taxes generated by development (up to 1 percent of governmental income is derived from land development). This was the first time that the government had taken such an active step to protect open space and earmark funds to make sure that there resources are available for conservation efforts to succeed (Sagi 2008; Han and Sagi 2009).[29]

In 2003, the Society for the Protection of Nature in Israel, the Nature and Parks Authority, the Ministry of the Environment, the Jewish National Fund, and the Planning Administration of the Ministry of the Interior published a document that aimed to define national policy and operational tools to preserve and use the country's open spaces in a sustainable manner. The document relates to economic, legislative, social, and other tools, in order to enrich the existing toolbox used for the protection of open spaces (Stern et al. 2003).

Behind the scenes in the implementation of national land-use policies, such as those included in NOP 35, there has been an ongoing struggle to minimize the gaps between policy and practice. Israel's planning system faces ongoing pressure to breach planning guidelines and allow more flexibility and more development. Moreover, in Israel there is considerable illegal development, much of which goes unpunished (Alfasi 2006). While there is no exact data about the amount of the illegal buildings or land uses throughout the country, a 2009 estimate of its extent suggests that there are about one hundred thousand illegal construction projects,[30] many of which are located in open space not zoned for development. Illegal activity includes building without permit or violations of building codes and approved uses, for example construction of buildings for commercial use (industrial or storage) on agricultural land approved only for greenhouse construction. Thus, even though the master plans offer strong protection for open spaces, they are far from being sufficient (Han 2004; Han forthcoming).

A number of new dilemmas have arisen concerning the protection of open space that reflects many conflicts between competing environmental goals; an example of such a conflict concerns land needed for renewable energy production. In 2009, the fuel mix for the production of electricity was largely based on fossil fuels, 70 percent of which came from coal-fired power plants (Mor et al. 2008). In May 2008, the Minister of Infrastructure announced that the target for renewable energies in the electricity production mix for 2010 would be 10 percent. At the Copenhagen climate change conference in December 2009, Israeli president Shimon Peres committed Israel to reduce its CO_2 emissions by 20 percent by 2020, using renewable energies as well as other solutions. These are ambitious goals, for in 2007 renewables accounted for only 0.1 percent of electricity in use. To achieve Peres's stated target, it will be necessary to establish renewable energy power plants with 8,300-megawatt capacity by 2030 (in relation to the overall installed production capacity of 11,000 megawatts in 2008). As a rule, infrastructure for producing electricity based on renewable energy technologies and solar power in particular requires significant landmass. Meeting the government's goal may translate into tens of thousands of dunams of natural open spaces and farmland needed for solar power stations, most of them in the south.

A new balance will be required, reconciling the wish for greater dependence on renewable sources for energy production and the need to protect open space. Environmental policy should give priority to solar energy generation in built areas, before converting open spaces and farmland to this use. Another important guideline for solar energy production is to direct development toward low-value areas contiguous to built areas, rather than toward the heart of open spaces.

Similar conflicts over space arise when planning the infrastructure required for the transportation and utilization of natural gas for energy production. In December 2009, following the discovery of natural gas reservoirs off of Israel's Mediterranean coast, the National Council for Planning and Building discussed the construction of an onshore receiving terminal for natural gas. As a cleaner alternative to coal and oil, there was full agreement among all members of the committee about the urgent need for natural gas in Israel, and therefore the urgent need to find a suitable location for the receiving terminal. But the desire that such infrastructure should be located in the limited and dense coastal zone of Israel made the decision very difficult. On the one hand, the desire to protect the coastal zone led to support of an alternative location for the terminal, namely offshore. On the other hand, this solution came with an environmental price of delay in integrating natural gas into energy production and an interim of increased reliance on coal.

Protecting open spaces in sufficient amounts and qualities in Israel's urban society indeed seems almost an impossible mission considering growth in population and economic well-being, and the attendant pressure for development. Still, great achievements have been recorded in Israel, mostly in the planning arena. The future of an even more dense and more developed country holds new challenges for planning and environmental agencies, as well as for NGOs. Innovative ideas, like those embodied in NOP 35 and newer ideas, will be required to resolve the many new dilemmas and challenges and to exploit future opportunities to protect invaluable open space. The key to establishing the balance between development in and protection of Israel's open spaces will be adherence to national planning policies. In addition, reform is needed in land-management policy so that it can better achieve the goal: open-space protection.

Currently, land management is development oriented, as reflected in the Israeli Land Administration Council decisions. Another final crucial element in the future of open spaces in Israel concerns agricultural land.[31] Most open space is considered agricultural, although only some of these lands (about 3.5 million dunam) are actually cultivated. Unless agricultural land is considered as a coherent part of Israel open spaces and is planned and managed based, inter alia, on environmental considerations, there will be no real future for open space in Israel.

Throughout Israel's history, the efforts to protect open spaces in this predominantly urban society have gone through periods with more or less success, reflecting the ever-changing challenges inherent in the country's dynamic demographic, economic, and political development. From conflicts between development and conservation, to unique circumstances of absorbing immigration and coping with emergencies, to present-day dilemmas between conflicting environmental goals, open-space preservation is an ongoing challenge. The coming years will likely raise new questions and new dilemmas, which will be even more difficult to solve than previous ones. The ability to protect open spaces in Israel's future, where population growth and urbanization may continue unabated, will depend on the capability of society to find innovative, smart, and sustainable solutions for meeting a diversity of land-use needs.

NOTES

1. See Campus Teva site, Tel Aviv University: http://campusteva.tau.ac.il/upload/ Biodiversity%20presentations/israel_biodiversity_part1.pdf; Ministry of Environment site, http://www.sviva.gov.il/bin/en.jsp?enPage=BlankPage&enDisplay=view&enDis pWhat=Zone&enDispWho=biodiversity_2010&enZone=biodiversity_2010. See OLI's presentation about open spaces in Israel: http://www.deshe.org.il/_Uploads/dbsAt-tachedFiles/OpenSpacesWithRemarks.pdf.

2. See http://www.parks.org.il/BuildaGate5/general2/company_search_tree.php.

3. See http://www.kkl.org.il/KKL/hebrew/nosim_ikaryim/doveret/ odaot_kodmot/2009/sukkot%202009%20summary.x.

4. See http://www.cbs.gov.il/shnaton60/sto2_14.pdf.

5. Beer-Sheva region—south from Beer-Sheva, the region contains approximately 60 percent of the country.

6. See http://www.cbs.gov.il/shnaton60/sto2_03.pdf.

7. See http://www.cbs.gov.il/shnaton60/download/sto2_01.xls.

8. See http://www.cbs.gov.il/shnaton60/st22_10.pdf.

9. See agreement in INRA site: http://www.ios.org.il/site/pdf/co-oper_army.pdf.

10. See http://www.mevaker.gov.il/serve/showHtml.asp?bookid=437&id=169&from page=83&contentid=8122&parentcid=8112&direction=1&bctype=1&frombutton=0& startpage=8&sw=1280&hw=730.

11. Statistical Abstract of Israel. http://www.cbs.gov.il/shnaton60/sto2_01.pdf.

12. See http://www.moia.gov.il/NR/rdonlyres/EF9DA37F-88F3-43CB-B2C917 F24656B9F7/0/sikum1999.pdf.

13. For further reading see Alterman 1995.

14. The plan, National Outline Plan 39, was approved by the government on November 27, 2005. The plan's documents are available at the Ministry of Interior website: http://www.moin.gov.il/. See also: http://www.teva.org.il/?CategoryID=268&ArticleID=3791.

15. About Nitzanim Field School in the SPNI website: http://www.teva.org.il/?CategoryID=257&ArticleID=320.

16. To read more about the environmental conflict around Lachish, see: http://www .teva.org.il/?CategoryID=530 and http://www.bimkom.org/communityView.asp?projectTypeId=1&projectId=139.

17. INPA official website: http://www.parks.org.il/BuildaGate5/general2/data_card.php?Cat=~~~660964978~Card13~&ru=&SiteName=parks&Clt=&Bur=41915268.

18. National Committee for Planning and Building final decision, http://mavat.moin.gov.il/MavatPS/Forms/SV2.aspx?tid=2.

19. See Ministry of Interior report: http://www.moin.gov.il/Apps/PubWebSite/MainMenu.nsf/4DF815EA4AC4E503C2256BA6002EE732/16C5835548859F59C225769B00251257/$FILE/News.pdf.

20. The poem was written by Nathan Altherman.

21. Details on plans for open spaces, as described before, are available in the Ministry of Interior website, www.pnim.gov.il.

22. See http://www.parks.org.il/BuildaGate5/general2/data_card.php?Cat=~~~660964978~Card13~&ru=&SiteName=parks&Clt=&Bur=736844153.

23. See http://www.teva.org.il/?CategoryID=219.

24. See www.moin.gov.il.

25. The free translation for the Hebrew term "Mirkam" is texture. Here we used the English term "typology," which explains better the meaning of the Hebrew term.

26. For presentation that includes figures and maps, see http://www.moin.gov.il/Apps/PubWebSite/mainmenu.nsf/4DF815EA4AC4E503C2256BA6002EE732/45C6D3CAA241AA89C22573600026DEEC/$FILE/News.ppt.

27. Information about those plans and their status is available in the Ministry of Interior website, http://www.moin.gov.il/.

28. The distinction between parks and reserves lies primarily in their designated use. National parks are generally areas of historic importance or high tourist value. They generally have more highly developed infrastructure to facilitate for visitors. Nature reserves are much broader swaths of area set aside for the protection of particular ecological phenomena, including unique species, ecosystems, or biologically important resources.

29. For further reading about Israel's land policy see Hananel 2010, Alterman 1999.

30. According to the State Comptroller and Ombudsman last reports.

31. For historic review see Feitelson 1999 and Alterman and Han 2004.

REFERENCES

Alfasi, N. 2006. "Planning Policy? Between Long-Term Planning and Zoning Amendments in the Israeli Planning System." *Environment and Planning A* 38: 553–68.

Alterman, R. 1995. "Can Planning Help in Time of Crisis? Planners Response to Israel Wave of Mass Immigration." *Journal of American Association of Planning* 61: 156–77.

———. 1999. *Between Privatization and Continued National Ownership: A Future Land Policy for Israel.* Jerusalem: Floersheimer Institute for Policy Studies.

Assif, S. n.d. "Principles of Israel's Comprehensive National Outline Plan for Construction, Development and Conservation (NOP 35)." http://www.moin.gov.il/apps/pubwebsite/MainMenu.nsf/ReplicationView/642611DA2DBF81E4C2257360002851110/$File/News.07.pdf?OpenElement.

Ben David, I. 2010. *Threats to Open Spaces in Israel, in Planning and Building Arena—Report to 2010.* Tel Aviv: Society for the Protection of Nature in Israel.

Frankel, A., and D. E. Orenstein. 2012. "Can Urban Growth Management Work in an Era of Political and Economic Change? International Lessons from Israel." *Journal of the American Planning Association* 78 (1): 16–33.

Gothelf, T. 2008. "Purchase of Land Rights in Order to Preserve Open Spaces." Tel Aviv: Open Landscape Institute. http://www.deshe.org.il/?CategoryID=225&ArticleID=181.

Han, I. 2004. "Non-Conforming Use of Open Agricultural Areas." Jerusalem: Jerusalem Institute for Israel Studies and Open Landscape Institute. In Hebrew; English summary.

———. Forthcoming. *Enforcement Policy of Illegal Development in Open Spaces.* Jerusalem: Jerusalem Institute for Israel Studies and Open Landscape Institute. In Hebrew.

Han, I., and Y. Sagi. 2009. "The Reform in Israeli Lands—The Environmental Aspect." *Mekarkein* 8 (6): 64–82. In Hebrew.

Hananel, R. 2010. "Zionism and Agricultural Land: National Narratives, Environmental Objectives and Land Policy in Israel." *Land Use Policy* 27: 1160–70.

Kaplan, M. 2009. "NOP 22, Policy Document." Jerusalem: KKL-JNF. In Hebrew; English summary.

Kaplan, M., L. Darom, R. Haklai, N. Vitman, S. Buckwald, H. Dean, and S. Caspi-Oron. 2007. *Patterns in the Utilization of Constructed Land in Israel.* Jerusalem: Jerusalem Institute for Israel Studies and Israel Ministry of Environmental Protection. In Hebrew; English summary.

Kaplan M., and T. Dayan. 1996. *Open Space in Israel—Israel 2020—A Master Plan for the 21st Century.* Haifa: Technion—Israel Institute of Technology. In Hebrew.

Levin, N., H. Lahav, U. Ramon, A. Heller, G. Nizry, A. Tsoar, and Y. Sagi. 2007. "Landscape Continuity Analysis: A New Approach to Conservation in Israel." *Landscape Urban Planning* 79: 53–64.

Mazor, A. 1996. *"Israel 2020"—Israel in the Years of 2000.* Haifa: Technion. In Hebrew.

Meffe, G. K., and C. R. Carroll. 1997. *Principles of Conservation Biology.* 2nd ed. Sunderland: Sinauer Associates.

Millennium Ecosystem Assessment (MEA). 2005. *Ecosystems and Human Well-Being: Synthesis.* Washington, DC: Island Press.

Mor, A., S. Sarusi, and Y. Laster. 2008. "Renewable Energy and Open Spaces." Tel Aviv: Open Landscape Institute. In Hebrew; English summary. http://www.deshe.org.il/_Uploads/dbsAttachedFiles/EnergyPaper.pdf.

Oren, A., and R. Regev. 2008. *Land in Uniform, Territory and Defense in Israel.* Jerusalem: Carmel. In Hebrew.

Orenstein, D. 2008. "We Changed Our Minds . . . " *Haaretz*, May 9. http://www.haaretz.com/print-edition/opinion/we-changed-our-minds-1.245503.

Sagi, Y. 2008. "Protecting Open Spaces in Israel—The Next Step: Managing the Land as Public Good." *Mekarkein* 7 (6): 38–42. In Hebrew.

Sar-Shalom, A., Y. Peled, I. Amit Cohen, A. Sasson, and R. Reich. 2010. *Cultural Landscape in Israel.* Jerusalem: National Reserve Authority.

Sharon, A. 1951. *Physical Planning in Israel.* Jerusalem: Government Print Office. In Hebrew; English summary.

Shkedy, Y., and E. Sadot. n.d. "Ecological Corridors—A Practical Conservation Tool." Nature and Parks Authority, Science Division. http://www.parks.org.il/sigalit/MIS-DRONOT.pdf. In Hebrew; English abstract.

Stern et al. 2003. "Preserving the Open Spaces in Israel—Policy and Tools: Operational Tools, Principles and Recommendations." Tel Aviv: JNF, INRA, Ministry of Environment, SPNI. In Hebrew; English summary. http://www.sviva.gov.il/Environment/Static/Binaries/index_pirsumim/p0216c_1.pdf.

Tal, A. 2008. "Space Matters; Historic Drivers and Turning Points in Israel's Open Space Protection Policy." *Israel Studies* 13 (1): 119–51.

Zalutzki, M. 2002. "Patterns of Recreation in Natural Settings in the Open Areas of the Judean Mountains." In *Environment and Policy—Environmental Policy Research Collection,* edited by A. Eidelman, A. Tal, and N. Ben-Aharon. Jerusalem: Jerusalem Institute for Israel Studies. In Hebrew; abstract in English.

CHAPTER EIGHT

THE BATTLE OF THE "TRUE BELIEVERS"
Environmentalism in Israeli Party Politics

Orr Karassin

ENVIRONMENTALISM HAS BEEN a very latecomer to Israeli politics, and it is arguable whether it has arrived at all. While other Western nations were already experiencing heated environmental political debate in the 1970s (Dryzek 1997, 203–6), not so in Israel: the terms "environmentalism" and "ecology" were relatively unknown to Israeli politicians at the time, nor were they cognizant of the grand ideas that stood behind them. In 1965, Israel's Minister of Finance and one of Israel's most influential politicians for two decades, Pinchas Sapir, conveyed the spirit of the times when he asked the then member of the Israeli Parliament Yosef Tamir, "what is that ecology *shmecology* you are constantly talking about?" (Eldar 2009; Greenpeter 2008). His rhetorical question not only reflected ignorance but also a disdain and alienation from environmental impulses. Sapir's sentiment was neither unique nor exceptional. It mirrored the predominant "development" ethos that had governed Zionist-Israeli society and politics since the 1930s (Tal 2002, 24; De-Shalit 1995).

Even if since the days of Pinchas Sapir, ignorance has been substituted by moderate knowledge about environmentalism, it is still far from a sweeping concern dominating the various corners of Israeli party politics. It has moved from the obscure to the eccentric and today sits comfortably as a niche issue promoted at times by no more than a handful of "true believers." Although since the new millennium two green national parties have emerged on the political scene, they have been unable to secure the needed votes to pass the

minimal electoral threshold and have been unsuccessful in placing representatives in the Knesset—the Israeli Parliament.

This chapter begins with a description of the party and ideological alignment of environmentalism in Israeli national politics. It places Israeli party
politics within a wider context of major political processes such as dealignment and realignment, thus creating the theoretical background for evaluating the broader role of environmentalism in Israeli politics. In this context an
attempt will be made to answer the recurring question Has environmentalism
been associated primarily with left-wing parties? It is stipulated that contrary
to the development of environmental politics in many Western nations, environmentalism in Israel has not been the sole domain of new (or old) leftist
ideologies. Indeed it has not been a party affair at all. Rather, it has emerged
as an individualistic agenda beyond partisan divisions, particular to a few
dedicated members of Knesset (MKs)[1] from various and at times opposing
political parties. This assertion is drawn through an in-depth description of
some of the exceptional figures that have colored Israeli environmental politics, along with their accomplishments and struggles.

Through the work of individual MKs, brief lessons are learned about a
few of the major environmental conflicts that received a degree of attention
from the Knesset. These political environmental struggles serve to illustrate
the ideological positioning of various actors, predominant discourses, ideologies, and interests that prevailed. Also, the chapter references some of the
legislative achievements of the various MKs through which one can learn
something about the active role individuals have played in promoting environmental regulation.

Finally, a brief description will be given of a relatively new phenomenon—
the establishment of two green parties. These parties have already participated
in national elections and have gained some holding in local-municipal elections. Whether green parties may in the future serve as a possible cure for
some of the shortcomings of environmentalism in Israeli party politics remains an open question.

AN OVERVIEW OF ISRAELI NATIONAL PARTY POLITICS

Israel is a parliamentary representative democratic republic with a multiparty
system. The Israeli Knesset comprises 120 members of Knesset who are elected
as party representatives on a national platform (Arian 2005). The prime minister is the head of government that is formed by a majority coalition (Arian
2005).

Since the nascent days of the Knesset, diversity and fragmentation have
been key characteristics in the political makeup (Peretz and Doron 1997).
From the first Knesset elected in February 1949 until the eighteenth Knesset

elected in February 2009, there have been at any time no less than nine and up to twenty elected factions represented (Knesset website).[2] Parties are usually seen as divided among right wing—moderate and nonmoderate; left wing—moderate and nonmoderate including a communist party; center party; religious (both orthodox and ultra-orthodox as well as representing Sefaradi Jews); and minority Arab parties (Arian 2005).

The first Knesset saw twelve parties and political groups elected, however the ruling party Mapai enjoyed a considerable dominance and maintained its domination until the ninth Knesset elections in 1977 (Peretz and Doron 1997, 78–79). The official policy of the party was "constructive socialism," based on pioneering idealism coupled with political pragmatism (85–86).

The elections to the ninth Knesset (1977) brought about a changeover in the ruling elite. The Likud, a right-wing party that consolidated several center right and far right-wing factions (Arian 2005, 139–50), had formed, for the first time, a right-wing government. The ninth Knesset also saw an increase in the number of factions represented rising to twenty (Knesset website, accessed August 2010). The turnover, dubbed as "Hamahapakh (i.e., the revolution), was the outcome of a complex set of conditions, among them the long, weakening dominance of the Labor Party, the legitimacy that the Likud had acquired gradually since the late 1960s; a demographic shift with a rise in the number of voters from non-European ethnic backgrounds, the public's annoyance at the shortcomings of previous governments, and the perceived failure of government in the 1973 "Yom Kippur" war (Arian 2005). It brought about many changes—in the character of the government, in economic policy, and in the status quo on issues of religion between the government and the Ultra-Orthodox Jewish parties (Eisenstadt 2004, 139–41).

The 1980s brought yet another political change, as the left and right wings became rather similar in size, along with a major economic crisis and the First Lebanon War, which drove the Likud and Labor to form two consecutive national unity governments (Koren and Shapira 1997, 308–31).The 2005 elections saw a significant shift to the center when Kadima became the first central party elected to rule and form the government (Shamir et al. 2008, 51–58). After the 2009 elections a reactionary shift to the political right occurred, when the Likud (led by Benjamin Netanyahu) was called upon to form the government after a majority of sixty-five MKs was attained by right-wing and religious parties (*Haaretz* February 2, 2009). Even though the government established a coalition with the Labor Party (*Haaretz* website March 31, 2009), the latter party's severely weakened position in the Knesset (thirteen representatives, an all-time low) and a lack of clear ideological standing severely compromised its overall political clout (Sternhell 2009).

DEALIGNMENT AND REALIGNMENT IN ISRAELI NATIONAL POLITICS

Two major processes, consistent with patterns of electoral change in Western politics, can be identified, to some extent, in the Israeli politics of the last two decades. First and foremost of these patterns is dealignment, the weakening of bonds between voters and their traditional partisan affiliation. These diminishing bonds have been attributed to several social and political processes. Political parties have lost their centrality in social life, while at the same time better education and increased political awareness have caused voters to abandon previous commitments to a particular party (Dalton et al. 1984; Dalton 2000). Shamir and Arian (2004, 41–47) establish that since the 1990s, Israel's political system has been experiencing partisan dealignment, which is characterized by increasingly inconsistent voting behavior, a decrease in the dominance of large parties, and an increased role of civil society.

Realignment has been described as a process concurrent to dealignment. The rise of "New Politics" divides (e.g., environmentalism or feminism) and a fundamental change in the balance of power between competing parties, translated in many Western democracies into higher voter turnout rates and increased ideological polarization (Dalton et al. 1984; Dalton 2000). The rise of New Politics brought about significant changes in the formally predominant political discourse and priorities in many Western nations (Lijphart et al. 2000). For example, in the recent 2009 elections to the European Parliament, disillusioned left-of-center parties' voters continued to gravitate to the Greens, which, coupled with the collapse of left-wing parties, caused a general rise in Green parties' representation (Carter 2010, 301).

In Israel, while the political system underwent a process of substantial dealignment, realignment did not reach the same degree of influence. It has been much slower, with smaller impact than in other Western democracies (Yael Yishay 2003, 67–70, 127–28; Van Der Heijden 1999). Substantive indications of this are decreasing voter turnout rates and the public's general sense that the major parties are similarly ideologically positioned (Shamir et al. 2008, 56–58; Arian and Shamir 2006, 79).

A notable attribute of the reduced influence of the realignment process has meant that environmentalism has never been considered a central political concern in national elections. Although individual MKs were aware of environmental issues even back in the 1960s (Tal 2002, 163–64), the environmental debate has not managed to climb up the ladder of political priorities in national elections. The prominent cleavages remained national security and territorial issues. This can be attributed to the fact that since its independence in 1948 Israel continues to be in a de facto state of war with many of its neighbors, with recurring hostilities and military clashes. Israel also remains until 2010 a country without internationally recognized borders and, hence, the prominence of the ongoing territorial dispute (Peretz and Doron 1997, 138–40). This situation is quite exceptional when compared with other Western democracies.

In industrialized democracies, "green ideas" made their prime entrance into intellectual and political circles as early as the 1970s (Richardson and Rootes 1995). Along with other "postmaterial" issues (Inglehart 1977), people started to notice that industrialism was taking its toll and producing deleterious environmental impacts. In Israel, much the same as in other developing countries, the predominant notion was that public policy and priorities could not "afford the luxury" of placing environmentalism and other postmaterial issues on the top of the political agenda (Lijphart et al. 1999). Israel even beyond the 1980s, was still a country in construction, pursuing the Zionist "ethic of development" (De-Shalit 1995, 75–76).

Although proportional electoral systems (such as the one that exists in Israel) are commonly perceived as favorable toward new and green parties (Karamichas and Botetzagias 2003 73; Richardson and Rootes 1995, 18), in the Israeli case, the so-called "advantage" of the proportional system has been almost entirely obscured by the dominant cleavages (security and territorial issues) exacerbating other political barriers (Doron and Moshe 1989). As a consequence, although between nine and twenty factions were represented in the Knesset throughout the years (Knesset website accessed August 2010), none of these factions ever placed the environmental agenda as a central goal.

While green parties "took advantage" of the dealignment and realignment processes, and achieved significant electoral accomplishments throughout Western democracies (Richardson and Rootes 1995; Dryzek 1997; Mair 2001; Carter 2010), Israel has yet to witness a green party gaining substantial electoral support in national elections. Furthermore, as stated no elected party has embraced a distinct environmental agenda, as has occurred in many Western democracies, where it is not uncommon that "gray" parties purloin ideas from green parties to capitalize on the "greens" electoral potential (Dryzek 1997).

SOLITUDE IN POLITICAL ENVIRONMENTALISM

Although green ideals did not receive a substantial place on party platforms or agendas, environmentally devoted MKs have played a significant role in Israeli politics. Notably, environmentally oriented MKs cannot be traced to one segment of Israeli political parties. They have been a rather eclectic bunch, coming from as far right as the Russian reactionary Israel Beiteinu Party to as far left as Hadash, the communist Jewish-Arab Party. Many MKs have had affairs with environmentalism, while others boasted a longer standing relationship.

From the mid-1960s to the early 1980s, the Liberal Party, later aligned to the Likud (Arian 2005, 148–50), hosted an extraordinarily committed environmental MK—the late Yosef Tamir. During the 1990s, MKs promoting an environmental agenda could be found in Meretz, the Zionist leftist party, which received a large portion of environmental activists' votes (Tal 2002, 395; De-Shalit 1994, 274–76). At the same time, devoted environmentalists were also to be found in the extreme right-wing party Israel Beitinu. The late Yuri Shtern a new immigrant with a doctorate in economics who was a member of the fourteenth to seventeenth Knesset, was such an MK (Yuri Shtern website;[3] Tal 2006, 549, 551). MK Michael Nudelman a professor of environmental economics also from Israel Beitinu (see Knesset website), was also devoted to environmental issues (see Adam Teva Vadin March 2006–March 2007, website;[4] Tal 2002, 395). Since the mid-2000s, environmentally dedicated MKs are to be found in Hadash, the Labor Party, and also seemingly in the right-wing Likud, some of whom even received official awards acknowledging their contribution (Life and Environment website).[5]

The following sections of the chapter will draw on an in-depth description of some of these exceptional figures that have colored Israeli environmental politics, along with their struggles and accomplishments, both legislative as well as others. The MKs that were chosen for the in-depth analysis do not by any means make up a comprehensive list of all prominent Israeli environmental parliamentarians. The limits of the chapter required selection of only a handful, which inevitably excludes many others worthy of mentioning.[6] Hence the description serves by no means as a complete historical overview, but rather as a means of analysis. Through the stories of a few of these MKs the chapter seeks to illustrate some of the major environmental struggles that received attention from the Knesset, predominant discourses, ideologies, and prevailing interests. Most importantly, their stories illustrate the nonpartisan nature of environmentalism in Israeli politics and the difficulties it has faced in the past and continues to face in the present.

FIRST SIGNS OF PARLIAMENTARY ENVIRONMENTALISM IN THE 1970s AND 1980s

Renowned in Israel as "Mr. Environment," MK Josef Tamir was an unlikely candidate for carrying the environmental torch. He was first elected to the sixth Knesset in 1965 as the secretary-general of the Liberal Party (Tal 2002, 251). The Liberals, oriented toward the bourgeoisie, gained their support from established landowners and businessmen (Arian 2005, 148–50). Many of the first founders and supporters of the party were sons of well-to-do orange grove farmers, part of the veteran Jewish economic elite that resided in Palestine before the independence of the State of Israel in 1948. The party promoted a libertarian worldview, much alienated from the predominant socialist philosophy of the ruling Mapai (Peretz and Doron 1997, 99–102). This political home was an improbable place for breeding Israel's pioneer environmental visionary.

Between 1974 and 1978 Tamir presided over the Parliamentary Internal Affairs and Environment Committee and the State Control Committee (Tamir 1985, 31–36). In 1973 he was among the founders of Gahal, the political alliance of the Liberals and the right-wing Herut, that later evolved into the Likud. Renowned for his writing and rhetoric, Tamir was soon appointed as head of the information and organization division of Gahal and later the Likud (42–44).

During the late '60s, while environmental concerns were gaining prominence around the world, the Knesset in Israel was still dominated by environmental indifference. No single parliamentary committee was responsible for environmental affairs. Tamir noticed the void and in 1970 promoted the establishment of the first parliamentarian nonpartisan lobby of MKs for the environment, which was quickly endorsed by sixteen MKs from across the political spectrum including MKs from the Communist Party (Maki) and the Jewish Ultra-Orthodox Party Agudat Israel (32). Later in 1972, after a concentrated lobbying effort, environmental affairs gained heightened recognition as the first subcommittee for the environment and ecology was formed (The Biosphere 1982, 12; Tamir 1985, 147). MK Tamir was appointed as the subcommittee's first chairman (Knesset website).

Finally, two years later Tamir's advocacy for a permanently binding parliamentary committee ended in success, after the parliamentary Interior Committee was formally transformed into the Interior and Environment Committee and was given the authority over environmental affairs. Tamir retained chairmanship of the Interior and Environment Committee for the duration of the eighth Knesset (Knesset website). Under this formal parliamentary umbrella, Tamir had ample opportunity to promote a great variety of national, and even regional, environmental initiatives through private law proposals, parliamentary questions, and parliamentary appeals to the public.

When asked why he decided to dedicate his parliamentary and later years to the environment, Tamir replied that two actions taken in the early days of the state by David Ben-Gurion, the first prime minister of Israel, caused a shift in his awareness. "The first was the annulment of the rural councils that were responsible for the conservation of open lands (Tamir during his youth was head of the Rural Council, Petach Tikva). The second was the draining of the Hula "swamp." The Hula wetlands that were vital in preserving the ecological and limnological balance of the Kinneret water basin were drained as part of the Zionist campaign to combat malaria and reclaim additional land for agriculture. The consequences however were disastrous (Tal 2002, 116). Tamir described the decision as "Stalinist in nature. . . . This was an action of unprecedented cruelty that hurt the natural world and the scenic environment on a global scale. I could not accept the position that perceived nature only as a tool for man's use" (Tamir 2006, 34). The draining of the Hula ultimately not only proved to be a turning point in Tamir's environmental consciousness, but has been described as a decisive moment in shaping the perspective of the founders of Israel's Society for the Protection of Nature, and later a fledgling environmental movement. As Tal colorfully put it: "A swamp is lost but a society is born" (Tal 2002, 115).

Tamir was one of the only MKs of his time to demand special sessions of the parliamentary plenum focusing on environmental issues. He was the first to raise many environmental issues but was particularly engaged with Israel's ever-growing water problems. In 1971 Tamir brought the issue of "the risks of contamination and ecological disruption of Lake Kinneret" to the parliament assembly (Goldshtein 2002, 51). The Kinneret, Israel's only freshwater lake supplying some 25 percent of water consumption, at the time was under threat of contamination, salification, and liminological disruption. After giving a heartfelt speech at the plenum, the Knesset assembly empowered the environmental subcommittee under Tamir's chairmanship to bring forth recommendations. In 1972 recommendations by the subcommittee were placed on the Knesset agenda that concluded, "immediate action needs to be taken to improve the quality of water in the Kinneret otherwise there is a substantial threat that its waters will become toxic and unsuitable for drinking." Among its operative recommendations, the committee called for an increase in the existing supervision over the various users of the lake waters including the municipalities around the lake basin, requiring them to use their authorities to prevent the discharge of wastewater into the lake (Goldshtein 2002, 54; Tamir 1985, 219–28).

Tamir was also preoccupied with conserving Israel's open spaces and especially preventing urban sprawl onto Israel's agricultural land. As he put it: "what we are seeing is a crawling extermination of Israel's most prized and irreplaceable asset. Land cannot be imported!" (Goldshtein 2002, 88). As early as 1965 he was among the initiators of an amendment to the Planning and Building Law that improved the legal protection of agricultural lands through the establishment of a special committee for the "Protection of Agricultural Lands" (65). The amendment required the approval of a special committee in addition to the regular planning committees, when changing the zoning of agricultural land to nonagricultural land.

Tamir also recognized another threat to open spaces and sustainable ur-

ban planning—namely unregulated, illegal building practices on public lands
(Tamir 1985, 326–37). Consequently one of the first initiatives he took in 1965,
as a novice MK, was to propose the inclusion of administrative orders that
would allow local planning committees to overcome the legal hurdles otherwise required to demolish illegal buildings. In 1977 the proposal was accepted
and the Planning and Building Law amended, allowing local planning councils to administer administrative orders to stop illegal building and require
the removal of illegal properties (Goldshtein 2002, 95; Planning and Building
Law [amendment no. 8] 1977).

Tamir was also among the most dominant political voices in what became
the first major national struggle against urban pollution in Israel: the struggle
against the establishment of Reading D (Tamir 1985, 358–67). In 1962 the National Electricity Company first introduced its plans to convert Tel-Aviv's existing, 36 megawatt "Reading" power plant to a 500-megawatt fuel-generated
plant on the sand dunes by the Yarkon River in northwest Tel Aviv. Only in
1967 were the plans brought before the newly appointed regional planning
council, which quickly rejected the proposed site. The council demanded a
prior inquiry and that consent be given by the Ministry of Health affirm-
ing that the plant would not pose additional health risks to Tel-Aviv's inhabitants (Tal 2002, 252–56). Tamir, quickly convened a hearing of the Knesset's
Interior Committee and discovered broad-based opposition to the site (Tamir
1985, 361–62).

To circumvent the decision of the regional planning council, the government drafted a bill that authorized itself to grant permission for planning and
building of the site without the required consent of the regional and local
planning authorities (Tal 2002, 253–54). The proposed law raised a public outcry. Two hundred thousand people signed a petition opposing the Tel Aviv site
for the plant—the largest public environmental campaign to date. But the effort was in vain, the ruling Mapai party enforced strict faction discipline, the
coalition voted in favor, and the law passed. In 1969 Reading D was opened.
Later Tamir commented: "never have so few decided to condemn so many to
pollution for so many years as did Levi Eshkol, the Prime Minister that stood
behind Reading D" (Goldshtein 2002, 123).

The campaign against Reading D and other environmental nuisances developed in Tamir a sense that a change in Israel's planning and development
policy was desperately needed. For the duration of his career, both as an MK
and later as founding chairman of Life and Environment, Israel's umbrella
organization for environmental NGOs, he advocated adopting a mode of sustainable rather than destructive development, as he noted in 1971: "The Israeli
citizen is perplexed. . . . He feels that economic growth when unaccompanied
by environmental planning and the protection of quality of life is like chas-

ing a dream that is accompanied by ever growing nightmares. Today there is increased recognition that development and environmental protection do not contradict one another but rather that a balance must be struck between them" (Greenpeace 2008, 22).

Tamir spent over a decade and a half in the Knesset promoting environmental awareness. At times he experienced the occasional satisfaction of success such as in the establishment of the Parliamentary Interior and Environment Committee or with regard to his campaign for protection of agricultural lands (Tamir 1985). But he was not oblivious to the difficulties of introducing new concepts of environmental protection to "a Knesset held captive by the conventional and the inefficient governmental institutions" (150). Tamir recognized the importance of nonpartisan action on environment issues and claimed that "partisan political action would have brought to the downfall of his efforts" (150).

Environmental nonpartisanship ultimately was not a completely effective solution. It could hardly be said that Tamir's environmental zealousness infected his party colleagues or other MKs of his generation. Ultimately, he remained an anomalous political figure. When asked, he often conveyed the feeling that during his parliamentary years and the preceding years in the Tel Aviv City Council he was a lone fighter on the environmental front (Tamir 2006). He mentioned with some irony that Menachem Begin, acclaimed leader of Gahal and later Likud and prime minister from 1977 to 1983, often said when asked that in "environmental affairs Josef Tamir represents me" (Paz 2000; Tamir 2006). This to Tamir was not necessarily a statement of personal trust, but rather an indication of Begin's indifference to environmental matters and as a result a testimony of the unfulfilled potential of his campaign for environmental awareness among the Israeli leadership of the time.

Tamir's dedication to environmental issues did not end with his Knesset tenure. He continued to act as a leader and the "great grandfather" of the environmental NGO community until his death at the age of 94 in 2009 (Eldar 2009). After his departure from the Knesset he was active in forming no fewer than four central environmental NGOs and continued writing and preaching on environmental affairs throughout his lifetime (Goldshtein 2002).

NONPARTISAN ENVIRONMENTAL POLITICS IN THE 1990s AND 2000s

Another unlikely story of environmental commitment is that of the Jewish Ultra-Orthodox MK Moshe Gafni from Yahadut Ha'torah (United Torah Judaism-UTJ), who has consistently been elected among the most environmental MKs in the yearly surveys conducted by the Israel Union for Environmental Defense.[7] MK Gafni was first elected to the twelfth Knesset (1988) as a parliament member for Degel-Hatora (Flag of the Torah), that merged with another Haredi-Hasidic party Agudat Israel to form UTJ in 1992 (Arian 2005, 150–152). Since its foundation UTJ has been the most austere Jewish Ultra-Orthodox religious party with representation in the Knesset. Traditionally, UTJ representation has been determined by the rabbinical council that governs its affairs and its agenda is dominated by promoting religious education, and other socio-economic interests of the Jewish Ultra-Orthodox sector (Arian 2005, 154). With this in mind it would therefore seem surprising that Gafni has shown such steady dedication to the environmental agenda over the years.

His green fingerprint is evident in the UTJ party platform, which includes "environmental protection" as one of the only nonreligious-oriented topics covered. As the party's platform for the 2009 elections states: "In recognition of the importance of environmental protection and out of the concern for ensuring the public's health the UTJ will act to prevent environmental hazards, ecological and aesthetic damages in the land, sea and along the shores of the country, in its rivers and water basins and in the air, and will act to ensure the natural beauty of our sacred land" (Knesset website).[8] Even so, it would be incorrect to assert that Gafni's environmental zealousness has "infected" the rest of the UTJ members. Indeed, his has remained a singular voice: an unorthodox perspective in this Ultra-Orthodox party.

MK Gafni has been reelected for seven consecutive terms, including the eighteenth Knesset in 2009 (Knesset website).[9] He chaired the Interior and Environment Parliamentary Committee during the fifteenth Knesset from 1999–2003 (Knesset website).[10] During this time he held countless meetings on environmental issues and was instrumental in advancing the preparation of the Private Law Proposal for the Mediterranean Sea (Protection Development and Conservation) 2002. The law evolved and was later accepted in the sixteenth Knesset as a governmental law, named the Law for the Protection of the Coastal Environment–2004 (Israel Ministry of Environmental Protection website).[11]

Gafni was also among the initiators of the Clean Air Law Proposal of 2005 (Reshumot 2005, 126).[12] Following three years of intensive negotiations and political maneuvering, the bill evolved and was confirmed as The Clean Air Law 2008 (Sidrei Hakika 2008, 752).[13] Contrary to what may be considered as the acceptable procedure for such substantial legislation, the law was not initiated by the government, but rather was a private endeavor undertaken by a group of MKs including Omri Sharon, Gafni, and later Dov Khenin, based on a draft received from an environmental NGO—the Israel Union for Environmental Defense (IUED) (Israel Ministry of Foreign Affairs 2008).[14] The law proposal constituted a major breakthrough. Since its passage in 2008, the Clean Air Law has been widely considered to be the most important piece of environmental legislation of the last decade (Ivry-Darel 2008).

Although it would appear that Gafni would not have much to gain from environmental stewardship, in light of his political affiliation and the sociodemographic profile of his voters, Gafni remains committed to this work. He claims his "pursuit and great interest in environmental affairs results from man's obligation to conserve the world in which he lives and prevent its destruction. This obligation has various roots in Jewish sources. . . . The obligation is both personal and public. . . . As a public figure and representative I have an obligation to deal with environmental issues as an integral part of my work." Although he feels that poverty and harsh living conditions prevent many Ultra-Orthodox Jews from noticing environmental problems, "even in this social sector environmental issues are increasingly acknowledged" (interview with M. Gafni, June 2, 2010).

During the 1990s and since the new millennium the left wing of the Israeli political map bred several prominent environmental MKs, but perhaps fewer than expected, in comparison with leftist parties in Western parliaments (Kitschelt 1988). Furthermore, until 2006, right-wing MKs led more environmental initiatives than did left-wing MKs (Tal 2006, 551). Among the most notable recent green "leftists" are MK Rabbi Michael Melchior, the leader of Meimad who aligned with the Labor Party, MKs Mossi Raz and Benny Temkin of Meretz, and more recently MK Dov Khenin from Hadash, and MK Nitzan Horowitz from Meretz.

Upon the commencement of the seventeenth Knesset (2006) MK Melchior was the dominant figure in establishing the first active Environmental MKs Lobby, which he cochaired with MK Omri Sharon from the Likud and later Kadima (son of former prime minister Ariel Sharon). Melchior continued his work through the lobby in the seventeenth Knesset and cochaired it with MK Dov Khenin. The environmental lobby, like other Knesset lobbies is an informal gathering of MKs that seeks to enlist the support of its peers and governmental decision makers to intervene in environmental issues and support pro-environmental policies.[15] It is an interesting fact that in the eighteenth Knesset the social-environmental lobby was one of the largest lobbies in the Knesset in terms of MK membership, consisting of twenty MKs from across the political spectrum (Knesset website). This serves as a possible indicator of the so-called consensual status of environmental issues that allows MKs from all parties and worldviews, through joining the lobby, to publicly declare their allegiance to environmental affairs, even if this is not practiced in fact.

Membership in the environmental lobby does not entail any formal commitment or obligation to vote in favor of environmental law proposals. This has allowed the lobby to become a convenient forum for MKs to orient themselves with an environmental worldview while retaining their freedom to conform to their party's policies, voters' interests, and other expediencies that might eventually clash with environmental values (Robinson 1992 chap. 6; De-Shalit 2000, 214–20).

As to the actual importance and effect of the environmental lobby, Yossi Sarid, a former MK, head of Meretz, and former minister of Environment commented: "It is good that there is an environmental lobby, if the alternative is that there won't be one. However if asked if this lobby has significant achievements the answer would have to be that being a member of a lobby doesn't count for much. What matters is the final vote count in the plenary—and there is no necessary link between the two" (interview with Y. Sarid, former minister of Environment and Meretz Party chairman, September 2009). A different view was expressed by former MK Mossi Raz from Meretz, who is convinced of the importance of the environmental lobby in creating a perception of prominence for environmental affairs: "The lobby creates common interests among MKs from different parties. This is an extremely significant achievement. It creates empathy and supports the Minister of Environment and in that way helps promote a wide environmental platform" (interview with M. Raz, September 2009).

MK Mossi Raz served as an MK in the fifteenth Knesset on behalf of Meretz for only a short period between March 2000 and February 2003 (Knesset website). However brief his tenure, Raz obtained an impressive environmental track record and was mentioned consecutively in IUED's list of excelling environmental MKs (IUED 2000–2001). He initiated several environmental law proposals that he was unable to see through, such as an amendment to the Bottles Deposit Law that was intended to widen the scope of the law and include large bottle containers. Raz is most notably remembered for his success in establishing formal representation of environmental NGOs in national statutory committees relating to environmental affairs. This was achieved through a law proposal accepted as the Law of Representation of Public Environmental Organizations 2002.[16] The law required the addition of environmental NGO representatives to public and governmental bodies and committees relating to environmental affairs—previously additions were only government and business representatives. When asked to attest to his greatest environmental achievement MK Raz replied: "It is with no doubt the Environmental NGO Representation Law, which does not compare to anything else I did. The fact that it has not only been successfully implemented but its scope widened since it was first legislated is the greatest measure of its success" (Raz interview 2009).

If legislative achievements are an indicator of the prominence of environmental MKs, then MK Dov Khenin holds a place of honor. First elected to the seventeenth Knesset in mid-2006, as a member of the communist Arab-Jewish Party, Hadash (Arian 2005, 162–63), Khenin entered the Knesset as an active leader in the environmental NGO community. Just weeks before elections he still formally held the position of chairman of Life and Environment, the umbrella organization of Israeli environmental NGOs. Although Khenin does not believe that dealing with environmental issues strengthened his political support he stipulates that "dealing with environmental issues is of utmost critical importance and in politics it is necessary to 'swim against the current' if needed" (interview with D. Khenin, June 2010).

Since his election Khenin initiated numerous proposals and amendments to existing laws, seven of which were accepted into law by 2010 (MK Dov Khenin website).[17] Two prominent examples of laws MK Khenin championed are The Polluter Pays Law 2008,[18] and the Law of Local Authorities (Environmental Enforcement—the Authorities of Inspectors) 2008.[19] The first law increased the variety of sanctions available to the environmental regulator by amending various environmental statues; it incorporated financial and administrative sanctions where previously lacking, and toughened penalties on facilities polluting without or in breach of a business license and provided a mechanism for authorizing payments by those given a license to pollute. The second law empowered the authorities of local government to enforce environmental legislation. In addition to the advancement of several important laws, MK Khenin has played an active role as cochairman of the Knesset's social-environmental lobby. In this capacity he initiated innumerous meetings and discussions on various local and national issues (Dov Khenin website) to ensure that the lobby was active and that environmental issues were constantly being raised in public profile.

DISCUSSION

The phenomenon of nonpartisan political environmentalism distinguishes the Israeli parliament from other Western parliaments, where "green ideas" and green parties are perceived to originate mainly from "new-left" ideologies (Kitschelt 1988; Mair 2001, 107; Gemenis 2009, 129).[20] As a unique feature of Israeli politics this environmentalism has brought together opponents and helped in the joining of forces, forming a singular nonpartisan effort in Israeli public domain. This uniqueness has been able to sprout unlikely partnerships, such as the one between the Communist party (Hadash) MK Dov Khenin and the Ultra-Orthodox party (UTJ) MK Moshe Gafni, who pooled their strengths in advancing the Clean Air Law. Finding such common ground would be unlikely, not only on political and security issues, but also regarding "civilian" issues like education, human rights, and even the economy.

This phenomenon is attributable to the convergence of several factors. The first is that the Knesset is an extreme example of what is referred to as the "representative democracy" model (Peretz and Doron 1997, 118–21). Parliamentarians' role is perceived first and foremost as the functional representation of their sector's interests, and not of national interests (Arian 2005, 205–7; De-Shalit 2004, 67–79). At the same time, environmental stances usually represent cross-sectoral interests or are of national importance and rarely do they embody the interests of one particular sector.[21] Hence, political capital that underlies environmental issues is extremely uncertain in Israeli politics. This is due to the coupling of the extreme representation model with the cross-sectoral nature of environmental concerns about the undiminished centrality of traditional divisions (Shamir et al. 2008, 57).

As to the political capital associated with environmentalism, in the mid-90s Dedi Tzuker, a leftist MK from Meretz, replied when asked why his party had never brought up environmental issues in any of the TV commercials before elections: "you are either crazy or naïve! No one will take me seriously if I talk about the environment" (De-Shalit 1994, 272). Less obtuse, but conveying no less the problem of political capital associated with environmentalism, MK Nitzan Horowitz from Meretz, when asked in 2009 if environmental accomplishments are a "winning ticket" in elections replied: "I can't say green issues are considered as a 'winning ticket.' They are basically considered as consensus and so it doesn't hurt the reputation of a candidate to demonstrate environmental commitment—it may even increase his personal popularity. But winning electoral gains from this is a whole different story. The public does not vote on environment in Israel. Electoral issues are essentially security, peace, to a lesser degree economics and the nexus between state and religion. But environment is and has always been a non-issue in national elections" (interview with N. Horowitz, September 2009). Dov Khenin put it directly: "Dealing with environmental issues does not to my mind strengthen the political support of those MKs that do deal with these issues" (interview with D. Khenin, 2010). Former minister of Environment Yossi Sarid bluntly commented: "Environmentalism is not and has never been a 'winning ticket.' There are MKs that deal with environmental affairs and some of them even do commendable work but their accomplishments and efforts have never gone rewarded" (interview with Y. Sarid, 2009).

The nonpartisan effort of individual MKs and the common effort exerted by the environmental lobby in the Knesset have produced important environmental legislative achievements and have been instrumental in enhancing the public profile of environmental affairs. However, environmental legislation often carries with it economic burdens and restrictions, such as taxing polluting behaviors or placing restrictions on the use of natural resources. These factors may deter some MKs from pursuing environmental legislation that they perceive as contradicting their voters' narrow interests (Robinson 1992, 169). In conclusion, it seems that the cross-sectoral character of environmentalism has attracted MKs from across the political spectrum, but in small numbers due to the dubious political capital that it offers.

THE RISE AND DEMISE OF GREEN PARTIES

There are those who contend the elevation of green issues above party politics has in fact been the downfall of Israeli political environmentalism. "Since they have not been under vigorous political debate, environmental concerns have not succeeded in becoming electoral issues. Tagging them as bi-partisan, has essentially meant that environmental issues have become a non-issue for the Israeli voter. People vote for issues that are under debate—not those that enjoy a so-called consensus," commented Mossi Raz former MK for Meretz.

The bleak reality of environmentalism as an irrelevant issue in the political party arena provided much of the motivation for the establishment of two green parties, each with distinct environmental platforms. The Greens were established in 1997, in partial response to the "tragic collapse of the bridge at the opening ceremony of the Maccabiah Games" (Greens website).[22] The collapse of the bridge was indeed one of Israel's notorious toxic-exposure disasters. Sixty-six athletes fell into the polluted waters of the Yarkon River, an event that ended with four fatalities, three of which were attributed to the exposure to the toxic mix in the river waters and riverbed (Tal 2002, 4).

One of the party's founders and an active member in its leadership, offered, however, a different account for the party's emergence: "'The Greens' were established for an almost trivial reason. Peer Visner (the head founder and party chairman), who had no previous environmental experience, had a tree cut down near his office, got annoyed and decided to establish a green party. He placed an ad in the newspaper saying that a green party had been formed" (interview with A. Lilian, member of The Greens leadership, September 2009).

The Greens ran consecutively in all national elections between 1999 and 2009. In the 1999, 2003, and 2009 elections they received the same mere 0.4 percent of the total vote count, which amounted to less than 30 percent of the votes needed to pass the threshold. In 2006 they came closest to achieving the electoral threshold when they received 1.5 percent of the total votes or 75 percent of the votes needed to pass the electoral threshold (table 8.1).

While they have failed time and again in national elections, the Greens achieved far greater success in local government elections. In 1998 they won two seats on the city council of Tel Aviv and later in the 2003 elections they were able to increase their representation to four seats. At the same time they obtained further representation in fourteen municipalities through local associated lists (Greens website). In the 2008 local elections they were able to secure some fifty representatives through twenty-two associated municipal

TABLE 8.1. Electoral outcomes for green parties in 1999–2009 national elections

THE GREENS				
	1999	*2003*	*2006*	*2009*
Number of votes	13,292	12,833	47,595	12,378
Percent of votes	0.4	0.4	1.5	0.4
Percent of electoral threshold	26	27	75	18.3
Electoral threshold (percent of votes)	1.5	1.5	2	2
Electoral threshold (number of votes)	49,672	47,226	62,742	67,470
THE GREEN MOVEMENT				
	1999	*2003*	*2006*	*2009*
Number of votes				27,737
Percent of votes				0.8
Percent of electoral threshold				41.2
Electoral threshold (percent of votes)				2
Electoral threshold (number of votes)				67,470

Source: Compiled from the Knesset central elections committee website, http://www.knesset.gov
.il/elections/index.html.

lists (Blander 2009), demonstrating a steady increase in local representation between 1998 and 2008.

In 2009 a group of environmental activists decided to form a new party called the Green Movement that would compete against the Greens in the 2009 national elections (Green Movement website).[23] The new party built on the undemocratic image of the Greens and the fact that it had never been embraced by the environmental NGO community and remained alienated from many of its prominent leaders. Justifying the formation of a competing party, respondents from the leadership of the Green Movement invoked several claims. First, and possibly most significantly, the Green Movement would be a transparent and democratically run party of activists with significant previous environmental achievements in civil society (in contrast with the Greens) (September 2009 interviews with I. Han, member of Green Movement leadership; E. Ben-Yemini, chairman of Green Movement; U. Shanas, member of Green Movement leadership; A. Dabush, member of Green Movement leadership). Some respondents stressed the ideological disparities between the Green Movement and the Greens, saying that the former had a significant focus on a social and economic agenda while the latter did not (2009 interviews with E. Ben-Yemini, A. Bell, U. Shanas). Most respondents claimed the Green Movement to be part of the Israeli Left in the orientation and profile of its members (2009 interviews with Ben-Yemini, A. Bell, U. Shanas).

In their first attempt at national elections, and just months after the Green Movement had been formally established, it formed a coalition with Meimad (headed by former MK Melchior) to run in the national elections. The Green

Movement won only 41 percent of the votes needed to pass the threshold. Although the rivalry between the Greens and the Green Movement might have impaired their chances, the fact remains that these parties did not receive together even 60 percent of the needed votes to pass the threshold, a figure less than what was achieved in the 2006 elections by the Greens alone.

Indeed after over a decade of green party politics the Greens and the Green Movement were unable to secure the needed votes to pass the electoral threshold in the national elections. Whether the successful results in municipal elections reflect possible trends in future national representation remains doubtful. Blander (2009) claims that the results of the 2008 municipal elections and later the 2009 national elections reinforce the existing trend of decoupling of local and national voting patterns (Blander 2009). While voters in municipal elections weigh local considerations, placing quality of life and the environment at the center of their decision, considerations are substantially different in national elections. In national elections the voters are much more likely to worry about national security and territorial issues; the environment remains a marginal issue. At the same time, as ideological identification with national partisan politics has subsided due to dealignment, national parties have lost their hold in municipal politics (Elazar 2001, 27–26).

Although Israel has seen some exceptional political leaders willing to dedicate their careers to environmental issues, they have remained an exception. These true believers have not come distinctively from parties associated with the Left and have forged unique political alliances and cooperation on environmental issues. They have demonstrated environment to be a nonpartisan agenda capable of producing one of the only consensual goals in Israeli politics.

At the same time the Israeli parliament has yet to see environmental activity by distinctively green parties. Dealignment weakened considerably the two largest Israeli parties (Shamir and Arian 2004, 41–48), but the realignment process did not substantially improve the prospects of green parties being elected. The dominance of the traditional political cleavages and especially security and territorial issues, has endured (Shamir and Arian 2004, 28–32), leaving environmentalism as a "peripheral" issue at best.

Israel's proportional electoral system has not contributed to the success of green parties as would have been expected (Richardson and Rootes 1995, 18). The so-called advantage of the proportional system has been almost entirely obscured by the dominant cleavages and the political barriers they create (Doron and Moshe 1989). Consequently, future developments in Israeli environmental party politics will greatly depend on whether there is a solution to the geopolitical conflicts that have characterized the region for over a century. If peace is to be achieved, there may be an opening for environmental issues to become more dominant in the national political agenda of parties and in the minds of the voters, possibly allowing for a green party to pass the electoral threshold in future elections.

NOTES

1. The Israeli Parliament is called the Knesset. Throughout this chapter members of the Israeli Parliament will be referred to as members of Knesset or MKs.

2. Knesset website: http://www.knesset.gov.il.

3. Yuri Shtern website: http://www.yurishtern.org.il.

4. Adam Teva Vadin website: http://www.adamteva.org.il.

5. Life and Environment website: http://www.sviva.net.

6. These MKs include, but are not limited to, Shimon Kanovich (see Tal 2002, 62), who was the legislator of the first air and noise pollution abatement statute; MK Yizhar Smilansky, a renowned novelist who was largely responsible for passing the landmark legislation that established the nature reserves system (see Tal 2002, 15); MK Yossi Sarid, who served as the fifth minister of Environment and assumed the role of the environmental icon of the 1990s (see Tal 2002, 297–317).

7. The Israel Union for Environmental Defense (IUED) is Israel's leading environmental advocacy organization. Since 2000 it has compiled periodical reports on environmentally related activities of Knesset members and factions. The reports rank environmental leaders and laggards among MKs according to various parameters such as, law proposals, voting records, parliamentary questions, and motions for the agenda. For example see IUED, *Summary Report for the Third and Forth Seats of the 15 from May 2001 to March 2002*, on file with author.

8. See http://www.knesset.gov.il/elections/knesset15/yahaduthatorah_m.htm; UJT 2009 platform. In Hebrew.

9. See http://www.knesset.gov.il/mk/eng/mk_eng.asp?mk_individual_id_t=35.

10. See http://www.knesset.gov.il/mk/heb/mk.asp?mk_individual_id_t=35.

11. Law for the Protection of the Coastal Environment 2004, http://www.sviva.gov.il/bin/en.jsp?enPage=e_BlankPage&enDisplay=view&enDispWhat=Object&enDispWho=Articals^l3422&enZone=mar_qual.

12. Clean Air Law Proposal, 111 *Reshumot-Law Proposals—the Knesset* December 19, 2005, p. 126.

13. Clean Air Law 2008, 2174 *Sideri-Hakika*, December 7, 2008, p. 752.

14. Israel Ministry of Foreign Affairs, *Knesset Approves Clean Air Law*, July 30, 2008. http://www.mfa.gov.il/MFA/Israel+beyond+politics/Knesset%20Approves%20Clean%20Air%20Law%2030-Jul-2008.

15. As such Knesset protocol does not interfere with the work of the lobbies. At the Knesset website, see Lobbies in the Knesset. http://www.knesset.gov.il/lexicon/eng/lobby_eng.htm.

16. Law of Representation of Public Environmental Organizations 2002, Book of Laws 1879 (25.11.2008), p. 118. http://www.sviva.gov.il/Enviroment/Static/Binaries/law/klali33_1.pdf.

17. Dov Khenin website: http://www.dovblog.org.

18. Law for Protection of the Environment (the Polluter Pays) (Law Amendments)

2008, Rules Book 2181 (August 11, 2008), p. 858. http://www.sviva.gov.il/Enviroment/Static/Binaries/law/klali60_1.pdf.

19. Law of Local Authorities (Environmental Enforcement—the Authorities of Inspectors) 2008, Rules Book 2155 (August 6, 2008), p. 534. http://www.sviva.gov.il/Enviroment/Static/Binaries/law/klali55_1.pdf.

20. It is important to carefully distinguish between "left" and "new left" ideologies, as a central assertion is that "green ideas" simply cannot be placed on the conventional left-right spectrum —"The conventional politics of left, right and centre are like a three lane motorway with all vehicles heading in the same direction. . . . Greens feel that it is the very direction that is wrong" (Porritt 1984, 43).

21. Referring to cross-sectoral interest does not mean that all sectors are hurt equally from environmental deterioration, rather that all sectors are hurt to some extent.

22. The Greens website: http://www.greenparty.co.il.

23. The Green Movement website: http://www.yeruka.org.il.

REFERENCES

Adam Teva Vadin. "The Environmental Quality Index of the Knesset March 2006–March 2007." http://www.adamteva.org.il/_Uploads/dbsAttachedFiles/madadsvivati.pdf.

Arian, A. 2005. *Politics in Israel: The Second Republic.* 2nd ed. Washington, D.C.: CQ Press.

Arian A., and M. Shamir. 2008. *The Elections in Israel 2006.* Jerusalem: Israel Democracy Institute.

Blander, D. 2009. "Is There a Connection between Local Elections in 2008 and National Elections in 2009?" Jerusalem: Israeli Democracy Institute. http://www.idi.org.il/breakingnews/pages/breaking_the_news_82.aspx.

Carter, N. 2010. "The Greens in the 2009 European Parliament Election." *Environmental Politics* 19 (2): 295–302.

Dalton, R. J. 1984. "Electoral Change in Advanced Industrial Democracies." In *Electoral Change in Advanced Industrial Democracies: Realignment or Dealignment?,* edited by R. J. Dalton, P. A. Beck, and S. C. Flanagan. Princeton: Princeton University Press.

———. 2000. "The Decline of Party Identifications." In *Parties without Partisans,* edited by R. J. Dalton and Wattenberg, 19. Oxford: Oxford University Press.

De-Shalit, A. 1994. "Where Do Environmentalists Hide?" In *Our Shared Environment, Conference Proceedings,* edited by R. Twite and J. Isaac. Jerusalem: IPCRI.

———. 1995. "From the Political to the Objective: The Dialectics of Zionism and the Environment." *Environmental Politics* 4: 70–87.

———. 2000. *The Environment: Between Theory and Practice.* Oxford: Oxford University Press.

———. 2004. *Red-Green: Democracy, Justice and the Environment.* Tel Aviv: Babel. In Hebrew.

Doron, G., and M. Moshe. 1989. "Hasamey Knisa." Tel Aviv: Papirus. In Hebrew.

Dryzek, S. J. 1997. *The Politics of the Earth.* Oxford: Oxford Press.

Eisenstadt, S. N. 2004. *Explorations in Jewish Historical Experience: The Civilizational Dimension.* Leiden: Brill.

Elazar, D. 2001."The Local Dimension of Governance and Politics in Israel." In *Hashilton Hamekomi Be'Israel*, edited by D. Elazar and H. Klehaim, 1–38. Jerusalem: Jerusalem Center for Public Affairs and the State. In Hebrew.

Eldar, E. 2009. "A Green Soul—Nobody Listened to Josef Tamir and Now We Are Paying the Price." *Maariv-Zeman* (Tel Aviv), February 9. http://www.nrg.co.il/online/1/ART1/935/097.html#after_maavaron.

Gemenis, K. 2009. "A Green Comeback in Greece? The Ecologist Greens in the 2007 Parliamentary Election." *Environmental Politics* 18 (1): 128–34.

Goldshtein, Y. 2002. *Betraying the Promised Land, the Socio-Economic Threat.* Ketter Pub.

Greenpeter, M. A. 2008. "Josef-Tamir—'Mr Environment'" *Epoch-Times, Israel*, December 12. http://www.epochtimes.co.il/news/content/view/10194/92/.

Inglehart, R. 1977. *The Silent Revolution: Changing Values and Political Styles Among Western Publics.* Princeton: Princeton University Press.

Israel Ministry of Foreign Affairs. 2008. "Knesset Approves Clean Air Law." http://www.mfa.gov.il/MFA/Israel+beyond+politics/Knesset%20Approves%20Clean%20Air%20Law%2030-Jul-2008.

IUED. Summary of 2000–2001 Report on Knesset, on file with author.

Karamichas, J., and I. Botetzagias. 2003. "Green Party Factionalism: The Case of the Federation of Ecologists Alternatives (FEA) of Greece." *South European Society and Politics* 8 (3): 64–92.

Kitschelt, H. P. 1988. "Left-Libertarian Parties: Explaining Innovation in Competitive Party Systems." *World Politics* 40 (2): 194–234.

Koren, D., and B. Shapira. 1997. *Coalitions.* Tel Aviv: Zmora-Bitan. In Hebrew.

Mair, P. 2001. "The Green Challenge and Political Competition: How Typical Is the German Experience?" *German Politics* 10 (2): 99–116.

Paz, D., ed. 2000. "Mr. Environment, 85 Jubilee Edition" ("Life and Environment" & the Israeli Economic Forum for Environmental Quality).

Peretz, D., and D. Gideon. 1997. *The Government and Politics of Israel.* Boulder: Westview Press.

Porritt, J. 1984. *Seeing Green.* Oxford: Blackwell.

Richardson, D., and C. Rootes. 1995. *The Green Challenge: The Development of Green Parties in Europe.* London: Routledge.

Robinson, M. 1992. *The Greening of British Party Politics.* Manchester: Manchester University Press.

Shamir, M., and A. Arian. 2004. "A Dominant Party in a Dealigning Party System?" In *The Elections in Israel 2003*, edited by M. Shamir and A. Arian. Jerusalem: Israel Democracy Institute. In Hebrew.

Shamir M., R. Ventura, A. Arian, and O. Kedar. 2008. "Kadima—Forward in a Dealigned Party System." In *The Elections in Israel 2006*, edited by M. Shamir and A. Arian, 25–61. Jerusalem: Israel Democracy Institute. In Hebrew.

Sternhell, Z. 2009. "Starting from the Beginning." *Haaretz*, August 23. http://www.haaretz.co.il/hasite/spages/1109383.html.

Tal, A. 2002. *Pollution in the Promised Land.* Berkeley: University of California Press.

———. 2006. *The Environment in Israel.* Tel Aviv: Hakibbutz Hameuchad. In Hebrew.

Tamir, J. 1985. *Haver Knesset. [Member of Knesset].* Jerusalem: Ahiabar. In Hebrew.

———. 2006. *The Enemy from Within.* In Hebrew.

Service for Environmental Protection. 1982. *The Biosphere* 11 (8): 12.

Van Der Heijden, H.-A. 1999. "Environmental Movements, Ecological Modernization and Political Opportunity Structures." *Environmental Politics* 8 (1): 199–221.

Yishay, Y. 2003. *Between Recruitment and Reconciliation: The Civil Society in Israel.* Jerusalem: Carmel. In Hebrew.

CHAPTER NINE

ENVIRONMENTAL CHALLENGES FACING ARAB SOCIETY IN ISRAEL

Hussein Tarabeih

A RAB SOCIETY IN ISRAEL is exposed to a unique array of environmental challenges that are due to the sector's political and economic status as minorities in the state. Before the establishment of the State of Israel in 1948, Arabs owned approximately 95 percent of the private land in Palestine (excluding what is now the Occupied Palestinian Territory or the West Bank and Gaza) (Khalidi 1992). Today, Arab society in Israel constitutes approximately 18 percent of the total population (2008 Report of the Israeli Central Bureau of Statistics), but it owns less than 4 percent of the total land area.[1] As will be discussed throughout the chapter, the issue of land confiscation is the driving factor behind the majority of environmental problems in the Arab sector. In addition, socioeconomic processes such as rapid urbanization of Arab-Israeli towns and the political climate (as evidenced by ongoing conflicts with the Occupied Palestinian Territories, Syria, and Lebanon) combine to intensify environmental conflicts. Due to urbanization, lack of immigration, high birthrates, increasing standards of living, and geographically constricted jurisdictions, Arab towns require additional land for residential developments, public institutions, commercial developments, environmental infrastructure, and public parks (Yiftachel 2000; Ozacky-Lazar and Ghanem 2003).

There is increasing pressure for construction and infrastructure development along roads. Projects routinely invade open space either without planning or without taking into account future plans, safety and environmental considerations, and nature, landscape, heritage and cultural values. Increased construction and infrastructure generate a wide range of environmental conflicts within the towns and in meeting zones with neighboring Jewish towns, causing substantial damage to quality of life and environment, partially evidenced by numerous complaints from Arab and Jewish residents (Sofer and Gal 1995; Towns Association for Environmental Quality-Agan Beit Natufa 2009).

Environmental conflicts that develop within and around Arab towns are intensified by the Jewish-Arab geopolitical dispute, governmental policy that perpetuates division between Arab and Jewish populations, and a belief within the Arab community that most of their land has been seized since the establishment of the state for developing the Jewish sector (Rouhana 1997; Hoffman 1982; Yiftachel 1995, 2000; Shmueli 2008; Tarabeih 2008). Clearly, environmental challenges in the Arab-Israeli community can be considered within the framework of environmental justice.

In this chapter, the environmental conditions experienced by the Arab population in Israel will be described along with the drivers for the disparities that exist between its reality and that of the Jewish majority.

TRADITIONAL ARAB LAND DEVELOPMENT

Spatial development of Arab villages in Israel and Palestine historically (and even as late as the 1990s) has followed a pattern of private land expanding in sections from a center in concentric circles. This spatial pattern of expansion is not planned through a municipality, but rather results from individual initiatives to construct additional family residences and to expand commercial and agricultural endeavors. The aggregation of individual building initiatives creates an urban disorganization that poses challenges for creating infrastructures for public services including drinking water, sewer-system drainage, trash collection, and transportation. The patchwork of various land uses also created, and continues to create, problems characteristic to traditional societies—problems that grew in complexity as populations grew (Tarabeih 2008). These problems were then compounded when the villages and towns sought to expand beyond their municipal boundaries. Villages did not have public land, and when towns grew to become small cities, local governments were unable to secure additional land to meet these needs, as will be discussed in the sections below.

ISRAELI ENVIRONMENTAL ADMINISTRATION AND THE ARAB SECTOR

Israeli history of addressing environmental challenges is primarily a history of its Jewish sector. The Israeli government acknowledged, in 1993, that environ-

mental progress in the Arab sector was behind that of the Jewish sector. Yossi
Sarid, the minister of the Environment at the time, delivered the following
statement to the Knesset (Israeli Parliament) during Environmental Quality
Week: "The Ministry of Environment is now emphasizing an increase in its
activity in the Arab sector. For years, the topic of environmental quality has
been neglected in this sector, at the levels of environmental administration,
environmental infrastructure and public awareness of this topic" (Sarid 1993).
This statement marked the beginning of environmental intervention in the
Arab sector, starting with the establishment of seven regional environmental-
quality units and town associations.

Before the establishment of the Ministry of Environment in 1989, town
associations and municipal environmental-quality agencies managed and implemented environmental programs under the Ministry of Interior. However,
these environmental-management programs did not include municipalities in
the Arab sector. The absence of environmental management in the Arab sector manifested itself in the disregard of environmental impacts in the sector's
planning processes. There are many examples[2] of infrastructure projects that
were approved without meeting basic environmental conditions that are req-
uisite according to national planning and building laws, including industrial
areas or environmental projects (Tarabeih 2008).

The subsequent establishment of environmental units in certain regions
of the Arab sector, including the Sakhnin Valley, Beit Hakerem Valley, Nazareth, the Northern and Southern Triangle, Carmel Ridge, Jat, Yanuh and
Kesra Smea, Tamra and Shfaram, Rahat, and others, has promoted awareness
of environmental issues among decision makers in Arab towns that had previously been neglected. A substantial proportion of environmental problems,
however, have yet to be resolved due to the lack of funding, approved plans,
and updated bylaws. Many development projects in the Arab sector continue
to occur without consideration of environmental impacts.

LAND OWNERSHIP AND THE GEOPOLITICAL CONTEXT

Because the politically motivated land confiscation and the restriction of Arab
development is the primary driver of Arab-Israeli environmental conflicts, we
must address how the geopolitical events unfolded since the founding of the
State of Israel in 1948. Table 9.1 is a time line that demonstrates the chronology
of important events and their impacts on the Arab Israeli environmental situation. As table 9.1 demonstrates, along with land confiscation came discriminatory policies that created a great disparity between Arab and Jewish towns
not only in land area, but also education, health, and environmental budgets.

TABLE 9.1. Time line of relevant events that intensified tensions between
the Arab minority and the State of Israel

Year	Event	Significance
1948	State of Israel established	Hundreds of thousands of Arabs and Palestinians displaced; their homes and lands seized for Jewish dispersion.
1969	Redistribution of land from Arab owners to State of Israel	Land belonging to Arabs living in Israel confiscated by the national government.
1970s	More Arab lands confiscated by the government	Arab towns begin urbanization process.
1970s	Ministry of Interior, Environmental Protection oversees environmental issues	The department establishes environmental units in the Jewish sector, but not in the Arab sector. Jewish land development, on confiscated Arab lands, has superior urban planning and zoning compared with Arab sector as authorities work to prepare infrastructure before residents locate to the area. This confiscation and development continues throughout the 1980s.
1976	Land Day occurs (from 1976, commemorated annually on March 30)	This marks first uprising against land confiscation within Israel. In parallel, Arab farmers begin planting olive trees on their undeveloped land to prevent Israeli government from confiscation (if nothing planted, then available for confiscation).
1980	Israel begins establishing Jewish regional councils that can solidify control and land confiscation from Arab towns	Arab citizens who own land now must get permission from Jewish regional councils and planning authorities to develop land for individual use requiring construction (e.g., home building, animal husbandry, etc.). This causes a shift in focus of the conflict from state level to regional level, as Arabs must turn to local Jewish authorities to get permission to expand municipal lands for public and private use.
1980s	Israel implements "Judaization" plan	Jewish settlements established adjacent to and encircling Arab towns (a plan known as Judaization of the Galilee, Negev, and Triangle—a geopolitical effort to infuse a majority of Jews into areas predominantly inhabited by Arabs). National funds channeled to development of the Jewish sector, resulting in growing disparity between Arab and Jewish budgets for education, health, and environmental programs.
1989	Ministry of Environment established	Indicative of paradigm shift in the Jewish sector, in which environmental impact is gaining governmental awareness.
1990s	Peace process between Arabs and Israel	Government policy starts to change, including encouraging establishment of regional environmental units, the first being in Sakhnin (in 1993, converted to a Towns Association as a statutory body in 1996).
2000	Second Intifada	Arab uprising against Israel state oppression results in increased violence, which causes further security measures to be implemented against the Arab population within Israel and Palestine; tensions increase.

Source: www.mossawacenter.org.

ENVIRONMENTAL PROBLEMS

Arab municipalities are plagued by problems that further exacerbate their environmental concerns. Poor availability and low quality of environmental infrastructure negatively affects the ability of the industrial and commercial sectors to meet environmental standards. Arab municipalities that try to allocate land beyond their jurisdiction for uses such as industry, occupation, leisure, animal husbandry, and environmental infrastructure are often unable to successfully negotiate with Jewish authorities that control most of the land surrounding Arab towns. Thus, the towns are becoming increasingly dense with a wide range of incompatible uses. For example, there are multiple examples of industries operating without business licenses, small factories and livestock farms located within residential areas, and sewage and waste-treatment infrastructure constructed without permits or environmental impact studies (Shenhar and Tarabeih 2003; Tarabeih 2008). The Arab sector also lacks pollution-reducing or efficient technology and lacks public awareness needed to demand the mitigation of harmful environmental impacts. Environmental hazards originating within Arab localities affect neighboring Jewish municipalities, which can create friction between the Arab and Jewish populations. Due to geopolitics and the struggle over land between Arab and Jewish communities, associated environmental conflicts threaten potential for coexistence of the two societies (Tarabeih 2008).

As Israel's Arab society transitions from rural to urban lifestyles, various new hazards are emerging, and existing environmental problems are worsening. Land, water, sanitation and animal husbandry issues, many of which are not major problems for Jewish municipalities, abound within this sector (Tarabeih 2008).

One predominant environmental nuisance is the transformation of traditional agricultural plots to yards of asphalt and concrete. Arab towns have fewer orchards than they did historically. Orchards were characteristic of the traditional rural setting but since the 1980s, Arab citizens have overdeveloped their urban properties because much of their land is confiscated and permission to develop land outside of Arab township limits is denied (even if the land is privately owned by Arabs). By removing orchards and garden areas of their residences to build homes for their families, they deplete the urban area of any open land.

Though vegetation is being planted, its extent is less than that in Jewish towns. Furthermore, Arab municipalities typically lack the capacity to maintain public gardens. The sector continues to have problems with animal farming within city limits. Most alarming is the serious problem of dumping waste within towns. The municipalities face a severe shortage of open public spaces because planning committees often do not consider urban open spaces important in light of landownership issues and lack of public awareness. Many areas also lack proper water drainage systems, which causes olfactory and mosquito nuisances. The illegal use of sewers intensifies disputes with the municipality since treatment facilities cannot handle the excess flow, particularly during the winter months. A related issue is drainage of olive oil residuals from modern olive oil presses to central sewer systems. Previously, the press comprised stones using animal labor, a dry technology that did not use water. In the current process, which requires water in the production process, the acidic content from the waste is detrimental to the wastewater-treatment process. Concerning sewage, the current effort to connect all homes to proper sewer systems requires infrastructure construction that will take several more years to be complete. There are also neighborhoods connected to central sewer systems without treatment facilities, causing severe groundwater pollution (Israel Ministry of Environment 2006, 2007; Adam Teva Vaden 2010 Report).

SOURCES OF ENVIRONMENTAL CONFLICTS

The lack of a competent, well-funded government-supported environmental management program in the Arab sector, combined with the environmental hazards described previously, yields a variety of environmental conflicts. These continue to simmer. Tension between Arab towns and their Jewish and Arab neighbors results from the perceived imbalances between environmental development and land distribution in the Arab and Jewish sectors (e.g., Karmiel and Misgav, a Jewish city and a regional council, that control 2,500 and 20,000 hectares of land, respectively, compared with 950 and 850 hectares in Sakhnin and Arrabe). As time goes on, Arab townships desire to attain environmental conditions similar to those typically found in Jewish communities, such as industrial areas, public gardens, and modern development and infrastructure.

Much of the land that Arab municipalities need to develop infrastructure for residential or public purposes falls under the jurisdiction of the Jewish authorities, as evidenced by the various conflicts between the Sakhnin Valley Arab towns (Sakhnin, Dier Hanna, Arrabe, and others) and the Misgav Regional Council. In the 1990s, the regional council of Misgav created an industrial zone on what was partially agricultural land privately owned by the Arab residents of Sakhnin (Sakhnin Municipality Planning Archive 2006). The Sakhnin Valley Arab municipalities seek to allocate land as industrial areas, sewage system plant areas, residential areas, animal husbandry areas, public parks, and so forth. Arabs who tried to utilize their private lands that had been subsumed by the industrial area were not allowed to access it for any purpose. Instead, the Arab lands are left as open space within industrial areas and cannot be developed.

For example, since 1995 the Arab towns within the Sakhnin Valley have struggled to convince the Misgav Regional Council to implement the Arab community's solution to the problem of animal husbandry within city limits—a major cause of environmental and health problems. The towns collectively determined to allocate a portion of their lands beyond the city limits, but that either belonged to Arab individuals or to the State of Israel, for the sole purpose of animal husbandry. These lands, including those of Arab private landowners, however, fall under the jurisdiction of the Misgav Regional Council. The council has continuously denied all requests by Arabs to use the lands outside of the city limits for any purpose (Tarabeih 2008). Because of this, the citizens within Arab towns are forced to continue their animal husbandry within the city limits, often in residential areas, further exacerbating existing environmental and health problems. This scenario is indicative of the situation for all Arab towns in Israel (Towns Association 2009).

One major root cause of environmental conflicts in meeting zones between Arab and Jewish populations is the reality of underallotment of land to Arab communities and overallotment of land to Jewish communities. Conflicts over land use and development occur between regional or municipal councils and local landowners. For example, Misgav Regional Council, which governs the lands surrounding Sakhnin municipality, controls 200,000 dunams for approximately 20,000 residents. This developed area includes businesses and recreational areas, including some of the best open spaces in the country. Neighboring towns such as Sakhnin, Tamra, Arrabe, and Shfaram, whose populations range from 20,000 to 60,000 each, manage a jurisdictional area of approximately 10,000 dunams each. These dense areas have a great shortage in industry, employment, public buildings, and services (interview with S. Osman, March 15, 2010).

The Israeli government has annexed thousands of dunams of Arab-owned land and declared them as nature reserves, national parks, and archeological sites in the Galilee triangle and in the Negev. Frequently, Arab landowners are under Jewish municipal jurisdiction or regional planning authorities or both. Regulatory bodies have also imposed limits on uses of private lands, which many Arab landowners understand as an imposition on their freedom[3] (Tarabeih 2008).

In most cases there is no open public land within the jurisdiction of Arab towns, so the only land potentially available for development or public use is under Jewish control. Arab towns with quickly growing populations are constrained in their ability to expand since the majority of land is either privately owned or controlled by the state or semigovernmental bodies. A substantial proportion of environmental conflicts between Arab and Jewish communities in Israel are intensified by the lack of available land for development of public infrastructure. Since the environmental conflict often revolves around land control, these disputes become a bone of contention in local communities, absorbing dimensions of geopolitical and majority-minority conflicts. Typically, when these conflicts are expressed, the Arab side has been represented by individuals, in contrast to the Jewish side, which is represented by the establishment—municipalities, regional councils, the Israel Land Administration, planning and building committees, the Jewish National Fund (JNF), the Nature and Parks Authority (NPA), and other bodies. The implications of this are that the Jewish sector has the more powerful negotiating position in all matters concerning land allocation, jurisdiction, and land use.

For example, from 2004 to 2008, the citizens of Wadi Salame participated in the first environmental mediation process in Israel regarding the declaration of Wadi Salame as a national park. This declaration would have resulted in the displacement of the residents from their homes (which their families had owned for two hundred years) and prevented the cultivation of their lands. After several rounds of negotiations in the mediation process between the stakeholders and the mediators, the Arab and Jewish parties agreed on several points, but not all the stakeholders signed the agreement for implementation. The decision that was made was that the citizens could remain in their existing homes, but would not able to expand their homes through additional annexes on to their current housing structures, and the next generations would have to relocate to surrounding villages. In addition, the current residents were not allowed to cultivate or develop their lands without the permission of the NPA. Within the park, the NPA would construct nature trails that dissect private lands along the stream (Tarabeih 2008).

To meet growing housing and infrastructural needs, all towns must apply for permits to increase intensity of use in open space and agricultural areas from external bodies as well as seek amendments to jurisdictional borders and national and regional land-use plans. However, Arab municipalities often face difficulties in obtaining such permission, which has significantly limited the usefulness of local planning efforts to accommodate the increase in housing and infrastructure demand. In general, Arab towns experience severe shortages of public and open land that hinder their ability to provide recreational areas, public gardens, and infrastructure. It is also increasingly difficult to meet local demand for land dedicated to animal husbandry, homes, and commercial or industrial development. Arab towns face great difficulties in negotiating joint industrial zones with Jewish communities, such as in the case of Misgav's Tardion industrial zone, as described above.

Below is a representation of how constraining the Arab-Israeli population's development to current city limits further exacerbates the geopolitical conflict and ethnic tensions between Jewish and Arab Israelis. What follows is a progression of typical Arab-Israeli land-development conflicts:

1. Arab-Israelis seek permits from municipality for animal husbandry, commercial, and industrial needs.
2. Arab municipality seeks permit from jurisdictional authority for land outside of city limits.
3. Jurisdictional authority denies permit for land outside of city limits.
4. Arab municipality denies permit for animal husbandry, commercial, and industrial purposes.
5. Arab Israelis conduct nonresidential activities from within their homes.
6. Construction and business activities within residential area lead to noise, olfactory, and sanitary complaints.
7. Complaints cause public outcry regarding Arab and Jewish land rights and environmental management imbalance.
8. Public outcry regarding imbalance leads to demonstrations in Arab sector.
9. Demonstrations in Arab sector lead to police and citizen skirmish.
10. Police and citizen skirmish results in violence and arrests.
11. Arrests increase tensions between Jewish and Arab-Israelis, deepening feelings of injustice and distrust, leading to additional confrontations and conflicts.

According to the Ministry of Environment, local enforcement departments receive a relatively large number of complaints related to animal farms and agricultural and traditional occupations within urbanized areas (Ministry of Environment, Annual Report, 2007).

In 2006, Tarabeih and Shenhar worked with the Sakhnin Valley municipalities to create a master plan to remove livestock from within the city limits to an appropriate distance from the urban areas. To do this, the master plans for towns under the Towns Association for Environmental Quality-Agan Beit Natufa (TAEQ) authority were thoroughly examined. The researchers conducted interviews with municipality leaders, planners, farmers, and representatives of farmers' associations to collect data on the problems and future needs regarding land, obstacles faced, and so forth. Stakeholders revealed that although livestock farms still provide a primary source of income for certain populations, the farms are also a source of many environmental nuisances and conflicts within the towns.

Farmers understood the environmental problems and have expressed willingness to cooperate to resolve them and avoid the negative impacts caused to the residents. At the same time, farmers were not confident that authorities would agree to prompt and equitable solutions. The aforementioned difficulties encountered in the Sakhnin Valley towns when their concerns involving animal husbandry were brought to the Misgav Regional Council serve as a good example of this phenomenon.

One analysis of the situation revealed that regional councils, planning authorities, and environmental bodies were unwilling to compromise and allocate additional land for animal husbandry outside of urbanized areas, which would reduce land pressure and environmental conflicts in the towns. It is important to note that the process of allocating land suitable for livestock rearing began in 1995. However, regional councils and the JNF objected to the allocation of land to solve environmental problems in the Arab sector. Relevant government ministries such as the Ministry of Agriculture and the Ministry of Environment are aware of the problem, although they have taken no effective action to implement solutions (Shenhar and Tarabeih 2003).

Arab towns and villages are essentially based on private landownership. Consequently, most of these built areas have an agglomeration of unregulated physical structures. Not until 1998 did the Israeli government begin initiating pilot projects for implementing urban planning and rezoning in thirty-six Arab towns (Khamaisi 2004a). As late as 2008, many Arab towns had yet to design or implement urban planning of any kind (Tarabeih 2008). This pattern poses difficulties for planning. Specifically, there are conflicts over public acquisition of land in order to build water, sewerage, electricity, and waste disposal infrastructure. Additionally, Arab municipalities have a severely limited ability to plan and manage land uses while honoring Arab traditions of private ownership, perceived as the "boundary of private sovereignty" (Khamaisi 2005). The outcomes of these public–private land conflicts are mixed land uses, forced construction of roads on private property, urban development on open space and agricultural land, and a shortage of waste and wastewater infrastructure. These outcomes result in a range of environmental hazards and nuisances such as water, air, and noise pollution; increasing exposure of the Arab population to environmental risks; and larger numbers of public complaints and conflicts between stakeholders.

Another inequality of access to natural resources is the lack of water quota allocation by the government for irrigation and agricultural development in the Arab sector. Although there is potential for irrigation with purified water from Arab towns, insufficient funding for sewer and waste treatment infrastructure has resulted in poor wastewater management, deterioration of general water quality, and increased involvement of residents in campaigns to rectify the situation.[4]

Until the 1990s, the Arab communities in Israel lacked infrastructure for wastewater treatment. Many did not have adequate municipal engineering departments. The Galilee Society was the first Arab nongovernmental organization to address environmental and health issues during the 1980s and 1990s. It provided financial support to the municipalities to plan a sewage system in the towns. Before these new systems were installed, the residents used septic tanks.

During the Oslo agreement period, the governmental policy shifted to provide funds for planning and infrastructure in Arab towns. In addition, environmental-management associations were founded during this time with funding provided by the Ministry of Environment and the Ministry of Infrastructure, which manages wastewater. From 1948 until 1993, Sakhnin was the only Arab town that had an established wastewater treatment plant, using its effluent for irrigation throughout the Sakhnin Valley. All other Arab towns sent their wastewater to Jewish kibbutzim. After 1993, when the policies changed, the Israeli government created regional solutions, although these continue to be managed by the Jewish sector.

Similar to other traditional societies throughout the world, the Arab-Israeli population is experiencing rapid modernization processes. Even villages undergoing urbanization continue to contain rural-familial elements such as the familial estate courtyard and agricultural elements such as orchards, vegetable gardens, chicken coops, cowsheds, and sheepfolds. On the intergenerational axis, the younger generation's aspirations for progress and change oppose the older generation's desire to retain traditional settings. This is manifested in a range of technologies. For instance, the older generation prefers stove chimneys, traditional charcoal-heated ovens (*taboons*), private septic systems, limited public areas, and animal husbandry; members of the younger generation do not widely share these preferences. Furthermore, the older generation tends to view the takeover of agricultural lands by commercial, residential, and industrial uses as an insult to their heritage (Khamaisi 2007), while the younger generation believes this is a natural part of the urbanization process.

Recent years have also seen a transformation in the economic means of production in Arab towns in Israel, which exhibit a dynamic similar to moshavim and kibbutzim in the Jewish sector. The number of nonagricultural jobs has increased while agriculture-related employment has decreased. As the contribution of agriculture as a means of production was declining, starting in the 1980s nonagricultural occupations began arriving in the towns.

Urbanization is also affecting those areas that remain rural; the spread of environmental hazards and nuisances into rural areas is often due to semi-industrial activities and increased private and commercial vehicle traffic. Hazards and nuisances attract the local population's attention and have become a source of conflict and public outcry (Sofer and Gal 1995; Shalev et al. 2000).

Municipalities are one of the governing bodies responsible for maintaining and improving local quality of life. Despite the anticipated benefits of decentralization and privatization (recommended by the central government), over the years Israel's central government has not provided the proper tools for achieving these goals including knowledge, local laws, and allocated budgets, to handle these responsibilities. As a result, most of the Arab townships have a problem with management and lack appropriate means and budget to properly start and complete many projects.

Improving the efficiency of public services by privatization and decentralization involves employee layoffs—a complex procedure that can have a "boomerang effect" and political consequences for the head of a municipality who chooses to fire employees. In this respect, the Arab sector is no different than the Jewish sector, except that the familial nature of the Arab sector causes elected representatives to have a strong sense of commitment to their extended family (hamula) members who may happen to be public employees. As long as the familial pull is more influential than political pressure, local enforcement and regulatory bodies remain ineffective, allowing environmental hazards and nuisances to multiply. Furthermore, when local officials lack professional training or have no commitment to an environmental agenda, the authorities' activity in the sphere of environmental regulation and planning is not effective (Khamaisi 2007).

Conflicts also occur within the Arab sector of Israel. Population growth in Arab towns is the result of high natural birthrates; this growth is accompanied by increasing consumption rates, market size, and purchasing power. Some towns undergo urbanization without changing their municipal status to a city, which results in less allocation of resources, budgets, and other services. In these cases, the town develops a form of "in situ urbanization" that is characterized primarily by the entry of urban functions into the rural space (Khamaisi 2004a; Brodnitz 1986; Kipnis 1976). In other cases, when towns grow enough to qualify for city status, they develop an "urban-village" pattern familiar in developing countries. This pattern gives rise to contradicting land uses, lifestyles and cultural, commercial, industrial, and residential patterns; when contradictions occur in close proximity, they can create a variety of environmental hazards (Kleniewski 1997). The increase in intra-town traffic, resulting from the entry of nonagricultural occupations, causes conflicts between nonagricultural and agricultural sectors. Such conflicts have a so-

cial component but are especially exacerbated by environmental hazards and
nuisances such as untreated waste and sewage, noise generation, unpleasant
odors, pests, and physical deterioration of infrastructure (Khamaisi 2004b).

The following are common environmental conflicts occurring within the
Arab sector of Israel (Tarabeih, Shmueli, and Khamaisi 2009):

1. Conflicts between neighbors regarding the positioning of cellular anten-
   nas on residential homes in the neighborhoods due to fear of radiation
   and cancer. These types of disputes can become violent, as reported by
   residents of Eilaboun, Arrabe, and Tamra, where conflicts over antenna
   location have resulted in incidents ranging from property damage to
   murder.

2. Conflicts between residents and municipalities or the Israel Electric
   Company or both regarding high-voltage power lines due to fear of
   health damage from electromagnetic radiation.

3. Conflicts regarding business and resident garbage cans that have not
   maintained proper hygienic standards resulting in olfactory nuisances,
   pests, deterioration of physical appearance, and so forth.

4. Conflicts regarding initiatives by municipalities or residents to pave
   access roads, which result in loss of land and environmental nuisances
   such as noise generation, dust, drainage problems, uprooting of old olive
   trees, and the like.

5. Conflicts regarding the connection of homes to different types of
   infrastructure (e.g., central sewer systems, water pipes, electric power
   supply, telephone lines). When lines or pipes cross private plots, there
   are often objections and conflicts.

6. Conflicts regarding planning processes conducted without public
   participation that result in mixed land uses and the entry of hazard-
   generating businesses (e.g., marble factories, welding and locksmith
   workshops, cowsheds, sheepfolds, carpentry workshops) into residential
   areas without legal business permits or licenses. This creates environmental nuisances and hazards that affect the neighbors. Additionally,
   construction of industrial zones and town markets as well as waste-
   and sewage-treatment facilities, often occurs without planning and
   consideration of the potential environmental impact.

7. Conflicts regarding social events, for example, noise from speakers at
   outdoor weddings and other events late at night and the use of fireworks
   during weddings, soccer games, and other occasions.

8. Conflicts concerning the shortage of parks, green areas, and community
   gardens in the neighborhoods.

9. Conflicts regarding the shortage of infrastructure and lack of waste management, which result in the creation of illegal waste sites in sensitive locations and disputes between different stakeholders.

CASE STUDY: SAKHNIN

In spite of the existence of environmental injustice, Israel's Arab sector has been home to numerous impressive environmental initiatives. Such an initiative is the environmental and educational programs implemented by the Towns Association for Environmental Quality in Sakhnin.

The Towns Association for Environmental Quality-Agan Beit Natufa (TAEQ) was established in 1993 as the first regional environmental unit in Israel's Arab sector. In 1996, it received formal statutory recognition according to Israel's Towns Association law. TAEQ serves six Arab towns in the Beit Natufa Basin: Sakhnin (which serves as home to the association's headquarter offices and environmental projects), Arrabe, Deir Hanna, Eilabun, Kaukab Abu El-Hija, and Bueina Nujidat, encompassing a population of approximately seventy thousand residents and a jurisdictional area of 6,000 hectares (15,000 acres). The TAEQ implements various educational and research programs to raise awareness within the Arab society regarding the need for environmental protection on all levels. TAEQ's activities are financially supported

FIGURE 9.1. The Center for Environmental Research and Education, Sakhnin. From the Center for Environmental Research and Education, Sakhnin; Hussein Tarabeih, director, TAEQ.

by various national and international organizations and institutions, including the Ministry of Environment, European Union, Beracha Foundation, Olive Stone Foundation, Karev Foundation, Green Net, and others.

Through technology implementation, management services, and consultation with the participating municipalities, TAEQ has initiatives in the following areas: environmental planning, solid-waste treatment, sewage treatment, agriculture and sustainable development, enforcement and supervision of environmental and planning regulations, education, research and development, and the demonstration of modern environmental technologies.

The TAEQ administers and implements its projects on three levels, simultaneously addressing needs at the local, regional, and transboundary international level. There are six Arab member towns within the association, with rotating responsibility for its municipal administration. This model immediately sets the stage for collaboration with representatives from the different townships. The regional dimension is manifested in the several projects that have been carried out in the Jewish sector and in partnership with other Jewish organizations and institutions. For example, TAEQ's educational initiatives began small in scope and only in the Arab community, but have since expanded to include Jewish schools, colleges, universities, and municipalities throughout Israel. About one-third of the participants in its educational activities come from the Jewish sector. Interestingly enough, this participation did not collapse even during periods of tension between the two ethnic groups during and after the Second Intifada of October 2000 (Tarabeih 2008). In fact, Shimon Peres visited the TAEQ headquarters in Sakhnin during this tense time. The Jewish-Arab cooperation achieved in the field of environmental education, in which there are broad understandings that are undisputed by the sectors, created the opportunity to include in the curriculum subjects and principles such as acknowledgment and respect for the other, and the significance of cooperation and dialogue as tools for the achievement of common goals (Tarabeih 2008).

Capitalizing on the success of the first two levels, TAEQ has in recent years won proposals to work across international lines, with countries including the Palestinian Authority, Turkey, Egypt, Jordan, and the United States, as well as the European Union.

In addressing the local and regional environmental challenges, TAEQ has had a series of successful programs throughout its fifteen years of existence. Based on its experience, it quickly became evident to TAEQ's leaders that environmental conflict resolution was a key to solving many environmental disputes both locally and regionally. The culmination of TAEQ's conflict resolution efforts, and the highlight of its international effectiveness, was its involvement in the 1994 peace talks between Israel, the Palestinian Authority, and Jordan. TAEQ staff participated in the bilateral negotiations on professional environmental topics that were part of the peace accord with Jordan. This led to the establishment of the Center for Environmental Technologies, which was developed as a cornerstone for regional professional cooperation. Thereafter, in 2007, as part of the preparations for the Annapolis peace conference, TAEQ's director participated in the bilateral Israeli-Palestinian committee that prepared a draft of the environmental accord between the parties. These occasions tapped into the constructive role that Arab-Israelis can play in promoting peace (Bang 2009).

Israel's Arab population continues to face environmental hazards within a geopolitical context and ongoing imbalances in programmatic support and government funding. Challenges surrounding governmental structure and resource allocation, rapid urbanization, and majority-minority relationships intensify the environmental conflicts experienced by Arab towns. The impact on land development can be seen in the extensive infrastructure construction, expansion of the built-up area of the towns, and increased business and economic activities. The process is occurring without environmental planning, which results in a mixture of incompatible land uses. The fact that businesses and factories do not meet environmental standards, along with the lack of sufficient enforcement of existing environmental regulations, generates environmental nuisances and hazards for residents and other stakeholders. Many of these environmental problems only began to surface in the 1990s. Accordingly, they are new and unique to Arab society, causing a new category of conflicts within the towns.

For the most part, there is insufficient infrastructure capacity to meet the constantly growing needs within Arab towns in Israel. Increasing population and construction pressures result in extensive loss of open space and spillover construction outside approved town jurisdictions. To a certain extent, the demand for additional land for construction outside Arab town jurisdiction is based on traditional construction patterns and the landownership structure (Khamaisi 2005).

Municipalities have not completed the construction of industrial zones that began approximately twenty years ago, although there remains significant unmet demand for such zones. This was the case for example in the communities of Sakhnin, Tamra, Arrabe, and Shfaram. In many other towns there are difficulties caused by the lack of allocation of land by the state, or in the planning of these areas, since most of the land is privately owned (e.g., the cases of Arrabe and Bu'ayna Nujeidat). As a result, many municipalities come to feel helpless with respect to what transpires in their jurisdiction, unable to provide viable solutions or answers to residents' environmental concerns. The result is increased potential for intra-settlement and regional environmental and political conflicts involving Arab localities.

The geopolitical Arab-Jewish conflict affects planning and environmental conflicts in the Arab towns; Israeli Arabs are marginalized socially, economically, politically, and geographically; and cultural differences between them and the Jews foster conflicts about regional planning and environmental quality. Confiscation of private land for public purposes is particularly problematic for the Arab community because of historical, cultural, and economic factors. All these factors make planning and urbanization in Arab towns in Israel extremely complex.

Municipalities have attempted to work around these challenges by resorting to planning tools that are more expensive and less suitable than optimal alternatives, such as the traditional environmental "Sulha." The results involve high private and public costs, numerous planning and environmental conflicts, and low rates of compliance with environmental regulations. These obstacles to sustainable development in Arab towns do not occur as frequently in the Jewish sector (Tarabeih et al. 2009).

To reduce and manage environmental conflicts, stakeholders share a common responsibility. All citizens deserve healthy lives free of environmental hazards, and the municipalities and relevant authorities must act in order to rectify policies that have perpetuated the asymmetry between the quality of lives of Arab and Jewish populations. From the perspective of environmental justice, it is imperative to empower local environmental management in the Arab sector through legislation, increased environmental awareness and enforcement, and incorporation of environmental assessments into the planning of any development project. At a minimum, Israeli ministries that bear the responsibility for allocating suitable land for development must enable the completion of the infrastructure necessary to reverse environmental degradation in Arab towns and prevent the creation of future environmental risks. This will have positive implications beyond the immediate quality of life for Israeli Arab communities.

NOTES

The author would like to thank the Beracha Foundation, and particularly Dr. Martin Weyl, for support of this research and TAEQ activities.

1. Of land within Israel, 93 percent is public, administered by the Israel Lands Authority; 3.5 percent comprises lands owned by Arab landowners, and 3.5 percent is owned by Jewish landowners.

2. For instance, waste-treatment facilities for Sakhnin, Arrabe, Dier Hanna, and the Sakhnin industrial zone, which were nonexistent or run-down.

3. See cases in Beit Jann, Ir HaKarmel (Carmel City), the Tzalmon Stream, Sakhnin, and Kaokab.

4. See cases of the Arrabe-Sakhnin sewage transfer station and the wastewater pipe between Sakhnin Valley towns and Karmiel, Towns Association, Agan Beit Natufa, Annual Report, 2005–2006.

REFERENCES

Bang, M. J. 2009. *Sakhnin—Portrait of an Environmental Peace Project in Israel.* Edinburgh: Floris Books.

Brodnitz, M. 1986. "The Suburbanization of Arab Settlements in Israel." *Horizons in Geography* 17-18: 105–24. In Hebrew.

Hoffman, J. E. 1982. "Social Identity and the Readiness for Social Relations between Jews and Arabs in Israel." *Human Relations.* 35: 727–41.

Israel Central Bureau of Statistics. 2008. http://wwwl.cbs.gov.il/reader/cw_user_view_Folder?ID=141.

Israel Ministry of Environment. 2006, 2007; Adam Teva Vaden 2010 Report.

Khalidi, W., ed. 1992. *All That Remains: The Palestinian Villages Occupied and Depopulated by Israel in 1948.* Ramallah: Institute for Palestine Studies.

Khamaisi, R. 2004a. *Barriers to the Planning of Arab Localities in Israel.* Jerusalem: Floersheimer Institute for Policy Studies. In Hebrew.

———. 2004b. "Urbanization Without Cities: 'The Urban Phenomena among the Arabs in Israel.'" In "Contemporary Israeli Geography." Special issue, *Horizons in Geography,* edited by J. O. Maos, M. Inbar, and D. F. Shmueli, 60 (6): 141–50. Haifa: University of Haifa.

———. 2005. "Urbanization in Arab Localities in Israel." *Horizon in Geography* 64–65: 293–310. In Hebrew.

———. 2007. *Between Customs and Laws Planning and Management of Land in Arab Localities in Israel.* Jerusalem: Floersheimer Institute for Policy Studies. In Hebrew.

Kipnis, B. 1976. "Trends of the Minority Population in the Galilee and Their Planning Implications." *Ir v'Ezo* 3: 54–68. In Hebrew.

Kleniewski, N. 1997. *Cities, Change, and Conflict: A Political Economy of Urban Life.* Belmont: Wadsworth Publishing.

Ministry of Environment, Israel. *Annual Report,* 2007. http://www.sviva.gov.il/Enviroment/Static/Binaries/ModulKvatzim/p0489_1.pdf.

Ozacky-Lazar, S., and A. Ghanem, eds. 2003. *The Orr Testimonies: 7 Professional Opinions. Submitted to the Orr Committee.* Jerusalem: Keter Publishing House. In Hebrew.

Rouhana, N. 1997. *Palestinian Citizens in an Ethnic Jewish State: Identities and Conflict.* New Haven: Yale University Press.

Sakhnin Municipality Planning Archive. 2006.

Sarid, Y. 1993. "Review by the Minister of Environment in the Knesset." Brochure submitted to Knesset members. In Hebrew.

Shenhar, H., and T. Hussein. 2003. *A Master Plan for the Sakhnin Valley Localities.* Eilaboun: Arab Center for Alternative Planning. In Hebrew.

Shmueli, D. 2008. "Environmental Justice in the Israeli Context." *Environment and Planning A* 40 (10): 2384–401.

Sofer, M., and R. Gal. 1995. "Environmental Implications of the Entrance of Non-
    Agricultural Businesses into the Moshavim." *Horizons in Geography* 42-43: 39–50.
    In Hebrew.

Tarabeih, H. *Final Report 2009*. Towns Association for Environmental Quality–Agan
    Beit Natufa, Sakhnin.

———. 2008. "The Management and Resolution of Environmental Conflicts in Split
    Societies: Towards the Formation of a Culturally Adapted Model: Case Analyses of
    Conflicts in the Galilee." PhD thesis, Department of Geography and Environmen-
    tal Studies, University of Haifa. In Hebrew.

Tarabeih, H., D. Shmueli, and R. Khamaisi. 2009. "Towards the Implementation of
    SULHA as a Cultural Peacemaking Method for Managing and Resolving Environ-
    mental Conflicts among Arab Palestinians in Israel." *Journal of Peacebuilding and
    Development* 5 (1): 50–64.

Yiftachel, O. 1995. "Arab-Jewish Relations in Israel: Policy, Disparities, and Political
    Geographical Implications." *Medina, Mimshal Veyachasim Benleumiyim* [Country,
    Government and International Relations] 40: 185–224. In Hebrew.

———. 2000. *Land, Planning, and Inequality: The Division of Space between Jews and
    Arabs in Israel*. Tel Aviv: Adva Center. In Hebrew.

CHAPTER TEN

A PROLONGED RECESSIONAL
The Continuing Influence of British Rule on Israeli Environmental Law

David Schorr

ISRAEL'S ENVIRONMENTAL LAW, despite its lack of salience in public consciousness (as well as in that of the professional lawyer class), has a long and rich history. It has dealt, with varying measures of success, with the full spectrum of environmental issues. These range from traditional ones, like water pollution and nature conservation, to relatively new issues, such as depletion of the ozone layer and cellular-phone radiation.

This chapter's aim is not to present a full account of environmental law's development in Israel; Professor Tal's book has already done so with masterful depth as well as breadth (Tal 2002). Nor will it take as the organizing principle for a historical survey the traditional media-based classification of textbooks and practitioners' guides: air pollution, water pollution, nature preservation, and so on. It argues, rather, for the relevance to the understanding of Israel's environmental-legal history of a certain historical fact: the country's past as a territory of the British Empire, and (perhaps more controversially) its continued postcolonial nature in the decades following the foundation of the state in 1948. Though "classic" environmental law is generally believed to be a product of the 1970s and later, this early-twentieth-century law has had a lasting and decisive influence on the shape and structure of Israeli environmental law—Kipling's "recessional" of Empire (Kipling 1897), from which the title of this chapter is taken, is not yet complete.

I will argue that the continuing influence of British colonial law can be felt far beyond the Mandate-era statutes that remain on the books. Israel's colonial past is evident in the very "DNA" of its environmental law, with even seemingly novel legislation hewing in many cases to the colonial models. Even radical departures from earlier templates can be profitably characterized, so I will claim, as the product of Israel's colonial past (though I do not mean to argue that they are solely the result of this heritage). Moreover, certain lacunae in Israel's environmental legislation can be understood to be the logical result of the structures developed under British rule, rather than of a divergence from the typical pattern of Western democracies to which it had conformed prior to the 1970s.[1]

Environmental law thus illustrates nicely Assaf Likhovski's argument on the continuity between Mandatory and Israeli law and the necessity of taking account of Israel's colonial past in understanding its legal system (Likhovski 1998). My claim also joins recent histories of American and British environmental law that stress the pre-1970 roots of environmental law. Accordingly it implies that in Israel there was no great watershed for environmental law around 1948, 1970, or any other date. "Modern" environmental law continued to drink from the wells that had been surveyed and dug in the 1920s and '30s.[2] This thematic presentation will necessarily give short shrift to other valid theoretical and narrative perspectives, and unfortunately leave the history of many laws unexamined and unexplained. I hope that these shortcomings will be partially compensated for by the provision of an overarching framework which can serve as a departure point or punching bag for other legal and environmental historians. Due to the limited scope of this chapter, it will focus mostly on pollution-control law, for the most part putting aside natural-resource and nature-preservation law in Israel, despite the similarly deep colonial roots of these fields of law.[3]

COLONIAL ENVIRONMENTAL LAW

Victorian Nuisance Regulation

Perhaps the most obvious sign of Israel's British Empire roots in its environmental law has been its ongoing reliance on concepts of nuisance law as the basis for pollution regulation. Nuisance is the traditional legal field that deals with disturbances caused by land uses to neighboring landowners and the public at large, and basically treats these disturbances as localized phenomena.

The Abatement of Nuisances Law, 5721-1961 (popularly known as the Kanowitz Law, after the legislator who introduced and promoted the bill in the Knesset) has for half a century been the centerpiece of Israeli air pollution law, considered the groundbreaking statute that initiated modern Israeli environmental lawmaking.[4] Yet a historical survey of the development of pollution law in Israel beginning in the Mandate period reveals that in reality the Kanowitz Law offered no more than a modest modification of traditional nuisance law.

For nearly the whole British period, the nuisance-law provisions of the *Mejelle*, the Ottoman civil code, remained in force (Hooper 1933, arts. 1199–1201), and Mandate courts supplemented the code with principles of nuisance law imported from the judge-made common law of England (Sick Fund of the General Federation of Jewish Labour in Palestine v. Taasiyah Chemith 1944, 43). Near the end of the Mandate, the nuisance provisions of the *Mejelle* were replaced with new legislation based on the English law of nuisance (Civil Wrongs Ordinance 1944, secs. 44–49).[5] In addition, the Criminal Code Ordinance, 1936 made the creation of a nuisance a crime (secs. 189, 198–199). Though the prohibitions on air and water pollution in the general criminal code have rarely been used, the private law of nuisance, imported by the colonial rulers from English law, has been the legal focus of a number of high-profile pollution cases (e.g., Hevrat HaHashmal v. Avisar 1969). Moreover, both the civil (private law) and criminal provisions remain on the books today (Penal Law 5737-1977, secs. 221–222; Civil Wrongs Ordinance [New Version] 1968, secs. 42–48).

More importantly, the nuisance approach pervaded Israeli environmental regulation throughout its history. One of the first significant legislative acts concerning pollution was the Palestine Municipal Corporations Ordinance, which mandated that municipalities take steps to prevent nuisances in general. It also referred to specific types of pollution, such as concentrations of sewage, waste, and the like (Municipal Corporations Ordinance 1934, sec. 96). These provisions were carried over into today's Municipalities Ordinance [New Version], sec. 242. Similarly, the Public Health Ordinance, 1940, still in effect today, defined a wide range of nuisances and empowered Local Sanitary Authorities (typically local governments) to issue abatement orders and otherwise act to prevent and remove smoke and other nuisances (Public Health Ordinance 1940, secs. 1, 53–64).

These laws paid particular attention to pollution's local effects, and empowered local government as the primary agent of implementation and enforcement. In this respect they were modeled (like contemporaneous English legislation) on the nineteenth-century British Public Health Acts (Public Health Act 1936; Public Health Act 1848; Public Health Act 1875; Public Health [Scotland] Act 1897).[6] The idea was not to regulate pollution of the environment as such, but to prevent or reduce the harm caused to residents by the by-products of industrialization and urban life. The focus on the local may have been based simply on blind transplantation of the metropolitan model of environmental regulation to the colony, or it may have reflected a conscious desire to foster local self-government.[7] Either way, it was a typically British approach, with its roots in the Victorian Era.

Moreover, this approach was carried over into post-independence legislation, particularly the Kanowitz Law. In the realm of private law, this law expanded somewhat the overly narrow boundaries of private and public nuisance, doing away with the tort of private nuisance's insistence on harm to immovable property and public nuisance's demand for pecuniary harm. It also extended a private right of action to parties disturbed by noise, smell, or air pollution, without regard to their rights in land or lack thereof or the nature of the harm (secs. 4, 13). In the criminal sphere, it allowed the ministers of Health and Interior to define by regulation pollution levels, which if exceeded would be deemed "considerable or unreasonable" (sec. 5).

It may have appeared as if the law was breaking free from the shackles of nuisance law and the need to prove localized harm, adopting a more modern, public-law and regulatory approach. This turned out not to be the case; even violations of ambient standards established by regulation could be proven by the defendant in court to not be "likely to disturb a person being in the vicinity or passersby," thus negating criminal and civil liability (sec. 10[1]). Thus was the localized, nuisance approach preserved; pollution of the environment as such, if not potentially disturbing to people, was not enjoined (Katin and Virshubski 1975; Marinov and Sandler 1993).

As a result, this strand of Israeli environmental regulation, though prominent in the literature, has never been of much practical significance. Yet the English model of regulating the environment primarily at the local level has remained strong in Israel, with local authorities and their agents responsible for much of the enforcement burden (Katin and Virshubski 1975; Marinov and Sandler 1993).

Continental-Style Licensing

Not all of Israel's environmental laws are of English origin: early on it adopted the Continental model of pollution licensing and has continued to rely on this model as a mainstay of its regulatory scheme. A Napoleonic decree of 1810, which had in effect codified the ancient régime institution of the *commodo et incommodo* inquest, required that licenses for businesses deemed (in decreasing order of seriousness of the risk) "dangerous, insalubrious, or incommodious" be issued only after due investigation by the authorities and the implementation of proper preventive measures (Reynard 2002). As opposed to the traditional English system, with its primarily reactive and penal measures, the French system envisioned the involvement of the state at the earliest stages of the establishment of a polluting facility, requiring the polluter to employ the best technology available to mitigate the harm (Morag-Levine 2011).

The French model spread through the Continent, eventually making inroads even in Britain (Morag-Levine 2011; Reynard 2002). Interestingly, despite fierce debates over the desirability of such Continental-style regulation at home, the British introduced this model into Palestine early on, in the Regulation of Trades and Industries Ordinance, 1927.[8] The ordinance conditioned the operation of businesses affecting public health or safety, including a list of polluting industries, on their receiving a license from the local government, valid for one year (secs. 4–5). Simply "Unhealthy Trades and Industries," such as manure depots and tanneries, required the approval of the Department of Health as well, while "Dangerous Trades and Industries," including asphalt factories and chemical-manufacturing plants, required approval of both this department and the police (sec. 6 and Sched. I). These departments could also attach conditions to the license in the interests of public health or order (sec. 7). The effect of this regulation was to potentially involve the state in a very intrusive way in the operation of polluting industries, allowing it to dictate terms under which they might operate. (Administrative control of this sort is precisely why this type of regulation aroused antagonism in Victorian England.)

This licensing scheme prohibited polluting activities unless the polluter was issued an individual permit. Officials were given wide discretion to grant those permits on a case-by-case basis, often with conditions attached. The ad hoc approach proved to be a mainstay of Israeli environmental regulation and was carried over into law in Israel's Business Licensing Law, 5728-1968. It also seems to have been the inspiration for other environmental regulatory schemes. The Kanowitz Law, for instance, granted the government the power to issue "personal directions," ordering potential polluters to take measures to prevent pollution (Abatement of Nuisances Law, 5721-1961, sec. 8); and heavy use is made of this legal tool, as well. Similarly, the 1971 amendments to the Water Law, 5719-1959, prohibited the pollution of any water source in the broadest possible terms, yet allowed the authorities to issue an "authorising order" to pollute under conditions to be specified in the permit (Water Law [Amendment No. 5], 5732-1971, secs. 20A–20B and 20K of amended law).[9] Though likely deriving most directly from American sources, Israel's environmental impact statement, required for many land-use plans, is likewise the intellectual descendant of the Napoleonic pre-licensing inquest (Planning and Building Regulations [Environmental Impact Statements], 5763-2003; Planning and Building Regulations [Environmental Impact Statements] 5742-1982; Reynard 2002).

Another aspect of Continental-style legislation the British imported was the conditioning of permits to pollute on adoption by the polluter of the best practical pollution-control technology (see Morag-Levine 2011). The Public Health Ordinance provided that nuisances would not be considered as such if the "best means" had been taken to prevent harm to the public health "as far as practicable" (Public Health Ordinance, 1940, sec. 53[m]). The "authorising order" allowing pollution under the Water Law may be issued when "the circumstances of the case leave no choice" but to authorize the discharge (Water Law [Amendment No. 5], sec. 20K[a][2] of amended law). In 1969 section 48B was added to the Civil Wrongs Ordinance, providing a defense against nuisance claims when the offending use was tolerable, required for the public interest, and reasonable steps had been taken to "reduce the damage as far as possible" (Land Law, 5729-1969, sec. 165). More recently, the regulations on sea pollution from land-based sources and permitting provisions of the Clean Air Law explicitly condition pollution permits on use of the best available technology (Prevention of Sea Pollution from Land-Based Sources Regulation, 5750-1990, regs. 6–7; Clean Air Law, 5768-2008, sec. 22).

The effects of this Continental approach, imported to Palestine by the British, are reflected in the fact that many, perhaps most, pollution-control measures are applied to businesses by the Ministry of Environmental Protection on a discretionary basis through business licenses and personal orders, rather than through norms of general application. (The ministry has, however, made an effort to standardize environmental conditions in business licenses across industry sectors.)[10]

Centralized Planning for the Environment

Alongside these two strands of British Empire law, Israeli environmental law has always envisioned a third, contrasting thread: centralized planning of the environment by the state bureaucracy. While the Common Law nuisance-based approach and the Continental-style licensing approach encouraged an ad hoc, case-specific approach to environmental law, other laws reflected a top-down, rationalizing and modernist approach to regulation. This approach was facilitated by the authoritarian nature of colonial government in Palestine, but it continued to develop and expand in the post-independence period as well.

The most obvious manifestation of this approach was the Palestine Town Planning Ordinance (1936), which provided for land-use planning by local governments, under the guidance and control of District Commissions staffed by officials of the central government. In 1965 the colonial legislation was replaced by the Planning and Building Law which added a further layer of administration, the National Board for Planning and Building. The law called for three levels of comprehensive plans—national, district, and local—with a clear normative hierarchy among them. Besides the law's application to clearly environmental issues, such as health, sanitation, open spaces, and the like (e.g., Town Planning Ordinance, 1936, sec. 12; Planning and Building Law, 5725-1965, sec. 49), the very institution of land-use planning and permitting created a powerful tool for environmental regulation. Polluting facilities, for example, could be refused approval for construction, sited so as to minimize harm, or have approval for their construction contingent on the adoption of technological or other standards.

The broad scope of Israel's land-use planning legislation and the accompanying extensive power vested in the planning authorities encouraged statutory plans to extend into the many lacunae in Israel's environmental legislation, and to become the primary legal tool for regulating a wide range of environmental issues (Marinov and Sandler 1993; Terlo 1973). These issues included solid-waste disposal, electricity generation, air pollution, and nature conservation, as well as classic land-use issues like the preservation of open space and coastal zone management. Many environmental-legal campaigns, and consequently much leading environmental case law in Israel, have been channeled into planning and zoning law.[11] The centrality of land-use law to environmental regulation is attested to by the deep opposition voiced by the environmental community to recent proposals to change the law in this area.

The field of water law, as well, was long dominated by the centralized planning approach, dating back to Mandate legislation. In a series of legislative moves in the late 1930s and early 1940s, the Palestine government took legal control over all of the colony's water resources to direct their development and use (Safeguarding of Public Water Supplies Ordinance 1937; Water Survey Ordinance 1938; Palestine [Amendment] Order in Council 1940; Drainage Surface Water) Ordinance 1942; Defence [Water Distribution] Regulations 1944). A couple of decades later, in the midst of massive hydroengineering projects that completely changed Israel's aquatic environments and settlement patterns, the state enacted an updated suite of laws, solidifying state control (Water Drillings Control Law, 5715-1955; Drainage and Flood Control Law, 5718-1957; Water Law, 5719-1959; Streams and Springs Authorities Law, 5725-1965). The ambition of the program was evident in the broad definition of the "water resources" owned by the public: "springs, streams, rivers, lakes and other currents and accumulations of water, whether above ground or underground, whether natural, regulated or made, and whether water rises, flows or stands therein at all times or intermittently, and includes drainage water and sewage water." The law also vested total control over these resources in the state's Water Commissioner (Water Law, secs. 2, 23–36). Its presumption to order nature can be seen in the grant of power to Stream Authorities to "define the course of the stream" (Streams and Springs Authorities Law, sec. 3[3]).[12]

In practice, the top-down planning model tended to be dominated by the entropy of the ad hoc licensing system, and centralized environmental planning never lived up to its promise in Israel. Though Israel's environment has been radically altered by water development and land-use changes, these have been carried out in a manner far more chaotic and unplanned than that envisioned by the statutes (see Alfasi 2006; Rosen-Zvi 2007; Schorr 2011). Yet the ideal of rational, centralized planning has continued to motivate and captivate Israeli policy makers and legislators to this day.[13]

Absent Standards

The dominance of the ad hoc licensing approach had as its corollary another prominent feature of Israeli environmental law: the relative absence of general emissions or technology standards. Such standards are consistent with classic command-and-control–style regulation, which is, in many systems, the core of environmental law. But they play a noticeably minor role in Israeli environmental law.

The law of the Mandate period allowed for the promulgation of regulations mandating general standards (Regulation of Trades and Industries Ordinance, 1927, sec. 9; Municipal Corporations Ordinance, 1934, secs. 96–99; Public Health Ordinance, 1940, sec. 70). Such authority, however, was infrequently used. The government did issue regulations under the Regulation of Trades and Industries Ordinance with the technology standard that businesses' chimneys rise at least two meters above the surrounding buildings and that furnaces consume their smoke as far as possible (Trades and Industries [Regulation] Rules, 1928, rule 14). Yet these rules were very primitive, very much part of the traditional nuisance-prevention approach discussed above.

The Kanowitz Law of 1961, despite its general nuisance-law approach, gave slightly more attention to the issue of general standards. It established in section 5 that the government "shall make rules for the implementation" of the prohibitions on considerable or unreasonable noise, smell, or pollution of the air, defining, inter alia, what would be deemed "considerable or unreasonable." In sections 7 and 18 it allowed the adoption of generic regulations to prevent pollution. After a lengthy struggle in and out of court, in 1971 a professor from the Technion succeeded in forcing the promulgation of ambient standards for six gaseous air pollutants (later expanded to twelve) (Abatement of Nuisance [Air Quality] Regulations, 5732-1971; Abatement of Nuisances [Air Quality] Regulations, 5752-1992).

These efforts were of limited legal effect. An inherent limitation of ambient standards as a regulatory tool is that while the quality of the air might exceed legally permissible values, it is typically impossible to assign legal responsibility for such violations to particular polluters. Legally enforceable restrictions on pollution would have required emissions or technology standards, but the government was stingy with these. Weak standards for automobile emissions and emissions-control technology were enacted relatively quickly (Abatement of Nuisances [Air Pollution from Automobiles] Regulations, 5723-1963; Abatement of Nuisances [Air Pollution from Automobiles] [Hartridge Test Standard] Regulations, 5724-1963), and emissions standards set for smoke and particulate matter a little later (Abatement of Nuisances [Air Pollution from Premises] Regulations, 5722-1962; Abatement of Nuisances [Emissions of Particulate Matter to the Air] Regulations, 5733-1972). But in the crucial area of emissions or technology standards for stationary sources emitting gaseous pollutants, such as sulfur dioxide and nitrous oxides, the regulators were silent.

Similarly, while detailed quality standards for drinking water were enacted into law in 1974 (Public Health [Sanitary Quality of Drinking Water] Regulations, 5734-1974), the government was painfully slow in enacting regulations containing water-pollution controls. The minister of Agriculture (later the minister of Environment) was granted broad authority to issue such regulations in the Water Law Amendments of 1971 (Water Law [Amendment No. 5], sec. 20D of amended law), but years passed before the government took steps to implement the law. Only in 1992 were regulations on cesspits and septic tanks promulgated (Water Regulations [Prevention of Water Pollution] [Cesspits and Septic Tanks], 5752-1992), and while more regulations have been issued since, they cover only solitary sectors or relatively few pollutants (e.g., Water Regulations [Prevention of Water Pollution] [Gas Stations], 5757-1997).

The lack of general emissions standards in Israeli law has been justified on the basis of the small size of the country, with relatively few polluters of any given type (Marinov and Sandler 1993). It is indeed not implausible that in the Israeli context, individualized, context-sensitive standards, issued through the licensing tools such as the Business Licensing Law and the personal directions of the Kanowitz Law, are more efficient and fair than general ones. Yet they also undeniably magnify the discretionary power of the authorities, in keeping with the historical themes outlined above.

Legal Overrides

Despite the uneven coverage of Israeli environmental law, and the generally discretionary nature of the power granted government authorities, officials have often chafed at the limits imposed by the law. An early example was the case of the Taasiya Chemith superphosphate fertilizer plant, established near Petach Tikva in the early 1940s, which polluted the air for miles around with noxious fumes, due to substandard raw materials and plant. When it became clear to nearby residents and workers that the authorities would not invoke their power to force the factory to stop polluting, nearby Beilinson Hospital brought a nuisance suit against the factory, winning an injunction. Unwilling to forgo the fertilizer produced by the plant, the government simply issued an order under wartime defense legislation, declaring the factory immune from any nuisance suit (Defence [Manufacture of Superphosphate] [Taasiyah Chemith Tel Aviv Ltd.] Order, 1945; Kupat Holim etc., 1946).

A similar story surrounded the building of the Reading D power plant in Tel Aviv in the 1960s. When the government-owned Israel Electric Corporation had its plans for the erection of the plant rejected for reasons of public health by the District Planning Commission under the new Planning and Building Law, the government quickly passed a special law ousting the planning authorities' jurisdiction over the power plant (Tel Aviv Power Station Law, 5727-1967; see Laster 1973). It explained, rather disingenuously, that the construction required the imposition of conditions not available under the planning and business-licensing statutes. It further rationalized that the special legislation would allow the government to tailor its regulations to the necessities of the new project (Tel Aviv Power Plant Bill, 5727-1967, explanatory note).

More recently, a similar phenomenon was evident in the 2002 amendment to the Planning and Building Law that created the National Committee for Planning and Building of National Infrastructures, over the intense opposition of environmental groups. The amendment allowed the government to exempt infrastructure projects from the normal planning process, directing them instead to an expedited procedure before the new committee, dominated by government representatives, with reduced opportunities for public input and environmental assessments (Planning and Building Law [Amendment No. 60], 5762-2002). The establishment of the committee, with its weakened protections for the environment, was attacked (unsuccessfully) by environmental groups as an unconstitutional infringement on the right to a healthy environment (IUED v. Prime Minister 2004).

Other environmental statutes had their overrides built directly into them, with no need for authorization from the Knesset (see Bader 1971). The Kanowitz Law proscribed air pollution, but allowed the ministers (today the minister of Environment) to exempt pollution from the law's provisions in the interests of protecting a public right. Less stringent local bylaws were also allowed to supersede national standards with the minister's approval (Abatement of Nuisances Law, 5721-1961, secs. 6, 16). The Water Law, as discussed above, banned all pollution but then allowed discharge of pollution when "the circumstances of the case leave no choice" (Water Law [Amendment No. 5], secs. 20A-20B, 20K of amended law).

Thus has Israeli environmental law been weakened not by its spotty coverage or by lack of enforcement, but in the very legal mechanisms for overriding
environmental provisions that the authorities found inconvenient.

POSTCOLONIAL ENVIRONMENTAL LAW

The Enforcement Crisis

Poor compliance with environmental regulations is a problem the world over.[14]
Yet the feeling among Israeli environmentalists seems to be that ineffective
enforcement, or at the least its scope, is a problem unique to the country (Tal,
Aharon, and Yuhas-Peled 2010). For decades policy makers have fretted about
the supposed enforcement gap, typically with invidious comparisons to the
superior situation of "civilized countries" (Hebrew: *medinot metukanot*), and
attempted a variety of solutions. This phenomenon may be viewed as a symptom of the systemic immaturity in the environmental-legal system of a state
struggling to escape its colonial past.[15]

As early as 1965, for instance, officials fretted that the fines for oil pollution of water sources were set too low for effective deterrence; fines were accordingly raised and summary procedures for payment of fines without trial
instituted [Oil in Navigable Waters Ordinance Amendment Bill, 5725-1965,
explanatory note; Oil in Navigable Waters Ordinance Amendment Law, 5726-
1966; Oil in Navigable Waters Ordinance Amendment Law [No. 2], 5733-1972).
Complaints that enforcement powers under this law and the Kanowitz Law
were too weak apparently led to the introduction of administrative enforcement measures in the Water Law amendments of 1971, which authorized the
Water Commissioner to promulgate orders to stop and remedy water pollution without judicial proceedings (Water Law [Amendment No. 5], secs. 20G–
20H of amended law; see Tamir 1971, 2275). These provisions for administrative enforcement were essentially copied into all subsequent environmental
legislation (Environmental Protection [Polluter Pays] [Amendments to Legis-
lation] Bill, 5767-2007, explanatory note), though the powers authorized by the
statutes seem to have been used infrequently.

Two further rounds of strengthening the government's enforcement powers ensued. In 1997 several central environmental statutes were amended to
increase the penalties applicable to environmental crimes; a decade later these
statutes and others were amended to further ramp up criminal penalties, as
well as standardize the extrajudicial powers available to the enforcing agencies
(Environment [Penal Methods] Amendments to Legislation) Law, 5757-1997;
Environmental Protection [Polluter Pays] [Amendments to Legislation] Law,
5768-2008).

Environmentalists' sense that the government was not enforcing the laws

also led to a secular effort to create "private attorneys-general" by granting
private parties powers to enforce the law. The Kanowitz Law aimed to turn
environmental enforcement into a concern of the central government (supplementing the local approach that preceded it). But at the same time it encouraged enforcement by private parties by recognizing the right of a private
citizen to initiate a criminal complaint; it also declared violations of the law
to constitute a private nuisance for purposes of civil suits (Abatement of Nuisances Law, 5721-1961, secs. 12, 13). Grants of power to initiate criminal proceedings to injured parties as well as environmental groups were later added
to many environmental statutes (e.g., Seawater Pollution from Sources on
Land [Prevention] Law, 5748-1988; Environment [Penal Methods] [Amend-
ments to Legislation] Law, 5757-1997).

The sense of lax enforcement also led to passage in 1992 of a major new law
to encourage civil lawsuits against polluters, by creating a freestanding cause
of action against violators of environmental statutes (without the need to
prove the elements of a tort) and by authorizing class-action lawsuits (Prevention of Environmental Nuisances [Civil Suits] Law, 5752-1992). Due to shortcomings in the design of the statute, such as the need for members of the class
to actively join the suit, limits on the ability to claim monetary damages, and
the inherent technical difficulty of proving many environmental violations,
the law proved to be of little practical value. These shortcomings were rem-
edied in the Class-Action Lawsuit Law, 5766-2006 (Sched. II, sec. 6).

Ironically, another trend in law reform seemed to seek to return environmental law to its Victorian roots—the devolution of powers to local governments. Israeli environmental law has always given a prominent place to regulation at the local level. Local governments have traditionally been perceived
as potentially important agents of enforcement. Their roles included serving
as sanitary authorities under the Public Health Ordinance, functioning as licensing authorities under Mandatory and Israeli business-licensing legislation, and using their power to bring criminal complaints under a variety of
statutes. Recent legislation has granted yet more enforcement powers to local
governments, apparently in an effort to make up for perceived lax enforcement at the national level (Local Authorities [Environmental Enforcement—
Inspectors' Powers] Law, 5768-2008; Local Authorities [Environmental Enforcement—Inspectors' Powers] Bill, 5768-2008, explanatory note).

The constant worry over insufficient enforcement that has characterized
the history of Israeli environmental law, and the recurring attempts to find a
legislative fix for the problem, can be seen as the symptoms of Israel's colonial
and postcolonial past. The fear of policy makers that citizens are not taking
the law seriously, and the attempts to educate them by ever-increasing penal-

ties and enforcement powers, seem to be the symptoms of a deep-seated anxiety over the efficacy and legitimacy of the law in a relatively young country.

Economic Tools

Although Israeli environmental law has been continuously and deeply influenced by its past, it also has seen much innovation. Yet even when apparently breaking free from the shackles of the past, environmental law has often displayed the characteristics of a postcolonial society, in its blind and sometimes crude borrowing of law reform measures from abroad. This borrowing arguably has been motivated by anxieties similar to those discussed in the previous section.[16] This phenomenon can be observed with regard to adoption of legal measures based on economic principles, an approach advocated largely in the American academia (e.g., Ackerman and Stewart 1985). As Oren Perez has pointed out, Israeli environmental law has made extensive use of economic rhetoric, but in practice has adopted the insights of economic analysis in a crude and often mistaken manner (from the economic point of view) (Perez 2009).

Perhaps the first legislative measures adopted in accordance with economic thinking were the amendments to the Oil in Navigable Waters Ordinance. The increased fines were motivated by the desire to increase economic deterrence for crimes which it was feared were all too worthwhile from the polluter's point of view (Oil in Navigable Waters Ordinance Amendment Bill, 5725-1965, explanatory note 1; Oil in Navigable Waters Ordinance Amendment Bill [No. 2], 5732-1972, explanatory note). Later, the creation of dedicated funds for environmental activities funded by polluter fees and fines—beginning with the Marine Pollution Prevention Fund in 1979, and followed a few years later by the Cleanliness Maintenance Fund—were portrayed as expressions of the "polluter pays principle" (Oil in Navigable Waters Ordinance Amendment Law [No. 3], 5737-1977; Oil in Navigable Waters [Establishment of Sea Pollution Prevention Fund] Regulations, 5740-1979; Maintenance of Cleanliness Law, 5744-1984; see Marinov and Sandler 1993). The "polluter pays principle" has also motivated the adoption of economic tools in several other contexts, including a bottle deposit scheme and solid-waste disposal fees (Beverage Container Deposit Law, 5759-1999; Maintenance of Cleanliness Law [Amendment No. 9], 5767-2007).

Fines and fees, however, in these cases as well as in the similar fee schemes adopted afterward, were almost always set without regard to the actual costs imposed by pollution on the environment, as would have been case under a system guided by the welfarist, Pigouvian approach (see Baumol and Oates 1988). Only in a few cases did the legislature direct some sort of systematic as-

sessment of the costs of pollution externalities, and little came of these efforts
(Perez 2009).

The 1997 and 2008 legislative overhauls of monetary penalties for environmental crimes, discussed above, were also motivated by the "polluter pays"
rhetoric that had seemed to have gained international acceptance. In Knesset debate over the 1997 law, for instance, the chair of the Interior and Environment Committee declared that the purpose of the law was to implement
a "modern approach" to environmental legislation, based on the "world-
renowned principle that the polluter pays" (Tarif 1997, 5819). The amendments,
however, increased deterrence simply by raising the maximum penalties imposed on violators of the law. There was little attempt to match the fines to the
harm caused to the environment (Environment [Penal Methods] [Amend-
ments to Legislation] Law, 5757-1997). Similarly, the 2008 amendments had
the "polluter-pays" term built into the title of the law, but the implementation
of the principle departed radically from its welfarist origins, in which the polluter's obligation to pay for the social costs of his pollution forces him to take
these costs into account, thus leading him to pollute at the socially optimal
level. Courts were directed to fine polluters in the amount they profited by
their violations, unrelated to the damage caused to the environment (Environmental Protection [Polluter Pays] [Amendments to Legislation] Law, 5768-
2008). This approach aimed to achieve maximal, not efficient, deterrence of
crime, since efficient violations of the law (where the marginal private utility of polluting exceeds its marginal social cost) would be deterred. Maximal
deterrence may indeed be the right policy when human health is at stake,
but this policy is something other than what is implied by the "polluter pays"
rhetoric.

Israel's experience with economic approaches to environmental law thus
displayed signs of an immature and postcolonial legal system, with sometimes
clumsy adoption of imported ideas viewed as superior, partly due to their foreign (particularly American) provenance.

History is ever present in Israel's environmental law. It has evolved considerably since the 1920s, yet in many ways it has not escaped the deep structural
legacies of British rule in the Mandate period. Beyond the colonial laws still
on the books, and notwithstanding the apparently modern statutes that are
essentially revised drafts of colonial legislation, the environmental law of Israel is colored throughout by the nation's history as a British-ruled colony. In
place of general regulations setting out the terms and conditions under which
pollutants may be emitted, the state retains immense discretionary power to
set standards on an individual, ad hoc, basis or to allow pollution without any
standards at all. Other trends in the law, the constant search for a fix to the

compliance problem, and the rush to economic tools, also expose Israel's colonial past, as signs of the legal system's attempts to put that past behind it and
join the cast of "civilized countries."

These structural legacies of the Mandate period can help explain one of
the central idiosyncrasies of Israeli environmental law, one that might call
to mind Kipling's "lesser breeds without the Law" (Kipling 1897)—its relative lack of general command-and-control–style emissions and technology
standards. There are presumably many reasons for this lacuna in the law, including political opposition of polluters and the difficulty of promulgating
regulations, but this history suggests another reason. With the plethora of
colonial-era tools available to the Israeli regulator, including expansive powers
to regulate through business licenses and similar pollution-permit schemes,
modern forms of regulation have not been deemed essential. Even the new
Clean Air Law, with its directions that the government promulgate general
regulations for polluting sources, retains the emphasis on individual permitting of stationary sources, thus largely adhering to the traditional forms of a
regulatory culture now nearly a century old.

NOTES

Thanks to Tal Avigdory, Gadi Ben-Dror, Hagit Brinker, Avigail Cohen, Bill Gutter-
man, and Mohammed Mawasi for research assistance; to Danny Fisch, Assaf Likhovski, Noga Morag-Levine, and participants in the TAU Law faculty seminar for
their valuable comments; and to Frank Uekoetter for helpful conversations. Research
funding was provided by the Law and Environment Program, the Vice-President's
Fund for Encouragement of Research, and the Cegla Center for Interdisciplinary Research of the Law, all at Tel Aviv University.

1. For the view that Israel became a "laggard" in environmental policy after the early
1970s due to international politics and its pattern of economic growth, see Vogel 1999.

2. For the classic American view, seeing 1970 as a crucial turning point, see Lazarus
2004. For an Israeli view, finding the origin of environmental law in the 1960s, see
Fisch 2002, 12. Newer research has begun to uncover the roots of post-1970 environmental law in the United States and Britain. See, e.g., Brooks 2009; Morag-Levine
2003; and Pontin 2007.

3. See, for instance, Schorr, forthcoming. In the interests of avoiding contorted
phrasings, and in keeping with the claim of this chapter that the environmental law of
Mandate Palestine and the State of Israel are best understood as a continuity, with no
rupture around 1948, the term "Israeli" will often refer herein not only to the law of the
State of Israel, but also to that enacted or in force before Israel's independence.

4. Fisch, 2002. The air-pollution provisions of the law were repealed as of January
2011 (Clean Air Law, 5768-2008, secs. 84, 93).

5. The nuisance provisions of the *Mejelle* were repealed, insofar as they were consistent with the Civil Wrongs Ordinance, 1944, by section 71 of the ordinance, and the
entire code was completely repealed in 1980 by the Foundations of Law statute (Foundations of Law, 5740-1980).

6. For the history of British public health legislation and its intimate connection with local government, see Hamlin 1994; Windham 1943.

7. See, e.g., the comment of Palestine's Legal Draftsman on the Municipal Corporations Ordinance, 1934 (Windham 1936, 188): "the encouragement and facilities which it provides for local self-government are an important step in the political development of Palestine."

8. The adoption of a French-influenced norm in Palestine ran counter to the general picture of the imposition of common-law–style norms, over the protest of nationalist Arab lawyers, discussed in Likhovski 2006. For the eclectic approach of the British to colonial legislation, see Schorr 2009.

9. See also, e.g., the power to attach conditions to water-production licenses (Water Law, secs. 20F and 25 of amended law), and the waste-disposal permits under the Prevention of Marine Pollution from Land-Based Sources Law, 5748-1988, secs. 2–3A.

10. According to the Ministry of Environmental Protection, in September 2009 nearly 17,000 businesses were operating with Ministry approval of their business licenses, in addition to several thousand licenses of other types issued by the Ministry. See Ministry website, http://tinyurl.com/mep-permits (in Hebrew). For examples of "personal directions" under the Kanowitz Law, see id., http://tinyurl.com/mep-conditions (in Hebrew). For industry-wide "framework conditions" for business licenses, see id., http://tinyurl.com/mep-frameworks (in Hebrew).

11. See, e.g., IUED v. Nat'l. Bd. for Planning & Building, 1996, dealing with construction of the Trans-Israel Highway; Association for Quality of Environment and Life in Nahariya v. Nahariya Municipality, 1998, dealing with asbestos-contaminated soil; Beer-Sheva Municipality v. Government, 1998, dealing with solid-waste disposal; IUED v. Minister of Interior, 2001, dealing with forestry practices.

12. My translation. The official translation is: "the fixing of an alignment for the stream."

13. See, e.g., sec. 5 of the Clean Air Law, 5768-2008, requiring as the first step of the law's implementation the preparation of a national air-pollution mitigation plan.

14. See, e.g., Duhigg, 2009, finding that the U.S. Clean Water Act was violated more than 506,000 times since 2004.

15. For a discussion of compliance and enforcement difficulties in postcolonial states, see Richardson, Mgbeoji, and Botchway 2006.

16. For a convincing argument that Americanization in Israel is rooted in the country's colonial past, see Frenkel and Shenhav 2003.

REFERENCES

Abatement of Nuisances Law, 5721-1961. *Laws of the State of Israel* 15: 52.

Abatement of Nuisances (Air Pollution from Automobiles) Regulations, 5723-1963. *Kovetz Takanot*, 1794. In Hebrew.

Abatement of Nuisances (Air Pollution from Automobiles) (Hartridge Test Standard) Regulations, 5724-1963. *Kovetz Takanot*, 92. In Hebrew.

Abatement of Nuisances (Air Pollution from Premises) Regulations, 5722-1962. *Kovetz Takanot*, 2168. In Hebrew.

Abatement of Nuisances (Air Quality) Regulations, 5732-1971. *Kovetz Takanot*, 380. In Hebrew.

Abatement of Nuisances (Air Quality) Regulations, 5752-1992. *Kovetz Takanot*, 972. In Hebrew.

Abatement of Nuisances (Emissions of Particulate Matter to the Air) Regulations, 5733-1972. *Kovetz Takanot,* 361. In Hebrew.

Ackerman, B. A., and R. B. Stewart. 1985. "Reforming Environmental Law." *Stanford Law Review* 37: 1333–65.

Alfasi, N. 2006. "Planning Policy? Between Long-Term Planning and Zoning Amendments in the Israeli Planning System." *Environment and Planning A* 38: 553–68.

Association for Quality of Environment and Life in Nahariya v. Nahariya Municipality. 1998. Admin. Petition (Haifa) 166/98. *Psakim Mechoziim* 5757 (1): 461. In Hebrew.

Bader, Y. 1971. *Divrei Haknesset* 60: 2276. In Hebrew.

Baumol, W. J., and W. E. Oates. 1988. *The Theory of Environmental Policy.* Cambridge: Cambridge University Press.

Beer-Sheva Municipality v. Government. 1998. HCJ 453/98. *Piskei Din* 52 (2): 13. In Hebrew.

Beverage Container Deposit Law, 5759-1999. *Sefer Hukim,* 170. In Hebrew.

Brooks, K. B. 2009. *Before Earth Day: The Origins of American Environmental Law, 1945–1970.* Lawrence: University Press of Kansas.

Business Licensing Law, 5728-1968. *Laws of the State of Israel* 22: 232.

Civil Wrongs Ordinance 1944. *Palestine Gazette,* no. 1380, supp. 1: 129. In Hebrew.

Civil Wrongs Ordinance (New Version). 1968. *Laws of the State of Israel* (New Version) 2: 5.

Class-Action Lawsuit Law, 5766-2006. *Sefer Hukim,* 264. In Hebrew.

Clean Air Law, 5768-2008. *Sefer Hukim,* 755. In Hebrew.

Criminal Code Ordinance, 1936. *Palestine Gazette,* no. 652, supp. 1: 285. In Hebrew.

Defense (Manufacture of Superphosphate) (Taasiyah Chemith Tel Aviv Ltd.) Order. 1945. *Palestine Gazette,* no. 1403, supp. 2: 414. In Hebrew.

Defense (Water Distribution) Regulations. 1944. *Palestine Gazette,* no. 1373, supp. 2: 1157. In Hebrew.

Drainage and Flood Control Law, 5718-1957. *Laws of the State of Israel* 12: 5.

Drainage (Surface Water) Ordinance. 1942. *Palestine Gazette,* no. 1204, supp. 1: 58. In Hebrew.

Duhigg, C. 2009. "Clean Water Laws Are Neglected, at a Cost in Suffering," *New York Times,* September 13.

Environment (Penal Methods) (Amendments to Legislation) Law, 5757-1997. 1997. *Sefer Hukim,* 132. In Hebrew.

Environmental Protection (Polluter Pays) (Amendments to Legislation) Bill, 5767-2007. 2007. *Hatzaot Hok HaKnesset,* 222. In Hebrew.

Environmental Protection (Polluter Pays) (Amendments to Legislation) Law, 5768-2008. 2008. *Sefer Hukim,* 858. In Hebrew.

Fisch, Daniel. 2002. "Environmental Law in Israel." Bnei Brak: Mahshavot. In Hebrew.

Foundations of Law, 5740-1980. *Laws of the State of Israel* 34: 181.

Frenkel, M., and Y. Shenhav. 2003. "From Americanization to Colonization: The Diffusion of Productivity Models Revisited." *Organization Studies* 24: 1537–61.

Hamlin, C. 1994. "State Medicine in Great Britain." In *The History of Public Health and the Modern State,* edited by D. Porter, 132–64. Amsterdam and Atlanta: Editions Rodopi.

Hevrat HaHashmal v. Avisar. 1969. Civ. App. 190/69. *Piskei Din* 23 (2): 314. In Hebrew.

Hooper, C. A. 1933. *The Civil Law of Palestine and Trans-Jordan*. Vol. 1. Jerusalem: Azriel Printing Works.

IUED v. Minister of Interior. 2001. HCJ 288/00. *Piskei Din* 55 (5): 673. In Hebrew.

IUED v. Nat'l. Bd. for Planning & Building. 1996. HCJ 2920/94. *Piskei Din* 50 (3): 441. In Hebrew.

IUED v. Prime Minister. 2004. HCJ 4128/02. *Piskei Din* 58 (3): 503. In Hebrew.

Katin, E., and M. Virshubski. 1975. "Environmental Law and Administration in Israel." *Tel Aviv University Studies in Law* 1: 197–238.

Kipling, R. 1897. "Recessional." In *Collected Verse*, 219. Cambridge: Cambridge University Press.

Kupat Holim Shel Hahistadruth Haklalith Shel Haovdim Haivrim Beeretz-Israel v. Ta'asiah Chemith Tel-Aviv Ltd. 1946. Motion 756/46. *Selected Cases of the District Courts of Palestine*. 1946: 662. In Hebrew.

Land Law, 5729-1969. *Laws of the State of Israel* 23: 283.

Laster, R. E. 1973. "Reading D: Planning and Building or Building and Then Planning?" *Israel Law Review* 8: 481–505.

Lazarus, R. J. 2004. *The Making of Environmental Law*. Chicago: University of Chicago Press.

Likhovski, A. 1998. "Between 'Mandate' and 'State': Re-thinking the Periodization of Israeli Legal History." *Journal of Israeli History* 19: 39–68.

———. 2006. *Law and Identity in Mandate Palestine*. Chapel Hill: University of North Carolina Press.

Local Authorities (Environmental Enforcement—Inspectors' Powers) Bill, 5768-2008. 2008. *Hatzaot Hok HaKnesset*, 112. In Hebrew.

Local Authorities (Environmental Enforcement—Inspectors' Powers) Law, 5768-2008. 2008. *Sefer Hukim*, 534. In Hebrew.

Maintenance of Cleanliness Law, 5744-1984. 1984. *Laws of the State of Israel* 38: 190

Maintenance of Cleanliness Law (Amendment No. 9), 5767-2007. 2007. *Sefer Hukim*, 88. In Hebrew.

Marinov, U., and D. Sandler. 1993. "The Status of Environmental Management in Israel." *Environmental Science and Technology* 27: 1256–62.

Morag-Levine, N. 2003. *Chasing the Wind: Regulating Air Pollution in the Common Law State*. Princeton: Princeton University Press.

———. 2011. "Is Precautionary Regulation a Civil Law Instrument? Lessons from the History of the Alkali Act." *Journal of Environmental Law* 23: 1–43.

Municipal Corporations Ordinance. 1934. *Palestine Gazette*, no. 414, supp. 1: 1. In Hebrew.

Municipalities Ordinance (New Version). 1964. *Laws of the State of Israel* (New Version) 1: 247.

Navigable Waters Ordinance Amendment Bill, 5725-1965. 1965. *Hatzaot Hok*, 376. In Hebrew.

Oil in Navigable Waters Ordinance Amendment Bill, 5725-1965. 1965. *Hatzaot Hok*, 376. In Hebrew.

Oil in Navigable Waters Ordinance Amendment Bill (No. 2), 5732-1972. 1972. *Hatzaot Hok*, 388. In Hebrew.

Oil in Navigable Waters Ordinance Amendment Law, 5726-1966. 1966. *Laws of the State of Israel* 20: 34.

Oil in Navigable Waters Ordinance Amendment Law (No. 2), 5733-1972. 1972. *Laws of the State of Israel* 27: 3.

Oil in Navigable Waters Ordinance Amendment Law (No. 3), 5737-1977. 1977. *Laws of the State of Israel* 31: 156.

Oil in Navigable Waters (Establishment of Sea Pollution Prevention Fund) Regulations, 5740-1979. 1979. *Kovetz Takanot*, 96. In Hebrew.

Palestine (Amendment) Order in Council. 1940. *Palestine Gazette*, no. 1093, supp. 2, p. 666. In Hebrew.

Penal Law, 5737-1977. *Laws of the State of Israel* 31: 4.

Perez, O. 2009. "The Influence of Economic Thought on Israel's Environmental Law: A Critical Review." *Tel Aviv University Law Review*, 429-87. In Hebrew.

Planning and Building Law, 5725-1965. 1965. *Laws of the State of Israel* 19: 330.

Planning and Building Law (Amendment No. 60), 5762-2002. 2002. *Sefer Hukim*, 157. In Hebrew.

Planning and Building Regulations (Environmental Impact Statements), 5742-1982. 1982. *Kovetz Takanot*, 502. In Hebrew.

Planning and Building Regulations (Environmental Impact Statements), 5763-2003. 2003. *Kovetz Takanot*, 800. In Hebrew.

Pontin, B. 2007. "Integrated Pollution Control in Victorian Britain: Rethinking Progress within the History of Environmental Law." *Journal of Environmental Law* 19: 173-99.

Prevention of Environmental Nuisances (Civil Suits) Law, 5752-1992. 1992. *Sefer Hukim*, 184. In Hebrew.

Prevention of Marine Pollution from Land-Based Sources Law, 5748-1988. 1988. *Sefer Hukim* 118, amended *Sefer Hukim*, 5765: 511. In Hebrew.

Prevention of Sea Pollution from Land-Based Sources Regulation, 5750-1990. 1990. *Kovetz Takanot*, 250. In Hebrew.

Public Health Act. 1848 (Eng.). 11 and 12 Vict. c. 63. In Hebrew.

Public Health Act. 1875 (Eng.). 38 and 38 Vict. c. 55. In Hebrew.

Public Health Act. 1936 (Eng.). 26 Geo. 5 and 1 Edw. 8, c. 49. In Hebrew.

Public Health Ordinance. 1940. *Palestine Gazette*, no. 1065, supp. 1, p. 87. In Hebrew.

Public Health (Scotland) Act. 1897. 60 and 61 Vict. c. 38. In Hebrew.

Public Health (Sanitary Quality of Drinking Water) Regulations, 5734-1974. 1974. *Kovetz Takanot*, 556. In Hebrew.

Regulation of Trades and Industries Ordinance. 1927. *Laws of Palestine* 2, cap. 143, 1454. In Hebrew.

Reynard, P. C. 2002. "Public Order and Privilege: Eighteenth-Century French Roots of Environmental Regulation." *Technology and Culture* 43: 1-28.

Richardson, B. J., I. Mgbeoji, and F. Botchway. 2006. "Environmental Law in Post-colonial Societies: Aspirations, Achievements, and Limitations." In *Environmental Law for Sustainability: A Reader,* edited by B. J. Richardson and S. Wood., 419-21. Oxford: Hart Publishing.

Rosen-Zvi, I. 2007. "Whose Garbage Is It Anyway?! Refuse Disposal and Environmental Justice." *Bar Ilan Law Studies* 23: 487-58. In Hebrew.

Safeguarding of Public Water Supplies Ordinance. 1937. *Palestine Gazette*, no. 711, supp. 1, 185. In Hebrew.

Schorr, D. B. 2009. "Questioning Harmonization: Legal Transplantation in the Colonial Context." *Theoretical Inquiries in Law Forum* 10: 49-53.

————. 2011. "Private Rights in Publicly Owned Water: The Pathology of Israeli Water Law." In *Water Policy and Law in the Mediterranean—An Evolving Nexus,* edited by S. Bogdanovic, 60–79. Novi Sad: Business Academy of Novi Sad.

————. Forthcoming. "Forest Law in the Palestine Mandate: Colonial Conservation in a Unique Context." In *Managing the Unknown,* edited by U. Luebken and F. Uekoetter.

Seawater Pollution from Sources on Land (Prevention) Law, 5748-1988, sec. 8. 1988. *Laws of the State of Israel* 42: 124.

Sick Fund of the General Federation of Jewish Labour in Palestine v. Taasiyah Chemith Tel-Aviv Ltd. 1944. Civ.Case (T.A.) 221/43. Selected Cases of the District Courts of Palestine, 1944: 37.

Streams and Springs Authorities Law, 5725-1965. 1965. *Laws of the State of Israel* 19: 149.

Tal, A. 2002. *Pollution in a Promised Land: An Environmental History of Israel.* Berkeley: University of California Press.

Tal, A., Y. Aharon, and H. Yuhas-Peled. 2010. "The Relative Advantages of Criminal versus Administrative Environmental Enforcement Actions in Israel." *Journal of Environmental Monitoring* 12: 813–21.

Tamir, Y. 1971. *Divrei Haknesset* 60: 2274. In Hebrew.

Tarif, S. 1997. *Divrei Haknesset* 162: 5818. In Hebrew.

Tel Aviv Power Plant Bill, 5727-1967. 1967. *Hatzaot Hok,* 208. In Hebrew.

Tel Aviv Power Station Law, 5727-1967. 1967. *Laws of the State of Israel* 21: 141.

Terlo, Z. 1973. "Environment and the Law in Israel." *Public Administration in Israel* 13: 11–24.

Town Planning Ordinance. 1936. *Palestine Gazette,* no. 589, supp. 1, p. 157. In Hebrew.

Trades and Industries (Regulation) Rules. 1928. *Palestine Gazette,* sec. 14. In Hebrew.

Vogel, D. 1999. "Israeli Environmental Policy in Comparative Perspective." *Israel Affairs* 5: 246–64.

Water Drillings Control Law, 5715-1955. 1955. *Laws of the State of Israel* 9: 88.

Water Law, 5719-1959. 1959. *Laws of the State of Israel* 13: 173.

Water Law (Amendment No. 5), 5732-1971. 1971. *Laws of the State of Israel* 26: 7.

Water Regulations (Prevention of Water Pollution) (Cesspits and Septic Tanks), 5752-1992. 1992. *Kovetz Takanot,* 784. In Hebrew.

Water Regulations (Prevention of Water Pollution) (Gas Stations), 5757-1997. 1997. *Kovetz Takanot,* 1121. In Hebrew.

Windham, R. 1936. "Review of Legislation, 1934—Palestine." *Journal of Comparative Legislation and International Law* 18 (3): 187–90.

————. 1943. "Review of Legislation, 1940 & 1941—Palestine." *Journal of Comparative Legislation & International Law* 25 (1): 248–50.

CHAPTER ELEVEN

MARINE-POLLUTION ABATEMENT ON ISRAEL'S MEDITERRANEAN COAST
A Story of Policy Success

Dorit Kerret

IN 2009 ISRAELI MEDITERRANEAN beaches were closed for 109 days due to severe marine pollution (Zalul 2009). This would come as a harsh blow to the scores of Israelis who love their beach. In such a small, crowded, cement-based country, the coast offers the ultimate escape from the hectic lives most Israelis live. In any weather, rain or shine, on weekdays and even at night there are always people at the beach and in the water. This special affection for the coastal environment tends to make Israelis unforgiving when it comes to polluting their primary and beloved natural resource, and makes it very popular to condemn the apparent failure of marine-pollution-abatement efforts. As a result, it is rare to describe the history of Israel's marine-pollution abatement as a success. Yet, as this chapter shows, environmental quality along Israel's coastline has improved significantly, making this aspect of Israel's environmental history a success story.

Much of this success, and the fact that Israel's marine environment has become dramatically cleaner, is due to the (small but influential) government agency Marine Pollution Prevention Department (later named the Marine and Coastal Environment Division [MCED]) in Israel's Ministry of Environmental Protection. This chapter suggests that the historical background of the establishment of MCED provides a compelling explanation to this success story. Moreover, international forces influenced the high capacity of MCED, manifested in its funding, organizational structure, motivation, and human

capital—factors that enabled the utilization of advanced policy tools that resulted in improved environmental outcomes.

In the absence of a formal marine-pollution regulatory strategy, the MCED
came up with innovative and creative solutions for addressing the sundry aspects of marine pollution. The most significant "boost" for combating marine
pollution came in the form of hierarchical regulation providing the MCED
with a variety of tools and authorities. Within the command-and-control
regulation that MCED had at its disposal, it implemented advanced policy
tools to improve environmental results. This chapter provides a snapshot
of the improvements in the state of the marine environment. Subsequently
the historical background for the establishment of MCED is described while
highlighting the components of the MCED's high capacity. The utilization
of advanced policy tools is then presented. The chapter concludes by drawing policy lessons from this story of success for other Israeli environmental
problems.

IMPROVEMENTS IN THE STATE OF THE MARINE ENVIRONMENT

The 2006 war with Lebanon, when oil depots off the Lebanese coast were destroyed, leaking oil onto the Beirut beaches, provided Israelis with a brief re-
minder of the black sand we used to have. As Tal describes in his book on Israeli environmental history: "During the 1960s and 1970s the stains on Israeli
beaches from the tarry petroleum residues reached disgusting levels. After
swimming, bathers had to scour the soles of their feet in kerosene to remove
the gooey black gobs of petroleum wastes" (Tal 2006). Today, generally speaking, Israeli beaches are white and clean. Monitoring data support this visual
observation: between 1975 and 1987 tar levels dropped from 3.6 kilograms per
front meter to 20 grams, according to the Oceanographic and Limnological
Research Institute (IOLR) (Tal 2006). Annual reports of the Ministry of Environmental Protection (MEP) state that beaches have been tar-free since 1985
(Ministry of Interior 1988).

Data provided by the MEP and the IOLR point to significant improvements of marine environmental quality, reflected in other environmental indicators as well (Malister and Mark 2006; Herut et al. 2008). For instance,
during the previous decade, heavy-metal concentrations decreased significantly in sediments, benthic organisms, and dust (Herut et al. 2008). Biological oxygen demand (BOD), as well as nutrient concentrations, decreased dramatically also (Malister and Mark 2006).

Nonetheless, there continues to be much room for improvement in the
quality of the Mediterranean marine environment in Israel. Particular recommendations for action are provided by the IOLR and stated in the work pro-

gram of the MCED of the MEP. In particular, the sludge of the Dan Region Wastewater Treatment Plant (Shafdan) is highlighted as the major source of pollution to the Mediterranean Sea, significantly larger than all other sources combined (MEP 2006a). Currently the Shafdan gradually reduces its discharges and according to the current plan, the discharge from the Shafdan to the ocean should cease by the year 2012 (according to the discharge permit dated June 2010).

Internationally, Israel is considered one of the leading countries in advancing and implementing Mediterranean pollution-abatement program (interview with R. Amir, November 26, 2009; Amir 2009b; Adler 2000; Tal 2008; Talitman, Tal, and Brenner 2003). In 2006 the head of the MCED was invited to Beijing, to the Second Intergovernmental Review of the Global Program of Action for the protection of marine environment from land-based activities, to share with other countries Israel's experience in combating marine pollution from land-based sources (interview with R. Amir, November 26, 2009). Among the Mediterranean countries, Israel has initiated some of the most stringent requirements and demanding international mechanisms for Mediterranean protection and has opposed any tendency for leniency in these requirements (interview with R. Amir, November 26, 2009). Israel's BOD levels (which is one of the comparative parameters for anthropogenic pollution factors) in the effluents discharged by Israeli sources into the Mediterranean are among the lowest of riparian nations (Tal 2008; UNEP MAP 2007).

What are the causes for the improvements in the quality of the marine environment? Although a comprehensive answer is difficult to provide and may require a causal research design, the following paragraphs suggest that effective and creative policy implementation by a highly capable regulatory unit offers a compelling explanation.

THE BACKGROUND SETTING FOR ADVANCED POLICY IMPLEMENTATION BY MCED

For understanding how the MCED came to initiate and employ advanced policy tools, it is important to take into account the historical context in which this unit was created and operated. There are two important variables that have affected its operations. The international context established the regulatory obligations and set Israel as a leading party in this context. The historical institutional capacity was affected by the international context and created a high-capacity unit, characterized by ample funding, an efficient institutional structure, a "can-do" spirit, and high-level human capital. The following sections present the components of the MCED, using the historical context of its establishment and operation.

THE INTERNATIONAL CONTEXT

In the 1970s, prior to the rise to prominence of environmental issues such as climate change and ozone depletion, marine pollution was one of the central environmental concerns in Israel with significant international implications. Ever since the early negotiations of the Barcelona Convention for the Protection of Mediterranean Sea Against Pollution, adopted in 1976, Israel took an enthusiastic and leading role in advancing regional protection of the Mediterranean marine environment (Talitman et al. 2003).

The international leader position, which was to a large extent adopted due to geopolitical considerations (Tal 2006; Talitman et al. 2003), has been preserved ever since. Israel remains one of the foremost proponents of adopting stringent international standards within the different international Mediterranean marine protection programs (such as the current MAP requirements for BOD standards) (interview with R. Amir, November 26, 2009). This historic role of an international leader in combating Mediterranean marine pollution seems to have had a crucial effect on the character and achievements of domestic marine-protection efforts in Israel, as described in the following paragraphs.

INSTITUTIONAL CAPACITY

Environmental capacity is defined as the ability to identify and solve environmental problems (Weidner and Janicke 2002). Funding, institutional structure, human capital, and motivation are significant elements of environmental capacity (Weidner and Janicke 2002). Although environmental capacity is usually studied at the state level, this chapter focuses only on the capacity of a single governmental unit.

Due to the international influence, the establishment of the MCED was characterized by the four aforementioned elements of environmental capacity (funding, institutional structure, motivation, and human capital), which affected its entire performance thereafter. To implement the ambitious protocols and action plans that the Barcelona Convention required, state funding was necessary. The legislative amendments for ratifying one of the Barcelona Oil Pollution Protocol as well as the MARPOL Convention, which seeks to prevent pollution of marine environment from the discharge of oil from ships, established an independent funding mechanism for treating marine pollution. Ship operators paid fines for noncompliance with the new Oil Ordinance as well as shipping fees to an independent Marine Pollution Prevention Fund. A designated fund for financing environmental activities was rare and surprising in the Israeli reality where an all-powerful and centralized Ministry of Finance always vigorously opposes the designation of fines for a particular activity. Miraculously, the provision slipped past the watchful eye of government economists and became law in 1980 (Tal 2006). This legislative finesse was not without its repercussions: subsequently, the Ministry of Environmental Protection was not capable of amending the Oil Ordinance, as the Ministry of Finance was always threatening cancellation of the Marine Pollution Prevention Fund (interview with N. Utitz, June 8, 1999). In its first year the fees generated $420,000 for the fund, an astronomical sum by the very modest standards of the time at the Environmental Protection Service (Tal 2006).

The money would enable the future MCED (established in 1983; see below) to run an enforcement program that included an independent legal framework with lawyers filing criminal indictments against marine polluters. By 1987 the fund was generating $650,000 a year. The money paid for necessary enforcement and response equipment as well as for the salaries of enforcement personnel (Tal 2006). By 2009 the fees generated around two million dollars (interview with R. Amir, 2009).

The "shadow" of international influence was also apparent in the historical structure of the MCED. Obviously, to implement Israel's international commitments funding was not enough; personnel capable of implementing it was also required. Therefore, in July 1983 the Marine Pollution Prevention Department (later named MCED) was established as part of the fledgling Environmental Protection Service (prior to the establishment of the MEP) (Tal 2006). It was the first department within the service—a precursor to the present ministry—that sat in the Interior Ministry and was therefore in charge of all aspects of regulating marine pollution. The historic structure of the MCED was preserved over the years, making it unique within the MEP, containing the four major components of capacity: funding, institutional structure, motivation, and human capital.

One of the unique institutional characteristics of the MCED is its status as the only environmental-medium-specific division under the supervision of the deputy director general of Enforcement (MEP Structure 2009). Additional parallel divisions are under the supervision of the deputy director general of Industries (such as Air Quality Division, Hazardous Substances Division) or the deputy director general of Infrastructures (such as Solid Waste Division and the Water, Sewage and Streams Division). This bureaucratic nuance may in fact strengthen a "built-in" enforcement orientation. The mission of the MCED is clearly defined: "to minimize and reduce to the maximal extent threats on Israel's Mediterranean coastal and marine environment" (MEP 2008).

Also unique to the MEP, the MCED has exclusive oversight over all aspects of marine protection. It enjoys responsibility and authority for permitting, enforcement, international cooperation, scientific research, and monitoring as well as policy setting. In the MEP, divisions responsible for regulating other environmental media, responsibilities, and authorities are usually divided between the central unit that sets the policies; the six districts that are in charge of monitoring, permitting, and implementing the policies; and the Green Police, which is in charge of criminal investigation. The integrative structure of the MCED created a sense of pride, unity, and ownership in addressing marine pollution (interview with Z. Shkalim, December 21, 2009). It avoided diffused and unclear priorities and transaction costs that can result from internal conflicts.

The unique spirit of the first years of the operation of the MEP was characterized by cooperation, teamwork, and devotion of the staffers to their mission (Tal 2006). Interviews with the MCED inspectors and extensive observations in their headquarters during 1999 revealed a government unit where all employees were enthusiastically engaged in their work. The inspectors, many of whom were graduates of elite combat units in Israel's navy, had a special bond with the Mediterranean. Zohar Shkalim, who served as the legal adviser of the MCED during 1998–2002, observed that the response of the inspectors to pollution of the marine environment was very personal: "They felt that the pollution hurt their beloved resource and therefore fought the pollution with all the enthusiasm and resources at their disposal. They had a sense of pride as an elite unit with a sacred mission at hand" (interview with Z. Shkalim, December 21, 2009).

In addition, since the beginning of its operation the MCED has been characterized as having a high quality of human capital. Most inspectors had earned academic degrees, which allowed the unit to set high standards in the collection of evidence and their ongoing work (interview with Z. Shkalim, December 21, 2009). In addition, the management of the MCED was characterized by highly qualified, academically trained personnel.

The high capacity of MCED, manifested in funding, structure, human capital, and spirit, was also reflected in policy implementation. The regulatory team had the sense of being an elite unit that could operate freely with clearly defined funding, policy priorities, and mandates. The performance of the MCED is characterized by strong regulatory implementation that created a meaningful deterrence, alongside new modes of governance, as will be described in the next sections.

MCED'S ADVANCED POLICY IMPLEMENTATION

The marine-pollution-prevention efforts started prior to a proper legislative framework. In the absence of mandatory regulatory standards and sanctions, the MCED was able to achieve cooperation from the polluters and reduce pollution in various areas. For instance, prior to the enactment of the Land Based Sources Law in 1988, they used the Oil Ordinance to achieve the coopera-tion of facilities that were possible sources of pollutants other than oil-related contaminants (interview with N. Utitz, June 8, 1999). The lack of regulatory authority remained problematic after the legislation of Oil Ordinance, as the Israeli Navy was excluded from its provisions. Inspectors secured the Navy's cooperation by approaching base commanders and convincing them of the importance of taking the marine environmental quality seriously (Talitman 2000).

Despite the combative spirit of MCED's devoted personnel, it was the es-tablishment of a formal regulatory framework that made a significant dif-ference in their efforts. The Oil Ordinance, enacted in 1980, provided the MCED with the authority to enforce restrictions on marine pollution with oil substances from all sources of pollution. The ratification of the Land-Based Sources (LBS) Protocol in the form of Land-Based Sources Marine Pollution Law in 1988 boosted significantly the efforts of MCED to prevent marine pol-lution as it eventually granted the authority to treat land-based source pol-lution from substances other than oil (Talitman et al. 2003). MCED tried to establish an equitable enforcement system that would regulate a variety of of-fenses. There were four main components to their enforcement strategy:

1. The regulatory procedure under the Oil Ordinance provided swift administrative penalties for minor oil spills, thereby reducing the burden of legal prosecutions (Talitman and Tal et al. 2003).

2. Another key aspect involved the MCED's institutional structure. Usually, the MEP legal department reviewed all completed investigation files prior to transferring them to external prosecutors who manage the legal proceedings. But prosecution files involving oil-pollution offenses were sent directly to the external prosecutor, without review by the ministry's legal department, therefore saving time and resources. This strengthened the regulations' deterrence effect (interview with Z. Shkalim, December 21, 2009).

3. Despite the relatively low penalties for environmental offenses, overall marine-pollution offences were among the more costly of these fines: while the mean penalty for noncompliance with marine-pollution statutes between 1990–1998 was $10,000 (Talitman et al. 2003), the mean penalty for other environmental offences during this period was only around $3,000 (Tal 2002). (It should be noted that there was a significant increase in the penalties for environmental offences over the previous five years.)

4. MCED enforced regulations evenly and equitably regardless of the identity of the polluters. For instance, strong enforcement efforts were directed at Israel's Navy, which was subject to the LBS statute (2000).

As a result of these measures, the MCED chalked up a string of concrete successes during its early years. Among these was the halting of sewage discharges from the Akko, Eilat, and Nahariya municipalities. In these cases criminal proceedings against municipal officials led to the establishment of sewage treatment plants. The reputation of MCED's enforcement encouraged the cooperation of additional actors in resolving their cases, such as proceedings against the Herzliya municipality and Atlit naval base (Amir 2009b). Amir also identifies significant improvements in maintenance practices of all coastal cities following the conviction of the Shafdan facility due to pollution discharge caused by maintenance failures. The lawsuit against the Shafdan was also a part of the enforcement efforts of the MCED.

ADVANCED REGULATORY TOOLS: NEW MODES OF GOVERNANCE IN OLD REGULATION

The recent history of environmental law includes new modes of governance, as a higher level of development has emerged within the environmental legal systems (Gunningham 2009; Fiorino 1999). New modes of governance include information and participation regulatory tools. These policy tools are based on cooperation and harnessing additional actors to the policy-making process (Gunningham 2009). In addition, Gunningham uses the concept of "license to operate" to explain the environmental behavior of environmentally regulated entities (Gunningham 2003). He claims that the interaction between societal, regulatory, and economic pressures creates a "license to operate" to which regulated entities respond. In other words, regulated entities take into account the societal, regulatory, and economic requirements of various actors in forming their behavior. The societal license to operate may be enhanced by the information and participatory regulatory frameworks (Gunningham 2004).

Despite the relatively difficult context in which the MCED operates, the relatively low capacity of both societal organizations and MCED's moderate regulatory authorities (Weinthal and Parag 2003; Kerret and Tal 2005; Kerret 2008), it was able to implement new modes of governance in its policy implementation. The implementation of participatory and information frameworks is a first step toward enhancing the social license to operate.

In retrospect, the most important contribution to MCED's operations was arguably the creativity it showed in harnessing additional actors to help it combat pollution. This is important because funding for environmental enforcement is never enough. Even with the additional sums from the Marine Pollution Prevention Fund it was still too small to ensure the detection of all violations. So inspectors of the MCED came up with creative solutions for raising their ability to detect violations. One such innovation involved harnessing different public groups as their informers: they approached port workers, diving clubs, fishermen, and surfing clubs and asked for their cooperation in detecting marine pollution. To encourage public participation some inspectors met with the potential informants and sent them letters of appreciation and complimentary T-shirts. These efforts seemed to be very fruitful, as 63 percent of marine-pollution criminal investigation files were opened due to public reporting of the offense (Talitman et al. 2003).

Another important factor that has influenced the success of MCED is the creation of evidence-based policy making. For this to be successful, two attributes are required: first, collecting the relevant information, and second, basing policies upon this relevant information. Both conditions were highly developed in MCED's operations. The money from the Marine Pollution Fund has been used for research and monitoring the state of the marine environment. Basic information, such as the identity of polluters and their emissions, started only later in other areas such as air pollution. For example, the 1998 Covenant regarding air pollution required potential air polluters to provide data regarding their potential pollution sources. Signing the covenant also revealed sources of pollution that were previously unknown to the MEP (Kerret and Tal 2005).

But contrary to information collection in other Israeli government systems, which often is not used for policy making (Gottlieb et al. 2009), data collected by the MCED are analyzed and major sources of pollution are identified. The priorities and work plans of the MCED are based on this information. For instance, IOLR monitoring identified the Shafdan—the country's largest sewage treatment plant—as the major pollution source in the marine environment.

These data enabled the MCED to approach the Shafdan and require it to cease the dumping of sludge. The land-based, alternative technology cost the facility around one billion shekels. Marine monitoring also highlighted the need for stopping TBT paint use on marine vessels, as it is considered a highly toxic biocide. It also set in motion a new policy to cease use of this toxin and encouraged its phasing out and the finding of alternatives. In addition, an index of the sensitivity of Israel's Mediterranean coasts to oil pollution was prepared by the MCED as a basis for calculating the cost for preventing, detecting, and cleanup of oil spills (MEP 2006a).

The IOLR has been monitoring the marine environment ever since the establishment of MPS (Prime Minister 1973), and its findings have provided a basis for policy since the establishment of MCED in 1983 (Ministry of Interior 1983). Currently the working program of the MCED focuses on implementation of the Mediterranean National Action Plan, which includes strategic planning and priorities based on relevant information (MEP 2006a; Amir 2009b).

MCED is very favorable toward public participation during policy formation and open to public criticism of its procedures. For instance, MCED opened all investigation files to the author's pursuit of research in 1998, when there was no legal obligation for them to do so. In response to findings from this research, the agency adopted some of the policy recommendations and even introduced others to the legal amendments to LBS statute.

This was not a unique experience. Through their website the MCED publishes the discharge permits and the decision of its permitting committees almost in real time (Amir 2009b). Moreover, when MCED prepares quality standards for the marine environment, even though there is no formal "notice and comment" process in Israel for secondary legislation, these criteria are opened for the public's response and debate. These indicators offer a basis for setting environmental standards, monitoring, and priorities (MCED 2002).

LESSONS LEARNED AND POLICY RECOMMENDATIONS

A snapshot of Israel's marine-pollution conditions may be misleading. The state of the Mediterranean marine environment in Israel has improved since the establishment of the MCED and the setting of its regulatory standards. While there is still plenty of work needed to improve the health of the marine environment, and to build environmental capacity (Weithal and Parag 2003), it seems that overall the story of marine-pollution abatement in Israel is a story of success.

How can this success be translated into other environmental arenas in Israel? It seems that an important attribute of the successful operation of the MCED has been its institutional capacity. The integrative structure and human capital, along with the extensive funding and the legal mandate to operate, made its operations smooth and effective. In addition, the "esprit de corps" and the functionality of an elite unit explain its impressive creativity and determination in fighting marine pollution.

While the international context and the capacity (funding, structure, spirit, and human capital) of MCED seem to explain to a great extent the policy success of Israel's marine-pollution-abatement efforts, there are two other important elements of the policy implementation of the MCED are worth noting.

One of these is the "shadow of hierarchy" (Heritiere and Lehmkul 2007). The MCED was able to establish enough deterrence to gain the cooperation of potential polluters. The shadow of hierarchy was created by the funding from the Marine Pollution Prevention Fund, the devotion and qualifications of the MCED personnel, and by establishing effective networks of informants to enhance enforcement capacity. These attributes could be fairly easily implemented in other environmental areas as well. In particular, galvanizing additional actors to improve capacity is a creative solution for improving enforcement.

Another important attribute is evidence-based policy making. Setting priorities on the basis of relevant scientific knowledge helped focus the efforts of MCED on priority polluters and remove the most acute threats during a relatively short period of time; this strategy is particularly important when resources are scarce.

This chapter leaves some interesting and important questions for further research, in particular regarding the background contextual variables. For instance, the leading international role Israel has come to play is far from obvious, particularly when compared with Israel's status in other global environmental arenas, such as climate change, biodiversity, or ozone depletion (State Comptroller 2009). It is still an open and important question—why did Israel take upon herself the role of an international leader in this marine-environment protection and not in others? It might have been the unique combination of factors that ultimately formed the sense of responsibility, pioneering, and leadership. Timing might have had a crucial role in shaping this leading role: it was the first time Israel participated in international efforts to save an environmental asset. The importance of taking a vital role in the destiny of an international asset (as opposed to our usual small role in other international environmental assets), suggests that geopolitical conditions contributed to the unique sense of duty and responsibility. In addition, the cultural conditions might have played an important role. The bond between the Israelis and the beach might have played a significant role in the desire to protect it. Arguably, the accumulation of these background factors resulted in the most important components of this success story: the answer to the above question has a great deal to do with the unique individuals who took on the challenge of marine enforcement and who were given the resources to get the job done. There is much to be learned from the marine-pollution success story whose lessons can be implemented in other environmental areas and in other countries. Yet, the story of Israeli marine protection is far from being concluded. Along with the yet unresolved pollution problems, new severe threats to the marine environment keep surfacing, particularly in light of the global change. Will the strong, impressive historical achievements of the MECD hold, under the new conditions? Only the future will tell. Certainly the MCED should take pride of their achievements so far and strive to be even stronger and more effective facing the challenges ahead.

REFERENCES

Fiorino, D. 1999. "Rethinking Environmental Regulation: Perspectives on Law and Governance." *Harvard Environmental Law Review* 23: 441.

Gottlieb, A., D. Kerret, and G. Menahem. 2009. "Environmental Information Management and Environmental Policy in Local Authorities in Israel." Policy Paper. Jerusalem: Hartoch School of Governance, Tel Aviv University.

Gunningham, N. 2009. "Environmental Law, Regulation and Governance: Shifting Architectures." *Journal of Environmental Law* 21 (2): 179.

Gunningham N., R. Kagan, and D. Thornton. 2003. *Shades of Green: Business, Regulation, and Environment.* Stanford: Stanford University Press.

———. 2004. "Social License and Environmental Protection: Why Business Go Beyond Compliance." *Law and Social Inquiry Journal of the American Bar Foundation* 29 (2): 307.

Heritier, A., and D. Lehmkul. 2007. "The Shadow of Hierarchy and New Modes of Governance." *Journal of Public Policy* 28 (1): 1.

Herut, B. 2008. "Environmental Quality of Israel's Mediterranean Coastal Waters in 2007, IOLR Report H52/2008." http://www.ocean.org.il/Heb/_documents/report2007.pdf.

Kerret, D. 2008. "ISO 14001 as an Environmental Capacity Building Tool—Variations among Nations." *Environmental Science and Technology* 42 (8): 2773.

Kerret, D., and A. Tal. 2005. "Green Wash or Green Gain? Predicting the Success and Evaluating the Effectiveness of Environmental Voluntary Agreements." *Penn State Environmental Law Journal* 14 (1): 31.

Malister, I., and O. Mark. 2006. "Multi-Annual Mediterranean Pollutants Balance 1998–2004." Ministry of Environmental Protection. http://www.sviva.gov.il/Enviroment/Static/Binaries/ModulKvatzim/p0421new_1.pdf.

Marine and Coastal Environmental Division (MCED). 2002. "Environmental Quality Standards for the Mediterranean Sea in Israel." http://www.sviva.gov.il/Enviroment/Static/Binaries/index_pirsumim/p0124_eng_1.pdf.

"MEP Structure." 2009. http://www.sviva.gov.il/Enviroment/Static/Binaries/odot Hamisrad/Structure-2008_1.pdf.

Ministry of Environmental Protection. (MEP). 2006a. "National Action Plan for the Reduction of Pollution of the Mediterranean from Land Based Sources." http://www.sviva.gov.il/Enviroment/Static/Binaries/index_pirsumim/p0349_1.pdf.

———. 2006b. "Marine Quality: Cleaner Seas and Coasts." *Israel Environment Bulletin* 32:8–13. http://www.sviva.gov.il/Enviroment/Static/Binaries/index_pirsumim/p0432_1.pdf.

———. 2006c. "Environmental Sensitivity Index." http://gis.sviva.gov.il/website/moe/Html/gis/interactiveMap1.htm#2$0&201.

———. 2008. "Enforcement Cluster, Summary of Activity." http://www.sviva.gov.il/Enviroment/Static/Binaries/ModulKvatzim/p0514_yam_vehofim1_1.pdf.

Ministry of Interior, the Service for Environmental Protection. 1983. "Environmental Quality in Israel." *Annual Report* 11 for 1983–1984.

———. 1988. "Environmental Quality in Israel." *Annual Report* 13–14 for 1985\6–1986\7.

Prime Minister Office, the Service for Environmental Protection. 1974. "Environmental Quality in Israel." *Annual Report* 1 for 1973.

State Comptroller Special Report. 2009. "Treatment of Green House Gases in Israel. Jerusalem." www.mevaker.gov.il.

Tal, A. 2002. "Assessing the Benefits of Noncompliance: The Role of Economic Analysis in Environmental Enforcement." In *Environment and Policy—Environmental Policy Research Collection*, edited by A. Eidelman, A. Tal, and N. Ben-Aharon, 11. Jerusalem: Jerusalem Institute for Israel Studies.

———. 2006. *The Environment in Israel—Resources, Crises, Campaigns and Policy— From the Birth of Zionism until the 21st Century.* Tel Aviv: Hakibbutz Hameuchad Publishing House. In Hebrew.

Tal, O. 2008. "Israel and the Barcelona Convention." Jerusalem: Knesset Research and Information Center. http://www.knesset.gov.il/mmm/doc. asp?doc=m02155&type=pdf.

Talitman, D. 2000. "Oil and the I.D.F.—Should the Prevention of Sea-Water Pollution by Oil Ordinance (1980) Apply to the IDF?" *Law and Army* 14: 143.

Talitman, D., A. Tal, and S. Brenner. 2003. "The Devil Is in the Details: Increasing International Law's Influence on Domestic Environmental Performance—The Case of Israel and the Mediterranean Sea." *NYU Environmental Law Journal* 11 (2): 414–78.

United Nations Environment Programme, Global Programme of Action for the Protection of the Marine Environment from Land-Based Activities (UNEP MAP). 2007. http://www.gpa.unep.org/content.html?id=345&ln=6.

United Nations Environment Programme, Mediterranean Action Plan. (UNEP MAP). 2007. "Regional Plan and Possible Measures for the Reduction of Input of BOD by 50% by 2010 from Industrial Sources." Athens: UNEP(DEPI)/MED WG 316/5.

Weidner, H., and M. Janicke. 2002. *Capacity Building in National Environmental Policy.* Berlin: Springer.

Weinthal, E., and Y. Parag. 2003. "Two Steps Forward, One Step Backward: Societal Capacity and Israel's Implementation of the Barcelona Convention and the Mediterranean Action Plan." *Global Environmental Politics* 3 (1): 51.

Zalul. 2009. "Summary of the 2009 Season." http://www.zalul.org.il/artical553.asp.

CHAPTER TWELVE

OLIVE GREEN
Environment, Militarism, and the Israel Defense Forces

Uri Gordon

M ILITARISTIC SOCIETIES ARE ones in which the armed forces enjoy a privileged material and cultural status, and where military priorities and frames of thinking play a key role in policy making and political culture (Vagts 1981; Newnham 1998). Militarism is not limited to direct governance by uniformed personnel ("praetorianism"), but may instead coexist with substantive democratic institutions (Ben-Eliezer 1997). Thus, contemporary societies described as militaristic are as politically diverse as Switzerland and Burma, North and South Korea, Jordan and Israel.

This chapter explores the interface between environmental and military issues in Israel, placing it within the context of the changing fortunes of Israeli militarism. In particular, it is argued that growing public willingness to challenge the military's environmentally destructive behavior in the last decades was linked to wider transformations in Israeli society. The Oslo Accords and the rise of liberal-individualist outlooks associated with globalization and consumer culture weakened the country's founding collectivist ideology in favor of material values associated with quality of life. In this context, the military lost its previous immunity to public criticism; and environmental concerns, formerly considered luxuries in comparison with security matters, were able to gain ground in the public sphere alongside other civil agendas.

The chapter begins by stating the case for viewing Israel as a militaristic society. It then surveys the military's environmental activity and the environmental destruction it has wrought, while also noting some early successes in the area of nature conservation. Finally, it discusses how, since the 1990s, the environmental movement and affected residents, as well as the Ministry of Environment and State Comptroller, have pushed the military to clean up its act.

THE IDF AND ISRAELI MILITARISM

The Israeli Defense Forces (IDF), commonly known in Israel by the Hebrew acronym TZAHAL, is a conscript army. National military service is mandatory for all non-Arab Israel citizens over the age of eighteen (including women, as well as Druze men), although exceptions are made on religious, medical, and mental health grounds. IDF service ranges from combat roles to logistics and auxiliary support, education, and intelligence. After completion of regular service of three years (two for women), the IDF may call up men for paid reserve duty of up to fifty-four days per three years (eighty-four days for officers), until the age of forty (forty-five for officers).

Between 1950 and 1966, Israel spent on average 9 percent of its GDP on security. The figure reached a high of about 30 percent in the 1970s, but has since returned to under 10 percent. As of 2008, Israel ranked fifth in the world in terms of military expenditure per GDP (7.0 percent), superseded by Oman (7.7 percent), Saudi Arabia (8.2 percent), Georgia (8.5 percent), and Eritrea (20.9 percent); and followed by Chad (6.6 percent), the United Arab Emirates (5.9 percent), Jordan (5.9 percent), Iraq (5.4 percent), Sudan (4.4 percent), and the United States (4.3 percent). Israel's expenditure includes military aid from the United States, which in 2008 was $2.38 billion (SIPRI 2009). In 2008, Israel spent just over $14 billion on its armed forces ($1,926 per capita), making it the country with the largest percentage of military spending as part of the national budget among all developed countries. In 2009, this budget was further raised by an extra 1.5 billion NIS to help address perceived threats from Iran's nuclear program, making it the highest total amount spent on security in Israel's history.

Israel is also among the world's largest arms exporters. According to Israeli Ministry of Security figures, in 2008 Israeli industries signed $6.3 billion worth of security export contracts, placing the country third in world rankings after the United States and Russia (Opall 2009). U.S. government data, on the other hand, place Israel at tenth place, with $400 million in exports (Grimmett 2009). The discrepancy is possibly due to the American report not including services such as training and technical support.

Finally, proportional to its size Israel has the world's most extensive military control of land. Over one third of the 22,072 square kilometers under Israeli civilian law (including the Golan Heights and East Jerusalem) are di-

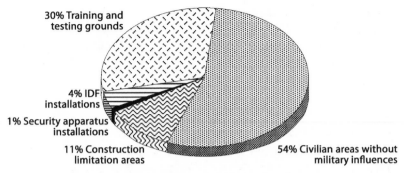

FIGURE 12.1. Military control or influence on land in Israel. Reproduced by permission from Oren and Regev, *A Land in Uniform*, 11.

rectly controlled by the IDF—mostly as training grounds. The military also places limitations on planning and construction around its installations; and certain, otherwise civilian, areas are designated for emergency use to gather forces and deploy weapons systems, enlarging the area controlled to almost half of the country (Oren and Regev 2008). Add the fact that the IDF is the sovereign in the occupied West Bank, and we find that military control exists over more than three-quarters of the territory between the Jordan and the Mediterranean.

With regard to construction and planning, the military functions as an all-but-autonomous entity. While the law requires security installations to receive building permits, the procedure for acquiring them is much shorter than for civilian projects, and requires only specifying the project's location and boundaries at a Committee for Security Installations (CSI) operating in every district (Baruchin, Oren, and Regev 2009). Moreover, Ministry of Security representatives sit on civilian Regional Planning and Building Committees, and may submit objections (whose substance need not be made public) to civilian projects that may conflict with existing or approved security installations.

The realities of role expansion, budget prioritization, control of land, and planning autonomy are the hallmarks of militarism. Nevertheless, only over the past decade has a critical discussion of this reality emerged in earnest.

Early Israeli scholarship on military matters took place within the structural-functionalist paradigm of "civil-military relations" imported from American academia, where it had been developed in the context of the Cold War (see Janowitz 1971; Huntington 1981). This framework assumes a functional differentiation in the modern democratic state between the civilian and military spheres, whereby the military is a professional service-provider to the state and does not take political stances as such, acting instead as yet an-

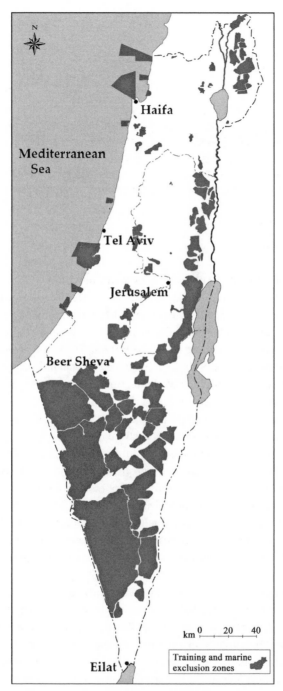

FIGURE 12.2. Training and marine exclusion zones in
Israel. Reproduced by permission from Oren and Regev,
A Land in Uniform, 19.

other interest group in the competition over state resources. On this account, military coups in modern states are the result of a pathological "role expansion" of the military, whereby it increasingly encroaches on a weakened civilian domain.

Israeli social commentators, eager to number the country among Western democracies, adopted this paradigm by and large (Perlmutter 1966, 1968; Peri 1977, 1981; Lissak 1983, 1984). At the same time, they could not ignore the overwhelming evidence for the expanded role of the IDF in Israeli society. This includes the regular "parachuting" of recently retired generals into senior political and managerial positions; the social networks among career officers and reservists that are carried over into civilian life; the promotion of the military by the school system, religious institutions, youth movements, cultural organizations, and the media; and the wide range of civilian roles played by the IDF, especially in education and immigrant absorption.

However, since no military coup had ever taken place in Israel, the aforementioned writers took for granted the health of civil-military relations, and proceeded to celebrate the IDF's role expansion as a functional contribution to democracy. The "civilianization of the military" (Perlmutter 1966, 102) and the partial militarization of the civilian sphere were explained as factors that by themselves mitigated the threat of praetorianism inherent to the prolonged Arab-Israeli conflict. All the while, the conflict itself was conceived as an extrinsic factor that places a strain on the social system from without, rather than as constitutive of Israeli society itself (see Peled and Shafir 1996).

This outlook has been increasingly undercut in the past two decades, as new scholarship has challenged previously unquestioned assumptions about the Zionist project and the role of the IDF (Ben-Ari, Rosenhek, and Maman 2001, 5–9). In contrast to earlier accounts, current studies tend to emphasize the constitutive role of the Arab-Israeli conflict in shaping Israeli society, and of the military in the construction of collective and individual identities (Ben-Ari 1998; Lomsky-Feder and Ben-Ari 1999).

Central to the reevaluation of Israeli militarism have been Uri Ben-Eliezer's studies (Ben-Eliezer 1997, 1998, 2001), which explain the blurring of the separation between Army and society in Israel by situating it as the latest in a series of "nations in arms"—France after the Revolution and again from 1870; Prussia from its defeat by Napoleon and until World War I; and Japan in the Meiji period (1868–1912). In common with these countries, there has never been overt military rule. Instead, role expansion "is manifested in the fact that the Army is not built as a professional force, separate from the society, but exists as the Army of the whole nation, with the idea of participation at its center. 'Everyone' is involved, first as conscripts, and afterward in the reserves" (Ben-Eliezer 2001, 146–47).

Newer scholarship has thus stressed how the IDF functions as a central mechanism in constructing differential levels of inclusion and exclusion in society via recruitment, assignment, and retention of personnel (Levy 1996, Rosenhek 1999). The gendered dimensions of Israeli militarism have also come under scrutiny, tying the military's central social role to the reproduction of masculinist worldviews, and analyzing women's service in the IDF not as an equalizing factor but rather as a mechanism for reproducing their subordination (Yuval-Davis 1985; Jerbi 1997; Izraeli 2001).

Kimmerling (2001, 215–16) argues that the ideological dimension of militarism in Israeli society amounts to a "civil religion of security," whereby "civilian leaders and constituencies regard primary military and strategic considerations as self-evidently the only or the predominant considerations in most of their social and political decision-making. . . . Once militarism penetrates the cognitive dimensions of a culture its suffuses both the structural and cultural state of mind of the collectivity . . . [the] institutional and cognitive orientation towards permanent war preparation in order to defend the collectivity's very existence [becomes] part of social routine and [is] no longer considered a matter of public debate or political struggle." On such a reading, the sense of "existential threat" prevalent in Israeli society—the perception that the only alternative to military victory is the total annihilation of the society—is artificial and functions to maintain the legitimacy of militaristic arrangements and the depoliticization of security (Ezrahi 1997; Pappé 2002).

As a result of these material and ideological dimensions of Israeli militarism, it is unsurprising that military priorities have regularly taken precedence over environmental ones throughout the country's history. We now move to assess the results of this precedence in terms of the military's environmental impacts.

THE IDF AND THE ECOLOGY OF WAR

By the time Israel was founded in 1948, a variety of local mammals in Palestine had already been hunted to the verge of extinction due to poor enforcement of the British hunting laws during the Mandate period. In view of the situation, a yearlong moratorium on all hunting was declared soon after the state's founding. Once it was lifted, however, it became clear that the major threat to wildlife was now IDF soldiers, who freely shot wild animals—especially gazelles—with their rifles. In response, the Joint Nature Protection Committee of the Zoology and Biology Societies (which would later evolve into the Society for Protection of Nature in Israel [SPNI]) wrote an impassioned plea to IDF chiefs. This resulted in a 1951 general order prohibiting all hunting of gazelles (Tal 2002, 158).

During the 1960s, an unlikely figure emerged from within the IDF as an early champion of conservation. Avraham Yoffe, an IDF general with a penchant for hunting, was appointed in 1965 as the first director of the Nature Reserves Authority, after a decade struggle by the SPNI to establish reserves. A larger-than-life figure with a forceful personality, Yoffe permanently gave up hunting, dedicating himself fully to conservation. He set out to maximize the number and size of areas designated as nature reserves, using his "combination of obstinacy, connections and charm" (Tal 2002, 170)—connections which were especially important in dealing with military counterclaims to land use. Within a decade of its founding the Authority's team of inspectors had grown tenfold, and by the end of Yoffe's tenure close to one hundred reserves had been declared.

Yet these early conservation successes have been an exception that indicates the norm. Overall, the IDF's environmental record has been negative and severe.

The environmental impacts of military conflict worldwide have been studied extensively, especially since the tactical oil spills of the first Gulf War where wildlife biologists documented high seabird mortality and pollution of tide flats important for migratory shorebirds (Evans, Symens, and Pilcher 1993; Sadiq 1993; Austin and Bruch 2000; Hulme 2004; Machlis and Hanson 2008). War regularly involves severe disturbances to habitats, uncontrolled extraction of resources, deforestation, and water contamination. Area-impact weapons such as napalm, cluster bombs, and fuel-air explosives are intentionally destructive over a wide area. Bombing of urban areas causes heavy smoke and dust pollution, which can be toxic when factories are targeted. Unexploded ordnance (such as landmines and cluster bombs) continues to kill and maim humans and animals long after hostilities have ended.

Such effects have been evident in Israel's experience of conflict. Since Israel has never carried out an assessment of its military's environmental impact, quantitative data on most of these aspects are sorely lacking. Evidence from elsewhere, however, indicates the likely impacts of military activities in Israel.

While no systematic information exists regarding the impact of country's major wars, widespread fighting in the Sinai Peninsula and Golan Heights during the 1967 and 1973 wars could only have damaged the local environment. Meteorological research indicates that fighting in the northern Sahara during World War II, in similar conditions to the Sinai, led to a tenfold increase in dust storms, as fragile desert vegetation and soils were disturbed (Machlis and Hanson 2008). To this day, the Golan Heights are littered with over two thousand minefields, including antipersonnel landmines that cause frequent animal and occasional human casualties (Heshmonai 2010). On the positive side, demilitarized zones established following the ceasefires in the

Jordan River basin and along the Syrian border serve as default nature reserves—although they are always vulnerable to resumed hostilities.

After the outbreak of the Second Intifada in October 2000, Palestinians alleged that the IDF was deliberately damaging the environment in the
West Bank. Such allegations included destroying trees and crops, damaging
wells and water infrastructure, and dumping of toxic waste in Palestinian-
controlled areas (Twite 2003, 567–69). Israel has argued that this damage was
a direct result of violence initiated by the Palestinian side, and was less serious
than the impact of the long-term neglect of the environment by the Palestinian Authority.

During the Second Lebanon War of 2006, Israeli jets bombed a power station south of Beirut, causing an estimated 15,000 tons of oil to spill into the
Mediterranean Sea. The oil spread rapidly, covering 150 kilometers of the Lebanese and Syrian coastlines, killing fish and affecting sensitive habitats. The
cleanup campaign was delayed five weeks until the ceasefire, making much
of the damage irreversible. Meanwhile, Hezbollah rockets caused major fires
in Northern Israel, burning a total of 52,000 dunams of forest to the ground
(Baror 2006; UNEP 2007).

The 2008 Gaza conflict, for its part, caused damage to wells and sewage
systems in the Gaza Strip, further polluting its already hyperstressed groundwater. According to an Amnesty International report, four water reservoirs,
eleven wells, and sewage networks and pumping stations were damaged and
20,000 meters of water mains were damaged or destroyed by Israeli tanks and
bulldozers. Sewage treatment plants in north and central Gaza were damaged,
resulting in raw sewage flooding more than a square kilometer of agricultural
and residential land, destroying crops and causing a health hazard (Amnesty
International 2009, 10). The Palestinians also accused Israel of using depleted
uranium shells and white phosphorus during the operation, a charge that Israel denies. Hamas rockets, for their part, have caused fires in both nature reserves and agricultural fields within Israel—both before and during the Gaza
conflict (Bereshkovsky 2006).

A more recent set of major environmental impacts caused by military
activity is related to the construction of the Segregation Barrier in the West
Bank, which is spread along hundreds of kilometers and incorporates extensive physical infrastructure. Alongside its human cost in terms of Palestinians' freedom of movement, livelihoods, and dignity, the barrier also has
important environmental impacts. According to the SPNI, these include the
fragmentation of previously continuous animal and plant populations or ecological corridors; direct damage to unique habitats; and damage to aquifers
and streams; and the disruption of migration routes (SPNI 2010).

IDF activities during peacetime also have many direct environmental costs. Modern war preparations include significant resource consumption, stockpiling of strategic materials, weapons testing, and training. Active training can lead to residual unexploded ordnance (UXO), chemical contamination, landscape cratering, vegetation removal, and soil erosion. The military's ecological footprint is even larger if we consider the inputs it requires in terms of water, fuels, food, and raw materials. Worldwide, war preparations alone utilize up to 15 million square kilometers of land, account for 6 percent of all raw material consumption, and produce as much as 10 percent of global carbon emissions annually (Machlis and Hanson 2008).

In Israel, everyday training activities take a serious toll on the landscape. Examples cited in the State Comptroller's report (2004) include the construction of training infrastructures such as mounds and ramparts, which alter water courses and wildlife corridors; the movement of heavy vehicles, which crush plants and animals and leave deep tracks in the ground; the discarding of waste food, packaging, and shells; and brushfires resulting from gunfire. The most recent example of this phenomenon is the 2007 fire, which raged in the Lachish region and destroyed 2,500 hectares of land (Oren and Regev 2008, 434).

It should be noted that 38 percent of lands in reserves overlap with military training grounds. In the Negev, half of the areas dedicated to nature reserves are located within training grounds, and a third of training grounds are within nature reserves (Oren and Regev 2008, 433–37). Under Section 23 of the National Parks and Nature Reserves Law, security forces are freed from complying with its provisions. This may well explain why the military has never been particularly obstinate about the declaration of reserves even when the land is already utilized for training. In practice the Authority tries to reach a consensus with the Army on the types of activities that take place, with tank training grounds suffering the most damage while the safety zones around the edges of firing ranges remain mostly unharmed (Tal 2002, 197).

It has been argued that the tracts of land that serve as a buffer between training grounds and civilian areas have led to the indirect protection of substantial habitats. While there is no direct evidence from Israel, studies from Camp Pendleton, California, highlight that the undeveloped shoreline has protected key habitats and now harbors significant biodiversity—1,250 species of plants and animals including 18 threatened or endangered species. Research from around U.S. military bases in Germany demonstrates that training activities have contributed to high biodiversity by creating disturbance heterogeneity (Machlis and Hanson 2008).

The State Comptroller's report (2004) identified a series of "faults, some of them fundamental, which point to a worrying state of affairs" with regard to the environmental oversight and regulation of the IDF's activities (State

Comptroller's Office 2004, 74). The findings identified seven problematic areas and indicated the degree to which the military had for years successfully dodged any meaningful external supervision of its environmental impacts, while leaving its internal mechanisms for environmental protection on a largely declarative level. These include:

- *Relations with the Ministry of Environmental Protection.* There has been a long-standing dispute over the applicability of environmental laws to the IDF. In practice, almost all military activities involving hazardous materials were carried out without Environment Ministry permits; the Ministry was not receiving necessary information; and its supervision of the IDF was "marginal and rare."

- *The Ministry of Security.* The Ministry's construction department was also responsible for supervising environmental protection, creating a potential conflict of interest. In addition, the Ministry's environmental committee lacked basic information on IDF environmental-protection activities, including the findings of local environmental monitoring systems and any unit or activity classified "Top Secret." The committee did not follow up on the implementation of many of its own decisions.

- *The IDF's administrative protocol.* While a generic environmental policy for the military was established in 1999, it has not been systematically implemented by High Command by 2004. Potential environmental hazards had not been identified; protocols had not been established for responding to and investigating emergency pollution events, and different bodies within the IDF were not sending representatives to the General Staff committee on environmental protection. In addition, the IDF was not required to report pollution events or environmental hazards to the Ministry of Interior Planning Directorate.

- *Fuel and oil pollution.* IDF fuelling stations, most of them in hydrologically sensitive areas, operated in contravention of water regulations— lacking fuelling platforms, fuel separators, and means for monitoring leaks. A 2001 inspection by the Water Commission of bases in northern Israel found dozens of cases in which the ground was saturated with fuels and oils, treatment platforms lacked proper funneling and collection, and containers were overflowing. These findings were discovered again in repeat inspections.

- *Sewage treatment.* Many sewage treatment and removal facilities in the IDF are based on absorption pools, and only limited steps had been taken to replace these with sealed septic tanks or with connection to the sewage system. The IDF did not adequately address faults found in its own inspections of evaporation pools.

- *Two ongoing large-scale contaminations.* The Ministry of Security's treatment of the contamination of the Hazor aquifer by the local Air Force base, and of the long-standing presence of discarded ammunition on the seabed opposite Tel Aviv's beaches, was limited to an assessment of the extent and causes of contamination, without pursuing any particular course of action.

- *Investigation and enforcement.* The IDF undertook a very limited number of actions to investigate environmental hazards caused by its units or to enforce environmental protection laws. A protocol approved in 2001 by the attorney general concerning the enforcement of environmental laws in the IDF was not implemented.

The IDF and Ministry of Security contested many of the report's findings. Regarding the disputes with the Ministry of Environment, for example, the IDF argued that the applicability of the hazardous materials law to the Army should be determined ad hoc for any given instance, rather than in advance for a list of various activities. It also argued that a comprehensive survey of environmental hazards in all Army units would be too costly and time-consuming, and thus assessments would be only carried out on a topical basis within certain units. At the same time, other findings were accepted: the IDF promised that fueling stations would in future be built according to legal requirements and existing hazards would be addressed as part of a multiyear plan. Six years after the report, the issue of sewage treatment remains a major bone of contention between the IDF and the Ministry of Environmental Protection, with the minister promising the IDF's imminent agreement to treat all of its sewage.

CIVIL SOCIETY, THE IDF, AND THE ENVIRONMENT

By the time the State Comptroller's report was released, the previously sacrosanct status of the military in Israeli society had already faced a number of important challenges. The growing environmental scrutiny of the Israeli Army should be seen in this evolving context.

In the late 1980s and early 1990s, Israel experienced a certain recoil from the "nation in arms" model, which signaled the beginning of a demarcation between military and society. Indications of this trend include an escalation of public and media criticism of the IDF following the Sabra and Shatila massacre in Lebanon and human rights violations during the first Intifada; a sharp decrease in the motivation of Israeli youth to join the military (Spiegel 2001); cases of entire units going AWOL over mistreatment; and intensified public intervention of soldiers' parents in military affairs, especially following the 1997 helicopter disaster, in which seventy-three soldiers were killed after two Sikorsky H3s transporting them to Lebanon collided and crashed.

The same period also saw the shrinking of the Israeli military-industrial complex, previously one of the main drivers of economic growth (Mintz 1985; Mintz and Ward 1989). The three government-owned arms manufacturers—the Israel Aircraft Industries (IAI), Israel Military Industries (Ta'as), and the Weapons Development Authority (Rafa'el)—all saw layoffs and a shrinking in domestic and foreign purchasing, following the peace agreements with Egypt and Jordan, the end of the Cold War, and a general trend toward subordinating the military to market considerations (Levy 2009).

Shafir and Peled (2002) explain the decline of militarism as part of a deeper process in Israeli society. Since the Labor Party lost its political hegemony in 1977, a series of economic reforms by Likud and national unity government effectively ended the state-managed economy and nurtured the rise of an independent business class not beholden to the state. This, along with the Oslo Accords (initially negotiated without military involvement) and processes of economic and cultural globalization, led to a fracturing of Israeli's once-pervasive republican ethos of citizenship, defined by an ideology of national unity and contribution to the "common good" (as defined by the ruling class). Instead, two competing discourses have emerged: a liberal-individualist discourse, inspired by consumerism and largely identified with the secular, Ashkenazi middle class, which emphasizes personal rights and quality of life; and an ethnonationalist discourse, largely identified with the Mizrachi working classes and the national-religious population, which essentializes inclusion in society in terms of Jewishness and views the Arab minority as an internal enemy.

It is within this process that the rise of mainstream Israeli environmentalism should be understood. Environmental contestation of military activities has primarily been the work of secular middle-class communities campaigning against hazards generated by adjacent military bases, grounded in concerns for health and quality of life. Rather than displaying environmental justice agendas, these campaigns have largely been a matter of Not-In-My-Back-Yard concerns (see Lake 1996). The following examples serve to illustrate this trend.

- *Ein Shemer.* In 1998, residents of the Menashe regional council undertook a public and legal campaign against the deployment, without CSI approval, of an Arrow anti-ballistic missile battery in the Ein Shemer base, citing health concerns surrounding the system's radar. After an appeal to the Supreme Court and following the intervention of the minister of Environment, a compromise was reached in 2003 between the regional council and the security apparatus, which limited the operation of the radar outside emergencies (Oren and Regev 2008, 239–40).

- *IMI facilities.* In the 1990s, three munitions factories belonging to the state-owned Israel Military Industries were closed in Tel Aviv, Jerusalem, and Herzeliya, leaving behind soil contaminated with heavy metals, organic pollutants, and explosives that also seeped into the water table. Though the IMI dragged its feet, heavy pressure from the public and the Ministry of Environment finally forced it to decontaminate the sites. In 1999, members of the Ramat Hasharon local council filed a class-action lawsuit against the IMI, claiming the largest and still-active facility was contaminating the town's drinking water. A subsequent water quality survey led to the closure of all the town's wells, which were connected to Tel Aviv's system. The facility was supposed to close by the end of 2010 as part of IMI's privatization; residents and litigators have meanwhile managed to freeze all plans for high-end housing in that area until it is decontaminated (Tal 2007; Netzer 2010).

- *Kishon River.* In 2000, a newspaper report revealed that over twenty former naval commando soldiers had contracted cancer, linking their illness to regular practice dives in the estuary of the Kishon River, which is highly polluted due to effluents from industries in the Haifa Bay. The former elite soldiers drew on powerful social networks to support their public campaign, forcing the military to cease dives in the Kishon and set up a committee of inquiry headed by former Chief Justice Meir Shamgar. While the committee determined that no direct link could be established between the diving and the cancer incidents, the IDF nevertheless recognized the soldiers who had become ill or died as disabled veterans or casualties, with the concomitant benefits (Nathan 2007).

- *Atlit.* In 2003, a local green NGO appealed to Haifa District Court against a construction project within the designated area of the Atlit naval commando base, located within a nature reserve (which is closed to the public due to the secrecy of the base). Concerned about damage to the marine environment, they initiated a legal process that ultimately saw the discussion returned to the CSI, where it was reapproved (Oren and Regev 2008, 240–42).

- *Hoshaya.* In 2003, residents of Hoshaya in the lower Galilee appealed to the Nazareth District Court against the construction of a new base nearby, which had been approved without their knowledge by the CSI in 1996. Citing damage to vistas, air and noise pollution, and harm to their quality of life, they also argued that the planned base contradicted regional development programs and demanded the right to view and comment on the plans. The long legal process finally reached the

Supreme Court. While the 2006 verdict did not cancel the construction, the judges did express severe discomfort with the nature of military exemptions in the planning process, emphasizing that the "sanctity" of security concerns was a thing of the past and underscoring the need to balance military needs with civilian and environmental ones (Oren and Regev 2008, 242–48).

- *Dimona.* In 2005, environmental concerns were central to opening up the debate over Israel's unacknowledged nuclear facility. It was issues of pollution and safety, rather than weapons proliferation, that prompted the first Knesset debate on the topic (Melman 2005). Meanwhile, the lawsuits of over forty reactor workers who claimed to have developed cancer following exposure to radioactive and toxic materials continue to be heard in the various courts (Shapira 2009; see Richter et al. 1997). The reactor's potential for decrepitude after four decades of use led to a series of provocative bills for its closure (Khenin et al. 2009).

- *The Segregation Barrier.* In 2006, hundreds of Jewish settlers from the Gush Etzion settlements took direct action to disrupt the clearing of the Abu Suda forest, a nature reserve dating back to the Mandate period, where a section of the barrier was to be constructed. The Kfar Etzion field school then petitioned the Supreme Court, offering an alternative route that would spare both the forest and 50 dunams of Palestinians' vineyards. The Ministry of Security accepted the new route. A year later, the SPNI led a parliamentary campaign against the construction of the 30-kilometer section of the barrier in the Judea desert, mostly within natural reserve areas. This led to the only documented case where a contested part of the barrier was actually cancelled and replaced with a network of electronic surveillance systems (Sharon 2007).

- *Tel Arad.* In 2008, a television report revealed Ministry of Health data according to which, between 1994 and 2001, seventeen soldiers at the Nahal Brigade training base in Tel Arad contracted Hodgkin's lymphoma—more than twice the rate of other infantry brigades. The report noted that the base was adjacent to the city of Arad's evaporation pools, which included waste from its industrial area. In response, parents of soldiers who were about to begin their service in the Nahal brigade launched a campaign of demonstrations and lobbying, demanding that the base be evacuated. Two parallel examinations by the IDF and the Ministry of Environment found no evidence of excess contamination in the training grounds. The parents rejected these findings, as did the Israel Union for Environmental Defense (IUED). Citing the precautionary principle as established by the Shamgar committee regarding the Kishon case, they petitioned the Supreme Court for the evacuation of the base. The case is still being heard (IUED 2009).

The most recent and highly publicized case in which military plans have been challenged on environmental grounds is that of Training Base City ("Ir HaBahadim"), a project designed to transfer nine IDF training bases for non-combat units (e.g., the Medical Corps and Military Police) from their current locations in central Israel to a single site near the Negev Junction (IUED 2009, 181–86, 269–86; Elad 2009). The plan covers 1,600 dunams of land, includes 250,000 square meters of buildings and is intended to house 11,000 soldiers. The project was promoted with the explicit goal of leveraging economic development in the Negev, creating jobs through auxiliary services, and persuading officers' families to relocate to the south (but see Svirsky 2007). In addition, the relocation would allow the IDF to sell off expensive real estate in the center of the country, particularly the Tzrifin base near Rishon LeZion, generating high revenues for the state.

The most important consideration for choosing the Negev Junction site was that it had already been designated for a military base in the 1980s. Yet this location is also within 8 kilometers of the Ramat Hovav industrial estate, Israel's major center for chemical and pharmaceutical industries and the location of its only approved hazardous waste disposal site. Ramat Hovav had been a target of concern among environmentalists for years due to the concentration of polluting industries, a number of accidents involving hazardous waste, and reports of high rates of cancer and lung diseases among Bedouins in adjacent unrecognized villages (Almi 2003). A 2004 epidemiological study by Ben-Gurion University, commissioned by the Ministry of Health, found that residential proximity to the industrial estate was associated with increased rates of mortality, chronic respiratory morbidity, and major congenital malformations among the Bedouin population (Bentov et al. 2006; Karakis et al. 2008; Karakis et al. 2009).

Citing the danger to the health of soldiers and the lack of adequate research of the potential hazards of the site, environmental NGOs such as the IUED initiated a vociferous public campaign against the project. In 2006, after a lengthy mediation process, the Ministry of Environment and representatives of the Ramat Hovav factories signed an agreement determining new measures for protecting air quality and a protocol for on-site treatment of their hazardous waste (Tal et al. 2006). This paved the way for a government decision approving the construction of Training Base City in April 2007, along with provisions for an epidemiological survey and the rehabilitation of the hazardous waste site—although these were to be completed after the base was already populated.

Environmental groups were, nevertheless, dissatisfied with what they considered superficial measures. And while bulldozers began to prepare the land for construction a number of demonstrations were organized by Green Course, a student environmental group, and parents of future conscripts. A coalition of NGOs appealed to the Beer-Sheva District Court, arguing that a project of such size should have been approved through the regular and not military planning channels, in which case a more comprehensive examination of environmental conditions would have been required. A lengthy legal process ensued, reaching the Supreme Court which required the state to prepare an assessment of the health risks associated with the base's proximity to Ramat Hovav, and to incorporate their conclusions into the plan, which would be returned to the District Planning Committee and open to public scrutiny.

The case of Training Base City, hailed as a victory by environmental NGOs, forms an important precedent in subordinating military planning to the same environmental standards required from civilian projects. Yet paradoxically, the case also indicates the continued force of Israeli militarism. It took a potential risk to soldiers' health to lead to regulation of pollution from Ramat Hovav, whereas the existing risk to residents of Beer-Sheva and the Bedouin population had failed to do so for years. It is also worth noting that due to the prevailing winds, Beer-Sheva residents are more likely to be exposed to pollution than the soldiers who will be living at the training base. The well-being of the armed forces still appears to retain more weight in the Israeli public sphere than the well-being of civilians, let alone Arab citizens.

In this context, and in closing, I would like to return to the ideological dimensions of Israeli militarism by looking at the IDF's framework for internal environmental education. This framework clearly displays the contingent terms on which environmental concerns have been incorporated into the military agenda, with the effect of defusing their civilian and potentially anti-militarist potential. The framework was issued in mid-2007 by the Education and Youth Corps (Israel Defense Forces 2007). Alongside its relatively banal operational directives (generating of educational materials and lesson plans, cleanup activities, nature hikes), the true interest of the document lies in its construction of a "green militarism"—a seamless mix of environmental and patriotic sentiments that reinforces the hegemonic political culture of Zionist militarism, even as it brings it up to speed with contemporary concerns over pollution and nature protection.

While briefly mentioning "protection of human life," "professionalism," and "compliance with the law" among the values driving the program, the document's detailed rationale explicitly couches environmental protection as a corollary of the requirement to "strengthen each soldier's connection to the land and his love of the motherland. Love of the motherland strengthens each soldier's commitment to protecting the State of Israel and its resources which have been entrusted to the IDF as a deposit" (Israel Defense Forces 9). Or, in the words of Chief of Staff Gabi Ashkenazi, "our duty [is] to educate for protection of nature, scenery, and antiquities, which are a testimony to the Jewish people's heritage and its historical right to maintain a sovereign Jewish state in the Land of Israel" (13).

In summary, it can be said that although environmental agendas have made an important contribution to challenging Israeli militarism, the IDF has also been agile in adapting to these pressures and has by no means lost its privileged material and cultural status. If anything, the last decade has seen a fortification of militarism and nationalism in the wake of major hostilities in the West Bank, Gaza, and Lebanon, and a strengthening of the ethnonationalist discourse of citizenship in Israeli society at the expense of the liberal-individualist one. The third option—a socialist-egalitarian discourse open to the universal claims of environmental justice—is heard from only a small minority on the radical left. Perhaps it is only with a final-status agreement with the Palestinians and the resolution of the Israeli-Arab conflict as a whole that we may hope for a true normalization of Israeli society; only then might environmental concerns finally receive the paramount place they deserve in public attention and policy.

REFERENCES

Almi, O. 2003. *No Man's Land: Health in the Unrecognized Villages in the Negev.* Tel Aviv: Physicians for Human Rights. http://www.phr.org.il/phr/files/article-file_1163421247181.pdf.

Amnesty International. 2009. *Thirsting for Justice: Palestinian Access to Water Restricted.* London: AI. http://www.amnesty.org/en/library/info/MDE15/028/2009/en.

Austin, J., and C. Bruch. 2000. *The Environmental Consequences of War: Legal, Economic, and Scientific Perspectives.* Cambridge: Cambridge University Press.

Baror, Y. 2006. *Assessment of Environmental Damage following the War in the North.* Jerusalem: Israel Ministry of Environmental Protection, Chief Scientist's Office.

Baruchin, A., A. Oren, and R. Regev. 2009. "The Planning Hegemony of the Security Apparatus." In *Space of Security*, edited by A. Oren, 97–116.

Ben-Ari, E. 1998. *Mastering Soldiers: Conflict, Emotion and the Enemy in an Israeli Military Unit.* Oxford: Bergham

Ben-Ari, E., Z. Rosenhek, and D. Maman, eds. 2001. *Military, State, and Society in Israel: Theoretical and Comparative Perspectives.* New Brunswick: Transaction.

Ben-Eliezer, U. 1997. "Rethinking the Civil-Military Relations Paradigm: The Inverse Relations between Militarism and Praetorianism through the Example of Israel." *Comparative Political Studies* 30: 356–74.

———. 1998. *The Making of Israeli Militarism.* Bloomington: Indiana University Press.

———. 2001. "From Military Role-Expansion to Difficulties in Peace-Making: The Israeli Defense Forces 50 Years On." In *Military, State, and Society in Israel*, edited by Ben-Ari et al., 137–72.

Bentov, Y., E. Kordysh, R. Hershkovitz, I. Belmaker, M. Polyakov, N. Bilenko, and B. Sarov. 2006. "Major Congenital Malformations and Residential Proximity to a Regional Industrial Park Including a National Toxic Waste Site: An Ecological Study." *Environmental Health* 5: 8.

Bereshkovsky, A. 2006. "Qassam Missile Falls in Be'eri Reserve, Causing Major Fire." *YNet*, July 3. In Hebrew.

Elad, N. 2009. "The Establishment of Negev Training Base City as a Lever for Environmental Regulation of Ramat Hovav Pollution." In *Space of Security*, edited by A. Oren, 228–36.

Evans, G., and J. Newnham. 1998. *The Penguin Dictionary of International Relations*. London: Penguin.

Evans, M. I., P. Symens, and C. W. T. Pilcher. 1993. "Short-Term Damage to Coastal Bird Populations in Saudi Arabia and Kuwait Following the 1991 Gulf War Marine Pollution." *Marine Pollution Bulletin* 27: 157–61.

Ezrahi, Y. 1997. *Rubber Bullets: Power and Conscience in Modern Israel*. Berkeley: University of California Press.

Grimmett, R. 2009. *Conventional Arms Transfers to Developing Nations, 2001–2008*. Washington, DC: Congressional Research Service.

Heshmonai, A. 2010. "Senior Officer: Hundreds of Minefields Are Unfenced." *Ma'ariv*, February 7. In Hebrew.

Hulme, K. 2004. *War-Torn Environment: Interpreting the Legal Threshold*. Leiden: Martinus Nijhoff.

Huntington, S. P. 1981. *Soldier and the State: The Theory and Politics of Civil-Military Relations*. Cambridge: Harvard University Press.

Israel Defense Forces. 2007. *Conception of Environmental Education in the Education and Youth Corps*. http://heschel.org.il/fellows/node/151.

Israel Union for Environmental Defense (IEUD). 2009. "Supreme Court Petition on Excess Sickness at the Nahal Training Base." http://www.adamteva.org.il/?CategoryID=373&ArticleID=820.

Izraeli, D. 2001. "Paradoxes of Women's Service in the Israel Defense Forces." In *Military, State, and Society in Israel*, edited by Ben-Ari et al.

Janowitz, M. 1971. *The Professional Soldier: A Social and Political Portrait*. New York: Free Press.

Jerbi, I. 1997. *The Double Price: The Status of Women in Israeli Society and Women's Service in the Military*. Tel Aviv: Ramot. In Hebrew.

Karakis, I., A. Bolotin, E. Kordysh, I. Belmaker, and B. Sarov. 2008. "Mortality in the Bedouin Population and Proximity to a Regional Industrial Complex." *Environmental Health Insights* 1: 21–29.

Karakis, I., E. Kordysh, T. Lahav, A. Bolotin, Y. Glazer, H. Vardi, I. Belmaker, and B. Sarov. 2009. "Life Prevalence of Upper Respiratory Tract Diseases and Asthma among Children Residing in Rural Area Near a Regional Industrial Park: Cross-Sectional Study." *Rural and Remote Health* 9: 1092.

Keren, M. 1999. "Israel's Security Intellectuals." In *Security Concerns: Insights from the Israeli Experience*, edited by D. Bar-Tal, D. Jacobson, and A. Klieman, 181–92. Stamford: JAI Press.

Khenin, D., M. Barakeh, H. Sweid, and A. Agbaria, MKs. 2009. *Bill: Closure of the Atomic Reactor in Dimona*. Jerusalem: Knesset. http://www.knesset.gov.il/privatelaw/data/18/238.rtf.

Kimmerling, B. 2001. *The Invention and Decline of Israeliness: State, Society, and the Military*. Berkeley: University of California Press.

Lake, R. 1996. "Volunteers, NIMBYs, and Environmental Justice: Dilemmas of Democratic Practice." *Antipode* 282: 160–74.

Levy, Y. 1996. "War Policy, Interethnic Relations and the Internal Expansion of the State: Israel 1948—1956." *Te'oria Uvikoret* 8: 203–24. In Hebrew.

———. 2009. "The Military and the Market: A Conceptual Framework." In *Space of Security*, edited by A. Oren, 59–74.

Lissak, M. 1983. "Paradoxes of Israeli Civil-Military Relations: An Introduction." *Journal of Strategic Studies* 3: 1–12.

———, ed. 1984. *The Israeli Society and Its Defense Establishment.* London: Frank Cass.

Lomsky-Feder, E., and E. Ben-Ari, ed. 1999. *The Military and Militarism in Israeli Society.* Albany: SUNY Press.

Machlis, G. E., and Hanson, T. 2008. "Warfare Ecology." *BioScience* 58: 729–36.

Melman, Y. 2005. "Sleeping Well at Night?" *Ha'aretz*, May 28. In Hebrew.

Mintz, A. 1985. "The Military-Industrial Complex: American Concepts and Israeli Realities." *Journal of Conflict Resolution* 29: 623–39.

Mintz, A., and M. D. Ward. 1989. "The Political Economy of Military Spending in Israel." *American Political Science Review* 83: 521–33.

Nathan, G. 2007. *State of Research on the Medical Consequences of Diving in the Kishon.* Background document for Y. Beilin, MK. Jerusalem: Knesset. www.knesset.gov.il/mmm/data/pdf/m01829.pdf. In Hebrew.

Netzer, R. 2010. "Bottom of the Sharon." *Globes*, January 14. In Hebrew.

Opall, B. 2009. "Israel 3rd Among World Arms Suppliers: MoD Numbers Conflict With U.S. Report." *Defense News,* October 5.

Oren, A., ed. 2009. *Space of Security: A New Approach to the Use of Land (Resources) for Security and Military Needs.* Jerusalem: Van Leer Institute. In Hebrew.

Oren, A., and R. Regev. 2008. *Land in Uniform: Territory and Defense in Israel.* Jerusalem: Carmel. In Hebrew.

Pappé, I. 2002. "Donning the Uniform: The Military and the Media in Israel." *Middle East Report* 223: 46–51.

Peled, Y., and G. Shafir. 1996. "The Roots of Peacemaking: The Dynamics of Citizenship in Israel, 1948–93." *International Journal of Middle East Studies* 28: 391–413.

Peri, Y. 1977. "Ideological Portrait of the Israeli Military Elite." *Jerusalem Quarterly* 3: 29–39.

———. 1981. "Political-Military Partnership in Israel." *International Political Science Review* 2: 303–15.

Perlmutter, A. 1966. *Military and Politics in Israel: Nation-Building and Role Expansion.* London: Frank Cass.

———. 1968. "The Israeli Army in Politics: The Persistence of the Civilian over the Military." *World Politics* 20: 606–43.

Richter, E., E. Ben-Michael, T. Tsafrir, and R. Laster. 1997. "Cancer in Thirty-Nine Nuclear Industry Workers: A Preliminary Report." *Environmental Health Perspectives* 105: 1511–17.

Rosenhek, Z. 1999. "The Exclusionary Logic of the Welfare State: Palestinian Citizens in the Israeli Welfare State." *International Sociology* 4: 195–215.

Sadiq, M. 1993. *The Gulf War Aftermath: An Environmental Tragedy.* Dordrecht: Kluwer.

Shafir, G., and Y. Peled. 2002. *Being Israeli: The Dynamics of Multiple Citizenship.* Cambridge: Cambridge University Press.

Shapira, R. 2009. "Dimona Nuclear Reactor Workers Who Developed Cancer Have Still Not Received Compensation." *Ha'aretz*, July 31. In Hebrew.

Sharon, R. 2007. "A Victory for the Greens: Construction of the Fence in the South to Be Frozen." *Ma'ariv*, January 9. In Hebrew.

Stockholm International Peace Research Institute. SIPRI. 2009. *The SIPRI Military Expenditure Database*. Stockholm: SIPRI. http://milexdata.sipri.org/.

Society for Protection of Nature in Israel (SPNI). 2010. *Building and Planning Threats to the Protection of Open Spaces in Israel*. Tel Aviv: SPNI. In Hebrew.

Spiegel, U. 2001. *Youth Motivation to Serve in the IDF*. Background document for Knesset Education and Culture Committee. Jerusalem: Knesset. http://www.knesset.gov.il/mmm/data/docs/m00132.doc. In Hebrew.

State Comptroller. 2004. *Annual Report 55a*. http://www.mevaker.gov.il/. In Hebrew.

Swirski, S. 2007. *Current Plans for Developing the Negev: A Critical Perspective*. Tel Aviv: Adva Center. http://www.adva.org/UserFiles/File/AdvaNegevJanuary2007.pdf.

Tal, A. 2002. *Pollution in a Promised Land: An Environmental History of Israel*. Berkeley: University of California Press.

Tal, A., A. Braverman, N. Hasid, and A. Zohar. 2006. "Regulating Ramat Hovav's Industrial Effluents: The Anatomy of a Mediation." Paper presented at National Ecology and Environmental Quality Conference, Haifa, June.

Tal, U. 2007. *Construction Plans in Haharon IMI Lands*. Background document for Knesset Internal Affairs and Environment Committee. Jerusalem: Knesset. http://www.knesset.gov.il/mmm/data/docs/m01706.doc. In Hebrew.

Twite, R. 2003. "A Question of Priorities—Adverse Effects of the Israeli-Palestinian Conflict on the Environment of the Region over the Last Decade." In *Security and Environment in the Mediterranean: Conceptualising Security and Environmental Conflicts*, edited by H. Brauch et al., 563–72. Berlin: Springer-Verlag.

United Nations Environment Program (UNEP). 2003. *Desk Study on the Environment in the Occupied Palestinian Territories*. Nairobi: UNEP.

——. 2007. *Lebanon Post Conflict Environmental Assessment*. Nairobi: UNEP.

Vagts, A. 1981. *A History of Militarism*. Westport: Greenwood.

Yuval-Davis, N. 1985. "Front and Rear: The Sexual Division of Labor in the Israeli Army." *Feminist Studies* 11: 649–76.

CHAPTER THIRTEEN

"GOING BEYOND ISRAEL"
Epistemic Communities, Global Interests, and International Environmental Agreements

Rachelle Adam

THE INTERNATIONAL COMMUNITY, recognizing the need for multistate co-operation to stop global environmental devastation, has adopted multilateral agreements as frameworks for action. Israel is among those joining these agreements, but to what end? Given the degree to which the Arab-Israeli conflict has historically shaped its identity, can Israel rebrand itself through a global environmental role? Can its strategic participation in several environmental agreements overcome political obstacles? Will its environmental diplomacy, in short, create a new identity for Israel?

Israel's small territorial dimensions—22,072 square kilometers—allegedly attest to the limits of its physical impact on the global environment (Statistical Abstract of Israel 2010). In light of its diminutive size, relatively small population—7,552,00 at the end of 2009—and lack of natural resources of global significance, Israel is apparently not made of the stuff of which major players in the international environmental arena are made. Yet Israel's substantially large-sized ecological footprint[1]—a result of a burgeoning population, strong economy, and high standard of living—makes the case for Israel going beyond its own domestic environmental problems (Bromberg and Twite 2001, 134–35).

This chapter offers two frameworks for thinking about Israel's role in international environmental agreements. One is exemplified by the Barcelona Convention for the Protection of the Marine Environment and the Coastal Region of the Mediterranean (Barcelona Convention 1995), a regional agreement addressing marine pollution and promoting sustainability. Because the issue is of critical concern to Israel—a consequence of its approximately 190 kilometers of coastline (Marine and Coastal Environment: Mediterranean Coast 2003)—it has been an active participant in the convention since its beginnings. The second framework is represented by an international multilateral agreement with almost universal state membership. The issues addressed in it do not pose a direct and immediate threat to Israel's environment, either because of their nature (e.g., protecting world heritage) or because Israel has developed scientific expertise in these areas and is considered a global expert (e.g., desertification). One example is the Convention Concerning the Protection of the World Cultural and Natural Heritage, hereinafter referred to as World Heritage Convention (World Heritage Convention 1972) operating under the aegis of UNESCO for the protection of cultural and natural heritage of "outstanding universal value." Another example is the United Nations Convention to Combat Desertification (UNCCD) (1994) geared to assist least developed countries against the ravaging effects of desertification.[2]

In addition to explicating Israel's historical role in international environmental affairs, this chapter has practical ramifications: Israelis are most familiar with the United Nations in the context of the Arab-Israeli conflict, an organization which many of them perceive as a symbol of discriminatory and unjust anti-Israeli sentiment (Israel UN Relations, Israel Ministry of Foreign Affairs, n.d.). However most are probably unaware that in the realm of the environment, the UN has assumed global leadership and mobilized the international community in addressing threats such as climate change, ozone depletion, dangerous chemicals, depletion of fisheries, and marine pollution. Israel, like other countries, certainly has an interest in the success of the UN in these areas. But does it have a role to play in this surge of international hyperactivity to stop and reverse these threats? Or, is Israel's identity so overwhelmingly shaped by the Arab-Israeli conflict as to confine this role to an elusive vision?

ISRAEL AND INTERNATIONAL ENVIRONMENTALISM

The Stockholm Conference

A milestone in the history of today's international environmental activism was the 1972 UN Conference on the Human Environment (Stockholm Conference), the first in a series of environmental megaconferences.[3] The Stockholm Conference marked the official launch of modern international environmental cooperation, with the UN serving as global environmental coordinator.[4] Together with another 112 countries, Israel participated in the conference with a delegation of twelve members, the head of which was Israel's foreign minister Abba Eban. If the overriding goal of the UN in organizing the Stockholm Conference was to raise awareness of countries to the human onslaught on the environment, as far as Israel is concerned, it can be judged a success (interview with U. Marinov, August 11, 2009). Following the conference's request that all countries submit national reports on the state of their environment, Israel for the first time had to locate, analyze, and assess almost nonexistent data, and synthesize them as its first national report on the environment (Marinov 2009). Its most profound and immediate impact was the March 1973 government decision creating the Environmental Protection Service (EPS) (Government Decision No. 563, March 20, 1973), the forerunner of the Ministry of Environment established in 1988 (Marinov 2009; Tal 2002, 259, footnote 89).

Under the leadership of the United Nations Environment Program (UNEP) that emerged from the Stockholm Conference, the international community began its remarkable labor of environmental treaty-making. Israel, through the EPS, was part of this process. It started out by signing, at the 1976 conference of plenipotentiaries held in Barcelona, the Barcelona Convention (Barcelona Convention 1995). Throughout the 1970s and 1980s Israel went on to ratify major international environmental conventions including the Convention on International Trade in Endangered Species of Wild Fauna and Flora (CITES) in 1979 (1973) and the UN Convention on the Conservation of Migratory Species of Wild Animals (CMS) in 1983 (1980). In 1984 it ratified the Protocol for the Prevention of Pollution of the Mediterranean Sea by Dumping from Ships and Aircraft of the Barcelona Convention (the Dumping Protocol) (Barcelona Convention 1995), and in 1987 the protocol concerning Mediterranean Specially Protected Areas (the SPA Protocol) (Barcelona Convention 1995).

To Ratify or Not to Ratify

With its establishment in 1988, Israel's Ministry of Environment has continued the EPS's active involvement in international agreements (International Cooperation 2004; Israel's Environmental Protection Minister 2009). While it has successfully prodded the government into joining all major agreements (Environmental Conventions 2004), the Ministry of Environment is not the final decision maker regarding ratification of environmental agreements nor are environmental factors the key considerations in making these decisions. Reviewing the ratification process for some of these agreements reveals a diverse range of motivations behind the decision to ratify or not to ratify.

Similar to the situation in other countries, ratification decisions are determined by politically stronger and less environmentally minded ministries such as the Ministry of Foreign Affairs, the Justice Ministry, and the Defense Ministry. Locked into the mind-set of the Arab-Israeli conflict and its implications for Israel's survival, these ministries historically have not differentiated between international policy in the area of the environment and other sectors. Consequentially, Israel's role in international environmental relations has habitually been defined by predetermined political preferences calculated on the basis of national self-interests amid fixed concepts of sovereignty. For example, objections of other ministries based on traditional politics of national sovereignty held up the ratification of the amended Barcelona Convention for over ten years[5] and continue to prevent Israeli accession to the UN Convention on the Law of the Sea (UNCLOS).

The opposite also can hold true. Political interests of other ministries may speed up the ratification process. The Ministry of Foreign Affairs' interests in ratifying the Kyoto Protocol because of the politically charged issue of climate change allowed for a relatively swift ratification process.[6] Israel's accession to the International Convention for the Regulation of Whaling (ICRW) (1947, 62 Stat. 1716, 161 U.N.T.S. 74) was the fortuitous result of the U.S.-versus-Japan politics of the convention, in which Israel supported the U.S. position for stronger measures to protect whales by maintaining the 1982 moratorium. The Ministry of Foreign Affairs supported the ratification after consulting with Environment Ministry officials, keen on joining the convention out of global considerations.[7] The proactive support of the Ministry of Foreign Affairs mobilized governmental agreement for the ratification. These incidents are noteworthy: they signify the mainstreaming of international environmentalism and the identification of environmental interests with political interests. Thus the increasing political weight of environmental agreements can influence the policy of ministries other than the Ministry of Environment.

Politics aside, a rule of thumb for decision makers in ratifying an agreement is the level of behavioral change required. Will ratification entail substantial change or will the situation remain one of "business as usual" (Downs, Rocke, and Barsoom 1996)? This approach is demonstrated in international biodiversity agreements. Characterized as weak and amorphous with few if any binding commitments, CITES, a regulatory agreement for trade in endangered species, is an exception—its ratification was a comparatively smooth procedure. In addition to CITES and the CMS (CITES 1973; CMS 1980), in 1995 Israel joined the Convention on Biological Diversity (Country Profiles: Israel 1992). Two years later it signed the Ramsar Convention on Wetlands of International Importance (Ramsar Convention 1971). In 1999 Israel completed ratification of five major biodiversity agreements by joining the World Heritage Convention (World Heritage Convention 1972; International Cooperation 2004). While these agreements were eminently "ratifiable" due to their lack of burdensome and binding requirements entailing major behavioral changes, this rule cuts both ways. For example, except for the African-Eurasian Migratory Waterbird Agreement (AEWA) (1995), Israel has not ratified other agreements under CMS precisely *because* these agreements are perceived as insignificant and additional financial and participation burdens could not be justified (Convention on Migratory Species: Agreement Summary Sheets, n.d.).

International trade, by contrast, is a crucial consideration in ratifying international agreements. Safeguarding Israel's trading relations and protecting its industries was the major factor for ratification of the Montreal Protocol on Substances That Deplete the Ozone Layer (1987) as well as the Basel Convention on the Control of Transboundary Movements of Hazardous Waste and Their Disposal (1989; International Cooperation 2004). These same considerations apply to the Rotterdam Convention on the Prior Informed Consent Procedure for Certain Hazardous Chemicals and Pesticides in International Trade (PIC) (1998) and the Stockholm Convention on Persistent Organic Pollutants (POPs) (2001), both major international agreements that entered into force in 2004. Israel is in the process of joining both, catalyzed by the threat to its international trade and by the resulting harm to domestic industries in the face of nonratification.

Yet perhaps the most salient reason for not ratifying all of these agreements is simply "treaty fatigue." The upsurge in their number imposes a burden on the majority of countries. For many governments, Israel included, having to find the additional human resources and funds to participate in a multiple number of agreements makes effective implementation a challenge (Ivanova and Roy 2007, 48; Muñoz, Thrasher, and Najam 2009).

Political Isolation

Another challenge facing Israel's participation in international environmental forums is its political isolation. A succinct example of anti-Israel polemics is illustrated by UNEP's Governing Council (GC) that has traditionally and consistently vilified Israel. A series of decisions disclose how Israel has been singled out for political attack in the guise of environmental concerns.[8] The 1983 GC session, decision 11/4 entitled "Israel's decision to build a canal linking the Mediterranean Sea to the Dead Sea," surfaced again at the 1984 GC session as decision 12/7; it requested the UNEP executive director to facilitate the monitoring of "the adverse effects on Jordan and on the Arab territories occupied since 1967, including Jerusalem, arising from the implementation of the Israeli decision to construct the canal" (Twelfth Governing Council 1984). The decision was approved by forty-seven votes with no abstentions. The only country to oppose was the United States, whose representative remarked that "the decision contained political elements which fell outside the competence of the Governing Council" (1984). The issue of the canal linking the two seas came up for a third round at the Thirteenth Governing Council Session. The vote was again adopted by forty-seven to one, again with the sole opposition of the United States: "The representative of the United States of America said that . . . it considered that the decision in question prejudged the matter on political grounds."

And in answer: "the representative of Jordan said he regretted that it had not proved possible to adopt the decision by consensus and called upon the Government that had voted against it to face up to its duties as a super-power concerned with maintaining the peace. It had become the philosophy of Israel to ignore United Nations resolutions, international law and the Geneva Conventions. The international community would have to put an end to such contumacy, including the canal project" (Thirteenth Governing Council Session: Israel's Decision to Build a Canal Linking the Mediterranean Sea to the Dead Sea 1985).

The 1987 Fourteenth GC session decision 14/11, entitled "The Environmental Situation in the Occupied Palestinian and Other Arab Territories," called on UNEP's executive director to help the Palestinian people protect their environment (Fourteenth Governing Council 1987). The final count was twenty-eight votes in support of the decision, seventeen abstentions, and one opposing (again, the United States) (1987). This time, the political nature of the decision was sufficiently palpable to make other participants uncomfortable, as attested by the remarks of the representative of Denmark: "speaking in explanation of vote on behalf of the EEC countries' members of the Council and on behalf of Switzerland, [he] said that those countries had abstained because political issues should fall within the purview of other forums. It was neither appropriate nor in the best interests of UNEP to burden the Governing Council with political matters" (1987, para. 61).

A particularly vitriolic exchange occurred at the 1989 fifteenth session:

> The speaker [for the Palestine Authority] continued that the environmental situation was deteriorating due to Israeli occupation and that the Israeli forces engaged in cruel and inhuman practices. Since the beginning of the Intifada, large numbers of Palestinians had been detained in camps, others had been evicted to Jordan and Lebanon, in violation of international codes and human rights, homes had been deliberately destroyed and the remaining population lived in intolerable conditions. In the West Bank and the Gaza Strip, olive and citrus trees and agricultural produce had been destroyed, land confiscated for Israeli use and wells poisoned. As was well known, Israel possessed nuclear plants and weapons and remained outside international control of its atomic wastes. . . . He called on the international community to put an end to

those practices and the Governing Council to condemn them. (Fifteenth Governing Council Session: Co-Ordination Questions, Summary and Suggested Action by the Governing Council 1989, para. 69)

In the face of these attacks, Israel's representatives at international forums see their primary role as defending Israel and preventing anti-Israel decisions or resolutions (interviews with Dr. Ellik Alder, August 20, 2009; U. Marinov, August 11, 2009). For example, when the same issue arose at the GC's seventeenth session, Israel's representative rejoined: "his delegation objected to both the spirit and the content of the draft. The draft . . . was politically motivated and irrelevant with respect to UNEP. . . . Such matters had to be discussed in other forums. The draft distracted UNEP from its task, and a dangerous precedent would be set if countries brought their conflicts to UNEP. . . . His delegation believed that the draft was hostile, political and anti-Israel, and he would treat it as such. He hoped that it would not receive support from the Council" (Seventeenth Governing Council Session: The Environmental Situation in the Occupied Palestinian and Other Arab Territories 1992, para. 120).

Beyond the anti-Israel polemics of UNEP's Governing Council, regional groups have been a determining factor in Israel's isolation. States' participation in international environmental agreements is largely based on the five UN regional geographical groups developed for facilitating elections to positions in UN bodies such as the Security Council and the Economic and Social Council (ECOSOC).[9] Regional groups have evolved as forums for consulting and caucusing among countries from the same geographical area. In the context of international environmental agreements, these groups operate as forums for determining regional policy with respect to the particular agreement, making up the basis for subsequent substantive discussion in plenary. The actual hands-on work in which operative decisions are taken occurs primarily in these regional groups. Geographically, Israel belongs to the Asian regional group. Yet due to the objections of Arab and Muslim member states, Israel has been blocked from joining this regional group in most environmental conventions. This has obstructed its full participation in these conventions and limited its representatives' ability to be elected to positions of influence in their governance (Crossette 2000).

Faced with the across-the-board dilemma of regional group association for Israel, geopolitical regional groups have become compromise solutions: WEOG (Western Europe and Others Group) (Crossette 2000; Weiner 2004); the Northern Mediterranean regional group as adopted by the UNCCD (UNCCD: Israel; UNCCD Regional Profiles, n.d.); the European and North America regional group under UNESCO (UNESCO: Europe and North America); and with respect to periodical reporting under the World Heritage

Convention—the subgroup of Mediterranean Europe (e.g., *Periodic Report and Action Plan* 2007). In January 2010 Israel was formally accepted into JUS-CANZ ("ADL Welcomes Israel's Entry into UN" 2010), a subgroup established under WEOG (composed of Japan, United States, Canada, Norway, Australia, and New Zealand) to counterbalance the other subgroup of EU member nations. Membership in JUSCANZ should enable Israel to take a more proactive role in these agreements. It remains to be seen if these compromise solutions can overcome Israel's historical exclusion from regional forums debating multilateral environmental agreements.

ISRAEL AND REGIONAL ENVIRONMENTAL CONVENTIONS

The Barcelona Convention was designed as the institutional legal framework to address the heavily polluted Mediterranean Sea and its environment. The original agreement, the Barcelona Convention for the Protection of the Mediterranean Sea against Pollution, was adopted in 1976 as the legal tool for the Mediterranean Action Plan (MAP). MAP, established in 1975 as the first Regional Seas Program under UNEP, addressed the Mediterranean's acute degradation (Cavanagh et al. 2007; Haas 1990, 4; Review and Assessment 2005; Skjaerseth 2002). In 1995, consistent with growing global awareness about the link between sustainable development and the environment, the original 1975 Action Plan was replaced by the Action Plan for the Protection of the Marine Environment and the Sustainable Development of the Coastal Areas of the Mediterranean (or "MAP Phase II") (1995). To ensure that the legal structure was in tune with the new action plan, the contracting parties amended the 1976 Barcelona Convention and renamed it the "Convention for the Protection of the Marine Environment and the Coastal Region of the Mediterranean" (1995).

To understand the underlying forces behind Israel's dynamic role in MAP and the Barcelona Convention, the following critical factors have been identified:

• *Regional versus international.* Israel's participation in the Barcelona Convention supports the contention that regional agreements are preferable to multilateral ones. The Barcelona Convention has created a collective regional identity and pride, expressed as "I am a Mediterraneaner," or, "I am a Mediterranean citizen" (interviews with R. Rotenberg, August 16, 2009; U. Marinov, August 11, 2009).[10] Because it contains a smaller number of countries, the regime is easier to administer, achieve coordination, and reach consensus. State representatives may become better acquainted and develop closer camaraderie, making for improved working relationships. The case of the Barcelona Convention is a compelling example of how the development of a regional identity in the context of an environmental problem has the potential to overcome a deeply entrenched and bitter political conflict. The smaller the number of participants in a collective arrangement, the greater the chance they can overcome mutual mistrust (Haas 1990, 37).

- *An issue of shared concern.* The Barcelona Convention's success is also attributable to its focus on an issue of deep concern to Israel and other Mediterranean countries (Focusing on the Mediterranean Environment 2003).[11] Mediterranean pollution indiscriminately affects all sectors of the economy. Most troubling is pollution's effect on the general public whether as a result of loss of recreational open space, a precious and scarce commodity in a heavily developed country (2003);[12] health hazards due to polluted beaches; or contaminated seafood. This shared concern over a regional problem creates links between the various member states that presumably can overcome suspicions and tensions that often hamper progress in larger, multilateral environmental contexts.

- *Collective action versus unilateral state action.* The Barcelona Convention demonstrates the role of international law in creating regional institutions to address a shared problem, requiring—or perceived as requiring—collective action.[13] Arguably, for an international agreement to succeed the problem to be solved must be subject to collective action; issues that can be addressed by unilateral state action are at a disadvantage since states have fewer incentives to comply with international commitments. Because cleaning up the Mediterranean is considered a classic tragedy of the commons (but see Haas 1990, 70–71), the convergence of shared interests overcomes states' fears in the face of uncertainty, leading to the establishment of cooperative regimes (Slaughter 2004, 25–29).

- *Full participation of all state members.* Achieving maximum participation of state parties in meetings of international regimes generates a process to which they all can contribute and to which they can claim ownership. This can create incentives for effective implementation and compliance. The Barcelona Convention has achieved full participation by funding participation costs of state representatives, ensuring that consistent participation is not the privilege of wealthy states but constitutes a right of all member states.[14] This further facilitates personal working relationships among delegates, creates a sense of partnership, and adds a personal stake in the meetings' outcome (Haas 1990, 155, 161–62, 171; interview with O. Livneh, August 13, 2009).[15]

- *Professional expertise.* Those interviewed for this chapter indicate that the key to Israel's successful participation in the Barcelona Convention has been its delegation's professional expertise and interests that transcend national interests. Their regional and global perspectives have dovetailed with those of other delegations, thereby enhancing Israel's status and upgrading the regime as well (interviews with V. Brachya, August 12, 2009; O. Livneh, August 13, 2009; U. Marinov, August 11, 2009; R. Rotenberg, August 16, 2009).

While the question remains open as to whether MAP and the Barcelona Convention are effective in improving the Mediterranean's environmental status,[16] they were undoubtedly effective in creating a "Mediterranean identity" that moderated some political conflicts.[17] Consequently, the Barcelona Convention has become a forum for Mediterranean countries to explore collective action for protecting a shared resource. From the beginning, Israel has gained legitimacy from its role in MAP and the Barcelona Convention (Haas 1990, 80) and its contribution has been recognized by the regime and its member states (interviews with Dr. Ellik Alder, August 20, 2009; V. Brachya, August 12, 2009; U. Marinov, August 11, 2009; R. Rotenberg, August 16, 2009). The Ministry of Environment's first director general was a highly respected participant in MAP at an early stage, and consistently represented regional interests. He defined participation in MAP as of highest importance for Israel's fledgling environmental institutions in spite of political differences with several parties to the convention (Haas 1990, 162; interview with Marinov 2009). Over the years, ministry officials have continued "going beyond" representing Israel in MAP, achieving recognition for their professional expertise.

For example, ministry experts have served as consultants to MAP and its constituent countries. The ministry's deputy director general for planning and policy prepared the preliminary documents on integrated coastal management, as well as an institutional analysis for the implementation of the coastal and offshore protocols (V. Brachya, pers. comm., June 16, 2010). She also served as a consultant to MAP for a training course on environmental impact assessment in Albania (Brachya 2010). The chief legal adviser consulted for MAP on coastal legislation for Montenegro (interviews with U. Marinov August 11, 2009; R. Rotenberg 2009). A staff lawyer from the ministry's legal department was actively involved in the preparation of the Integrated Coastal Zone Management Protocol (ICZM protocol) (Marinov 2009; Rotenberg 2009), and another served as a member of the working group for a compliance mechanism.

The Ministry of Environment's marine and coastal environment division has been especially active at the international level. At the invitation of MAP, the head of the division lectured on Israel's land-based sources strategy at the Global Programme of Action for the Protection of the Marine Environment from Land-Based Activities that took place in China in 2006 (R. Amir, pers. comm., June 16, 2010). In the same year the division organized a MAP capacity-building workshop in Slovenia, and in Montenegro in 2007 (Amir). In 2008 it organized a marine ecosystem workshop for the Nairobi Convention on implementing an ecosystem approach for the marine environment.[18] The head of the division has also authored manuals for MED POL on "Guidelines for Enforcement and Compliance" as part of a marine-pollution enforcement system (Amir, n.d.). Thus ministry officials are recognized not only as Israeli experts, but more importantly have earned the distinction of being MAP experts. By participating in working groups, meetings, workshops, and conferences, by preparing both national and international legislation, manuals and guidelines, and by working as consultants, they are constructing a regional Mediterranean identity that to a certain degree has transcended national identities.

ISRAEL AND THE WORLD HERITAGE CONVENTION

Another example of Israel's successful participation in the international environmental arena is the World Heritage Convention, an international multilateral agreement concerned with protecting cultural and natural sites, each located under the territorial sovereignty of an individual state yet considered of "outstanding universal value" (World Heritage Convention, 1972, Preamble). In force since 1976, the convention calls for international cooperation to conserve the world's heritage in the face of its ongoing devastation. It contains two lists: one for sites of cultural and natural heritage considered of universal value (World Heritage Convention 1972, Art. 11.2) and another for those listed sites judged as endangered (World Heritage Convention 1972, Art. 11.4).

The World Heritage Convention operates under the aegis of UNESCO. As Israel's UNESCO Commission is under the Ministry of Education, this ministry has also been charged with the convention's domestic implementation. In addition, the Ministry of Foreign Affairs has become heavily involved in Israel's participation in this convention. In marked contrast to the Barcelona Convention in which Israel is represented by government officials, Israel's focal point[19] for the World Heritage Convention is Professor Michael Turner, the UNESCO chair in Urban Design and Conservation at Bezalel, Academy of Arts and Design, Jerusalem ("Research and Publishing: PUSH" n.d.). An internationally recognized expert on cultural world heritage, Professor Turner has represented Israel at the convention since its ratification in 1999. In 2005, he was elected a member of the highly coveted twenty-one member World Heritage Committee by state parties to the convention and two years later was elected its vice chair. Considering that the World Heritage Convention has a membership of 186 member states (World Heritage List 2010), this constitutes an impressive diplomatic achievement (Nahmias 2005; "Results of Election to World Heritage Committee" 2005).

With its representative in a key position in the convention's governing institution, Israel has undertaken a proactive role in the convention. For example, it was one of the organizers of an international meeting on world heritage and buffer zones held in Switzerland and of a workshop held in India ("Indo-Israel Workshop" 2006). Israel hosted an international seminar on the conservation of historic urban landscapes,[20] and of particular note, an international expert meeting for serial world heritage sites in the Great Rift Valley (interview with M. Turner, August 11, 2009).

An underlying explanation for Israel's successful participation in the World Heritage Convention is the dominant role of Daniel Bar Elli, the secretary general for Israel's National Commission for UNESCO. Under his dynamic direction Israel has achieved international recognition in the area of world heritage (interview with M. Turner 2009).[21] Critical components in his successful strategy include creating and strengthening relationships between Israel, member states, UNESCO, and other international organizations, while ensuring that Israel is consistently represented by leading experts (Turner). Crucial to Israel's successful participation in the convention was the return of the United States to UNESCO in 2003, which helped alleviate traditional anti-Israel consensus (Turner).

ISRAEL AND THE DESERTIFICATION CONVENTION

The United Nations Convention to Combat Desertification (UNCCD) was created to address the growing threat of desertification (Tal and Cohen 2007), estimated as impacting over 250 million people and threatening about 1 billion more in over one hundred countries ("Problem of Land Degradation" 2005). Desertification is a direct result of overexploitation of natural resources and destructive land-use practices including overirrigation, forest devastation, overgrazing, and unsustainable agriculture (Tal and Cohen 2007; "Problem of Land Degradation" 2005).

Despite this environmental focus and attesting to its political weight, in Israel the UNCCD operates under the Ministry of Foreign Affairs rather than the Ministry of Environment. Israel's focal point to the convention since joining in 1996 has been Professor Uriel Safriel, former head of the Blaustein Institutes for Desert Research (BIDR) of Ben-Gurion University of the Negev. Professor Safriel is a world-renowned ecologist, one of the team of four core writers of the Millennium Ecosystem Assessment, Ecosystems and Human Well-Being: Desertification Synthesis (World Resources Institute 2005). Under his leadership, Israel has assumed a proactive role in the UNCCD, marked by hosting several international conferences. In 1997, the BIDR was the venue of an international conference on synergies among the Convention on Biological Diversity, the UN Convention on Climate Change, the UNCCD, and the Forest Principles. In 2006, it hosted the UNCCD's international conference on "Deserts and Desertification: Challenges and Opportunities" (Deserts and Desertification 2006). Based on its success, in December 2008 and in November 2010 Israel hosted follow-up international conferences under the heading of "Drylands, Deserts, and Desertification" (Drylands, Deserts, and Desertification 2010). These academic conferences, with hundreds of participants from over fifty dryland countries, have enhanced Israel's status in the UNCCD and emphasized its contribution to the international effort to stop desertification. In this context, Israel has arguably broken free of its dominant identity as a belligerent in the Middle East conflict. It has accomplished this by persuading other countries to view it as capable of effectively dealing with desertification on the domestic and international levels (Drylands, Deserts, and Desertification 2010).

Comparable to the regional relationship between Israel and its Mediterranean neighbors in the context of Mediterranean pollution, Israel is building regional relationships with its African neighbors who suffer from desertification, by offering them capacity building. Thus although the UNCCD is a multilateral international agreement, Israel's actual role is perhaps most effective at this regional level (interview with A. Tal, August 20, 2009).

ISOLATING THE CRITICAL FACTORS

Similar to the review of the Barcelona Convention, the following is an attempt to isolate those critical factors for Israel's successful participation in the World Heritage Convention and the UNCCD.

- *Professional expertise.* Israel's focal point to the World Heritage Convention is an internationally recognized architect with expertise in the area of cultural heritage. Similarly, its focal point to the UNCCD is a world-renowned ecologist who contributes professional advice on a diverse array of ecological issues and desertification in particular. Generally, Israeli achievements in water management, drip irrigation, arid-land afforestation, solar energy development, desert agriculture, and aquaculture are perceived as creative and instructive for developing dryland nations.

- *Academic nongovernmental representatives.* Israel's delegates to the World Heritage Convention and the UNCCD are also affiliated with academic institutions, in contrast to the government officials who are Israel's representatives to other environmental agreements. Their nongovernmental status frees them from conventional political mind-sets. Unlike government officials, who are barred from expressing opinions not in line with official government policy, nongovernmental or academic representatives generally have more freedom to express global views (Haas 1990, 73–74). Another advantage of academics as focal points to these forums is the consistency and stability of their representation. This critical mass of accumulative experience allows for a greater in-depth understanding of the issues concerned.

- *Support of the Ministry of Foreign Affairs.* Linking to the above factors, and as indicated by the significant number of references on its website,[22] the Ministry of Foreign Affairs has become an enthusiastic supporter of Israel's active involvement in these two conventions, emphasizing Israel's expertise as a contribution to the international community.[23] Regarding the UNCCD, in addition to sponsoring international conferences, in 2007 Israel's Ministry of Foreign Affairs through MASHAV—the Center for International Cooperation—sponsored an event at the eighth UNCCD conference of the parties in Madrid.[24] Represented again by MASHAV, in the same year Israel and UNEP signed a memorandum of understanding for capacity building for developing countries in environmental areas such as water resources management, waste management, food security and agriculture, and desertification.[25]

Thus we see evidence of "rebranding" Israel; the Ministry of Foreign Affairs understands the possibilities of international environmental diplomacy based on the expertise of widely respected Israeli academics, for improving Israel's standing in the international community.[26] The Ministry lobbied extensively for the election of Professor Turner to the World Heritage Committee.[27] Its support for Israel's active participation in the agreement required a change of mind-set regarding Israel's role in international forums[28] and the World Heritage Convention in particular in light of UNESCO's history of anti-Israeli resolutions.[29] When elections for a new UNCCD executive secretary were held in 2008, the Ministry of Foreign Affairs even went so far as to quietly float the candidacy of the internationally acclaimed ecologist Professor Uriel Safriel who has been Israel's focal point to the convention since its inception.[30]

The Ministry of Foreign Affair's initial fears of the World Heritage Convention have apparently been replaced by an international "rebranding"[31] of Israel, thanks to the persuasive efforts of Israel's focal point and other members of Israel's World Heritage Committee, and in particular, to the secretary general of Israel's UNESCO Commission. Their major achievement with respect to the Ministry of Foreign Affairs was convincing it to think outside of the box of the Arab-Israeli conflict, and persuading its officials that Israel could and should be recognized internationally for its contribution to global interests. In short, they succeeded in gaining the support of the Ministry of Foreign Affairs by capturing the imagination of its officials as to Israel's potential leadership role in the World Heritage Convention.[32]

- *The role of the epistemic community.* Running like a red skein through Israel's participation in the Barcelona Convention, the World Heritage Convention, and the UNCCD, is the key contribution of epistemic communities to its active engagement with these agreements. Their members succeeded in constructing new international identities for Israel, using discourse and persuasion to transform traditional beliefs and values and remold them in the shape of their own (interviews with V. Brachya, August 12, 2009; U. Marinov, August 11, 2009; M. Turner, August 11, 2009). They also believe that to promote global environmental well-being, countries must transcend their political borders and domestic concerns to focus on how globally interconnected ecosystems reveal the interdependency of these countries (Haas 1990, 76).

Israel's strong and proactive participation, both in the World Heritage Convention and the UNCCD demonstrate that Israel's historic pariah status at UN-associated institutions is not ineluctable. It also shows the advantages of relying on internationally recognized experts associated with Israeli academic institutions as its representatives in international agreements. These case studies further demonstrate the advantages of the involvement of the Ministry of Foreign Affairs and its vast institutional network of political contacts. On the whole, what could be described as a positive model of international proactivism for Israel has gained a foothold and early findings are encouraging.

ISRAEL AND ENVIRONMENTAL DIPLOMACY

The following factors are proffered as critical in enhancing Israel's future role in environmental diplomacy:

- *Representing global interests.* Israel should continue to go beyond the exclusive representation of domestic interests, contributing to international cooperation in solving global environmental problems. It should recognize its ability as well as its responsibility to further these efforts, and use environmental diplomacy (interview with V. Brachya, August 12, 2009) to strengthen its international status as a major player. Its recognition as a major player in the agreements discussed here demonstrates the benefits that Israel has accrued from its policy of "going beyond Israel."

Extending this policy to other environmental issues could increase these benefits.

- *Expertise is everything.* A requirement for Israel's representatives in international environmental forums is a high level of expertise in the relevant issue. Without it, they cannot bring anything new to the table, and risk either being ignored, or worse, being defined in the traditional political context of the Arab-Israeli conflict.

- *Nongovernmental representatives from academic institutions.* In light of the obstacles to active and consistent participation in international forums, Israel should rethink using government officials exclusively as delegates to these forums, and consider appointing internationally respected Israeli experts as focal points for environmental agreements. Besides ensuring consistency and stability in Israel's representation, such appointments would serve to raise Israel's profile, increase its visibility, and allow it to play a more active and substantive part in resolving key international environmental challenges.

Of all these factors, the most salient appears to be professional expertise.[33] Israel's environmental capabilities and know-how should be harnessed and utilized to promote environmental diplomacy, and thus contribute in battling global environmental devastation. However, this assessment comes with a caveat. Contributing expertise does not stand alone; rather, it is persistently shaped by the political situation in which other actors toss aside cooperation with Israel for the sake of an all-consuming regional conflict. Despite the successful use of international environmental law to bridge deeply entrenched and historical animosities, the political reality remains an independent factor that will not fade away (interviews with Dr. Ellik Alder, August 20, 2009; O. Livneh, August 13, 2009). Still, as demonstrated by the three case studies making up the focus of this chapter, enhancing Israel's role in international environmental agreements is proving an effective counterbalance to its historical identity in one of the most bitter, deeply entrenched, and tragic conflicts of international politics.

NOTES

1. In terms of its ecological footprint, Israel is listed as number 11 out of a list of 55 countries worldwide, falling between Great Britain and Switzerland. See Indicator: Ecological Footprint 2001, n.p.

2. See generally Tal and Cohen 2007.

3. It was followed by the 1992 United Nations Conference on Environment and Development (UNCED) held in Rio de Janeiro and the 2002 World Summit on Sustainable Development (WSSD) held in Johannesburg.

4. See Principle 26 to the Stockholm Declaration, "Cooperation through multilateral

or bilateral arrangements or other appropriate means is essential to effectively control, prevent, reduce and eliminate adverse environmental effects resulting from activities conducted in all spheres" (UN Conference on the Human Environment 1972, p. A/ CONF 48/14/Rev 1).

5. The amended convention was adopted in June 1995, came into power in July 2004, and was ratified by Israel in September 2005. The lengthy period of time that passed until the amended convention came into power shows that other countries also delayed its ratification (Barcelona Convention 1995 [as of April 2010]).

6. The process began at the end of 2002 and was completed in February 2004. Protocol Kyoto entered into force a year later in February 2005 (Status of Ratification, Kyoto Protocol, n.d.).

7. As based on the personal experience of the author regarding the ratification of biodiversity conventions.

8. Uri Marinov noted that the main consideration of Israel's representatives at GC sessions was to defend it against anti-Israel polemics and prevent adoption of anti-Israeli decisions (Eleventh Governing Council Session: Israel's Decision to Build a Canal Linking the Mediterranean Sea to the Dead Sea 1983; Twelfth Governing Council Session: Israel's Decision to Build a Canal Linking the Mediterranean Sea to the Dead Sea 1984; Thirteenth Governing Council Session: Israel's Decision to Build a Canal Linking the Mediterranean Sea to the Dead Sea 1985; Fourteenth Governing Council Session: The Environmental Situation in the Occupied Palestinian and Other Arab Territories 1987; Fifteenth Governing Council Session: Co-Ordination Questions, Summary and Suggested Action by the Governing Council 1989; Sixteenth Governing Council Session: The Environmental Situation in the Occupied Palestinian and Other Arab Territories 1991; Seventeenth Governing Council Session: The Environmental Situation in the Occupied Palestinian and Other Arab Territories 1992; interview with U. Marinov, August 11, 2009). But despite the isolation at formal meetings and conferences, on an informal and personal basis, Israeli delegates succeeded in creating a significant number of international contacts with environmental colleagues from various countries, using environmental diplomacy (Marinov 2009). On environmental diplomacy in particular, interview with Valerie Brachya, former senior deputy director general for policy and planning of the Ministry of the Environment and presently director of the Environmental Policy Center at the Jerusalem Institute for Israel Studies (August 12, 2009). On the anti-Israel animosity in international forums, interview with Dr. Ellik Adler, Regional Seas Programme coordinator, UNEP, former head of the Coasts and Marine Division of the Environment Ministry (August 20, 2009).

9. See http://www.jewishvirtuallibrary.org/jsource/UN/Jennings.html.

10. Ms. Ruth Rotenberg, former chief legal adviser of the Ministry of the Environment, noting the creation of a regional Mediterranean identity (interview, August 16, 2009). Also, Uri Marinov noting regionalism as a factor for Israel's active role in the Barcelona Convention (interview, August 11, 2009). Generally the interviewees agreed that the characteristic of regionalism (in contrast to global multilateralism) together with professional expertise were dominant factors for the agreement's success (Marinov 2009; Rotenberg 2009).

11. When asked why Israel should take such an active role in regional efforts to protect the Mediterranean environment, Mr. Rani Amir is unequivocal: "The Barcelona Convention and its protocols have led to an immense improvement in the level of pol-

lution entering the sea and in our preparedness to treat this pollution. If there were no Barcelona Convention and only other marine environmental conventions such as MARPOL 73/78, we would have remained somewhere in the 1950s—with inadequate legislation, with raw sewage flowing into the sea, with toxic emissions of industrial plants into the Kishon River and from there to the Sea, with oil spills in our sea and tar on our shore. Today, anyone visiting our beaches knows that tar is a thing of the past. If it weren't for the Mediterranean Action Plan, the Mediterranean may well have turned into a Dead Sea due to its physical characteristics and the enormous anthropogenic burden of some 250 million people along its coasts. If the Barcelona Convention and MAP did not exist, we would simply have had to invent them" (Focusing on the Mediterranean Environment 2003).

12. "In 1948 each citizen of Israel had 31 cm of coast; today only 2.5 cm of coast remain per citizen" (Focusing on the Mediterranean Environment 2003).

13. "Many officials thought that pollution was a commons problem and thus required coordinated action throughout the region . . . only later did studies reveal to marine scientists that currents were too weak to fully exchange the wastes between the northern and southern shores: regional pollution was not a true collective good, and it could be managed bilaterally or subregionally" (Haas 1990, 70–71).

14. However, MAP does not fund participation of state parties in conference of the Parties (COPs).

15. Ori Livneh, former head of the International Relations Division of the Ministry of the Environment, discussing "ownership of the process" as an important component in effective participation (interview with O. Livneh 2009).

16. See generally Jon Skjaerseth, classifying the Barcelona Convention as "a regime of low effectiveness" (Skjaerseth 2002, viii). See also Executive Summary, "while the Mediterranean Sea and its coastal zone still suffer from serious problems and their long-term sustainability is not yet fully secured" (*External Evaluation of MAP* 2005, UNEP(DEC)/MED WG.270/8), and Downs et al. 1996, 396.

17. Additional conflicts to that between Israel and the Arab countries are Turkey and Greece, France and Algeria, and Algeria and Morocco (Haas 1990, xxi; CITES 1973).

18. "The Nairobi Convention provides a mechanism for regional cooperation, coordination and collaborative actions . . . towards solving interlinked problems of the coastal and marine environment" (Nairobi Convention, n.d.).

19. "Focal point"—"an official or agency designated by a government to serve as the focus or channel of communications for a particular issue or agreement" (List of Acronyms and Glossary Terms, n.d.).

20. Interview with Professor Michael Turner, August 11, 2009. Turner was Israel's focal point to the World Heritage Convention, chairman of Israel's World Heritage Committee and professor of architecture at the Bezalel Institute of Art and Design, and Vice Chair of the international World Heritage Committee.

21. Interview with Professor Michael Turner, August 11, 2009.

22. Website references include "Israeli Statement at Beijing Conference Combating Desertification," http://www.mfa.gov.il/MFA/Foreign+Relations/Israel+and+the+UN/ Speeches+-+statements/Israeli%20statement%20at%20Beijing%20Conference%20 on%20Combating%20Desertification%2022-Jan-2008; "MASHAV-sponsored event at UN Convention to Combat Desertification in Madrid," http://www.mfa.gov.il/MFA/ Foreign+Relations/Israel+and+the+UN/Issues/MASHAV-sponsored+event+at+UN

+Convention+to+Combat+Desertification+in+Madrid+10-Sep-2007.htm; "UN conference at Ben-Gurion University highlights Israel's leadership in desert research,"
http://www.mfa.gov.il/MFA/Israel+beyond+politics/UN%20conference%20at%20
Ben-Gurion%20University%20highlights%20Israel%20leadership%20in%20desert%20
research%208-Nov-2006.

23. See http://www.mfa.gov.il/MFA/About+the+Ministry/MFA+Spokesman/2007/
Election+of+Prof+Turner+as+Vice-Chairman+of+UNESCO+World+Heritage+Comm
ittee+3-Jul-2007.htm. Interview with Michael Turner, August 11, 2009.

24. See "MASHAV-sponsored event at UN Convention to Combat Desertification in
Madrid."

25. For memorandum, see January 17, 2007, at http://www.mfa.gov.il/MFA/
About+the+Ministry/MFA+Spokesman/2007/Israel+signs+cooperation+agreement.

26. See http://www.mfa.gov.il/MFA/Israel+beyond+politics/Putting+Israels+hi
storic+sites+on+the+UNESCO+World+Heritage+List+18-Sep-2005.htm. See also
http://www.mfa.gov.il/MFA/Foreign+Relations/Israel+and+the+UN/Speeches+-
+statements/Israeli%20statement%20at%20Beijing%20Conference%20on%20
Combating%20Desertification%2022-Jan-2008.

27. See http://www.ynetnews.com/articles/0,7340,L-3153957,00.html;
http://www.mfa.gov.il/MFA/About+the+Ministry/MFA+Spokesman/2007/
Election+of+Prof+Turner+as+Vice-Chairman+of+UNESCO+World+Heritage+Comm
ittee+3-Jul-2007.htm.

28. The chairman of Israel's World Heritage Committee believes that a factor for
Israel's proactive role in the World Heritage Convention was due to the Ministry of
Foreign Affairs agreeing that Israel should not be recognized as a one-issue country
(interview with Michael Turner, August 11, 2009).

29. See http://www.mfa.gov.il/MFA/Foreign%20Relations/Israels%20Foreign%20
Relations%20since%201947/1984-1988/113%20UNESCO%20General%20Conference%20
Resolutions%20on%20the%20t.

30. Comment of Professor Alon Tal, August 2009.

31. Comment of Professor Alon Tal, August 2009; interview with Valerie Brachya.

32. Interview with Mike Turner, August 11, 2009.

33. Interviewees generally agreed that the key to Israel's role in the global environmental arena is its emphasis on expertise.

REFERENCES

Action Plan for the Protection of the Marine Environment and the Sustainable Devel-
    opment of the Coastal Areas of the Mediterranean. 1995. United Nations Envi-
    ronment Programme. http://www.unepmap.org/index.php?module=content2&ca
    tid=001001004.
"ADL Welcomes Israel's Entry into U.N. Coalition of Liberal Democracies." 2010.
    Anti-Defamation League, January 26. http://www.adl.org/PresRele/UnitedNations
    _94/5698_94.htm.
African-Eurasian Migratory Waterbird Agreement. 1995. http://www.unep-aewa.org/
    map/parties.htm.
Amir, R. n.d. "Part IV—Guidelines for Enforcement and Compliance—General Issues
    and Strategies." Marine and Coastal Environment Division (MCED), Ministry of
    the Environment, Israel.
Barcelona Convention for the Protection of the Marine Environment and the Coastal

Region of the Mediterranean. 1995. Barcelona: United Nations Environment Programme.

Basel Convention on the Control of Transboundary Movements of Hazardous Wastes and Their Disposal. 1989. *International Legal Materials* 28 (3): 649–86.

Bromberg, G., and R. Twite. 2001. *Regional and International Cooperation* (Israel NGO Shadow Report). "Paths to Sustainability," 130–44. Johannesburg: World Summit on Sustainable Development. http://www.worldsummit2002.org/download/ISRAELRegCoop.pdf.

Cavanagh, R., C. Gibson, World Conservation Union (IUCN), IUCN Centre for Mediterranean Cooperation, IUCN Species Survival Commission, and IUCN Shark Specialist Group. 2007. *Overview of the Conservation Status of Cartilaginous Fishes (Chondrichthyans) in the Mediterranean Sea.* Gland, Switzerland: IUCN and the IUCN Centre for Mediterranean Cooperation.

Contracting Parties to the Ramsar Convention on Wetlands. n.d. Ramsar Convention on Wetlands. http://www.ramsar.org/cda/ramsar/display/main/main.jsp?zn=ramsar&cp=1-36-123^23808_4000_0__.

Convention Concerning the Protection of the World Cultural and Natural Heritage. 1972. *1037 U.N.T.S.* http://whc.unesco.org/en/conventiontext/ (World Heritage Convention).

Convention on Migratory Species: Agreement Summary Sheets. n.d. Convention on Migratory Species: Agreement Summary Sheets. http://www.cms.int/publications/agr_sum_sheets.htm.

Convention on Wetlands of International Importance Especially as Waterfowl Habitats. 2008. State of Israel, Ministry of Environmental Protection. http://www.sviva.gov.il/bin/en.jsp?enPage=e_BlankPage&enDisplay=view&enDispWhat=Object&enDispWho=Articals^l2561&enZone=bi_int (Ramsar Convention).

Country Profiles: Israel. n.d. Convention on Biological Diversity. http://www.cbd.int/countries/?country=il.

Crossette, B. 2000. "Israel's Bittersweet Moment: One Step Out of Isolation at U.N." *New York Times.* http://www.nytimes.com/2000/06/01/world/israel-s-bittersweet-moment-one-step-out-of-isolation-at-un.html.

"Deserts and Desertification: Challenges and Opportunities." 2006. American Associates Ben-Gurion University of the Negev. http://www.unccd.int/IYDD/documents/iydd_docs/Israelconferencenov2006.pdf.

Downs, G. W., D. M. Rocke, and P. N. Barsoom. 1996. "Is the Good News about Compliance Good News about Cooperation?" *International Organization* 50 (3): 379–406. doi:10.1017/S0020818300033427.

Drylands, Deserts, and Desertification: The Route to Restoration. 2010. Third International Conference on Drylands, Deserts, and Desertification: the Route to Restoration. http://www.entersymposium.com/ddd/site/.

Eleventh Governing Council Session: Israel's Decision to Build a Canal Linking the Mediterranean Sea to the Dead Sea. 1983. New York: United Nations Environment Programme. http://www.unep.org/Documents.multilingual/Default.asp?DocumentID=61&ArticleID=1323&l=en.

Environmental Conventions. 2004. State of Israel, Ministry of Environmental Protection. http://www.sviva.gov.il/bin/en.jsp?enPage=e_BlankPage&enDisplay=view&enDispWhat=Zone&enDispWho=conv_int&enZone=conv_int.

External Evaluation of the Mediterranean Action Plan (MAP), Executive Summary.

2005. Evaluation Report on Implementing the Action Plan for the Conservation of Marine Vegetation in the Mediterranean Sea (p. 127). Athens: United Nations Environment Programme. http://195.97.36.231/acrobatfiles/05WG270_Inf25_Eng.pdf.

Fifteenth Governing Council Session: Co-Ordination Questions, Summary, and Suggested Action by the Governing Council. 1989. New York: United Nations Environment Programme. http://www.unep.org/Documents.multilingual/Default.asp? DocumentID=71&ArticleID=985&l=en.

Focusing on the Mediterranean Environment: Facts to Remember. 2003. *Environmental E-Bulletin* (1). http://www.sviva.gov.il/Enviroment/bin/en.jsp?enPage=bulletin& infocus=1&enDisplay=view&enDispWhat=object&enDispWho=News%5El1892&e nZone=june_bull04&enVersion=0&.

Fourteenth Governing Council Session: The Environmental Situation in the Occupied Palestinian and Other Arab Territories. 1987. New York: United Nations Environment Programme. http://www.unep.org/Documents.Multilingual/Default.asp? DocumentID=100&ArticleID=1599&l=en.

Haas, P. 1990. *Saving the Mediterranean: The Politics of International Environmental Cooperation.* New York: Columbia University Press.

Indicator: Ecological Footprint—2001. 2001. *Globali-Indicator-Global Virtual University.* http://globalis.gvu.unu.edu/indicator.cfm?IndicatorID=13&country=IL#ro wIL.

Indo-Israel Workshop on the Management of World Heritage Sites and Jewish Heritage in India. 2006. UNESCO World Heritage Centre. http://whc.unesco.org/en/ events/320/.

International Convention for the Regulation of Whaling (ICRW). 1947. 62 Statute / 161 U.N.T.S. http://www.iwcoffice.org/commission/members.htm.

International Cooperation. 2004. *Environmental E-Bulletin* (11). http://sviva.gov.il/ Enviroment/bin/en.jsp?enPage=bulletin&enDisplay=view&enDispWhat=Zone&en DispWho=june_bull04&enZone=june_bull04&p=bulletin.

Israel UN Relations, Israel Ministry of Foreign Affairs. n.d. *Israel Ministry of Foreign Affairs.* http://www.mfa.gov.il/MFA.

Israeli Statement at Beijing Conference on Combating Desertification. 2008. Israel Ministry of Foreign Affairs. http://www.mfa.gov.il/MFA/Foreign+Relations/ Israel+and+the+UN/Speeches+-+statements/Israeli%20statement%20at%20 Beijing%20Conference%20on%20Combating%20Desertification%2022-Jan-2008.

Israel's Environmental Protection Minister: Israel Prepared to Serve as Regional Laboratory and Center of Excellence for Climate Change Adaptation. 2009. State of Israel, Ministry of Environmental Protection. http://sviva.gov.il/Enviroment/bin/ en.jsp?enPage=e_BlankPage&enDisplay=view&enDispWhat=Object&enDispWho =News^l4834&enZone=e_news.

Ivanova, M., and J. Roy. 2007. "The Architecture of Global Environmental Governance." In *Global Environmental Governance: Perspectives on the Current Debate,* edited by L. Swart, P. Estelle, and C. F. U. R. Education, 48–66. New York: Center for UN Reform Education. http://www.centerforunreform.org/system/files/ Ivanova+and+Roy+GEG.pdf.

List of Acronyms and Glossary Terms. n.d. United Nations Environment Programme. http://www.unep.org/dec/onlinemanual/Resources/Glossary/tabid/69/Default .aspx?letter=F.

Marine and Coastal Environment: Mediterranean Coast. 2003. *Environmental E-Bulletin* (1). http://sviva.gov.il/Enviroment/bin/en.jsp?enPage=bulletin&infocus=1&enDisplay=view&enDispWhat=object&enDispWho=News%5Eli1011&enZone=july_bulletin&enVersion=0&.

Montreal Protocol on Substances that Deplete the Ozone Layer. 1987. *International Legal Materials* 26 (6): 1541–61.

Muñoz, M., R. Thrasher, and A. Najam. 2009. "Measuring the Negotiation Burden of Multilateral Environmental Agreements." *Global Environmental Politics* 9 (4): 1–13.

Nahmias, R. 2005. "Israel Gets Unesco Committee Seat." *Y-Net News*. http://www.ynetnews.com/articles/0,7340,L-3153957,00.html.

Nairobi Convention. n.d. "The Convention." http://www.unep.org/Nairobi Convention/The_Convention/index.asp.

Preamble to Convention Concerning the Protection of the World Cultural and Natural Heritage. 1972. *1037 U.N.T.S.* http://whc.unesco.org/en/conventiontext/.

The Problem of Land Degradation. 2005. United Nations Convention to Combat Desertification. http://www.unccd.int/convention/text/leaflet.php.

Protocol Concerning Specially Protected Areas and Biological Diversity in the Mediterranean. 1995. Adopted June 10, 1995, entry into force December 12, 1999. http://www.unepmap.org/index.php?module=content2&catid=001001001 (replaced the original Spa Protocol).

Protocol for the Prevention and Elimination of Pollution of the Mediterranean Sea by Dumping from Ships and Aircraft or Incineration at Sea. n.d. http://195.97.36.231/dbases/webdocs/BCP/ProtocolDumping 95_Eng_pdf.

"Research and Publishing: PUSH." n.d. Bezalel Academy of Arts and Design, Jerusalem. http://www.bezalel.ac.il/en/about/research/push/.

Results of the Election to the World Heritage Committee. 2005. UNESCO World Heritage Centre. http://whc.unesco.org/en/news/195/.

Review and Assessment of National Strategies for Sustainable Development in the Mediterranean Sea. 2005. United Nations Environment Programme.

Rotterdam Convention on Prior Informed Consent Procedure for Certain Hazardous Chemicals and Pesticides in International Trade. 1998. 2244 U.N.T.S. http://treaties.un.org/pages/ViewDetails.aspx?src=TREATY&mtdsg_no=XXVII-14&chapter=27&lang=en.

Seventeenth Governing Council Session: The Environmental Situation in the Occupied Palestinian and Other Arab Territories. 1992. New York: United Nations Environment Programme. http://www.unep.org/Documents.Multilingual/Default.asp?DocumentID=55&ArticleID=196&l=en.

Sixteenth Governing Council Session: The Environmental Situation in the Occupied Palestinian and Other Arab Territories. 1991. New York: United Nations Environment Programme. http://www.unep.org/Documents.Multilingual/Default.asp?DocumentID=55&ArticleID=196&l=en.

Skjaerseth, J. 2002. "The Effectiveness of the Mediterranean Action Plan." In *Environmental Regime Effectiveness: Confronting Theory with Evidence*, edited by E. Miles, 311–30. Cambridge: MIT Press.

Slaughter, A. M. 2004. "Theory: A Prospectus." In *The Impact of International Law on International Cooperation: Theoretical Perspectives*, edited by E. Benvenisti and M. Hirsche, 16–49. Cambridge: Cambridge University Press.

Statistical Abstract of Israel. 2010. Central Bureau of Statistics, Israel. http://www.cbs
.gov.il/reader/shnatonenew_site.htm.

Status of Ratification, Kyoto Protocol. n.d. *Status of Ratification, Kyoto Protocol*. http://
unfccc.int/kyoto_protocol/status_of_ratification/items/2613.php.

Stockholm Convention on Persistent Organic Pollutants. 2001. http://www.pops.int/
documents/signature/signstatus.htm.

Tal, A. 2002. *Pollution in a Promised Land: An Environmental History of Israel*. Berkeley: University of California Press.

Tal, A., and J. A. Cohen. 2007. "Bringing 'Top-Down' to 'Bottom-Up': A New Role for
Environmental Legislation in Combating Desertification." *Harvard Environmental
Law Review* 31 (1): 163–217.

Thirteenth Governing Council Session: Israel's Decision to Build a Canal Linking the
Mediterranean Sea to the Dead Sea. 1985. New York: United Nations Environment
Programme. http://www.unep.org/Documents.multilingual/Default.asp?Documen
tID=59&ArticleID=341&l=en.

Twelfth Governing Council Session: Israel's Decision to Build a Canal Linking the
Mediterranean Sea to the Dead Sea. 1984. New York: United Nations Environment
Programme. http://www.unep.org/Documents.multilingual/Default.asp?Documen
tID=75&ArticleID=1100&l=en.

UN Conference on the Human Environment. 1972. United Nations Environment Programme. http://www.unep.org/Documents.Multilingual/Default.
asp?documentid=97.

UN Convention to Combat Desertification in Those Countries Experiencing Serious
Drought and/or Desertification, Particularly in Africa. 1994. *International Legal
Materials* 33 (5): 1328–82.

UN Convention on the Conservation of Migratory Species of Wild Animals. 1980. *International Legal Materials* 19 (1): 11–32.

UN Convention on Wetlands of International Importance Especially as Waterfowl
Habitat. 1971. *996 U.N.T.S.* http://www.un-documents.net/ramsar.htm.

UNCCD Country Information Database: Israel. n.d. United Nations Convention to
Combat Desertification. http://www.unccd.int/regional/menu.php.

UNCCD Regional Profiles. n.d. United Nations Convention to Combat Desertification. http://www.unccd.int/regional/menu.php.

UNESCO Worldwide: Europe and North America. n.d. United Nations Educational,
Scientific and Cultural Organization. http://www.unesco.org/new/en/unesco/
worldwide/unesco-regions/europe-and-north-america/.

Weiner, R. 2004. "Israel Wins Membership on WEOG." *Jewish Virtual Library: A Division of the American-Israeli Cooperative Enterprise*. http://www.jewishvirtual
library.org/jsource/UN/weog1.html.

World Heritage List. 2010. UNESCO World Heritage Centre. http://whc.unesco.org/
en/list.

World Resources Institute. 2005. *Millennium Ecosystem Assessment: Ecosystems
and Human Well-Being: Desertification Synthesis*, edited by L. Bledzki and
C. J. Cleveland. World Resources Institute. http://www.eoearth.org/article/
Ecosystems_and_Human_Well-being:_Desertification_Synthesis_(full_report).

CHAPTER FOURTEEN

TOWARD SUSTAINABLE DEVELOPMENT
Mainstreaming Environment in Israel

Valerie Brachya

THE STATE OF A COUNTRY'S environment is not determined by its environ-mentalists but by its developers. Of this, Israel is an extreme case: its rapid rate of population growth and economic development has been the crucial driving force determining the level of protection its environmental resources have received. The essential issue has been and remains "to what extent can en-vironmental considerations be effectively integrated into the decision-making processes which governed the location of housing, the alignment of roads, the generation of electricity and the type of industry?" "Mainstreaming" the en-vironment into investment and development activities was a key element in Israel's environmental management (Ministry of Environment 1992; Pruginin and Glass 1992).

Israel's economy is urban and industrial. Over 90 percent of its population resides in urban areas, and employment is 16 percent in industry and 57 per-cent in services (Central Bureau of Statistics 2009). Population expansion has been rapid, not only as a result of the influx of waves of immigration but also as a result of the high rate of natural growth, unlike countries in Europe that are currently stable or even experiencing negative population-growth rates. As income has risen, so has the standard of living, expressed in floor space per person, rates of car ownership, electricity consumption, and domestic-waste generation. Israel is facing a range of internal environmental problems typical of most Western countries today, including urban air pollution largely generated by traffic, the loss of green and open spaces, risks caused by the use of chemicals and the storage of hazardous materials, and the management of wastes and effluents. In addition, it is facing global issues as an active member of global society and taking on increasing responsibilities concerning climate change, protection of the global commons, and biodiversity (Ministry of Environment 2004).

A crucial framework that provided a platform for the incorporation of environmental aspects in development and the prevention of pollution was the land-use planning system, a regulatory system originally established under the British Mandate and revised under the Planning and Building Law 1965 (Marinov and Brachya 1979). It was a well-established institutional framework when environmental management began to gain public attention in the early 1970s and was forward-looking, able to anticipate, and therefore prevent, environmental deterioration. It did not have the capabilities of halting or remediating existing environmental degradation. That came later through harnessing the Law for Business Licensing 1968 and through prosecution of offenders under the Environmental Nuisances Act of 1961.

Not all countries have linked their environmental and planning systems together. Research on planning systems (Pritej 2009) has actually indicated that they have often evolved separately and only recently sought how to better synchronize sustainability into planning procedures and tools. In a new, small country, where professional civil servants met each other frequently, formally and informally, and especially when located within the same ministry (as were land-use planning and environment between 1976–1988), it is not surprising that colleagues frequently exchanged information about where they found helpful examples from around the world and their relevance. Senior Israeli heads of planning were willing to adopt new approaches (Feitelson 1998; Forester, Fischler, and Shmueli 2001) and environmental heads of planning sought every window of opportunity to incorporate additional aspects of environment into decision making (Brachya 1993; Amir 1985; Ministry of Environment 1989).

TRANSFORMATION OF THE REGULATIVE PLANNING FRAMEWORK

The Israeli regulatory land-use system is based on the fundamental principle that development rights belong to the state and consequently a developer has to request approval for any activity defined as requiring a "building permit." The definition is wide. Other than agricultural activity, drainage, and internal changes within an existing building, all land-use changes (on and offshore), earthworks, buildings, and infrastructure require a building permit. A permit cannot be issued unless in accordance with an approved plan, which has to be in accordance with the highest plan in the three-tiered hierarchy of master plans: national, regional, and local. Wherever a plan submitted does not comply with an existing, approved plan, it requires the approval of a higher level in the planning hierarchy. The national planning level includes two special committees of environmental significance: for protecting agricultural land and open space and for protecting the coastal environment. All plans are deposited for public comment for sixty days, during which time legal objections can be submitted. Some changes have been made and are being proposed to speed up the planning system. In 2010, a major reform of the planning and building law was under discussion in the parliamentary committee for internal and environmental affairs, following frequent criticism as being overly bureaucratic and causing delays, especially concerning the delivery of public infrastructure. However, the process and principles basically remain the same.

In a rapidly developing country, where floor space doubles itself in a twenty-year time span, the planning system is confronted with huge risks and opportunities for protecting the environment. At the outset, in the early years of the state, the emphasis of the governmental planning system was on enabling development and promoting dispersion to avoid a Tel Aviv city-state. The small country was regarded by early planners as empty, and efforts were taken to decentralize development to the periphery. Environment in the 1950s and 1960s received attention through proxy policies, such as policies for the protection of agricultural land (all open space capable of cultivation), and directly through the designation of specific sites for nature protection, national parks, antiquities, and historic sites.

The 1970s marked the real start of environmental awareness in the planning system, when signs of pollution were becoming apparent (e.g., air pollution in Haifa Bay, risk of eutrophication of Lake Kinneret, tar on beaches, landscape damage by quarries). It was also the decade when several major development proposals came under discussion, including the continuation of a cement quarry on the Carmel mountain ridge or at an alternative new quarry site at Tamra, the construction of an oil (later changed to coal) power station at Hadera, and the expansion of Ben-Gurion Airport. These set precedents in the recognition of the importance of landscape protection, pollution prevention, and abatement (air quality and noise exposure) in the planning debates (Brachya 1980, 1996).

The first step toward a more sustainable approach to physical development was taken in 1973 by a government decision to establish the Environmental Protection Service (EPS), which included the appointment of its director, Dr. Uri Marinov as an adviser to the National Board for Planning and Building (NBPB) (Environmental Protection Service 1974). This was not in itself controversial. Controversies arose later when opinions were expressed by the environmental adviser concerning specific master plans or planning proposals.

Whatever the differences of opinion, the EPS gained credibility as a professional body at the national level of planning, with the encouragement of the then director general of the Ministry of Interior and chairman of the National Board, Mr. Haim Kubersky, who promoted the integration of environment into the land-use planning system (see Introduction to EPS 1982).

The appointment of environmental advisers to the six regional planning committees came later as the volume of work increased and as the planning system showed willingness and interest in receiving advice on environmental issues. The transformation of the regulative planning system during the 1970s and 1980s was achieved through promoting consultation and providing advisory services. The environmental planners had no formal legal authority.

In 1988, with the establishment of the Ministry of Environmental Quality, the status of the environmental advisers to the planning authorities was changed—they became full-fledged voting members of the NBPB and later, by statutory amendments, became voting members of the regional planning committees and nonvoting members on the local planning committees, under amendment 43 to the Planning and Building Law in 1994. This structural change effectively created a new professional cadre of "environmental planners." By the year 2000 there were some sixty environmental planners in Israel's national, regional, and local planning institutions and about the same number in private consultancies, providing consultative services to developers and to opponents of development.

Much of the transformation was achieved through incorporating environmental considerations in national and regional master plans (officially termed National Outline Scheme [or NOS], which gave environmental planners the opportunity to impose environmental regulations on specific issues covering the whole of the country, such as for roads or quarries, or for a whole region (Feitelson 1998). Later sections of this chapter illustrate the influence of the environmental planners on planning policy in relation to sectorial issues: residential and industrial development, transportation infrastructure, and energy infrastructure.

The governmental decision that established the EPS also required the establishment of a system of Environmental Impact Statements. It was modeled on the U.S. concept under the National Environmental Policy Act (1970) but was integrated into the British-based land-use planning system (Rotenberg 1992). This was an awkward hybrid, as the U.S. concept was based on requiring consideration of all possible alternatives and on enabling public access to the information as a basis for submitting a case to court. The planning system in Israel adopted Environmental Impact Statements in 1982 in the form of regulations under the Planning and Building Law with a focus on mitigation, without questioning the validity of the planning proposal or possible alternatives to the plan proposed. The statements also did not require planning authorities to check if all reasonable steps had been taken to prevent or reduce the likely negative impacts of the planning proposal as submitted by the developer.

The result resembles the Environmental Impact Assessment systems established under the EU directive of 1985. The main advantage of the interlinkage between planning and environment was that the planning authorities had to require an Environmental Impact Statement (EIS) for projects where it was mandatory by law, and usually required one for all activities considered of concern. It did not take long for EIS to emerge as a major element in formulating decisions. The alternative would have been to establish a separate system under a separate law for EIS, but that would not have guaranteed that the EIS would be seriously considered by decision makers in the planning committees (Brachya 1980; Brachya and Marinov 1995; Brachya 1996).

The first set of regulations regarding EIS (1982) imposed a requirement on specific types of major development projects and required the statement to include five sections, including the measures to be taken to reduce or to prevent impacts, with tailor-made guidelines prepared by EPS for each plan. Many of the EIS at that time concerned proposals for new roads, despite the fact that preparing EIS for road plans was not mandatory since the Ministry of Transport had voiced strong opposition to their being included as mandatory in the regulations. Other EIS prepared were on waste-disposal sites, quarries, power stations, and coastal development projects. The proponent of a development plan was responsible for the preparation of the EIS, using consultants as necessary. The EPS (and later the Ministry of Environmental Quality or Environmental Protection) reviewed each EIS and then submitted its opinion and recommendations to the planning authority (Ministry of Environment 1997; SPNI and Ministry of Environment 1997).

The EIS regulations were amended to Environmental Impact Assessment (EIA) regulations in 2003 to widen the list of cases where an EIA process was required. The new procedures did not just require a statement, but added an important stipulation that asked how sustainable development would be ensured, such as the efficient use of land, water, and energy. Another key provision required developers to consider alternatives to the project, including the implications for the environment that the project or plan would not be permitted at all.

The revised regulations imposed requirements on the consultants involved in the preparation of EIS to improve the professional standard of submitted EIS. The revised regulations gave statutory status to the review procedures by the Ministry, including a right to refuse an EIS if it did not meet professional standards or supply the required information. This right has in fact been used on several occasions.

Experience in EIA in Israel to date suggests that it does ensure that the environmental review of all major development proposals takes place and that it has undoubtedly improved conditions imposed on plans concerning pollution prevention and reduction and minimizing resource degradation. Nonetheless, the process is often criticized for serving the interests of the developer, rarely leading to rejection of a plan.

A notable example is the EIA procedure on the Trans-Israel Highway (Route 6), which contributed significantly to the environmental aspects of the detailed alignment and to its integration into the surrounding landscape, but did not question whether the highway was the right solution as compared with transportation alternatives (Maizlish 2005).

The transformation of the planning system in the 1990s was largely generated through the expansion and strengthening of nongovernmental environmental organizations and the rise of the environmental movement. Since 1975, an environmental NGO representative was appointed as a formal member of the NBPB but not in the other planning authorities. As the environmental movement intensified its activities versus development proposals, submitted objections, and took developers and the planning committees to the courts, focus turned on how to manage environmental conflicts (Feitelson 1996; Ministry of Environment 2002; Shmueli and Ben-Gal 2004). Major conflicts included proposals for the U.S. radio relay station in the Arava, a road connection across the Matlul Zurim range to link Karmiel with Tefen, a hydroelectric power station at Kfar Hanasi, and the Herzliya marina. After several years of exerting pressure on the planning authorities through conflicts, in 2002 the environmental movement joined the decision makers through the appointment of statutory representatives to planning authorities at the national and regional levels. While this did not prevent NGOs from filing legal objections with regard to specific proposals, it ensured that their perspective would be heard in all major planning decisions.

Although the integration of environmental policies in planning evolved over the years, a chronological description would produce a confusing picture of a wide range of concurrent activities. The evolution of environmental policy in planning in Israel is therefore presented according to the major sectors that it influenced: residential development, industrial development, transportation infrastructure, and energy infrastructure. Finally, the question will be raised as to whether the planning authorities have generated a system that promotes sustainable development.

In a rapidly developing country, where solutions had to be found to accommodate waves of immigration as well as a high natural population growth and increasing household split (separation of generations), the distribution and relative density of residential development were crucial issues in the efficient use of limited land resources and in the feasibility of successful public transport.

In the early years of the state, emphasis was placed by the planning authorities on the dispersion of development to the periphery, when undeveloped open space was seen as empty areas. By the 1990s, it was recognized that the scarcity of open space was a crucial issue in a small country so the question was rephrased as how to build: whether urban or rural, central or peripheral. A few environmental experts suggested that Israel should reconsider its policy of open doors for immigration and consider the limitations on its carrying capacity; but most of the environmental community promoted a policy of "concentrated dispersal," which would allocate land for urban expansion, preferably within or contiguous to existing urban centers (Israel 2020).

When pressures for development increased in the 1990s in response to the need for housing during the wave of immigration from ex-Soviet Union countries (Brachya and Levy 1992), the Israeli environmental movement widened its attention. Rather than merely protecting specific sites for nature or landscape value, it sought to protect the "continuity" of open space and prevent its fragmentation—to enable the survival of habitats and ecosystems and to protect ecological corridors (Kaplan and Zalutsky, n.d.). The sensitivity and the continuity of open-space protection were adopted by the national planning authorities in the comprehensive short- and long-term plans for residential development in Israel (National Master Plan NOS 31 and later NOS 35).

The Ministry and the environmental movement turned their attention to the urban scene and voiced objections to any proposals promoting widespread low-density development as being unsustainable and proposed that development be concentrated in and around existing urban areas, at urban densities. They realized that a mistake had been made in the early 1990s during the wave of immigrant absorption when permission had been granted, through the national Master Plan 31, for major expansions of all rural villages, consequently promoting development of single-story housing at low densities, dependent on car usage for accessibility. The requirement for "contiguous" development and for minimum residential densities in NOS 35 were seen as major steps forward.

Commuting became a major issue in planning, since traffic congestion at the entrance to cities at peak hours had become a concern to transportation and urban planning.[1] The nonstatutory planning think tank of "Israel 2020" and the following national NOS 35 paid particular attention to the need to link transportation and urban planning to prevent further sprawl, especially in the central region, and to strengthen existing urban centers. They faced a conflict with the desire of the population to own and use their private cars. Car ownership increased from 70,000 vehicles in 1960 to over 2.4 million in 2008 (Central Bureau of Statistics 2009). The use of the private car for commuting had been encouraged through taxation and pension systems, which had encouraged employers to pay part of their employees' salaries through non-pensionable benefits, particularly car benefits. Commuter preference to use the private car was further promoted by the provision of cars leased by employers in preference to purchased automobiles, which reduced even further awareness of the real costs of travel to work (Transportation Today and Tomorrow 2009).

So as congestion built up and time delays were the focus of transport considerations, the government invested hugely in improving the road system, widening existing roads, adding multilevel junctions, and adding new road alignments. Expansion of the road system enabled commuting and encouraged urban sprawl (Mindali, Raveh, and Salomon 2004). The emphasis on private vehicles undermined the viability of public transport and encouraged modal split to favor the use of the private car, reducing the use of public transport. It not only generated more congestion but also caused more severe urban air pollution and noise. The main pollution problem in the Tel Aviv metropolitan area was not industrial pollution but traffic-generated pollution, which affected air quality over a much wider area as far away as Jerusalem (Ministry of Environmental Protection website, http://www.sviva.gov.il—air pollution).

The Ministry of Transport has now recognized the mistakes of the past and is directing major investments to improving urban public-transport systems (e.g., light rail in Jerusalem, fast bus in Haifa, and underground lines in Tel Aviv). Parking standards in city centers are now being reduced and nonvehicular transport in cities is being encouraged, particularly cycling. Sustainable urban transportation is now recognized as a key issue in promoting the revitalization of urban centers, preventing low-density urban sprawl, and reducing public preference for the car-centered lifestyles of rural villages.

In the early years of the state, establishing new villages—kibbutzim and moshavim—was seen as a national goal and viewed with pride. However, since the 1990s, the environmental movement has emphasized that there is no justification for dispersed rural settlement. If rural development is encouraged, it should be through raising housing densities in existing villages. Its opposition to new village locations was based on the allocation of undisturbed "greenfield" areas for building, fragmentation by new infrastructure, and the need to concentrate public investment in improving services in existing villages, including investment for sewage treatment and waste disposal.

In recent years, the government has proposed new villages in Lakish, the Galil, and in the northern Negev and has also permitted some individual homesteads, promoted as fulfilling the Zionist mission of settling the land. It was strongly opposed by environmentalists, including by the Ministry of Environmental Protection. Planning authorities did not entirely accept either position, refusing some but permitting others. Opposition by the Ministry and environmental groups succeeded in preventing the approval of several proposals, including a new village named Michal on the Gilboa in 2006, which threatened the endemic iris flowers, but the settlement of Kadita on Mount Meron was permitted.

Local authorities differed in their positions; some saw the establishment of a new village as a way to attract government funding and new residents to the area. Others recognized that in the long term, the costs of service provision would be higher than the immediate benefits. The Nature and National Parks Authority surprisingly supported the proposal of Michal, even though the major impact would have been the loss of part of the habitat of a highly valued natural species. Their claim was that the approval of the new village would enable the Local Authority's agreement to designate a large area of the Gilboa as a nature reserve. Members of their internal scientific committee objected to such a position, but the decision to refuse the development proposal was ultimately the result of strong public opposition generated by the environmental movement.

Environmentalists had hoped that the planning authorities would take steps to promote the revitalization of inner-urban areas, which in many cases were suffering from a loss of population to the more attractive new outer suburbs or rural villages. This was a main argument by opponents to the proposed western expansion of Jerusalem (known as the "Safdi plan," as it was planned by the well-known architect), which was refused by the NBPB after a massive public campaign in favor of encouraging revitalization within the existing urban area of Jerusalem.

The Coalition for the Protection of the Jerusalem Hills was founded in 2003 to fight proposals for development, including the Safdi plan. In addition to media exposure and public demonstrations, they prepared a detailed review of the availability of dwelling units (Barsheshet 2008). The report and the review of an independent expert were highly influential in the NBPB reaching its decision in February 2007 to refuse approval of the Safdi plan.

Revitalization at high densities has, however, frequently raised conflict with environmentalists within urban areas, particularly where urban renewal at very high densities was claimed necessary on economic grounds but would cause a loss of urban parks and open spaces and historic or architecturally valuable buildings. The environmental movement occasionally finds itself in conflict when it opposes redevelopment within the existing urban fabric and at the same time opposes the development of greenfield sites. All of the above cases concern the allocation of land for development and the protection of land as open space, for which the land-use planning system was recognized by all stakeholders as the framework in which such issues should be discussed and decided. Although the same system governs the issuance of building permits and therefore has a major role to play concerning the regulation of construction, the issue of "green building" did not enter the stage until very recently. The environmental movement in Israel concentrated its attention on planning rather than on building and construction. The only exception was the attention paid to building materials. Construction in Israel is predominantly based on aggregates, stone appropriate for cement and concrete. These are the only available sources of local building materials and there is no reasonable alternative to them. However, at issue is where to permit quarries that would have the least impact on the protection of open space and areas of high landscape value and that would not cause dust and noise disturbance to local residents.

Many disputes have occurred concerning the location of aggregate and cement quarries and the reclamation of the damage they caused and the often-approved proposals by planning authorities for aggregate quarries in highly sensitive areas (Enis and Schechter 1971; Brachya 1979). Planning policy has become more sensitive to the adverse impacts of quarries and, under the more recent national NOS 14, preferred the intensification of production at existing quarry sites to the opening of new sites. Underground quarrying, which could be a better solution, is still considered prohibitively expensive. The recycling of building waste should be encouraged as a source of raw materials to stop its uncontrolled disposal as waste, but recycled waste would only provide a small proportion of the demand for building materials.

Surprisingly, perhaps, Israeli environmentalists did not recognize the role they could have played in the use of building materials and in the promotion of green building. The only significant exception Israel can claim is the widespread use of solar domestic water heating, which has been compulsory since it was required under planning regulations in 1974. The importance of green building is now becoming apparent in relation to measures for reducing greenhouse gas emissions by means of energy efficiency in building. In 2005, the Israel Standards Institute established a green-building standard, which is currently under revision; it is a voluntary guideline and has as yet had little impact. Several local authorities have also taken on the subject: Kfar Saba, for example, has issued guidelines for green construction but these are not part of a statutory document under the planning and building law. The Tel Aviv regional planning authority has passed a policy document promoting green building in their area. The ministries of Environmental Protection and Housing and Interior, as of 2010, were seeking ways to promote green building through mandatory planning and building regulations and through the revision of the national Master Plan 35.

The planning authorities have not been major players in determining the type of industrial development in Israel or in integrating environmental considerations into its development. Their role has been significant concerning activities relating to the extraction of raw materials and to the location of industries identified as being "noxious" or siting industries where they would not interfere with conditions for residential development.

Phosphates offer an example of the problematic environmental implications of quarrying for industrial raw materials in a small and scenic country. Israel's considerable phosphate reserves are not of a high quality and require enriching processes before their transportation to the fertilizer industry. Environmental impacts of phosphate quarrying are substantial and severe— huge quarries, the enormous overburden of overlying strata that have to be removed prior to extraction of the relevant strata, landscape deterioration, dust and fine particles from extraction and processing, and water pollution by effluent.

The phosphate industry operates under conditions originally established by the British Mandate and because of their distant location in the south, they have operated for many years with little respect for the environment. The Society for the Protection of Nature in Israel led public concern, in the 1990s and again in 2004, which largely focused on industry damage to the landscape and lack of landscape reclamation and even questioned whether the industry should be allowed to continue to exploit natural resources in such a wasteful and polluting way. The industry responded by establishing a reclamation fund for previous landscape damage and accompanied its newer proposals with landscape management plans to significantly reduce damage during operations.

The issue of dust generated by phosphate quarrying and the enrichment process came into the public arena when the phosphate company requested permission to open a new quarry in close proximity to Arad, where residents feared air pollution, especially as Arad has been a location favored by asthma sufferers. The company's bad environmental record demonstrated to the residents that they had good reason to oppose the opening of a new phosphate field beside them. The company revised its environmental responsibility over the last decade and still hopes to convince the planning authorities to permit the opening of the new quarry at Sde Barir near Arad, since the EIS prepared in 2006 shows that theoretically they should be well within the pollution controls required by the Ministry of Environmental Protection. Their alternative is to open a quarry at West Hatzeva, which falls within a nature reserve. The conclusion is perhaps that there is no space in Israel today for any industrial activity that does not exercise a high level of environmental responsibility and fails to achieve a high level of public acceptability, even if it claims that it can abide by the current legal standards.

The Dead Sea Works (DSW), which utilizes solar energy to extract or mine natural salts and minerals from the Dead Sea, has also come under intense public criticism concerning its impacts on the environment. Its process involves transporting water from the northern basin of the Dead Sea to the southern evaporation ponds from which the minerals are extracted, processed, and sent on to other chemical-processing industries. Contrary to much misinformed public opinion, this process is only responsible for about 12 percent of the water removed from the Dead Sea and its corresponding drop in sea level, which is now at a rate of over a meter a year. Three-quarters of the loss of water to the Dead Sea is from the diversion of water sources, including the Israel national water conduit, which once supplied its water input (Jerusalem Institute for Israel Studies 2006).

When the DSW requested permission from the planning authorities to expand its activities, one of the conditions was that it would not increase its intake of water from the northern basin. The planning authorities have been more concerned about the impacts of the DSW on the southern basin (which is an evaporation pond and not the Dead Sea itself), along whose shores exists a major tourist resort. The hotels depend on the DSW for maintaining the water body, but the buildings themselves are at risk from the rise in water level as salts settle on the bed of the basin and, consequently, surrounding embankments are raised. The government recently established a new government company to determine whether to create a separate lagoon to protect the hotels or to require the DSW to remove salts from the bed of the basin in a massive dredging operation, instead of raising the embankments.

Both the phosphates company and the DSW demonstrate the complex situation between public and private interests and to what extent environmental externalities are fully internalized. They are both important employers in areas that otherwise have limited employment prospects. The planning authorities have been interested in promoting opportunities for development, but the environmental price has been high.

The main role the planning authorities have played in relation to industrial development in Israel has concerned the relocation of what were termed "noxious and polluting" industries. Chemicals are a major industrial sector in Israel, accounting for some 26 percent of its net export value (Central Bureau of Statistics 2009). Oil refining and chemical industries in the Haifa Bay were the first major pollution "hotspot." The response of the planning authorities to such industries in the 1950s was to designate areas for their relocation to the south, then seen as empty space and as an area to which employment opportunities must be directed. The south was then considered in a similar way to developing countries—the urgent need for employment opportunities overrode concerns about environmental damage for this or future generations.

One of the areas established for such industry was Ramat Hovav, an area south of Beer-Sheva, which was designated as a special industrial zone in which seventeen chemical industries were established in 1975, and in which a site was developed for the treatment of Ramat Hovav's hazardous wastes. The area became a major environmental disaster, suffering from noxious industrial emissions, effluents, wastes, smells, fires, and high risks to health and safety.

No serious control measures were taken until the Ministry of Defense announced its plans to move its training bases from valuable real estate in the center of the country to a location some nine kilometers south of Ramat Hovav. Following warnings of health and exposure risks, the Ministry of Defense took major steps to back the Ministry of Environment's requirements for pollution abatement, which were supported by a government decision in 2004. The Ministry of Environmental Protection then imposed severe restrictions on the business licenses of the industries (the main means for imposing regulatory controls on industry), who subsequently went to court.

The case was settled by mediation in 2005 and significant improvements in the treatment of chemical effluents have already been made by the industries and by the hazardous-waste-disposal facility. Future action will be taken in accordance with a government-backed decision to bring air emissions from the chemical plants under control to comply with best available technology (BAT), as commonly practiced in Western countries. In hindsight, there is no valid reason why such steps were not taken many years before and why a proposed development of the Ministry of Defense was the trigger to attaining environmental compliance. However, it demonstrates that the southern area was seen by many, including the planners, as being a vast, empty area, where environmental controls were less important—a concept that has since become outdated.

The last decade or so of industrial development in Israel has been in the area of high-tech, which now composes some 50 percent of the value of national exports. On the whole, this industry has little environmental impact and the planning authorities welcome its development, which does not conflict with residential development. However, some so-called high-tech industries are actually chemical industries. Intel, for example, in Jerusalem and in Kiryat Gat, is in fact a high-tech chemical industry. Nonetheless, the company takes intensive actions to maintain a very high standard of corporate environmental governance, beyond best international standards; as a sign of this commitment, Intel was included in the 2009 index for Corporate Social Responsibility prepared by the Maala organization.

The way forward for improving environmental performance in the industrial sector is likely to be promoted by Israeli companies that trade on international markets and are obliged to comply with the requirements of the supply chain, such as the EU REACH Directive or ISO 14000. It imposes environmental requirements on Israel's chemical industries. Similarly, international sources of funding and investment increasingly require evaluation of environmental risks as financial risks before making financial resources available. As Israel becomes more economically integrated into the developed world, in particular as a result of its accession to the OECD, it will be obliged to incorporate similar environmental obligations as others do when competing in global markets (Coren 2010).

INTEGRATING ENVIRONMENTAL CONSIDERATIONS INTO ENERGY INFRASTRUCTURE

The planning authorities have assumed, and still do, that their role is to enable energy providers to establish the necessary infrastructure to supply the growing demand for energy. The rise in electricity consumption and production was seen in the early years of the state as a sign of freedom from manual labor and as a symbol of economic progress; and, in consequence, the construction of additional power stations was interpreted as positive. Their focus was primarily on the location of the power stations, where their concerns focused on the adverse impacts of electricity production on residential development and on the protection of the coastal waterfront for recreation and public access. Planning authorities objected to the location of Reading D power station, just north of the then-built-up area of Tel Aviv, mainly on the grounds of potential air pollution and noise. Their protest was dismissed by government by the enactment of a special law (Laster 1973).

Historically, a major criterion in Israel's energy policy was diversification of energy sources, which led to the import of coal for electricity production. Until then, Israel had been dependent on oil for electricity production. A major power station at Hadera, constructed in 1981, was originally planned to operate on oil but was changed to coal, for which multiple sources of fuel were and still are available that do not pose a security risk. Greenhouse gas emissions during the 1980s were not yet on the global agenda. Discussions at the National Planning and Building Board focused on the location of the power station—whether at the mouth of the Hadera River or at the Taninim River further north, the former adjacent to an urban area and the latter to a nature reserve (Hill and Alterman 1974; Brovender 1979). The urban location was preferred and attention then focused on the environmental conditions needed to prevent pollution or at least to minimize damage (Environmental Protection Service 1982).

The environmental regulations relating to air pollution, noise, fly-ash disposal, and the prevention of marine pollution constituted a precedent and acted as the model for future power stations. They included monitoring of air and marine pollution and of coastal erosion. The NBPB took the risk of direct coal unloading instead of the more conventional solution of unloading coal at an existing port. A local environmental unit was established for monitoring the impacts and ensuring compliance, and a planning subcommittee was empowered with enforcement. The residents of the urban area were awarded "compensation" for accepting the power station on their doorstep, by the promise of a park, which was only established many years later and has not truly provided environmental compensation (Brachya 1996).

A second coal-fired power station was built further south in Ashkelon on a very similar model of conditions and operations. Compensation to residents of the city consisted of a major financial contribution by the electricity company to construction of a marina, which was seen as a symbol to strengthen the tourist image of the city. Both the Hadera and Ashkelon power stations were outstanding examples of the extent to which environmental concerns were adopted by the NBPB; and their monitoring requirements were the basis for establishing environmental associations of local authorities to ensure compliance.

The energy scene has evolved over the last few years, as the issue of climate change has come onto the Israel agenda. A proposal to add further coal-fired units to the Ashkelon power station might have been immediately accepted in the past as a necessary part of national infrastructure. However, it is currently the focus of a major dispute in the planning committees where environmental representatives, government and nongovernment, are voicing objections on the basis of greenhouse gas emissions and air pollution, including mercury. They argue that no further coal-fired units should be permitted until clean-coal technology is available. Local authorities, including Ashkelon itself, have joined the opposition. While the electricity company, backed strongly by the Ministry of National Infrastructure and the Ministry of Finance, claims that it can only guarantee electricity supply if further coal-fired units are added, the planning authorities have so far delayed giving permission for the project, awaiting government plans for mitigating greenhouse gas emissions, which would bring Israel in line with Western countries.

The claim that Israel had no alternative to coal was rendered false with the discovery of offshore natural gas. The offshore natural gas fields began to supply a source of energy from 2004 and will enable a change in Israel's energy footprint. Natural gas not only provides a cheaper source of fuel for electricity production but also is far cleaner in terms of emissions and requires less space. Over the last two years further offshore natural gas fields have been discovered and it is now accepted by energy and environmental parties that the proportion of natural gas in the energy mix will rise to at least 70 percent—with another 10 to 20 percent from renewables (Mor 2012).

The environmental risks may then come from a different medium—the risks and hazards of a terminal for receiving liquefied natural gas to ensure continuity and diversification of natural gas supply from multiple sources. Natural gas is already being supplied by pipeline from Egypt and will be increasingly supplied from Israel's offshore fields. A national natural gas grid was approved by the planning authorities and is under construction to bring power stations, such as that in Haifa, online with gas instead of oil, and to bring several major industrial companies online with gas. This structural change of the energy infrastructure of Israel is one of the most predominant environmental issues of the country at present.

Both government and the environmental movement would like to see more energy coming from renewable sources. Renewable energy derived from domestic solar boilers on rooftops has historically saved some 3 percent of demand for electricity. Photovoltaic units are now being installed on large rooftops particularly in the southern region, encouraged by government financial incentives. The planning authorities permitted in 2009 a thermal solar power station at Ashelim in the northern Negev and waived restrictions on granting building permits for rooftop photovoltaic units. In contrast, when considering the efficient use of limited space and the protection of nature and landscape as overriding planning criteria, authorities are very reluctant to permit ground-level solar units that have a huge space requirement per unit production. These solar installations, when combined with wind turbines in the north and some waste-to-energy infrastructure, may bring Israel's renewable energy up to some 10 percent of electricity demand, but they are highly unlikely to provide a major source of its energy requirements in the foreseeable future.

The question therefore turns to whether there is a place for energy demand management. While attitudes have changed from regarding electricity consumption as a symbol of social advance to understanding that electricity should be saved (like water conservation), these attitudes have not been effectively translated into practice. Minimum efficiency standards have been imposed by government regulation on many household appliances, and an incentive is planned to encourage replacement of old and wasteful air conditioners. However, attention will increasingly be paid to improving energy efficiency in new construction (as mentioned above under planning for residential development), since it is now clear that the major increase in demand is from the acclimatization of buildings, with a peak demand for electricity on hot summer afternoons. The government decided in 2008 to set itself a target of 20 percent energy conservation but as yet has no action plan by which it hopes to achieve the target and is unlikely to achieve it without major intervention.

Until the last decade, almost all investment in ground transportation in Israel was directed toward expanding and improving the road network. New alignments and the widening of existing roads carried a heavy environmental toll. Traffic congestion caused increasing air pollution and noise, in spite of improvements in vehicle technology and fuel quality. The rapid rise in transport volume including freight transport overtook all attempts at technological improvement. Economic sector ministries and local authorities regarded road development as essential infrastructure, whatever the impacts and environmental costs.

New road alignments have caused fragmentation of natural habitats, loss of wildlife attempting to cross roads, and major adverse impacts on sensitive landscapes through the choice of poor alignments and lack of attention to and investment in landscape planning. Unnecessary cutting of natural slopes, lack of willingness to even consider tunnels and bridges, and inconsiderate disposal of waste material scarred many attractive landscapes.

While the planning authorities had taken steps to impose environmental requirements on the interurban road network through the national master plan for roads, NOS 3 amendment 7, and had frequently required Environmental Impact Statements on roads even when not statutorily required under the EIS regulations, environmental considerations in road alignment and construction were inadequate until the Trans-Israel Highway, Route 6, was approved and constructed. Route 6 was designated on the national plan for roads approved by the government in 1976, but its actual construction was proposed in the early 1990s as a major north–south highway.

Planned as a toll road in 1993 and opened in the early 2000s in stages, Route 6 was strongly objected to by environmental organizations on the grounds that it would disturb undeveloped open landscape and they called for investment in public transport. The professional staff of the Ministry of Environment did not object to the highway in principle, but claimed that investment in public transport in the Tel Aviv metropolitan area should come first, to strengthen the existing urban fabric and to avoid attracting residential and economic development to the outer suburban areas.

During the course of the road's approval process, ministers of the Environment held various positions regarding the road; two sided with the environmental organizations, others supported the road but with increased emphasis on environmental considerations. Apart from the overall question of whether the highway should be constructed at all, environmental conflicts focused on particularly environmentally sensitive sections of the road. Protests included considerable civil disobedience and multiple appeals to the Supreme Court. Neither the protests nor the litigation changed the decisions of the planning authorities and the government to approve the plans, and the road was ultimately constructed (Maizlish 2005).

The environmental standards incorporated into the Trans-Israel Highway's planning and construction were far higher than those of any previous infrastructure plan and, in retrospect, set new standards for the country. The innovations included tunnels and bridges, overpasses and underpasses for wildlife crossings, landscaping in harmony with the natural surroundings, and the careful relocation of trees and geophytes. The innovations were partly due to the willingness of the Trans-Israel Highway Company and the Derech Eretz Highways (who won the tender when the project was privatized and became the country's first toll road). The innovations were also partially the results of requirements of the Ministry of Environment's very close supervision of the team accompanying the detailed planning and construction of the project. The environmental measures were undoubtedly a response by the developers to criticism of the environmental organizations—to demonstrate that a major infrastructure could be constructed in an environmentally sensitive way. It was a turning point for environmental considerations in cross-country transportation projects, whether road or rail, showing what could and should be done.

When proposals were made for improving the rail system, environmentalists were sometimes unsure how to encourage investment in rail systems as environmentally friendly transport on the one hand, but, on the other, to object when the improvement of existing lines and the alignment of new lines conflicted with landscape and nature protection. The improvement of the old rail alignment to Jerusalem, which slowly winds its way along the Sorek valley, had disastrous consequences on the mountainous landscape as bends were straightened to speed up the travel time (still over an hour following improvements, and therefore still not a serious competitor to road transport). However, the new alignment proposed for a much faster connection between Jerusalem and Tel Aviv ran into a severe conflict led by the Nature Reserves and National Parks Authority. It initiated a study of an alternative—a long, low-level tunnel—that would not damage an unspoiled natural area of the Itla stream. Even when well supported by professional evaluation and public pressure, their objection was not accepted by the planning authorities, who gave preference to the rail company's claim that the work involved in preparing plans for the alternative alignment would cause a delay of at least three years. The planning authorities perhaps considered that they had gone far enough toward the environmental organizations and were not willing to take one step more, even when well justified.

Planning authorities, however, have been very conducive to incorporating environmental considerations in very problematic large-scale development proposals. The proposed plans for operating the runways of Ben-Gurion Airport in the 1980s generated a huge conflict with affected communities concerning noise disturbance. The country has multiple airports for defense use, but civilian air traffic is predominantly concentrated at Ben-Gurion Airport, with subsidiary activity at Sde Dov in north Tel Aviv and in the south at the Eilat Airport. Intensive international and defense flights from Ben-Gurion inevitably led to noise impacts on the surrounding towns and villages under the flight paths.

The question was whether to concentrate the noise disturbance along one flight path or distribute the noise impacts between several affected areas. The Environmental Protection Service (pre-Ministry) led the discussions within the planning authorities, which eventually agreed to spread the noise impacts, impose controls on the operation of the flight paths, and establish measures to limit new construction in areas sensitive to noise impacts—those above 30 Ldn (measure of day-night average sound level, with a weighting on night noise to account for higher level of sensitivity) (Brachya 1996). Measures were taken to incorporate noise insulation in schools and educational institutions. The plan had included proposals to insulate affected residential dwellings but these were refused by the property owners, who submitted claims for compensation (the district court overruled the local court in 2010 and supported the claims for compensation—a decision that will now be challenged in the Supreme Court).

A night curfew was imposed in 1997 on departures from the airport but may be lifted shortly to enable runway improvement. The lifting of the ban followed the opinion of Ministry of Environment noise experts that the concentration of flights before and after the curfew caused more serious noise impacts than flights under no curfew. Affected local authorities continue to oppose a lifting of the ban.

This early case and the later plans for the expansion of ground facilities at the airport, including a new terminal, demonstrate that in some cases environmental considerations became the main factor in planning decisions. However, unlike the Trans-Israel Highway Company, the Airports Authority did not propose an environmentally acceptable solution but was forced to accept environmental constraints imposed by the planning authorities. It could be concluded that this was just a matter of time, since the airport plans far preceded the highway plan.

However it could also be suggested that the various government infrastructure authorities do not necessarily act in a similar way with regard to environmental considerations, and that progress may be dependent on an individual or an institutional attitude toward the protection of the environment. The Airports Authority regarded itself as literally and metaphorically "above" the environment.

It is interesting to compare the airport experience with a maritime port case. Ashdod port was constructed in the 1960s to provide major marine transport infrastructure and be an addition to the existing port at Haifa. No consideration was given at the time to its likely impacts on the coastal environment. Monitoring of sediment around marine structures showed that the port was responsible for the accumulation of some 4.5 million cubic meters of sand on its southern side with consequent loss of sand supply to shores north of the port (Golik et al. 1997). When proposals were made to expand the port and extend the main breakwater to deeper waters to enable larger ships to enter the port, an environmental impact statement was required with particular attention to the consequences for coastal erosion. The planning authorities accepted the need for the expansion of the port as essential national infrastructure, but the approval was conditional on the construction enabling the sediment, which is transported along the Israeli shore by long-shore currents, to bypass the obstacle of the port breakwaters and continue north to supply sand to the beaches.

This case represents an example of cooperation between transport and environmental authorities and their mutual recognition of the importance of integrated coastal-zone management. The agreement was achieved through negotiations between the Ports Authority and the Ministry of Environment, with the assistance of an international expert who held a public hearing together, to check if the proposal would be acceptable to the environmental organizations. Once accepted, the plan gained the immediate approval of the planning authorities. It perhaps demonstrates that discussions between the relevant parties prior to the submission of a plan can save time and achieve a better solution than plans characterized by conflicts fought in the planning authorities or in the courts.

Clearly, the planning authorities in Israel have constituted the main institutional structure for preventive measures for environmental protection. They have certainly played a role in making development more sensitive to potentially adverse impacts on the environment, including prevention of damage to nature and landscape, reduction of pollution at source, and frequently (though not always) restrained development in areas exposed to environmental degradation and risks. The mainstreaming of environment into the planning system through environmental advisers to the planning authorities, statutory regulations, and environmental considerations in master plans, has undoubtedly created a strong interface between spatial planning and environmental considerations.

Some of the policies that have emerged can also be recognized as promoting sustainable development and not just preventing pollution. Particularly noteworthy is the emphasis on the efficient use of land, through residential building at higher urban densities and through concentration of new development contiguous to existing infrastructure and services.

However, many of the issues associated with sustainable development, which, as defined by the Brundtland Commission in 1987, is development that "meets the needs of the current generation without compromising the ability of future generations to meet their own needs," have not yet been sufficiently integrated into the planning system. As in many countries, coming to terms with mitigation of and adaptation to climate change has not yet expressed itself through the spatial planning system. Nor has the concept of sustainable consumption entered into the planning dialogue, which requires consideration of whether current consumption patterns can be continued and how demand for renewable and nonrenewable resources can be reduced.

The concepts of sustainable development are entering the arena in Israel through economic development rather than through physical, spatial development (Ministry of Environment 1999). A government decision in May 2003 established an interministerial framework that included a requirement for each ministry to prepare a strategy for the activities it would undertake to promote sustainable development. This wide-ranging decision was the forerunner of many specific actions taken by such ministries as Industry, Trade and Labor, Agriculture, and Tourism, and includes greening government procurement, incorporation of environmental risks as financial risks by the financial regulators, and the integration of environmental considerations into agricultural policy (Ministry of Environment 2005, 2006, 2007, 2008).

Sustainable development at the local authority level did not enter the arena through the local planning and building commissions but through a voluntary commitment to reduce greenhouse gas emissions. In 2008, the leading fifteen municipal local authorities and another three who joined the initiative, signed the International Council for Local Environmental Initiatives (now known as Local Governments for Sustainability) committing themselves to a target of 20 percent reduction of greenhouse gas emissions. It was a declaratory step at first, initiated and encouraged by the NGO Heschel Center for Environmental Learning and Leadership, but it developed into an opportunity for a wider agenda, using the stimulus of climate change to promote the reduction of air pollution, conservation of energy and water, sustainable transport, and the reduction of wastes.

Future greening of the economy, greening development, and greening infrastructure in Israel are likely to come from driving forces outside the planning system. Environmental governance around the world is increasingly influenced by international commitments, market forces, public awareness, and the active role of civil society. Environmental directives in Europe affecting the supply chain are generating improved environmental performance of industry in Israel; commitment to greenhouse gas mitigation may further stimulate green building and promote sustainable transport. And the environmental movement will no doubt continue to fight, not only for the protection of nature and landscape, but increasingly for the protection of biodiversity and ecosystems.

The planning authorities will, it is hoped, take on further commitments within their discussions or processes of decision making, demonstrating that institutional structures can reform themselves from within. As they have demonstrated over the past thirty years, Israel's planners are capable of adopting an environmental agenda.

NOTE

1. CBS statistics on car ownership: 6.3 cars per 1,000 people in 1951, 254.4 cars per 1,000 in 2008. The steepest rise was until 2000 at 7.8 percent a year, and then the rate of increase reduced to 2.3 percent a year. Israel is still far below the rate of car ownership in Europe (in France, e.g., the rate is 498 per 1,000).

REFERENCES

Amir, S. 1985. "Environmental Quality Protection through Land Use Planning." *Environmental Policy Law* 15: 56–63.

Brachya, V. 1979. "Towards the Integration of Planning for the Extraction and Reclamation of Quarries." Selected Papers on the Environment in Israel no. 7. Jerusalem: Environmental Protection Service, Ministry of Interior.

———. 1980. "Environmental Planning in Israel." IFHP News Sheet prepared for Thirty-Fifth Congress in Israel.

———. 1993. "Environmental Assessment in Land Use Planning in Israel." *Landscape and Urban Planning* 23: 167–81.

———. 1996. "Environmental Management through Land Use Planning in Israel." Special Bulletin on Planning in Israel, prepared for 32nd ISoCaRP Congress in Israel, Jerusalem, October 13–16.

Brachya, V., and S. Levy. 1992. "Environmental Management at a Time of Rapid Development." In *Planning and Housing in Israel in the Wake of Rapid Changes*, edited by Y. Golani, S. Eldor, and M. Garon. Ministry of Interior and Ministry of Housing and Construction for 41st IFHP conference in Israel, Jerusalem, September.

Brachya, V., and U. Marinov. 1995. "An Analytical Comparison of the Environmental Impact Statement System in Israel Compared to Other Countries." *Horizons in Geography* 42–43: 71–78. In Hebrew.

Brovender, S. 1979. "Power Station: Dilemma of Location." *Teva Vearetz*, January–February. In Hebrew.

Central Bureau of Statistics. 2009. Statistical Abstract of Israel.

Coren, O. 2010. "OECD Rules Forcing Israel's Industrial Polluters to Improve." *Haaretz*, August 31. http://www.haaretz.com/print-edition/business/oecd-rules -forcing-israel-s-industrial-polluters-to-improve-1.311178.

Enis, R., and M. Schecht. 1971. *Quarries and Landscape*. Haifa: Technion Center for Urban and Regional Studies.

Environmental Protection Service. 1974. *Annual Report on Environment in Israel*, no. 1. In Hebrew.

————. 1982. "Energy and Environment." *Annual Report on Environment in Israel,* no. 9: 205–13.

Feitelson, E. 1996. "A Model of the Evolvement of Environmental Conflicts in the Metropolitan Area and Its Planning Implications." Jerusalem: Jerusalem Institute for Israel Studies and Ministry of Environment. In Hebrew.

————. 1998. "Muddling towards Sustainability: The Transformation of Environmental Planning." *Israel Progress in Planning* 49: 1–53.

Forester, J., R. Fischler, and D. Shmueli. 2001. *Israeli Planners and Designers: Profiles of Community Builders.* Albany: State University of New York.

Golik, A., D. Rosen, M. Shoshany, D. DiCastro, and P. Harari. 1997. "Ashdod Port's Effect on the Shoreline, Seabed and Sediment." In *Proceedings of 25th ICCE* 4: 4376–89.

Hill, M., and R. Alterman. 1974. "Power Plant Site Evaluation: The Case of the Sharon Plant in Israel." *Journal of Environmental Management* 2: 179–96.

"Israel 2020: Master Plan for Israel in the 21st-Century." ftp://ftp.sni.technion.ac.il/Israel2020/Israel%202020_Taktzir.pdf.

Jerusalem Institute for Israel Studies. 2006. Policy Document on The Dead Sea Basin, Assessment of Current Situation and Prospects for the Future under Continued Dead Sea Water Level Decline Prepared for the Ministry of Environment and Ministry of National Infrastructure.

Kaplan and Zalutsky. n.d. "Methodology for Assessing Open Space Sensitivity and Value." Ministry of Environment website. In Hebrew.

Laster, R. 1973. "Reading D: Planning and Building or Building and Planning." *Israel Law Review* 8 (4): 481–505.

Marinov, U., and V. Brachya. 1979. "New Trends in Land Use Planning—The Environmental Input." In *New Trends in Urban Planning,* edited by D. Soen. New York: Pergamon Press.

Maizlish, M. 2005. *The Struggle against the Trans Israel Highway—Documenting an Environmental Struggle.* Jerusalem: Jerusalem Institute for Israel Studies. In Hebrew.

Mindali, O., A. Raveh, and I. Salomon. 2004. "Urban Density and Energy Consumption: A New Look at Old Statistics." *Transportation Research Part A* 38 (2): 143–62.

Ministry of Environment. 1989. *Annual Report on Environment in Israel* 15 [noise] 379–415, [environmental planning] 579–601. In Hebrew.

————. 1992. "The Environment in Israel" (National Report to the UN Conference on Environment and Development).

————. 1997. "Articles on Environmental Impact Statements. " In Hebrew.

————. 1999. *Towards Sustainable Development.*

————. 2002. *The Management of Conflicts in Planning, Development and Environmental Quality.* In English and Hebrew.

————. 2004. *A Look at Environment—The Environmental Situation in Israel 2003/4.* In Hebrew.

————. 2005. *The Path Towards Sustainable Development in Israel.*

————. 2006. *The Path Towards Sustainable Development in Israel.*

————. 2007. *The Path Towards Sustainable Development in Israel.*

————. 2008. *The Path Towards Sustainable Development in Israel.*

Pritej, R. M. 2009. "The Impact of Environmentalism on the British Land Use Planning System." Master's thesis, University of Toronto.

Pruginin, A., and J. Glass. 1992. *Environmental Quality in Israel 2000–2025*. Jerusalem: Jerusalem Institute of Israel Studies and Ministry of Environment.

Rotenberg, R. 1992. *A Decade's Experience in Implementing a Land Use Environmental Impact Assessment System in Israel in View of the American and European Experience*. Boulder: Natural Resources Law Center, University of Colorado School of Law.

Shmueli, D., and M. Ben-Gal. 2004. "The Potential of Framing in Managing and Resolving Environmental Conflict." In *Advancing Sustainability at the Sub-National Level: The Potential and Limitations of Planning*, edited by E. Feitelson, 197–216. Aldershot, Hants, England, and Burlington: Ashgate.

Society for the Protection of Nature in Israel (SPNI) and Ministry of Environment. 1997. "The Future of Environmental Impact Statements." In Hebrew.

Topol, N., and T. Keinan. 2009. *Green Commuting*. http://www.transportation.org.il/sites/default/files/pirsum/hamadrich_lamaasikim_0.pdf.

CHAPTER FIFTEEN

ANTHROPOGENIC CLIMATE CHANGE IN ISRAEL

Lucy Michaels and Pinhas Alpert

Do not damage or destroy my world; for if you do, there will be
no one to repair it after you.

—ECCLESIASTES RABBAH 7:13

CLIMATE AND ARCHAEOLOGICAL records from the last ten thousand years show that there has always been significant climate variability in the East Mediterranean (Issar and Zohar 2004). As we enter the twenty-first century, however, Israel's climate is entering a new period of uncertainty. Over the last forty years, the unexpected ways in which humans influence the climate have become increasingly evident. This chapter surveys how researchers have come to understand Israel's climate, with a focus on the significant science and policy challenge posed by global warming.

While we now have a fairly clear picture of the likely effects of global warming in Israel and the Middle East, successive Israeli governments have been slow to recognize the need to address it: slow to allocate research funding, slow to introduce policies to reduce greenhouse gas (GHG) emissions, and slow to introduce adaptation strategies to protect Israel against the changing climate. While the Ministry of Environmental Protection has been quietly working on this issue since 1989, only in the run-up to the 2009 UN climate conference in Copenhagen did Israel's leaders begin to recognize the need for action and the additional health, security, and economic benefits of doing so. Where the Israeli government has faced significant barriers to action, at the forefront of addressing climate change in Israel have been scientists, entrepreneurs, environmental NGOs, municipalities, and civil society.

CLIMATE CHANGE SCIENCE IN ISRAEL

Scientific debate about the changing climate in Israel began in the mid-1970s. The initial focus was on how direct human activity, namely irrigation, had changed weather patterns in central-southern Israel (Alpert and Mandel 1986; Otterman et al. 1990; Ben-Gai et al. 1993). From the early 1990s onward, Israeli researchers also began to explore the likely influence of global warming on the Eastern Mediterranean region, with particular concern for how it might affect the water balance. Since then, global climate models (GCMs) have become more sophisticated, observed data have been analyzed, and there is greater understanding of how the region's climate is influenced by other local and major climate systems. Israeli climate researchers have also carried out groundbreaking research on the effects of anthropogenic aerosols on urban pollution and rainfall patterns, as well as cloud seeding (e.g., Alpert, Halfon, Levin 2008; Givati and Rosenfeld 2004, 2005; Levin, Halfon, and Alpert 2010).

While the impact of carbon dioxide and other GHGs in the atmosphere has been the source of scientific debate since the mid-twentieth century, it was concern about an observed warming trend in the late 1970s that initially widened the scientific and public debate. By the summer heat waves of 1988 the issue was firmly on the public stage, with the UN Intergovernmental Panel on Climate Change (IPCC) founded that year.[1]

Against this background, in 1989 the newly founded Israeli Ministry of Environmental Quality nominated a National Committee for Research on Climate Change. The committee was mainly responsible for the organization of an international workshop on "The Regional Implications of Future Climate Change" at the Weizmann Institute of Science in Rehovot in May 1991. The workshop demonstrated Israel's particular concern about global warming, clearly summarized by Professor Joshua Jortner, president of the Israeli Academy of Sciences and Humanities in his opening address: "As Israel is a very small country on the edge of a desert, the consequences of global change may have much greater effects regionally than those observed globally . . . especially with respect to the future of water sources in the region" (Graber, Cohen, and Magaritz 1994).

While the climate models presented at the workshop diverged in their predictions as to the regional effects of climate change, all identified an impact on water availability (Druyan and Rind 1994; Kay 1994; Segal et al. 1994). Segal et al. (1994) performed the first runs of regional climate models in the East Mediterranean to study the potential impacts of doubling carbon dioxide (CO_2) on several rainfall-bearing cyclones. While the results suggested that a doubling of CO_2 in the atmosphere would result in only a small *average* change in the amount of winter rainfall, the major changes would come with the distribution of that rainfall (e.g., less rainfall in the south and more in the north). Other interesting findings were the large increase of surface evaporation that would influence significantly the water balance in the region and the disappearance of Jerusalem snow, with large snow reductions over the northern mountains of Israel. These very preliminary results essentially indicated the potential of the desert zone to advance northward.

The workshop highlighted the need to undertake the basic and comprehensive research necessary to build more effective regional climate models and to understand the local and regional water cycle. Yet despite the alarming predictions and the apparent concern of both government and scientists, the funding for a dedicated research program remained unavailable for nearly another decade.

In 2000, funding finally became available for extensive research on regional climate impacts through the German government–funded GLOWA-Jordan River project. This ongoing project brings together Israeli, Jordanian, Palestinian, and German researchers to "explore the future of the water scarce Jordan river basin under the impact of climate and global change" (GLOWA-Jordan 2009). Since 2005 the Ministry for Environmental Protection has also made research funds available. These funds have massively improved the state of the art in research in Israel, bringing it up somewhat closer to what has been done in the North America and Europe.[2]

According to Israel's Water Authority, the years 2005 to 2010 represent a severe period of drought, although there have been longer and more severe periods of drought in the last one hundred years (Rom et al. 2006).[3] The current dry years concur with global trends, showing that the decade ending in 2009 was the warmest on record (NASA 2010).

Data from meteorological stations around Israel demonstrate that the country has experienced a warming trend from the beginning of the 1970s, with some parts experiencing decreasing rainfall and rising aridity (Bruins and Kafle 2009). While the coastal plain has not been significantly affected, this trend has certainly been observed in the Arava desert. Although their research has not yet extended for a long enough period to show a long-term trend, Ginat and Shlomi (2008) demonstrate that annual rainfall in this hyperarid zone has decreased by 25 percent–50 percent in the fifteen years from 1994 to 2009 compared with the period 1960–1993. In addition, rainfall events have become less frequent, more localized, and of higher intensity, while average summer temperatures have risen.

Another area where the impact of climate change has been clearly observed is in northern Israel at Lake Kinneret, the country's major freshwater reservoir. Research shows that there has been a distinct decline in the average winter flow in the upper Jordan River (which flows into Lake Kinneret) since 1936 (Alpert and Ben-Zvi 2001; Givati et al. 2010).

The first study to analyze extensively surface temperature observations in forty Israeli weather stations (1964–1994) was conducted by Ben-Gai et al. (1999). This study shows a complex, changing pattern but essentially demonstrates that Israel's summers have become warmer (although the increase of the minimum summer temperature is more pronounced than the increase in maximum temperature) while the winters have become colder (with the decrease in the maximum temperature in winter greater than the decrease in the minimum). Ziv et al. (2005) demonstrate that the warming trend has expressed itself throughout the Mediterranean Basin through the increase in the number and duration of "hot days" between June and August (1976–2002) compared with the previous twenty-seven years. They ascribe this increase in summer temperature to global warming, arguing that it is consistent with global trends.

In contrast to predicted global trends, however, between 1964 and 1994, Israel also experienced somewhat colder winters (Ben-Gai et al. 1999; Alpert 2004). Further, despite an observed and predicted decrease in total rainfall over the whole Mediterranean and the rest of the Middle East, total rainfall has increased in central-southern Israel (Ben-Gai et al. 1993; Yosef et al. 2009), and the country is experiencing more extreme rainfall events (Alpert et al. 2002). Data from sixty rainfall stations across Israel from the 1930s onward reveal appreciable changes in temporal and spatial rainfall distribution patterns with the north of the country becoming drier, along with more frequent, heavier rainfall years (Ben-Gai et al. 1998). While heavy rainfall contributed approximately 23 percent of the annual rainfall in the 1950s, by the 2000s it was contributing 33 percent of annual rainfall (Yosef et al. 2009).[4]

Alpert (2004) argues that these seeming temperature and rainfall paradoxes can be explained by the fact that global warming is not only directly affecting Israel's climate, but also all the major and local circulation patterns that influence it. These patterns include localized phenomena such as Sahara dust, the Red Sea Trough, and the Persian Trough; major tropical systems such as the El-Niño Southern Oscillation (ENSO), the South Asian Monsoon and hurricanes; as well as the North Atlantic Oscillation and the East Atlantic/West Russia pattern (Alpert et al. 2006; Saaroni et al. 2010). As noted earlier, the increase in irrigation in the Negev desert (central-southern Israel) has also affected local rainfall patterns.

Israel's average temperatures are expected to rise by 1.5 degrees Celsius by 2020 and by up to 5 degrees Celsius by the end of the century compared with 1960–1990, based on moderate IPCC scenarios for global warming and regional climate modelling (Alpert et al. 2008).[5] Rainfall is also expected to decrease by 10 percent by 2020 and up to 35 percent by the end of the century, with extreme weather events becoming longer and more frequent, including drought years, floods, and heat waves. Since Israel depends on reliable seasonal rainfall, this clearly poses a threat to its already limited water resources (Jin, Kitoh, and Alpert 2010).

Israeli agriculture could suffer considerably from changes in rainfall and temperature. While a mild increase in climate could be beneficial in allowing farmers to supply early fresh produce to international markets, a drastic change would be disastrous, with crops threatened by a loss of soil moisture and new pests suited to the warmer climate (Fleischer, Lichtman, and Mendelsohn 2007).[6] An increase in heavy rainfall events could also increase topsoil erosion and soil salinity which damage plant health. Israel is already experiencing an increase in farm animal diseases, which originate from mosquitoes and pests. This increase could be caused by a number of factors, including global warming which may be making conditions more conducive to mosquito populations. Besides an increase in pest-borne diseases, heat stress and flood events related to global warming threaten public health. Paz has identified emergence of two pest-borne diseases in Israel, West Nile Virus and Vibrio Vulnificus disease, which she argues can be connected to global warming (Paz et al. 2007; Paz 2009).

As hinted at in initial studies, changes in temperature and rainfall regimes would also significantly affect the transition zone between the Mediterranean and Desert Belt ecosystems that cross Israel. Under global warming, the desert line is expected to move northward and Mediterranean flora and fauna, which are less resilient to dryness, are expected to rapidly migrate north increasing the risk of desertification and species loss (Safriel and Pe'er 2000).

Israel is also vulnerable to sea level rises. Klein, Lichter, and Tzviely (2004) present a scenario of a 50-centimeter rise in sea level by 2050, increasing to 1 meter by 2100. They claim that this could lead to coastline retreat of 2–10 meters and the loss of 0.4-2 square kilometers of coastal area every ten years. In addition to the damage to coastal ecology, archaeological sites, and tourism, this loss of coastal area would have a serious impact on Israel's narrow Mediterranean coastal strip, where 60 percent of Israel's population, vital infrastructure, and a recharge aquifer are concentrated.

Based on these findings, the Ministry of Environmental Protection estimates that inaction with regard to climate change would carry a high economic price. By 2020, inaction over water scarcity could cost the economy around 450 million NIS (shekel) a year, while flood damages could cost 340 million NIS a year (Bar-Or and Golan-Angelko 2008). The Israel Electric Corporation (IEC) is also now beginning to build climate scenarios into its long-term planning, expecting electricity demand for both heating and cooling appliances to grow due to global warming. Not only will this have cost implications but, considering Israel's reliance on fossil fuels, will only contribute to Israel's growing greenhouse gas emissions.

A super-high-resolution climate model of the whole Middle East region suggests that decreased rainfall and a severely reduced stream flow in the region's major rivers could contribute to the total disappearance of the area known as the Fertile Crescent by the end of the twenty-first century (Kitoh, Yatagai, and Alpert 2008). Rain-fed and flood-based agriculture led to the Fertile Crescent becoming the "Cradle of Civilization," and permits subsistence farming there today. Even a moderate rise in the average global temperature of 2.6 degrees Celsius, however, could threaten agriculture and livelihoods in the region. It is ironic that this region will be one of the first to be dried out by human activities in modern times. Jin et al. (2010) extended this study to six major rivers flowing into the Mediterranean, forecasting significant decreases in all, except the Nile.

Friends of the Earth Middle East (Freimuth et al. 2007) makes equally pessimistic predictions, referring to climate change as a "threat multiplier" that would exacerbate water scarcity and tensions over water both within and among nations linked by hydrological resources, geography, and shared political boundaries. Scenarios conducted by the United Nations Environment Program (UNEP) and other organizations indicate that a half-meter rise in sea level could displace nearly 2–4 million Egyptians by 2050. Rising sea levels would also further contaminate the only drinking water source of 1.5 million Palestinians in Gaza. Economic unrest across the region, due to a decline in agricultural production, could lead to greater political unrest, threatening current regimes and internal and cross-border relations (Freimuth et al. 2007).

Brown and Crawford (2009) also seem doubtful about the prospects for Middle East peace in a climate-constrained world. They claim that the history of conflict in the region could prevent the transboundary cooperation necessary for adapting to climate change. They also predict that countries might be less inclined to part with territory containing freshwater resources. Israeli-Syrian negotiations have broken down over access to Lake Kinneret and its sources in the Golan Heights, and the Sheba'a Farms area currently annexed by Israel contains one of the headwaters of the River Jordan. Water is also a final-status issue for Israeli-Palestinian peace. Regional scientific collaborations such as GLOWA–Jordan River are, however, making their best efforts to engage policy makers in thinking regionally in future resource use.

The scientific evidence that the global climate is warming is now "unequivocal," based on observations of global average air and ocean temperature increases, the widespread melting of snow and ice, and rising sea levels (IPCC

2007). It is also "very likely" that this warming has been caused by human activities, especially anthropogenic emissions of CO_2 (ibid.). There are still, however, some dissenting voices. Leading skeptics in Israel include Hebrew University atmospheric scientist Nathan Paldor and astrophysicist Nir Shaviv. Shaviv argues that CO_2 may only have a secondary role in driving climate over geologic timescales. Instead he claims that variations in galactic cosmic ray flux (energetic particles in space) interacting with solar activity have been the major driver of Earth's climate for the last 545 million years (Shaviv 2005).

This skepticism has created some controversy and, as a result, the Israeli media regularly presents the "other side" of the climate change story. This media exposure contributes to the public belief that the science is still unclear on the causes of global warming (see Boykoff and Boykoff 2004), and may be the reason why the 20 percent of the Israeli public who are aware of the issue believe that climate change primarily has natural rather than anthropogenic causes (Waldoks 2009b).

Kliot, Paz, and Kaidar (2008) interviewed over ninety Israeli scientists for their opinions about climate change, finding only a handful who disagreed with the IPCC consensus. Some argue that climate variability has always been a feature of the Middle East, taking the Genesis story of the seven years of plenty and seven years of drought as a case in point. They argue that observed recent anomalies should not be automatically ascribed to anthropogenic global warming, especially since interannual rainfall variability in Israel is considerable and land-use changes and complex climate phenomena like the Red Sea Trough can have unexpected influences. Such a view, however, reflects unawareness of the basic fact that recent increases in GHG concentrations in the atmosphere have reached levels unseen in Earth's history for the last several hundred thousand years.[7]

CLIMATE POLICY IN ISRAEL

Despite their professed concern, Israel's leading policy makers displayed an almost complete lack of interest in global warming until the early 2000s. This was underlined by the failure of Prime Minister Shamir to join 117 heads of state attending the 1992 United Nations Conference on Environment and Development (UNCED), known as the "Earth Summit" in Rio de Janeiro. Uri Marinov, the director general of the Environment Ministry was Israel's most senior delegate to the Earth Summit.

Partly as a result of its low profile at the summit and because of the rapid influx of nearly a million Russian immigrants to the country in the early 1900s, Israel was recognized as a non-Annex 1 or "developing" country to the United Nations Framework Convention on Climate Change (UNFCCC) initiated in Rio. This has meant that Israel's only obligations to the international community have been to keep a national inventory of GHG emissions and to formulate and implement a national mitigation program. It is thus not surprising that Israel was quick to ratify the UNFCCC in 1996 and to become a signatory to the Kyoto Protocol in December 1998, ratifying it in February 2004. Israel did establish an Inter-Ministerial Committee on Climate Change in 1996, but this did not report until 2000.

In November 2000, Israel submitted its First National Communication on Climate Change to the UNFCCC. In the ten years from 1990, Israel's population had grown 29.4 percent and it had achieved one of the highest GDP growth rates in the developed world (6 percent). As a result, Israel's GHG emissions skyrocketed in the early 1990s. The First National Communication demonstrates that Israel's CO_2 emissions, almost predominantly from fossil fuel combustion for vehicle and energy use, constituted by far the largest source of its GHGs. Methane and nitrous oxides, mostly from agriculture, waste production, and industrial processes were responsible for the rest, which accounted for 17 percent of Israel's total GHG emissions (measured in kilotons of CO_2 equivalent or CO_2eq).[8]

Based on 1998 research by the Samuel Neaman Institute, the document lists a number of policy recommendations by which Israel could reduce these emissions. These include switching from coal to natural gas;[9] improving energy efficiency; promoting renewable energy; reducing industrial emissions; promoting green building and appliance efficiency; improving vehicle efficiency and public transport; addressing private vehicle use through urban planning measures; and promoting composting and improving animal feed to reduce methane emissions. The report also highlights the urgency of addressing water scarcity through both conservation and generation of new sources and effective land management to prevent desertification.

The report is optimistic that significant measures can be taken without requiring major structural changes to the economy, while also delivering additional benefits such as reducing air pollution and traffic congestion. The report is also a rallying cry for the leading role that Israel could play in global adaptation efforts.

It would not be true to say that Israel has done nothing to fulfill this potential; the figures, however, speak for themselves. In 1996, Israel emitted 62.7 million tons of CO_2eq while by 2007 this had risen to 76.7 million tons (Israel Central Bureau of Statistics figures), with GHG emissions rising significantly in the energy, agricultural, and transportation sectors. The global management consultancy firm McKinsey and Company (2009) predicts that emissions will only increase; under its "business as usual" (BAU) scenario, Israel will double its carbon dioxide emissions by 2030. This is predominantly due to rising population and affluence and a range of existing policies described below. While emissions are actually falling in major developed countries, Israel's pattern of emissions growth closely resembles those patterns observed in "recently developed countries" such as Spain or Greece (Yanai, Koch, and Dayan 2008).

Since the First National Communication, Israeli academics, think tanks, and NGOs have proposed numerous policy options to reduce Israel's GHG emissions. Avnimelech (2002), the Israel Union for Environmental Defense (IUED) (2007), and the NGO coalition Life and Environment (Porat 2009) all come to similar conclusions that reinforce those highlighted in the First National Communication: that by implementing existing technologies across a wide range of sectors as part of a national strategy, Israel could reduce its emissions by as much as 43 percent (IUED 2007). Other researchers have explored how carbon taxation and emissions trading could be effective in Israel (Tiraspolsky, Schechter, and Palatnik 2008; Dagan 2008).

Despite over ten years of discussion, the first policy recommendations by the Environment Ministry to the Israeli Government came in January 2009, when it circulated an economic analysis of potential policy options (Axelrod 2010). This research identified that Israel could with relative ease reduce its emissions by 31.7 million metric tons of carbon dioxide equivalent (MtCO2eq) a year. With a new environment minister, Gilad Erdan, taking the office in March 2009, a further cost-benefit analysis was commissioned, this time from the global management consultancy firm McKinsey and Company. In their report, published in November 2009, McKinsey employs its widely used greenhouse gas abatement cost curve to model for Israel the abatement potential of various different measures or levers to reduce greenhouse gas emissions, and the relative cost or benefit to the economy.

McKinsey suggests an abatement potential of 45 $MtCO_2eq$ a year after having switched to low-carbon energy sources and improving energy efficiency (sound familiar?). Behavioral changes such as reducing use of lighting, increasing public transport and bicycle use, increasing average building temperatures, and reducing meat consumption could achieve a further reduction of 7 $MtCO_2eq$. McKinsey argues that the total net cost to the economy of implementing these measures would be approximately zero by 2030. Although some measures would require significant up-front investment, almost all the measures would save money in the long term. McKinsey notes that Israel has less emissions reduction potential than some countries because it lacks a heavy industry and has little possibility for hydroelectric power or carbon capture and storage.

McKinsey's emissions reduction target for Israel is based on a formula dif-

ferent from those proposed by most countries where targets either aim to reduce emissions below a given baseline year (EU and U.S. approach) or to reduce the carbon intensity per unit of GDP (Indian and Chinese approach).
Israel's target is based on the prediction that under its "BAU" scenario, its
emissions would double by 2030. By taking the measures proposed, McKinsey
argues that instead of doubling its emissions, Israel will only increase them by
one-third by 2030, that is, the target is to reduce emissions by 64 percent below
its BAU levels by 2030.

While characterizing it as a step in the right direction, environmental
NGOs have criticized the McKinsey process as being too rushed. They are
critical of the unambitious targets, which essentially permit an increase in
GHG emissions and the lack of attention to additional behavioral changes,
which could yield far greater reductions.[10]

The Israeli government has made a number of important decisions regarding climate change. These include a 2001 commitment to voluntarily reduce
emissions of GHGs (Government Decision 2913); a 2002 commitment to significantly expand renewable energy to 2 percent of total electricity production
by 2007 (Government Decision 2664); a 2003 commitment to a national strategy for sustainable development (Government Decision 246); and ratification
of the Kyoto Protocol by government resolution in 2004. (For a detailed list
of relevant government decisions see Porat 2008 and Axelrod 2010.) In December 2009, a climate bill was also proposed to introduce ambitious GHG
emissions reduction targets, although it failed to reach a preliminary reading
in the Knesset.

The 2001 commitment to voluntarily reduce GHG emissions also established Israel as a participant in the Clean Development Mechanism (CDM).
The CDM is an arrangement under the Kyoto Protocol by which developed
countries with emissions reduction targets can invest in projects that reduce
emissions in developing countries instead of having to undertake more expensive reductions in their own countries.[11]

As a de facto "developing" country under the Kyoto Protocol, Israel can
receive CDM financing for its emissions reductions, and it plays this paradox
to its advantage. The Ministry of Environmental Protection advertises Israel
as "an excellent venue in which to develop CDM projects because although
categorized as a developing country under the Kyoto Protocol, it has all the
characteristics of a developed country" (Ministry for Environmental Protection 2006, 17).

Israel CDM projects, financed by the UK and Germany, include collecting
methane from landfills and agriculture; introducing technology to reduce industrial emissions; and promoting efficiency and fuel switching in industrial

sectors. Israel claims that its sixteen UN-registered CDM projects have re-duced national emissions by an estimated 1.8 $MtCO_2eq$ a year, while the forty-six additional projects submitted for approval would reduce over 6 $MtCO_2eq$ (Inbar 2008).

While the CDM may have materially reduced Israel's GHGs by 1.2 percent a year, it is still a highly problematic framework, widely criticized by environmental and climate justice groups for failing to deliver promised reductions globally, delaying necessary structural changes in developed countries, and being open to corruption (Bachram 2004).

Israel's 2003 decision to pursue a national strategy based on sustainable development was the result of a commitment made at the 2002 World Summit on Sustainable Development in Johannesburg. In order to monitor whether Israel could live up to this commitment, especially on climate change, the "Paths to Sustainability" coalition was established by the Israeli environmental NGO community. The coalition now has over forty member organizations; it coordinates NGO lobbying efforts as well as producing yearly reports on Israel's progress to sustainable development.

In its 2008 report, the Paths to Sustainability coalition criticized the government's failure to implement a strategic master plan for sustainable development across ministries or to give adequate budgetary expression to relevant decisions. Even modest objectives, such as a 2 percent target for renewable energy, were not met. The report argued that the government was also making contradictory decisions such as investing both in public transport and road construction.

Yet the policy decision that has been identified as a "litmus test" indicating whether Israel is truly committed to sustainable development has been whether the government would give the go-ahead for two additional coal-fired units at the Rotenberg D power plant in Ashkelon.

In August 2001, plans were announced for the construction of a $1.3 billion additional coal-fired power station in Ashkelon, to be completed by 2007–2008.[12] The plans met with immediate opposition from local residents and environmental groups with the IUED obtaining an interim injunction from Israel's Supreme Court blocking construction of the plant until the government justified its position.

A revised plan for the power plant was sent for review to the National Infrastructures Committee (NIC)—a controversial fast-track procedure for major infrastructure projects that bypasses established environmental and public overview safeguards. In November 2004, the Infrastructure Ministry blamed "interventions by environmental organizations" for delaying the plan.

In 2008, after a one-day public hearing and a heavily criticized Environmental Impact Assessment, the NIC approved the plan. Again environmental groups petitioned the High Court of Justice for a full review of the environmental and health risks, as well as requesting full transparency as to why the NIC had given the go-ahead despite concerted opposition. By August 2009, the NIC received over twenty thousand planning objections in response to a deposition of detailed construction plans. Environment Minister and Ashkelon native, Gilad Erdan, and President Shimon Peres, also actively opposed the plant.

The Israel Electric Corporation (IEC) has argued that the additional power plant is necessary to address the national rise in electricity consumption—the company is operating at maximum capacity and facing a constant rise in demand, with a very narrow reserve and a high risk of blackouts. IEC also argues that relying on coal is vital for energy security—there are many more potential coal suppliers than gas suppliers from countries that are friendly to Israel, and suppliers can be easily switched. In addition, the IEC argues that it can reduce air pollution from its existing coal-fired plants; but to install the new equipment will require that each plant is shut down for six months, making the extra capacity from the new Ashkelon plant essential.[13]

Underlying this debate is the ongoing tension between the IEC, Israel's sole public electric utility, and Prime Minister Netanyahu who has signalled that he would like to see the IEC privatized and the whole sector liberalized. The IEC currently faces serious financial difficulties partially due to artificially low electricity prices set by the Public Utilities Authority, the supervising government body. However, the IEC is actively resisting privatization, partly to maintain its monopoly over energy production. It is Israel's largest single employer with over twelve thousand employees, a powerful union, and wages 2.2 times that of Israel's average (Tishler et al. 2008). Detailed economic analysis also suggests that Israel's privatization plan could be disastrous, resulting in higher prices for consumers and making the production of electricity from gas economically unviable (Tishler et al. 2008).

At the beginning of 2011, the Environment Ministry and Infrastructures Ministry finally reached a compromise deal that the new Ashkelon power plant would run primarily on natural gas, but switch to coal in case of emergencies. However, in July 2011, the Finance Ministry gave permission for a dual fuel plant, stipulating instead that the choice of fuel (gas or coal) should be based on economic and strategic needs. The matter is by no means resolved.

Despite setbacks and controversies, improved solid-waste disposal and CDM projects have modestly slowed the increase in Israel's GHG emissions during the 2000s. Israel has also begun to switch its generating capacity to natural gas through a 2004 agreement to buy Egyptian gas. The gas agreement with Egypt has faced considerable political, security, engineering, and supply-side challenges. In 2011 following the fall of the Mubarak regime, the gas pipeline was sabotaged twelve times. In 2009, however, substantial natural gas reserves were discovered in Israeli territorial waters, and it is now anticipated that by 2014, this locally sourced gas will be Israel's primary fuel for electricity generation (Ministry of Energy and Water Resources 2011). After years of parliamentary debate, in 2008 Israel's Knesset passed a Clean Air Law that could also be used as a tool for regulating GHG emissions when it comes into force in 2011.

Late 2008 saw a flurry of potentially ambitious policies relating to energy use, including a commitment to reduce electricity consumption by 20 percent by 2020 (Government Decision 4095) and for 10 percent of energy to come from renewable sources by 2020 (Government Decision 4450. (For a full list of government decisions see Porat 2008 and Axelrod 2010.) Expansion in the solar energy sector will be facilitated by government approval for the promotion of renewable energy in the Negev and Arava regions, reasonable feed-in tariffs for producers, and a special interministerial committee focused on the development of solar energy in Israel, established in December 2009 and headed by the prime minister.[14]

The Environment Ministry has also supported research into the impacts of climate change and adaptation strategies. Research was commissioned in 2005 and 2008, which included investigation into likely climate scenarios for 2030 (see also Axelrod 2010). In 2011, the Ministry established an Israel Climate Change Knowledge Center on adaptation to climate change to gather and coordinate scientific knowledge about the likely impacts of climate change in Israel and the region. The center presented concrete recommendations on climate change adaptation policy in March 2012.

Over the years, Israel has invested significantly in research and development to overcome the country's lack of natural resources and its arid climate. Israeli scientists have developed cutting-edge technologies in fields such as drip irrigation and wastewater reuse, desert agriculture and afforestation, and desalination and solar energy as well as innovative strategies to address desertification. There is growing recognition that these technologies could be useful both for "technology transfer" to developing countries and for export to European countries projected to suffer from increased aridity.

Although the 2009 Copenhagen Climate Summit itself failed to establish a new binding global agreement on GHG reduction targets, it nevertheless put the issue on the Israeli national agenda. The appointment of Gilad Erdan, an enthusiastic advocate for climate change mitigation policy, as Environment minister, has focused attention on the issue, as has Israel's recent membership in the Organization for Economic Cooperation and Development (OECD), which will commit Israel to reduce GHG emissions in line with other developed countries.

While Environment Ministry Director General Yossi Inbar claimed that setting ambitious reductions targets was "effectively saying we must close the country down," efforts were made to prepare the country for Copenhagen (Rinat 2008). In May 2009, a government committee was established to formulate a national climate change policy, headed by the Finance Ministry which inspired hope that climate change would be addressed more seriously than in the past, since the Ministry for Environmental Protection is one of the weakest and least funded of all government ministries. This was followed by the commissioning of the McKinsey report (see above) and the Samuel Neaman Institute to assist with policy analysis. In December 2009, a "Green Regulation Package" was introduced to the Knesset, and the summit may well have also tipped the scales against the new Ashkelon plant.

In the run-up to Copenhagen, Israel's leaders finally began to acknowledge the need to address climate change, also recognizing the potential trade and PR opportunities in promoting Israel's adaptation and mitigation technologies. At a UN climate meeting in September 2009, Erdan argued that Israel should be recognized as a developed country and take responsibility for its emissions. He also said that Israel was prepared to serve as a regional laboratory and center of excellence for climate change adaptation and renewable energy (Erdan 2009). A month later, Prime Minister Netanyahu stated that in ten years Israel aimed to develop "a practical, clean, efficient substitute for oil" (Netanyahu 2009). At the summit itself, President Shimon Peres announced that by 2020, Israel would make its "best efforts" to reduce its CO_2 emissions by 20 percent compared with its "business as usual" scenario, and openly voiced his opposition to the Ashkelon plant (Ministry of Environmental Protection 2009).

Despite these positive developments, just before the 2009 summit, the State Comptroller criticized the government for not having implemented even the basic actions necessary for dealing with climate change: Israel had not formulated a national mitigation plan or collected sufficient data to inspect and supervise its emissions. The country was also ill-equipped to monitor long-term changes (Rinat 2009a).

In November 2010, the Israeli government finally approved a national greenhouse gas emissions reduction plan. It committed NIS 2.2 billion over the following decade to replacing inefficient appliances; improving vehicle efficiency; some limited green building measures; and issuing tenders for emissions reductions in the industrial, commercial, and public sectors.

While these measures can be welcomed in and of themselves, they were primarily based on win-win measures that would have a direct, quantifiable, and immediate benefit to the economy. They therefore did not include more structural measures related to green building and transportation. In addition, most critics agree that they are unlikely to meet Israel's modest 2020 targets, which in any case represent a net growth in emissions.

While the Israeli government is only just waking up to the economic opportunities offered by climate change, Israeli businesses, especially those operating in Europe where they are already subject to climate legislation, have already begun to take advantage of them. Israel is home to world-class renewable energy innovators such as Ormat Technologies, Inc., Solel, Zenith Energies, and BrightSource, Inc. In recent years, Israel has also started to showcase cutting-edge renewable technologies ranging from the electric car to concentrated photovoltaic (CPV) technology. Israel was been ranked in the top five of Cleantech countries, behind Denmark, Germany, Sweden, and the UK in 2009 by a leading analyst (Lesser 2009), with five Israeli companies listed in the top one hundred Cleantech companies, based on a poll of corporate leaders (*Guardian* 2010).

Major corporations have taken note. In late 2009, German engineering conglomerate Siemens bought Solel and a 40 percent share in the Arava Power Company. Meanwhile, the Israel Corporation, the country's largest multinational company, has established its own renewable energy subsidiary with former chairman Idan Ofer becoming chairman of international electric car infrastructure company, Project Better Place. Oil company Paz established Paz Solar to market and install photovoltaic technology. Attractive feed-in tariffs have also attracted multinationals such as SunEdison.

A 2009 Israel-U.S. agreement to promote cooperation on renewable energy has generated international hype around Israel as a unique innovation hub for cleantech, with conferences taking place in Israel, Texas, and California and leading U.S. venture capitalists visiting Israel (Israel Ministry of Foreign Affairs 2009). Israeli venture capital firms, green consultancies, and carbon-trading firms now support the burgeoning industry.

While Israeli renewable energy companies run commercial projects worldwide this is not yet the case in Israel. In December 2009, the UNEP criticized Israel for sitting at the bottom of the list of countries producing solar electricity for national consumption, with only 0.1 percent coming from renewable sources (Rinat 2009b). The CEO of Solel, Avi Brenmiller, recently argued that Israel was a decade behind Germany and Spain in instituting public policy to support renewable energy (Kordova 2008). While four sites in Israel have been designated for solar energy plants, by mid-2010 construction had yet to begin, draft policy had only been recently completed, and already the new plants faced administrative difficulties. Business leaders are also concerned that the government "cap" on the total amount of megawatts that can be produced by solar energy production, currently set at a total of 300 megawatts for medium-sized fields, will seriously limit market growth (Waldoks 2010).

Some commentators have identified a lack of available land as the primary reason for Israel not developing solar energy fields, as most suitable sites are under military control. Others argue that land owned by kibbutzim, moshavim, and even by Bedouin families would permit Israel to produce more than enough solar energy.[15] Furthermore, some more visionary commentators have heralded the potential for regional solar energy production, which could also contribute to Israel's energy security through interdependence rather than dependence on Arab neighbours. Such collaboration could provide the basis for improved political relations and be facilitated through the Desertec supergrid, which plans to supply solar and wind energy from North Africa and the Middle East to Europe (Levy 2010).

Israel's Water Authority has dramatically changed its perception of climate change since the mid-1990s. Global warming is considered to be a major factor in the reduction of water in the Kinneret drainage basin and is now taken into account in strategic water planning (Bar-Or and Golan-Angelko 2008). Israel's response to the current drought has been to massively scale up its water desalination efforts; by 2012 desalination will constitute a serious climate adaptation strategy for Israel, providing for nearly half of all household water consumption.

The irony of Israel's considerable breakthrough in desalination technology is that this "adaptation" method employed to address water shortages caused by climate change is actually contributing to the problem. Despite using cutting-edge energy-recovery systems for reverse osmosis, desalination is extremely energy intensive. The Ashkelon Desalination Plant consumes around 55 megawatts of energy a year, which is equivalent to the energy needs of a city of 45,000 residents (Tal 2009).

CIVIL SOCIETY: NGOS, SUBNATIONAL EFFORTS, AND THE GENERAL PUBLIC

As a relatively young movement, Israeli environmental NGOs have generally focused more on local issues, such as air and water pollution, than on global issues, such as climate change. As a result, until recently climate change has not emerged as a priority campaign for green organizations, other than as an additional concern raised, for instance, in the controversy around the Ashkelon power station.

Israel has participated in global climate change awareness-raising events such as the global Live Earth concert in 2007 and the yearly Earth Hour event, a one-hour voluntary lighting "blackout" by residents of major cities. In the run-up to Copenhagen, the 350.org day of coordinated global action saw wide Israeli participation with nine events listed including a rollerblade tour and a joint demonstration on the Israeli, Palestinian, and Jordanian shores of the Dead Sea.[16] The Jewish National Fund (JNF) now also promotes its long-term afforestation efforts as carbon offsetting, although primarily to a Diaspora audience. The lack of concerted public campaigning and media coverage of the issue until the Copenhagen conference, however, is reflected in the fact that around 28 percent of Israelis are either unaware of climate change or have only heard the expression (Waldoks 2009b). According to the Gallup World Poll, this places Israel alongside Eastern and Southern European countries, rather than the United States and Western Europe in terms of climate change awareness (Pugliese and Ray 2009).

Campaigning on climate issues in Israel is marked primarily by good collaboration among NGOs and a focus on influencing government policy. The Paths to Sustainability coalition has written a number of in-depth critical reports and coordinates lobbying efforts at the Knesset.[17] The IUED drafted the climate bill (see earlier), and representatives of both the Heschel Center and IUED sit on the Inter-Ministerial Committee on Sustainable Development. Friends of the Earth Middle East has written a handbook on climate change for policy makers and organized workshops for government and the media.

A delegation of over thirty Israeli NGO representatives attended the Copenhagen Summit, including individuals from Israel's Arab community. The delegation actively participated in events, including organizing two well-received workshops on sustainable cities and the Ashkelon campaign. This participation provided a big boost in confidence for the Israeli environmental movement, connecting what had until then been local struggles to the wider global movement. An additional boost came at the end of 2009, with public funds made available for the first awareness-raising campaign on climate change in Israel.

As has been observed worldwide, where national governments have failed to implement effective climate legislation, subnational groups, such as municipalities, have led the way (Betsill and Bulkeley 2007). Israel's Forum 15 network of fifteen financially independent municipalities plus Jerusalem, Ashkelon, and Bat Yam are members of the International Council for Local Environmental Initiatives (ICLEI) and in February 2008 they signed on to a Convention on Climate Protection. This requires local municipalities to identify the major GHG sources in their cities and to develop local action plans to reduce emissions by at least 20 percent by 2020 from 2000 levels, with the support of environmental organizations and universities. While some municipalities, especially Ra'anana, have begun to implement measures to reduce emissions, what measures these municipalities can ultimately take are limited by both budget and the centralized nature of energy and transport planning in Israel (Bass Specktor, Rofe, and Tal 2009).

A significant portion of Israel's GHG emissions derives from everyday behaviors and lifestyle choices. For example, energy use in commercial, residential, and public buildings accounts for 61 percent of Israel's total electric power demand. Of this, lighting, heating, electrical appliances, and air-conditioner use account for at least 75 percent of energy consumption (2005 figures cited by McKinsey and Company 2009). Due to Israel's reliance on fossil fuels, this translates directly into carbon dioxide emissions. In addition, transportation accounts for 18 percent of all greenhouse gas emissions (2005 figures cited by McKinsey 2009). Methane from landfills and nitrous oxide from industry and agriculture also contribute significant amounts of GHGs. Despite its comparatively tiny (0.3 percent) contribution to global GHG emissions, Israel's per capita emissions are relatively high. In 2006 Israel's per capita emissions were 9.15 tons of CO_2—higher than the per capita emissions of many European countries such as the UK, Italy, and France. This indicates that addressing industrial emissions and improving technology will not be sufficient to reduce Israel's carbon footprint. Israeli lifestyles and behaviors, from transport patterns to waste disposal and energy usage at home, must also be tackled. Therefore, future work on climate change must engage the Israeli public.

A public opinion survey conducted by Ben-Gurion University in November 2009 revealed some perhaps surprising results concerning Israelis, priorities and concerns around global warming. Of the Israelis who are aware of climate change, almost all (96 percent) want to see the international community taking action on climate change, with 73 percent wanting to see substantial action soon; 74 percent also want Israel to sign up to serious long-term emissions reduction targets, with 54 percent endorsing this position very strongly (Waldoks 2009). One could hardly imagine a more encouraging environment in which to introduce ambitious climate policy.

The survey results suggest that concern about climate change is connected to a wider concern about the drought and water shortages that Israel is currently facing. Climate change is thus perceived as something real, immediate, and threatening. Translating this concern into action, however, is the challenge now facing policy makers and environmentalists.

Climatologists are in no doubt that global warming is already altering Israel's climate and that in the coming years the changing climate could bring with it potentially devastating impacts. Yet a powerful combination of circumstances and institutional culture has kept global warming off the public and policy agenda in Israel for the past twenty years. It is perhaps understandable that Israel's leaders have chosen to focus on security issues that appear more immediate and pressing, yet it is also clear that global warming has been deprioritized as an "environmental issue" rather than one pertaining to the long-term future of the country.

As a result Israel is poorly equipped to confront climate change. In terms of mitigation, Israel's ever-growing carbon footprint results from a fossil fuel–based economy, inadequate investment in public transportation, escalating traffic congestion, weak or nonexistent building standards (especially concerning energy conservation), increasing reliance on high-energy-consuming desalination projects, and high rates of economic and population growth. Israel's leaders have also failed to recognize the additional economic, public health, and energy security benefits of addressing climate change. In terms of adaptation, while the Environment Ministry is pushing forward with research and a national plan there has been little preparation on the ground.

Reviewing the history of anthropogenic climate change in Israel should be a call to action to all those who care about this land and its long-term future. The social and economic transformations required to address climate change may seem overwhelming, but in the end, they are the only means to secure Israel's future. The sooner the country embarks on a sustainable path, the easier that transition will be.

NOTES

This chapter uses the following terms in its scientific definitions: "global warming," the increase in the Earth's average surface temperature due to an increase in anthropogenic greenhouse gases in the atmosphere and its consequences; "climate change," a long-term change in the Earth's climate, or of a region on Earth, including very localized changes. In the policy discussion, climate change and global warming are used interchangeably. The authors ask readers to bear in mind that while the science section is primarily based on peer-reviewed journal articles, the policy section relies on a range of sources, including statements by politicians that should be handled with more caution than data presented from a peer-reviewed journal article.

1. The IPCC was founded to synthesize the state of the art of climate research on "a comprehensive, objective, open and transparent basis" for policy makers; see the IPCC Fourth Assessment Report (4AR) (IPCC 2007).

2. This funding includes some of the work of Pinhas Alpert, one of the authors of this article. He founded GLOWA-JR in Israel along with M. Shechter, Haifa University, and J. Ben-Asher, Ben-Gurion University.

3. Dr. Amir Givati, Israel Water Authority, pers. comm., August 2, 2010.

4. Such tendencies are even stronger over other Mediterranean regions (Italy, Spain). See Alpert et al. 2002.

5. The IPCC (4AR) identifies four scenarios (based on different approaches to climate regulation and economic growth) for projected global warming until 2100. These would result in moderate to extreme temperature rises.

6. See GLOWA-JR 2010.

7. This period is probably the first in the history of Earth's climate in which the air concentrations of GHGs and consequent global warming caused by anthropogenic activities have yielded the term "anthropocene." This term was proposed by the Nobel Prize Laureate Paul Crutzen (Crutzen and Stoermer 2000; Zalasiewicz et al. 2008).

8. Carbon dioxide equivalents (CO_2eq) is a quantity that describes, for a given mixture and amount of greenhouse gas, the amount of carbon dioxide that would have the same global warming potential (GWP), when measured over a specific timescale (generally one hundred years). It allows comparison of the relative contribution of different greenhouse gases.

9. Natural gas, while still a fossil fuel, produces considerably less carbon dioxide on combustion than do coal or oil.

10. These were some of the conclusions of wide-ranging discussions at the Climate Change Mitigation Policy Workshop held at Ben-Gurion University, May 25, 2010, in response to the McKinsey report. Contributors included NGO participants, academics, business representatives, and ministry officials.

11. See Clean Development Mechanism, http://cdm.unfccc.int/about/index.html.

12. See IUED website for a detailed overview and timeline of the Ashkelon power plant, http://www.adamteva.org.il/?CategoryID=392&ArticleID=473.

13. For detailed overview of IEC position regarding Ashkelon power plant, see Knesset Internal Affairs and Environment Committee Meeting Protocol 391, June 29, 2008.

14. The Inter-Ministerial Committee had, however, still not met by the end of July 2010. Yosef Abramovitz, president, Arava Power Company, pers. comm., July 25, 2010.

15. Yosef Abramovitz, pers. comm. July 25, 2010.

16. For more information, see http://www.350.org.

17. Paths to Sustainability Coalition Activities, http://www.sviva.net/develop/eng/Info.php?docId=new_activities_sustainable; IUED Activities on Climate Change http://www.adamteva.org.il/?CategoryID=436.

REFERENCES

Alpert, P. 2004. "The Water Crisis in the E. Mediterranean and Relation to Global Warming?" In *Water in the Middle-East and N. Africa*, edited by F. Zereini and W. Jaeschke, 55–61. Berlin: Springer.

Alpert, P., T. Ben-Gai, A. Baharad, Y. Benjamini, D. Yekutieli, M. Colacino, L. Diodato, C. Ramis, V. Homar, R. Romero, S. Michaelides, and A. Manes. 2002. "The Paradoxical Increase of Mediterranean Extreme Daily Rainfall in Spite of Decrease in Total Values." *Geophysical Research Letters* 29 (11): 311–14.

Alpert, P., and A. Ben-Zvi. 2001. "Climate Change Impact on the Availability of Water Resources in Israel." *Water–Water Engineering* [*Mayim–Handasat Mayim*] 51 (October): 10–15.

Alpert, P., N. Halfon, and Z. Levin. 2008. "Does Air Pollution Really Suppress Precipitation in Israel?" *Journal of Applied Meteorology and Climatology* 47 (4): 933–94.

Alpert, P., S. O. Krichak, H. Shafir, D. Haim, and I. Osetinsky. 2008. "Climatic Trends to Extremes Employing Regional Modeling and Statistical Interpretation over the E. Mediterranean." *Global Planetary Change* 63: 163–70.

Alpert, P., and M. Mandel. 1986. "Wind Variability—An Indicator for a Mesoclimatic Change in Israel." *Journal of Climate and Applied Meteorology* 24: 472–80.

Alpert, P., C. Price, S. O. Krichak, B. Ziv, H. Saaroni, and I. Osetinsky. 2006. "Mediterranean Climate and Some Tropical Teleconnections." *Nuovo Cimento Della Societa Italiana Di Fisica C-Geophysics and Space Physics* 29 (1): 89–97.

Avnimelech, Y. 2002. *Alternatives for Reducing Greenhouse Gas Emissions in Israel.* Jerusalem: Samuel Neaman Institute for Advanced Studies in Science and Technology. In Hebrew.

Axelrod, M. Y., ed. 2010. *Israel's Second National Communication on Climate Change: Submitted under the United Nations Framework Convention on Climate Change.* Jerusalem: Ministry of Environmental Protection.

Bachram, Heidi. 2004. "Climate Fraud and Carbon Colonialism: The New Trade in Greenhouse Gases." *Capitalism Nature Socialism* 15 (4): 5–21.

Bar-Or, Y., and I. Golan-Angelko. (2008) 2009. *Israel's Adaptation to Climate Change, Chapter A: Impact of Climate Change in Israel and Interim Recommendations.* Translation edited, condensed, and updated by M. Yanai and S. Gabbay. Jerusalem: Ministry of Environmental Protection. In Hebrew.

Bass Specktor, S., Y. Rofe, and A. Tal. 2009. "Cities for Climate Protection Initiative in Israel: Assessing the Impact of Urban, Economic, and Socio-Political Factors on Program Implementation." Paper presented at Low Carbon Cities: 45th ISOCARP Congress, Porto, Portugal, October 18–22.

Ben-Gai, T., A. Bitan, A. Manes, and P. Alpert. 1993. "Long-Term Change in October Rainfall Patterns in Southern Israel." *Theoretical and Applied Climatology* 46: 209–17.

Ben-Gai, T., A. Bitan, A. Manes, P. Alpert, and S. Rubin. 1998. "Spatial and Temporal Changes in Annual Rainfall Frequency Distribution Patterns in Israel." *Theoretical and Applied Climatology* 61: 177–90.

———. 1999. "Temporal and Spatial Trends of Temperature Patterns in Israel." *Theoretical and Applied Climatology* 64: 163–77.

Betsill M., and H. Bulkeley. 2007. "Looking Back and Thinking Ahead: A Decade of Cities and Climate Change Research." *Local Environment* 12: 447–56.

Boykoff, M. T., and J. M. Boykoff. 2004. "Balance as Bias: Global Warming and the U.S. Prestige Press." *Global Environmental Change* 14: 125–36.

Brown, O., and A. Crawford. 2009. *Rising Temperatures, Rising Tensions: Climate Change and the Risk of Violent Conflict in the Middle East.* Winnipeg: International Institute for Sustainable Development.

Crutzen, P. J., and E. F. Stoermer. 2000. "The 'Anthropocene.'" *Global Change Newsletter* 41: 17–18.

Dagan, R. 2008. "Emissions Trading as a Tool for Air Quality Control in Israel." Paper presented at the workshop on Voluntary GHG Emissions Reporting, Jerusalem, February 13–14.

Druyan, L. M., and D. Rind. 1994. "Implications of Climate Change on a Regional Scale." In *Regional Implications of Future Climate Change. Proceedings of an International Workshop, Weizmann Institute of Science,* edited by M. Graber, A. Cohen, and M. Magaritz, 75–78. Jerusalem: Israeli Academy of Sciences and Humanities and State of Israel, Ministry of Environment.

Erdan, G. 2009. Statement at the UN Special Summit on Climate Change, New York, September 24. "Israel Prepared to Serve as Regional Laboratory and Cen-

ter of Excellence for Climate Change Adaptation." http://www.sviva.gov.il/bin/
en.jsp?enPage=e_BlankPage&enDisplay=view&enDispWhat=Object&enDispWho
=News%5E14834&enZone=e_news.

Fleischer, A., I. Lichtman, and R. Mendelsohn. 2007. "Climate Change, Irrigation,
and Israeli Agriculture: Will Warming Be Harmful?" World Bank Policy Research
Working Paper 4135. Washington, DC: World Bank.

Freimuth, L., G. Bromberg, M. Mehyar, and N. Al. Khateeb. 2007. *Climate Change: A
New Threat to Middle East Security*. Amman: Friends of the Earth Middle East.

Ginat, H., and Y. Shlomi. 2008. "Climate Change Trends in an Extreme Arid Zone
Southern Arava (Israel and Jordan)—Initial Results." Paper presented at Desertification Conference, Jerusalem, Ben-Gurion University of the Negev, December.

Givati, A., and D. Rosenfeld. 2004. "Quantifying Precipitation Suppression Due to Air
Pollution." *Journal of Applied Meteorology* 43: 1038–56.

———. 2005. "Separation between Cloud-Seeding and Air-Pollution Effects." *Journal
of Applied Meteorology* 44: 1298–315.

Givati, A., R. Samuels, A. Rimmer, and P. Alpert. 2010. "Using High Resolution Climate Model to Evaluate Future Water and Solutes Budgets in the Sea of Galilee."
Journal of Hydrology.

GLOWA-JR. 2010. "Economic Analysis of Global and Climate Change Impacts on Agriculture in Israel." http://www.glowa-jordan-river.de/uploads/OurProducts/Brief-
ing_10.pdf.

Graber, M., A. Cohen, and M. Magaritz, eds. 1994. *Regional Implications of Future Climate Change: Proceedings of an International Workshop, Weizmann Institute of Science, Rehovot, Israel, April 28–May 2, 1991*. Jerusalem: Israeli Academy of Sciences
and Humanities and State of Israel, Ministry of the Environment.

Guardian. 2010. "Global Cleantech 100." Environment section. http://www.guardian.
co.uk/globalcleantech100/list and http://www.guardian.co.uk/globalcleantech100/
by-country.

Inbar, Y. 2008. "Climate Change in Israel: Programs of Activities under the CDM."
Presentation to German Environment Ministry. www.sviva.gov.il/Enviroment/
Static/.../climatechange-yossi_2.ppt.

IPCC. 2007. "Summary for Policymakers." In *Climate Change 2007: The Physical Science Basis. Contribution of Working Group I to the Fourth Assessment Report of the
Intergovernmental Panel on Climate Change* ("4AR"), edited by S. Solomon, D. Qin,
M. Manning, Z. Chen, M. Marquis, K. B. Avery, M. Tignor, and H. L. Miller. Cambridge: Cambridge University Press.

Israel Ministry of Foreign Affairs. 2009. "US-Israel Sign Agreement of Cooperation
in Renewable Energy." http://www.mfa.gov.il/MFA/Israel+beyond+politics/US-Is-
rael%20sign%20agreement%20of%20cooperation%2026-Feb-2009, February 26.

Israeli Union for Environmental Defense (IUED). 2007. *The Forecast Is in Our Hands.
Climate Change in Israel: Possibilities, Influences and Policy Directions*. In Hebrew.

Issar, A., and M. Zohar. 2004. *Climate Change: Environment and Civilization in the
Middle East*. Berlin: Springer-Verlag.

Jin, F. J., A. Kitoh, and P. Alpert. 2010. "Global Warming Projected Water Cycle
Changes over the Mediterranean, East and West: A Comparison Study of a Super-
High Resolution Global Model with CMIP3." *Philosophical Transactions Royal So-
ciety A* 368: 1–13.

Kay, P. A. 1994. "Scale and Precipitation Patterns in the Eastern Mediterranean in a CO_2-Warmed Climate." In *Regional Implications of Future Climate Change: Proceedings of an International Workshop, Weizmann Institute of Science, Rehovot Israel April 28–May 2 1991*, edited by M. Graber, A. Cohen, and M. Magaritz, 79–83. Jerusalem: Israeli Academy of Sciences and Humanities and State of Israel, Ministry of the Environment

Kitoh, A., A. Yatagai, and P. Alpert. 2008. "First Super-High-Resolution Model Projection that the Ancient Fertile Crescent Will Disappear in This Century." *Hydrological Research Letters* 2: 1–4.

Klein, M., M. Lichter, and D. Tzviely. 2004. "Recent Sea-Level Changes along Israeli and Mediterranean Coasts." *Contemporary Israeli Geography: Special Issue of Horizons in Geography* 60-61: 167–76.

Kliot, N., S. Paz, and O. Kaidar. 2008. "Frame & Framing Analysis for the Study of Preparedness for Climate Change in Israel." In Hebrew; unpublished.

Knesset Internal Affairs and Environment Committee Meeting Protocol 391, Climate Change Bill June 29. 2008. http://www.knesset.gov.il/protocols/heb/protocol_search.aspx.

Kordova, S. 2008. "Policies Restrain Potential of Israel's Renewable Energy Say Researcher Though Technology Is Ready." *Ha'aretz*, May 23.

Levin, Z., N. Halfon, and P. Alpert. 2010. "Reassessment of Rain Enhancement Experiments and Operations in Israel." *Atmospheric Research* 97: 513–25.

Lesser, S. 2009. "The Top 10 Cleantech Countries of 2009." November 9. http://www.israel2lc.org/briefs/isreal-is-no-5-on-top-10-cleantech-list.

Levy, D. 2010. Climate Change and Clean Tech in Israel, Climate Inc. January 12. www.climateinc.org.

McKinsey & Company. 2009. "Greenhouse Gas Abatement Potential in Israel." November. http://www.sviva.gov.il/Enviroment/Static/Binaries/index_pirsumim/p0560_1.pdf. In Hebrew and English.

Michaels, L. 2011. "Public Opinion about Climate Change in Israel: Results of National Survey." PhD thesis, Ben-Gurion University, June.

Ministry for Environmental Protection. 2006. *Israel Environment Bulletin* 31. Jerusalem: Ministry for Environmental Protection, October.

———. 2009. "Copenhagen Climate Change Conference: The Israeli Perspective." December 23. http://www.sviva.gov.il/Enviroment/bin/en.jsp?enPage=e_BlankPage&enDisplay=view&enDispWhat=Object&enDispWho=News%5El4902&enZone=e_news.

Ministry of Energy and Water Resources. 2011 "The Natural Gas Sector in Israel." http://energy.gov.il/English/Subjects/Natural%20Gas/Pages/GxmsMniNGEconomy.aspx.

NASA press release. 2010. "2009: Second Warmest Year on Record; End of Warmest Decade. NASA." January 21. http://www.giss.nasa.gov/research/news/20100121/.

Netanyahu, B. 2009. Speech at the President's Conference, Prime Minister's Office. October 20. http://www.mfa.gov.il/MFA/Government/Speeches+by+Israeli+leaders/2009/Speech_PM_Netanyahu_President_Conference_20-Oct-2009.htm.

Otterman, J., A. Manes, S. Rubin, P. Alpert, and D. O'c. Starr. 1990. "An Increase of Early Rains in Southern Israel Following Land-Use Change?" *Boundary Layer Meteorology* 53: 333–51.

Paz, S. 2009. "Warming Tendency in the Eastern Mediterranean Basin and Its Influence on West Nile Fever Outbreaks." In *Global Warming, Green Energy and Technology*, edited by I. Dincer, A. Midilli, A. Hepbasli, and T. H. Karakoc, 526–34. New
York: Springer. doi:10.1007/978-1-4419-1017-2_34.

Paz, S., N. Bisharat, E. Paz, O. Kidar, and D. Cohen. 2007. "Climate Change and the
Emergence of *Vibrio Vulnificus* Disease in Israel." *Environmental Research* 103:
390–96.

Porat, S., ed. 2008. *The Government of Israel and Climate Change—Complying with
Government Decisions and Meeting International Obligations*. Report by the Paths
to Sustainability Coalition. Tel Aviv: Life and Environment.

———. 2009. *Israel and the Climate Crisis: Risks and Opportunities. Report by the Paths
to Sustainability Coalition*. Tel Aviv: Life and Environment.

Pugliese, A., and J. Ray. 2009. "Awareness of Climate Change and Threat Vary by Region." Gallup WorldPoll December 11. http://www.gallup.com/poll/124652/aware-
ness-climate-change-threat-vary-region.aspx.

Rinat, Z. 2008. "Environment Ministry Official: Israel Has No Ability to Reduce the
Amount of Greenhouse Gas Emissions" *Ha'aretz*, November 9.

———. 2009a. "Comptroller: Israel Ill-Prepared for Tackling Climate Change."
Ha'aretz, December 6.

———. 2009b. "UN: As World Leader in Solar Energy, Israel Must Cut Fossil Fuel Use."
Ha'aretz, December 9.

Rom, M., D. Berger, L. Kronbetter, and B. Taltash. 2006. "Changes and Trends in the
Hydrology of the Pooling Lake of the Kinneret (1970–2006)." Presented at The
Influence of Climate Change in Israel—Towards a National Action Plan, June. In
Hebrew.

Saaroni, H., B. Ziv, I. Osetinsky, and P. Alpert. 2010. "Factors Governing the Interannual Variation and the Long-Term Trend of the 850 hPa Temperature over Israel."
Quarterly Journal of the Royal Meteorological Society 136: 305–18.

Safriel, U., and G. Pe'er. 2000. *Climate Change: Israel National Report under the United
Nations Framework Convention on Climate Change. Impact, Vulnerability and Adaptation, October 2000*. Jerusalem: Ministry of Environment, Blaustein Institutes
for Desert Research, Ben-Gurion University of the Negev

Segal, M., P. Alpert, U. Stein, and M. Mandel. 1994. "On the 2x CO_2 Potential Climatic
Effects on the Water Balance Components in the Eastern Mediterranean." *Climatic
Change* 27: 351–71.

Shaviv, N. 2005. "Cosmic Rays and Climate." *PhysicaPlus—The Journal of the Israel
Physics Society* 5. http://physicaplus.org.il/zope/home/en/1105389911/1113511992_en/.

Tal, A. 2009. "Building a Hydrological Future." *Ha'aretz*, May 26.

Tiraspolsky, A., M. Schechter, and R. Palatnik. 2008. *Incorporating Economic Incentives in Reducing Greenhouse Gas Emissions under the Kyoto Protocol: The Case of
Israel*. Haifa: University of Haifa.

Tishler, A., J. Newman, I. Speckerman, and C. K. Woo. 2008. "Assessing the Market for
Competitive Electricity Market in Israel." *Utilities Policy* 16: 21–29.

Waldoks, E. Z. 2009. "Israelis Support Urgent Action on Climate Change." *Jerusalem
Post*, November 25.

———. 2010. "Is the Sun Setting on the Solar Energy Boom?" *Jerusalem Post*, June 25.

Yanai, M., J. Koch, and U. Dayan. 2008. "Trends in CO_2 Emissions in Israel—An International Perspective." *Climatic Change* online edition, October 2009.

Zalasiewicz, J., et al. "Are We Now Living in the Anthropocene?" *GSA Today* 18 (2): 4–8.

Ziv, B., H. Saaroni, A. Baharad, D. Yekutieli, and P. Alpert. 2005. "Indications for Aggravation in Summer Heat Conditions over the Mediterranean Basin." *Geophysical Research Letters* 32.

CHAPTER SIXTEEN

NATURE KNOWS NO BOUNDARIES?
Notes Toward a Future History of Regional Environmentalism

Stuart Schoenfeld

WORK TOWARD ARAB-ISRAELI peace in the 1990s involved activities at dual levels. While there were formal negotiations, there was also work to build popular support for peace through projects that would show the benefits of cooperative rather than hostile relations. Formal negotiations led to agreements between Israel and the Palestinian Authority (PA), and to the Peace Treaty between Israel and Jordan. Work to build cooperative projects with mutual benefits took a variety of forms, including building links between civil society groups and creating new settings to bring Israelis, Palestinians, Jordanians, and others together. Environmental issues—water, energy, pollution, biodiversity, and habitat protection—were acknowledged at both the formal and civil society levels. Formal agreements included sections on these topics. Cooperative projects not only addressed environmental issues, but also involved the creation of a small civil society network to promote regional environmental research and policy formulation.

This chapter describes initiatives that have fostered regional environmentalism in the Eastern Mediterranean at both the formal and civil society levels. It is not history written in hindsight with perspective, but, rather, notes toward a future history of an initiative whose outcome is still very much uncertain. The uncertainty comes not only from inherent limits of forecasting, but also from the awareness of, on the one hand, frustration and failure, and, on the other hand, the perseverance and commitment of those who are working to make environmental initiatives ultimately a success.

Formal peacemaking has yet to be successful. The promise of robust official environmental cooperation is still unfulfilled. Some environmental civil society efforts faltered, but some work continues. Their continuation and promise is the primary focus of this chapter. The chapter is partly a historical narrative, but it also asks how some organizations have continued to do environmental peace-building for well over a decade, despite the official frustrations and the failure of other initiatives. The concept of "resource mobilization," taken from the study of social movements, provides an analytical framework through which to account for the perseverance of environmental cooperation. There are various kinds of resources that social movements need in order to survive and work toward their goals (Edwards and McCarthy 2004). Understanding how environmental groups working toward regional cooperation were able to mobilize the resources needed to persevere may be useful to understanding how other groups may sustain their efforts to work toward peaceful cooperation when formal peacemaking has stalled.

How, then, was the idea of promoting regional environmental cooperation initiated? What role did it play in regional negotiations and treaties? What were the civil society aspects of this initiative? What happened when regional environmentalism was challenged by intensified hostilities? How have some environmental civil society initiatives persevered?

INTRODUCING THE FRAME OF REGIONAL ENVIRONMENTALISM[1]

The 1980s and early 1990s were a period of high visibility for global environmentalism. Dramatic events—Bhopal, Chernobyl, the discovery of the depletion of the ozone layer and anthropogenic global warming, fires in the Amazon, the Exxon Valdez oil spill, and the collapse of the Atlantic cod fisheries—were framed by activists and the media not as idiosyncratic individual occurrences, but as iconic markers of the human degradation of the planet. Many grassroots organizations emerged to address local issues. National governments, including those in the Eastern Mediterranean, established ministries of the environment. Transnational environmental NGOs—notably the World Wildlife Fund, Greenpeace, and Friends of the Earth—extended their reach by developing international centers that coordinated the work of national chapters (Wapner 1995). International diplomacy addressed environmental issues through conferences and treaties. The United Nations brought "development" and "environment" agendas together by promoting "sustainable development" and was gearing up for the 1992 Earth Summit (International Institute for Sustainable Development 2007).

This extensive activity around environmental concerns was in the background as a major diplomatic initiative in the Middle East was under way. In the aftermath of the fall of the Berlin Wall, the first Gulf War and the apparent emergence of the United States as "the world's only remaining super-power," the United States worked with its allies to convene peace negotiations in Madrid in 1992 involving Israel, Syria, Lebanon, Jordan, and the Palestinians (Israel Ministry of Foreign Affairs 2007). The Madrid framework discussions for Middle East peace included multilateral negotiations in five tracks: refugees, water, regional security, environment, and economic development. Working groups in each track produced documentation and proposals that framed these issues as regional ones, with solutions to be similarly regional.

Just as the Brundtland Report released five years earlier had promoted "sustainable development" as the synthesis of the environment and development agendas, the Madrid process brought together regional peace and development agendas. Just as there was rhetoric in the United States of a "peace dividend" following the Cold War, in the Middle East regional peace was promoted as a strategy for diverting resources from destruction to development. Within that perspective, environment was identified as a shared regional concern, and water separated out for special attention.

ENVIRONMENTAL ISSUES IN FORMAL AGREEMENTS

While the Madrid conference did not lead to a comprehensive regional peace agreement, back-channel Palestinian-Israeli contacts led to the bilateral Oslo Declaration of Principles in 1993. The declaration, signed in front of the White House by the Yitzhak Rabin and Yasser Arafat, established a five-year transitional period during which permanent status negotiations were to resolve difficult outstanding issues. The first step would be an interim agreement establishing a Palestinian Authority governed by an elected council, which would establish, among others, water, environment, and electrical authorities. The Declaration of Principles (Israel Ministry of Foreign Affairs 1993) continued the Madrid linkage between peace and development, identifying specific steps that could begin immediately to develop cooperative projects while the final-status negotiations were taking place.

Annex III of the Declaration of Principles specifies a joint Israeli-Palestinian Committee on Economic Cooperation to prepare joint water, electricity, and energy development programs (the first three items on the list) and (much further down the list) an environmental protection plan. Annex IV notes continuing multilateral peace efforts, and lists examples of possible elements of a Regional Economic Development Program:

- a joint Israeli-Palestinian-Jordanian Plan for coordinated exploitation of the Dead Sea area;
- the Mediterranean Sea (Gaza)-Dead Sea Canal;
- regional desalination and other water development projects;

- a regional plan for agricultural development, including a coordinated regional effort for the prevention of desertification;
- interconnection of electricity grids; and
- regional cooperation for the transfer, distribution, and industrial exploitation of gas, oil, and other energy resources (Israel Ministry of Foreign Affairs 1993).

Two years after the Declaration of Principles, the government of Israel and the Palestinian Liberation Organization signed the Interim Agreement, which formally established the Palestinian Authority (Israel Ministry of Foreign Affairs 1995). Some seventeen years later, it may be instructive to review just how detailed the approach taken to environmental issues in this lengthy document was. Article IV reaffirms the importance of economic cooperation, particularly to encourage Palestinian economic growth, while also noting that economic growth should take environmental protection into consideration. Article V calls for agricultural cooperation, including technical cooperation on water and related issues, extensive environmental cooperation to be implemented under an Environmental Experts Committee; and energy cooperation, with an emphasis on alternative energy and conservation.

Annex III of the Interim Agreement contains forty detailed articles regarding the PA's powers and responsibilities for civil affairs, including articles on agriculture, electricity, environmental protection, forests, nature reserves, quarries and mines, and water and sewage. In the areas of electricity and water, pending a final agreement, Israel would maintain responsibility for supply with the PA taking responsibility for distribution. The Interim Agreement calls for a Joint Electrical Subcommittee, a Joint Committee of Experts on nature reserves, and an Environmental Experts Committee.

Article 40 in Annex III "Water and Sewage" is the most detailed of all. It formally recognizes Palestinian water rights in the West Bank, obligates Israel to maintain the existing water supply and to increase water allocations by specified amounts to specified localities, mandates various technical areas of water cooperation, and obligates each side to protect water quality and infrastructure. A separate schedule ensures Israeli control of water and sewage services for its Gaza settlements, and Palestinian control of water and waste management in other areas. A Joint Water Committee is described in detail. The Joint Water Committee would have an equal number of representatives from each side. The development of water sources and systems, new wells, new water sources, new sewage systems, and modification of existing systems require prior approval by the Joint Water Committee. All decisions are to be reached by consensus (Israel Ministry of Foreign Affairs 1995).

The negotiations on water were supported by the work of officially sanctioned teams of Palestinian and Israeli water experts. Professors Eran Feitelson from Hebrew University and Marwan Haddad from el Najah University led an academic effort to consider coordination in the field of water. The Feitelson and Haddad (1994, 1995) and Haddad and Feitelson (1995, 1996) volumes reported shared research over a series of years. Expert cooperation went as far as proposing a specific management structure based not on the political calculations that produced the Interim Agreement but on expert knowledge about how cooperative water management could actually work (Feitelson and Haddad 1998).

In addition to substantive issues, the Interim Agreement also responds to the criticism that neither the Palestinian nor the Israeli publics are prepared to embrace cooperative peaceful relations after decades of animosity and hostility. Israel and the PA committed themselves to fostering "mutual understanding and tolerance" (chapter 4, article XII) and agreed to develop programs of cooperation. Annex VI describes in detail a wide range of anticipated cooperative programs. Environmental protection is the first area listed (article II), but it was subsumed, along with agriculture and energy, within the plans for economic cooperation. Article VIII endorses the "People-to-People" initiative from Norway, to "enhance dialogue and relations between their people."

Environmental issues are also a significant part of the Israeli-Jordanian Peace Treaty (Israel Ministry of Foreign Affairs 1994) that followed the 1993 Israeli-Palestinian Declaration of Principles by slightly more than a year. In contrast to the length, complexities, and unresolved differences in the 1995 Palestinian-Israeli Interim Agreement, the Israeli-Jordanian Peace Treaty is relatively brief. As in Israeli-Palestinian agreements, environmental issues are identified as areas for cooperative relations. The peace treaty between Jordan and Israel writes of "a comprehensive and lasting settlement of all the water problems" between the two states (article VI) and notes the "great importance" of "matters relating to the environment" (article XVIII). These articles are elaborated in Annex II and IV, respectively.

In addition to various provisions for cooperation, including a Joint Water Committee (specified in much, much less detail than the committee established by the Palestinian-Israeli Interim Agreement), Annex II commits Israel to providing additional water to Jordan. Annex IV lists broad areas for environmental cooperation, with specific reference to the Gulf of Aqaba and the Jordan rift valley that extends from Aqaba through the Arava Valley to the Dead Sea and then up the Jordan River to the Sea of Galilee.

Jordanian-Israeli negotiations formalized existing cooperation and built a mechanism for a public common future. The governments of Israel and Jordan had long had departments responsible for water supply and planning. While nominally at war, the sides held off-the-official-record talks on water

(Zak 1995; Haddadin 2000). This hidden cooperation was driven by perceived necessity since the Jordan River system is a primary source of water for both states. In contrast to these secret relations, the peace treaty was public, intended to shift the framework from water as an object of conflict to water management as a common task that could reinforce regional peace and long-term sustainability.

TOWARD REGIONAL ENVIRONMENTALISM: CIVIL SOCIETY

Globally, a broad, diffuse social movement has driven awareness of environmental issues and the promotion of ecological sustainability. Much environmental activism has taken place within national boundaries, but issues such as water, energy, natural resource limits, pollution, and biodiversity are very often transnational, and environmentalism inherently draws people toward transboundary and global perspectives. The environmental movement has correspondingly often taken a transnational form. Civil society groups connecting Israelis, Palestinians, and Jordanians promoted not only bilateral environmental cooperation, but also a vision of the Eastern Mediterranean as a region whose peoples face shared problems of water, energy, waste, pollution, natural resource management, biodiversity, and sustainable development.

The institutional legitimacy given to environmental issues by Middle East peacemaking efforts in the 1990s and the growing transnational activism of environmentalism opened a space for civil society environmental organizations with a regional perspective. Environmental initiatives could also build on the changing nature of environmentalism in the region. Prior to the 1990s, the region's nature conservation groups, the Society for the Protection of Nature in Israel and the (Jordanian) Royal Society for the Conservation of Nature, were the most visible forms of environmentalism in the Eastern Mediterranean. This situation was changing, with new or more activist groups in Israel, Jordan, Lebanon, and the PA focused on water, wildlife, agriculture, resource management, pollution, environmental law, and other related issues. The attention given to environmental issues in the political agreements created an intersection between the Israeli peace movement and the Israeli environmental movement. Those at this intersection had the opportunity to reach out to Palestinian and Jordanian partners. From the late 1980s to the late 1990s, a series of civil society initiatives supplemented formal peacemaking efforts with initiatives for environmental cooperation. The initiatives discussed below were the most prominent or active.

Israel-Palestine Center for Research and Information: IPCRI opened under joint Israeli and Palestinian directors in 1989 during the first Intifada. Before the Madrid negotiations, IPCRI had working groups on economic issues, water, and Jerusalem, and has had at different times working groups on peace education, final-status negotiations, and other issues. IPCRI established a formal Water and Environment Program under retired British diplomat Robin Twite in 1994. A 1993 edited book presented Palestinian and Israeli perspectives on water cooperation (Baskin 1993). Between 1994–1996 IPCRI held workshops on "Our Shared Environment" and published three volumes of papers from the workshops (Twite and Isaac 1994; Twite and Menczel 1995, 1996; Chaitin et al. 2002, 74). Shared research projects, an initiative on environmental mediation, and a number of seminars followed (Twite 2005, 250–51). More recently, IPCRI's Water and Environment Program took the lead in organizing a 2004 International Water for Life Conference held in Turkey, where over five days about 130 participants from the region were joined by about 50 international water experts. The conference was cochaired by Israeli and Palestinian professors, assisted by a 14-member Palestinian and Israeli steering committee (Twite 2005, 16–17, 251), with sixty-four of the ninety papers presented subsequently published in two volumes (Shuval and Dwick 2006) and other supporting material posted on the IPCRI website. More recently, IPCRI undertook a study of the management of the transboundary Nahal Alexander–Wadi Zomer basin; participated in the GLOWA-Jordan River Project, a study of the impact of climate change on the Jordan River basin; and conducted a pilot project to treat wastewater with a filtration system using wetlands rather than chemical methods (Twite 2009).

EcoPeace/Friends of the Earth Middle East (FoEME) was founded in 1994 as EcoPeace, an organization that was envisaged as a meeting place for Palestinian, Egyptian, Jordanian, and Israeli environmental NGOs, and became an affiliate of Friends of the Earth (FoE) in 1998. Affiliation with FoE placed FoEME in the context of global environmentalism but also preserved its autonomy. Like Greenpeace and the World Wildlife Fund for Nature, FoE has an international headquarters and chapters in many countries. Of these three large transnational environmental NGOs, Friends of the Earth is the most decentralized. It is essentially a mutually supportive federation of autonomous groups that share a broad outlook and agenda.

FoEME uses regional language in its rationale: "The people and wildlife of our region are dependent on many of the same natural resources. Shared surface and sub-surface freshwater basins, shared seas, common flora and fauna species and a shared air-shed are some of the characteristics that necessitate regional cooperation" (Friends of the Earth Middle East 2009). FoEME has had Israeli, Palestinian, and Jordanian codirectors since it began, and until 1998 had an Egyptian codirector. Over the past few years, FoEME has moved from an institutional agenda of discussions, awareness building, and conferences to a more operational orientation. Its present projects include a major initiative to establish a transboundary peace park in the Jordan Valley, coordinated climate change initiatives, and a Good Water Neighbors project that connects Israeli, Palestinian, and Jordanian communities in efforts to preserve shared water resource integrity (Bromberg and Qumsieh 2005).

The proposal to establish the Arava Institute for Environmental Studies came from Alon Tal, a scholar with a PhD in environmental policy who had founded Adam Tevah v'Din—the Israel Union for Environmental Defense (IUED) in 1990. With colleagues, he brought together Kibbutz Ketura (in a remote part of the Negev desert south of the West Bank, east of Gaza, and just across the valley from Jordan), where he was a member, and Tel Aviv University, where he was a faculty member, on a project to establish an institute for university-level environmental studies. Students from Israel, Jordan, Palestine, Egypt, and overseas would spend one to two semesters living together and earning university credits. The institute opened in the 1996–1997 academic year and has since established research centers, alumni activism programs, and a joint master's degree program with Ben-Gurion University's Blaustein Institutes for Desert Research. The formal vision statement of the institute is explicitly regional: "The Arava Institute for Environmental Studies will provide the Middle East a new generation of sophisticated professionals that will meet the region's environmental challenges with richer and more innovative, peace-building solutions" (Arava Institute 2009).

As the rhetoric in its name indicates, the Palestinian-Israeli Environmental Secretariat (PIES), founded in 1997, was an ambitious bilateral initiative. Its founding partners were the Palestine Council on Health, the Society for the Preservation of Nature in Israel—both mainstream institutions in their respective societies—and the Israel Economic Cooperation Forum, which was part of the formal Israeli structure to develop Israeli-Palestinian economic cooperation (Zwirn 2001, 118). In its initial year, PIES received financial support from a number of governments and from U.S. Jewish charities (119). PIES developed programs on environmentally safe production standards for the business sector and environmental education programs for youth.

People-to-People Programs and Joint and Cooperative Environmental Programs were set up as follows: The first Oslo negotiations were held secretly and announced without a popular mandate; subsequently, international funding was made available, first from Norway and then as an outcome of the Interim Agreement, for People-to-People (P2P) initiatives to "deepen the peace" by bringing together Palestinians and Israelis to encounter and learn to understand each other. One source reports about 500 P2P projects involving over one hundred organizations, and tens of thousands of Israelis and Palestinians from 1993 to 2000, at an estimated cost of US$20–30 million (Herzog and Hai 2005, 15). A number of ventures, some identified as People-to-People projects, implemented the Interim Agreement's agenda of environmental cooperation. A study of Palestinian-Jordanian environmental cooperative initiatives (Chaitin et al. 2002) identified environmental cooperation undertaken by three joint Israeli-Palestinian environmental NGOs, twelve Palestinian NGOs, nineteen Israeli NGOs, two academic institutions, and an Israeli government department.

OFFICIAL ENVIRONMENTAL COOPERATION: SETBACKS AND LIMITED CONTINUITY

Although Palestinian-Israeli agreements and the Jordanian-Israeli Peace Treaty acknowledge a variety of environmental issues as transboundary concerns, these bilateral agreements have not led to regional environmental cooperation. The Palestinian-Israeli Interim Agreement has not led to a formal peace ("final-status") agreement that could turn the promise of cooperation in the Interim Agreements into reality. The "cold peace" between Egypt and Israel, the absence of peace treaties between Israel and Syria and Lebanon, and the limited relations Jordan established with Israel in the absence of other Arab peace treaties have restricted the development of formal regional environmentalism.

Shortly after the Interim Agreement, Palestinian-Israeli reconciliation—already challenged by "rejectionist" mobilization and violence from both societies—became even more problematic. Following the assassination of Prime Minister Rabin, Benjamin Netanyahu's Likud, which had opposed the Oslo Accords, won the 1996 elections. Militant Palestinian resistance escalated to suicide attacks. Israeli Defense Force retaliation intensified, checkpoints proliferated, and settlements expanded. In a context of continuing tension, intermittent violence, and accusations of bad faith, the negotiations toward a final-status agreement stalled. The elaborate mechanisms for formal cooperation stipulated by the Interim Agreement mostly broke down. The Second Intifada began in September 2000 following the failed personal intervention by U.S. president Clinton at the Camp David summit in July.

Environmental cooperation between Israel and Jordan continued, although strained (Eisenberg and Caplan 2003). Through the late 1990s Jordanian public sentiment had become increasingly pro-Palestinian and anti-Israel. Anti-normalization blacklists had (and continue to have) a chilling effect. Nevertheless, the peace treaty stands and continues to be a framework for environmental cooperation. The dispute in the late 1990s over guaranteed water allocations to Jordan was settled within the framework of the treaty. Work continues on the peace park planned along the Jordan River. Despite the reservations by some water experts and environmentalists about the plan to build a water conduit from the Red Sea to the Dead Sea, there has been considerable Israeli cooperation on the project, which is a Jordanian priority in its long-range water planning (Schoenfeld, Abitbol, and De Chatel 2007; Abitbol 2009).

The armed Palestinian uprising of the Second Intifada was accompanied by a diplomatic campaign against Israel in which Palestinian civil society groups and overseas solidarity movements played a major role. NGOs took the lead in the campaign to vilify and isolate Israel at the 2001 World Conference on Racism in Durbin, a campaign continued by Palestinian environmental NGOs at the 2002 World Summit on Sustainable Development (Greenspan 2005). The Palestine Environmental NGO Network (PENGON), a coalition of twenty-one groups formed in 2000 shortly after the Second Intifada began, rejected environmental cooperation with Israel and took a strong adversarial position in its "apartheid wall" campaign. Similarly, Palestinian environmental NGOs support the Boycotts, Divestment and Sanctions campaign that was formally launched in 2005.

The turn away from environmental cooperation is seen in the 2003 United Nations Environment Program (UNEP) study on the environment in the Palestinian territories and in the reaction to the study. In 2002 the Governing Council of the Global Ministerial Environment Forum, in response to "alarming reports related to the pollution of water, dumping of wastes, loss of natural vegetation and pollution of coastal waters" unanimously called on UNEP to investigate environmental conditions in the Palestinian territories (United Nations Environment Programme 2003, 4). The move to involve the United Nations marked a departure from the bilateral environmental mechanisms envisaged by the Interim Agreement. Instead, in the atmosphere of the Second Intifada, the call for a UN investigation fit the new Palestinian approach of promoting international condemnation of Israel.

The 2003 UNEP report noted "the full cooperation and support both from the Palestinian Authority and the Government of Israel." In introducing its detailed review of freshwater, wastewater, solid waste, hazardous waste, and conservation and biodiversity issues, the report proposed that "environment could be seen as a bridge-building element, building the confidence between the two parties" and wrote, "environmental cooperation could play a key role in the process towards a lasting peace" (United Nations Environment Programme 2003, 9–10). The Israeli government welcomed the report, but no initiatives for environmental cooperation followed. PENGON issued a highly critical response, writing that it was "gravely concerned that the report quietly neglects the illegality of the Occupation while encouraging complicity with its institutions and practices." PENGON stated "emphatically its concern at the worldwide trend of utilizing environmentalism as a tool to de-politicize what is at its core a political issue. Perhaps more appropriately stated, utilizing environmental issues outside of their context is not only counterproductive, but may be seen as serving particular interests that are ultimately harmful to the environment. Supporting Israel's de facto policy of de-development in the Occupied Territories supports and encourages such a policy" (Palestine Environmental NGO Network 2004).

Despite the stresses of the Second Intifada, Palestinian-Israel agreements did produce some significant results, particularly in the area of water. There has been progress, but also continuing frustrations on both sides.[2] Under the specific terms of the Interim Agreement, Israel increased allocations to Palestinians from the water sources it controls. The impact, however, is hardly recognizable because the Palestinian water shortage is so great (Tal and Abed Rabbo 2010). The Palestinian-Israeli Joint Water Committee, established to manage (pending a final-status agreement) the pressing problems of water and sewage in Palestinian territories and to foster cooperation in water and sewage, is the only joint committee envisaged by the Interim Agreement that has managed to survive. It has approved many projects to improve Palestinian water and sewage, leading to some improvement in the West Bank. However, many proposals have not been approved, and of those approved not all have been implemented, leaving a great many remaining deficiencies in the West Bank as well as in Gaza (Jayousi 2010). Although the Joint Water Committee's meetings have become much less frequent since 2000, it continues to meet, with its professional members maintaining contact outside of meetings. During the Second Intifada, Palestinian and Israeli water authorities agreed on the importance of preserving water infrastructure from harm and the Joint Water Committee issued a statement calling on combatants to avoid damage to water infrastructure.

Formal Palestinian-Israeli agreements have not produced robust water and sewage cooperation or a noticeable improvement in conditions on the West Bank, and serious problems of water and sewage in Gaza remain as a consequence of restrictions on imports and the direct damage to infrastructure in the December 2009 fighting. Outside of on-again, off-again Palestinian-Israeli negotiations, Palestinians have no direct voice in Israeli water and sewage planning. The asymmetries of Palestinian and Israeli conditions of everyday life and the Israeli control of the situation on the ground are marked. Nevertheless, modest improvements have been made, professional networks have been established, and a formal structure for cooperation has survived, with the potential to be used for greater impact.

SETBACKS TO CIVIL SOCIETY ENVIRONMENTAL COOPERATION

The mobilization of Palestinian civil society groups in the campaign to isolate Israel severely disrupted civil society environmental ties. In the context of a turn toward overtly hostile relations, PIES, which had close official ties, lost its funding and organizational activity stopped (Chaitin et al. 2002; Zwirn 2001). People–to-People projects could not cultivate an agenda of reconciliation in tension with adversarial popular opinion and political leadership (Herzog and Hai 2005; AbuZayyad and Schenker 2006). As travel between the Palestine and Israel became dangerous or highly limited, the physical obstacles to cooperation became substantial. Writing about joint environmental projects in the early months of the Second Intifada, Chaitin et al. state that "most of this work came to a standstill" (2002, 64–65) and in 2004 they report, "When we contacted NGOs to see whether or not they were carrying on with joint work, we learned that almost all projects had stopped" (540).

Failed negotiations undermined IPCRI's pre-Oslo position that progress could come through mutual Israeli-Palestinian recognition. The Arava Institute was faced with challenges of student recruitment and financing. The FoEME office in Jerusalem was closed for several months during the Second Intifada (Zwirn 2001, 122), with staff having to work from home. The Palestinian Hydrology Group withdrew from FoEME and took the lead in forming the PENGON, which subsequently applied for membership as a national organization in Friends of the Earth and was accepted (Chaitin et al. 2002; Zwirn 2001), with FoEME continuing in affiliated status.

THE PERSISTENCE OF REGIONAL ENVIRONMENTALISM IN CIVIL SOCIETY ORGANIZATIONS

Notwithstanding the setbacks to environmental cooperation that accompanied the Second Intifada, the logic for cooperation on water, energy, pollution, biodiversity, and related issues is strong. Drought and other impacts of climate change; expensive and polluting energy sources; release of dangerous effluents into air, land, and water; and the disruption to habitat are all transnational issues and can be better addressed through coordinated action. FoEME, the Water and Environment Program in IPRCI, and the Arava Institute have persevered, with some difficulty, through and after the Second Intifada.

These three that persisted have characteristics of environmental movement organizations. Environmental movement organizations, like other social movement organizations, understand themselves as formally organized nodes in networks that have constructed distinct collective identities in struggles over social change, in opposition to others and in conflict with them (see, e.g., Della Porta and Diani 2006, 21–22; 135–62). Social movement organizations have the agenda of influencing governments rather than supporting government positions. FoEME, the Water and Environment Program in IPRCI, and the Arava Institute have their own goals and structural independence, making them more resilient to the changing situation than PIES and P2P projects. Each of these three, in its own way, continue to model a regional understanding that is not yet widely shared and is opposed by many in their respective societies. It is possible to get a better understanding of what they do and why they persist through the lens of resource mobilization theory as it has developed in the study of social movements.

While the resource mobilization perspective has been in use in social movement studies for decades, Edwards and McCarthy have noted that the identification of resources has been underconceptualized. They elaborate this perspective by specifying various kinds of resources social movements need: moral, human, cultural, financial and material, and social organizational (Edwards and McCarthy 2004). Advocates of regional environmentalism face the challenge of mobilizing resources that are necessary for them to survive and advance their agendas. It is possible to understand the persistence of the civil society organizations that promote regional environmentalism through the ways they have managed to mobilize these various resources. A description of each type of resource and the challenges of mobilizing each are noted in the discussion that follows.

Moral resources legitimate the goals and means of social movements, either directly or through endorsement. In explaining why the movement they promote should receive support, regional environmentalists refer to the growing environmental concern in the world in general and in the Eastern Mediterranean in particular. Regional environmentalists share a common language of environmental issues as transboundary concerns, although there is some variation in emphasis, representing the internal debates within environmentalism (Guha 2000). There is, especially, a wide understanding that water is a regional issue.

Endorsements add to the legitimacy of regional environmentalism. Regional environmental groups publicize the recognition they have received within the region from King Abdullah of Jordan, Shimon Peres, president of Israel,[3] and Abu Ala, the speaker of the Palestinian legislature. Foundations, news sources, and celebrities in Europe and America have also praised their work.

The contentiousness of regional environmentalism may be seen in the challenges it faces in mobilizing moral resources. Although regional environmental NGOs are well known within the environmentalist networks of each national society, the vast majority of people in the region do not know them or their work. Environmental consciousness in the region is still developing and it is often articulated through frameworks antagonistic to cooperation. Leading political movements are more concerned with control of scarce resources rather than environmental planning and cooperation. Strong ideological resistance to Arab-Israeli cooperation shapes what is reported in the mass media. Consequently, discourses of natural resource competition and environmental (in)justice are very common and contrast sharply with discourses of common interests in a shared region (Schoenfeld 2005).

The human resources that social movements require include leaders, trained staff members and participants, and supporters of various kinds. Social entrepreneurs are needed to start up and lead through crises. IPCRI, FoEME and the Arava Institute were each begun by immigrants to Israel who came intending to commit their careers to social activism. Idealistic and committed Arab environmentalists were equally essential partners in establishing regional environmental initiatives. These dedicated entrepreneurs patiently recruited others to help, secured funding, and worked long hours to keep their projects going during difficult times. IPRCI successfully recruited a retired British diplomat to head the Water and Environment division. Kibbutz Ketura became a source of personnel for the Arava Institute. Establishment of the Arava Institute as a credit-granting university program was important for recruiting faculty and students. FoEME and IPRCI have been able to provide internships and paid positions and train people on the job. FoEME, through its links to Israeli, Palestinian, and Jordanian environmental organizations and in view of its decentralized structure, has been able to recruit from its three constituencies. The Arava Institute, in view of its special mandate for training the next generation of regional environmentalists, has become a source of personnel for other regional environmental initiatives, including IPCRI and FoEME, and has cultivated networking among its alumni since early in its existence.

Building a human resource base in a conflict zone is challenging (see e.g., Abitbol and Schoenfeld 2009). There are social and political pressures within Palestinian and Jordanian society against cooperating with Israelis, and those who participate in joint programs may be professionally and socially stigmatized. Neither society, however, is homogeneous in its rejection of cooperative work. In the "liberal" section of Israeli society, work on peace and environmental issues carries some prestige, and there is practical support for cooperative work. In the initial period of the Second Intifada, the Israeli military imposed tight restrictions on Palestinian ability to remain overnight in Israel, leading to a sharp drop in enrollment at the Arava Institute. The Arava Institute responded to military controls on Palestinian residency by joining Hebrew University (which was supported by all but one of Israel's universities) in an ultimately successful court challenge to the blanket military ban.

There are also incentives for participation in cooperative environmental work. Palestinians, Israelis, and Jordanians participate in the practical local work of the Good Water Neighbors project of FoEME under the auspices of NGOs in their respective societies. Palestinian, Jordanian, and Israeli students at the Arava Institute attend on scholarship and improve their English, their curriculum vitae, and their prospects for further professional education. The Arava Alumni Peace and Environment Network (AAPEN), which held its first meeting in Aqaba in 2005, provides a structure of mutual support for a network of young professionals committed to regional environmentalism (see Friends of the Earth Middle East 2009; Cohen 2006; Alleson and Schoenfeld 2007; Zohar, Schoenfeld, and Alleson 2008; Schoenfeld and Zohar 2009).

Cultural resources are needed to spread the perspective of a social movement. FoEME, IPCRI, and Arava Institute publications vary in the audiences that they address. Some publishing—the volumes of Arava Institute conferences published by Springer, the two volumes from the IPRCI "Water for Life" conference, and various technical studies done by FoEME—is directed toward professionals and policy makers. Some documents, like annual reports and brochures, are addressed to current and potential supporters. FoEME has devoted much care to fostering a cultural presence for regional environmentalism. It releases periodic statements to the press, holds events designed to attract media attention—such as the joint Jordan River swim of Palestinian, Jordanian, and Israeli mayors—and maintains an environmental peacemaking listserv. The FoEME website is detailed, covering a wide range of projects. Projects deal with particular geographic features—the Jordan River valley, the Dead Sea, the Gulf of Aqaba and Eilat—water, and environmental policy. In addition to its projects, the front page of the FoEME website has links to the texts of peace agreements and proposals and many links to Jordanian, Palestinian, and Israeli environmental organizations, international environmental organizations, organizations that work on international cooperation, and organizations that work on regional or cross-border cooperation.

This work of FoEME, IPCRI, and the Arava Institute has established a cultural space in which environmental issues in Israel, the Palestinian territories, Jordan, and adjacent countries can be understood as issues of shared concern. In this space, proposals for addressing shared problems can be developed. Others participate in this cultural work: The *Green Prophet* blog expands this space with articles from Israel and elsewhere in the Middle East; the website *Environment and Climate in the Middle East* reports regional environmental news and provides resources on environmental peace building.

This cultural space, however, is limited, with significant challenges to extending it. The ideological barriers and political opposition to Arab-Israeli cooperation noted above restrict the opportunities for expansion of the culture of regional environmentalism. Nevertheless, regional environmentalists continue to work for that cultural change, despite the current ascendance of the culture of hostility.

The culture of regional environmentalism is also mainly produced in the

English language. On the one hand, this is understandable. English is a shared language. Educated professionals working on environmental issues in the region are likely to use it. Environmentalists are likely to read and understand it. External funders and politicians, whose support is needed, are important audiences for English-language materials on regional environmentalism. On the other hand, while English-language material makes regional environmentalists visible to external audiences, it only reaches those limited Arabic or Hebrew speakers who also routinely use English.

Financial and material resources for regional environmentalism have come primarily from government agencies, foundations, and charities in the United States, Europe, and Canada. As with virtually all NGOs and educational institutions, IPCRI, FoEME, and the Arava Institute have developed a range of avenues to various kinds of financial resources. The Arava Institute, for example, has income from overseas students' tuition, research grants, government grants, and the American "Friends of the Arava Institute." Dependence on funding from outside the region is an obvious challenge, but regional environmentalism is hardly in a unique position. External support is common for this region, where grants, subsidies, institutional support, project funding, and other similar mechanisms channel financial support to governments and a wide variety of civil society groups. Indeed, one of the significant structural features of politics in the Eastern Mediterranean is the widespread dependency of all sorts of movements on external financing.

Social organizational resources include networks that support the work of social movement organizations. In the organizational network of regional environmentalism FoEME, IPCRI, and the Arava Institute occupy different niches. Each organization builds its own network, extending the flows of information and support. The IPCRI strategic affairs unit, the water and environment department, and the peace education department are each heavily engaged in organizing public meetings, extended discussions, and joint activities. FoEME, as an advocacy group, is a frequent participant in regional public policy discussions, routinely organizes public events, and has a well-developed network of its own. The Jordanian director of FoEME, Munqueth Mehyar, for example, founded the Jordanian Society for Sustainable Development and continues to sit on its board. The Good Water Neighbors project is notable in the development of "grassroots" networks that build a shared understanding of how local residents are part of larger systems. The Arava Institute, because its organizational form blends university education, research, and activism, is able to participate in university-based and environmental networks and to draw resources from both of them. The institute's staff, students, research partners, and conference participants have come both from university-based and environmental networks inside and outside of the Eastern Mediterranean. The Arava Institute and FoEME are members of Life and Environment, the umbrella network of Israeli environmental organizations.

Regional environmentalists have cultivated allies outside the region, including the European Union (EU) and European and American government agencies. In the United States, the Arava Institute, FoEME, and IPCRI are members of the Alliance for Middle East Peace (ALLMEP), which has met in Washington since 2005 and has collectively lobbied the U.S. government.

OTHER APPROACHES TO REGIONAL ENVIRONMENTALISM

Environmental cooperation in the Eastern Mediterranean could be developed in other ways besides direct transboundary environmental contacts in the region. The World Wildlife Fund, Greenpeace, and Friends of the Earth—the three high-profile transnational environmental NGOs—have structures with international headquarters and national chapters that work on coordinated agendas. The impact of these transnational environmental NGOs in the Eastern Mediterranean, however, is limited. The World Wildlife Fund does not have chapters in Jordan, Israel, the Palestinian Authority, Lebanon, Syria, or Egypt. Greenpeace has Israeli and Lebanese chapters and orients itself to the region through its Mediterranean project.[4] FOE International, having accepted, as noted above, both FoEME and PENGON, is in the peculiar position of having regional affiliates who have opposite views on environmental cooperation.

There are other developing environmental networks that have relevance for the Eastern Mediterranean (Schoenfeld and Rubin 2011). The EU launched the Euro-Mediterranean Partnership (also known as the Barcelona Process) in 1995 to manage its southern border through a formal multinational structure in which shared interests would be identified, coordinated policies developed, and a shared regional identity promoted. For a variety of reasons (see Pace 2006; Jones 2006; Adler et al. 2006; Calleya 2009; Botetzagias, Robinson, and Venizelos 2010), promoting coordinated action on shared problems was difficult, and this initiative was relaunched in 2008 as the Union for the Mediterranean. Pollution, energy, sustainable futures, and climate change are highly visible as common Mediterranean problems and potential areas of cooperation (Lesser 2009).

The EU has not been the only advocate for Mediterranean environmental coordination. Since 1976, there has been a UN convention on protecting the Mediterranean from pollution and a Mediterranean Action Plan within UNEP. The World Bank has established the Middle East and North Africa (MENA) Region Water Resources and Wastewater Network. The EU and the UN support the Information Office for Environment, Culture and Sustainable

Development (MIO-ECSDE)—the federation of Mediterranean environmental NGOs, which was formed in 1996. There was hope that these Mediterranean initiatives would influence the dynamics of conflict in the Eastern Mediterranean by providing a framework in which Israel, Jordan, the Palestinian Authority, and other states in the Eastern Mediterranean could work together on regional environmental issues. They have yet to do so, but potential is still there.

A recent initiative promotes the environment as a shared Arab concern. The Arab Federation for Environment and Development, formed in 2006, represents a pan-Arab network of experts, educators, civil servant, politicians, and businessmen. The perspective in its first two reports (Tolba and Saab 2008, 2009) is amplified by the UNDP's *Arab Human Development Report* (Regional Bureau for Arab States 2009). The 2009 *Arab Human Development Report* paid particular attention to the environmental challenge facing Arab countries, addressing it in detail as the first of seven threats to Arab human security, and listing as its elements: "demographic pressures, the overexploitation of land, water shortages, desertification, pollution, and climate change" (Regional Bureau for Arab States 2009, 2). The recommendations echo those of AFED.

The implications that a call for joint Arab environmentalism has for environmental cooperation in the Eastern Mediterranean are uncertain. On the one hand, Arab initiatives exclude cooperation with Israel—for example, there is discussion of a transnational energy grid in which Israel would not participate—on the other hand, the 2008 AFED report included a chapter on "Environmental Impact of Wars and Conflicts." This topic was discussed as well in the *Arab Human Development Report*. Within these documents, continuing conflict is presented as both a direct and indirect factor in environmental degradation and a challenge to sustainable development. Palestinian issues are placed in a broader Arab context of concerns over sustainable development and avoiding the high environmental costs of continuing hostilities. From this approach, a strong case can be made for perceiving the continuation of the Palestinian-Israeli conflict as a barrier to urgently needed regional environmental stewardship.

TOWARD A FUTURE HISTORY

Environmentalism has arrived in the Middle East. Water, pollution, the meaning of "sustainable" economic development, the looming threat of climate change, depleting biodiversity, and related issues are on the regional agenda. Environmental concern is institutionalized in ministries of environment, in civil society organizations, in the articulation of regional environmental professionals with international professional networks, and in shifting routines of everyday life. The region is producing a substantial generation of environmentally engaged scientists, educators, architects, media professionals, and business people who recognize that solutions to many of their environmental challenges require transboundary coordination. An environmentalist outlook is increasingly pronounced in the region's scientific, media, and political cultures. Increasing resources—although arguably far from enough—are being devoted to a wide range of environmental problems. Regional environmentalists are linked to networks of support through a range of international agencies. The EU Mediterranean initiative and nascent pan-Arab environmentalism also share a transboundary environmental perspective and could be places where recognition of the environmental costs of continuing conflict could stimulate connections and cooperation.

However, the shift to a regional environmentalism in which Israel is an ally rather than an adversary of its neighbors is still undeveloped. The failure of the Palestinian-Israeli Environmental Secretariat and the collapse of many cooperative programs during the Second Intifada showed the difficulties of making the shift. Opposition to "normalizing" relations with Israel on the part of Arab governments and civil society groups acts as a continuing obstacle. Nevertheless, the civil society groups profiled here continue with their agenda of building regional environmentalism. The moral resources that legitimate regional environmentalism are substantial. Human resources for regional environmentalism are developing from the alumni of the Arava Institute, the communities brought together by FoEME, and the professional networking of IPCRI. Regional environmentalist publications, Internet presence, news reports, and honors contribute to a cultural change. Consequently there is a growing awareness among experts, social activists, overseas supporters, and others of the importance of seeing the environmental challenge in the Eastern Mediterranean as regional and responding regionally. Regional environmentalists have established channels to develop financial and other material resources on a continuing basis. Networks of allies amplify and support regional environmental work.

Those committed to regional environmentalism seem to share common fears and hopes. They share fears that without a regional perspective of collective environmental stewardship, the costs will be very high. They share hopes that the ethic of restraint that is the moral foundation of environmentalism (Guha 2000, 115) may have a greater influence on the shaping of regional politics. In a context of increasing global and regional environmental stress, the challenge is immense. Perhaps due to the work of regional environmentalists, future historians will be able to report the successful response to this challenge.

NOTES

The author would like to acknowledge with thanks comments and suggestions from Asaf Zohar, Eric Abitbol, Itay Greenspan, Robin Twite, Gidon Bromberg, and David Lehrer.

1. Some material that follows has appeared previously in Schoenfeld 2010.

2. See Jayous 2010 and Kerret 2010 for more detailed presentations of Palestinian and Israeli perceptions of the impact of Palestinian-Israeli water agreements. The volume edited by Tal and Abed Rabbo 2010, in which their work appears, is itself an indication of continuing discussion among Palestinian and Israeli water experts.

3. Peres is also a former prime minister, Nobel Peace Prize recipient, and chair of his own peace-building foundation. The Peres Center for Peace was established 1996, with the goal of bringing "Israel and its Arab neighbours closer by means of peacebuilding projects which focus on common social and economic interests" (Peres Center for Peace 2009). The "five pillars" of the Peres Center—people-to-people dialog and interaction, capacity building through cooperation, nurturing a culture of peace, business and economic cooperation, and humanitarian responses—do not explicitly mention environmental work. Environmental concerns are brought into its agenda through the "Agriculture, Water and Environment" department. A continuing series of projects have dealt with agricultural technology and training, export partnerships, standards, cooperation on pest control, and water planning. While this is a more restricted agenda than that of those proposing a holistic regional environmentalism, the Peres Center's work on more efficient use of water and the shift to more efficient, environmentally sustainable agricultural practices gives both practical support and high-level legitimacy to a regional environmentalist perspective.

4. Greenpeace Mediterranean has project headquarters in Malta and offices in Istanbul, Tel Aviv, and Beirut. Greenpeace identifies the goals of its Mediterranean campaign as a nuclear-free Middle East, "peaceful energy," and defending the Mediterranean Sea. Focusing on the Mediterranean, nuclear weapons, and green energy is consistent with its past initiatives. Greenpeace began with an ocean nuclear protest, and it has worked on ocean-related issues, in opposition to nuclear proliferation, and as an advocate of green energy throughout its almost forty years. Its activities in the Eastern Mediterranean are also consistent with its past practices. Without a presence in Jordan or the Palestinian Authority, Greenpeace Mediterranean has not been involved in the efforts to build Israeli-Palestinian-Jordanian cooperation. In Israel, where it has been more active than in Lebanon, Greenpeace has been particularly active in advocating in opposition to building coal-fired power plants.

REFERENCES

Abitbol, E. 2009. "Developing Water and Marginalising Israel/Palestinian Peace: A Critical Examination of the Read Sea-Dead Sea Canal Feasibility Study Process." *Journal of Peacebuilding and Development* 5 (1): 35–49.

Abitbol, E., and S. Schoenfeld. 2009. "Adaptive Visions of Water in the Middle East: Lessons from a Regional Water Planning Initiative." In *The Jordan and Dead Sea Basin: A Regional Environmental Challenge, Establishing a Basis for Cooperative Management,* edited by D. Sandler and C. Lipchin, 297–316. Berlin: Springer.

AbuZayyad, Z., and H. Schenker, eds. 2006. "People-to-People: What Went Wrong and How to Fix It?" Special issue, *Palestine-Israel Journal of Politics, Economics, and Culture* 12 (4)–13 (1).

Adler, E., B. Crawford, F. Bicchi, and R. A. Del Sarto. 2006. *The Convergence of Civilizations: Constructing a Mediterranean Region.* Toronto: University of Toronto Press.

Alleson, I., and S. Schoenfeld. 2007. "Environmental Justice and Peacebuilding in the Middle East." *Peace Review* 19: 371–79.

Arava Institute. 2009. www.arava.org.

Baskin, G., ed. 1993. *Water: Conflict or Cooperation.* Jerusalem: IPCRI.

Botetzagias, I., P. Robinson, and L. Venizelos. 2010. "Accounting for Difficulties Faced in Materializing a Transnational ENGO Conservation Network: A Case-Study from the Mediterranean." *Global Environmental Politics* 10 (1) (February): 115–51.

Bromberg, G., and V. Qumsieh. 2005. "Advancing Human Security through the Sharing of Water Perspectives in the Middle East." In *Palestinian and Israeli Environmental Narratives: Proceedings of a Conference Held in Association with the Middle East Environmental Futures Project*, edited by S. Schoenfeld, 257–61. Toronto: York University Centre for International and Security Studies.

Calleya, S. C. 2009. "The Union for the Mediterranean: An Exercise in Region Building." *Mediterranean Quarterly* 20 (4) (Fall): 49–70.

Chaitin, J., F. Obeidi, S. Adwan, and D. Bar-On. 2002. "Environmental Work and Peace Work: The Palestinian-Israeli Case." *Peace and Conflict Studies* 9: 64–94.

———. 2004. "Palestinian and Israeli Cooperation in Environmental Work during the 'Peace Era.'" *International Journal of Politics, Culture, and Society* 17(3): 523–42.

Cohen, M. 2006. "The Arava Institute for Environmental Studies: Nature Knows No Borders." In special issue, *Palestine-Israel Journal of Politics, Economics, and Culture* 12 (4)–13 (1).

Della Porta, D., and M. Diani. 2006. *Social Movements: An Introduction.* Hoboken: Wiley and Sons.

Edwards, B., and J. D. McCarthy. 2004. "Resources and Social Movement Mobilization." In *The Blackwell Companion to Social Movements*, edited by D. A. Snow, 116–52. Malden: Blackwell.

Eisenberg, L. Z., and N. Caplan. 2003. "The Israel-Jordan Peace Treaty: Patterns of Negotiation, Problems of Implementation." *Israel Affairs* 9 (3): 87–110.

Feitelson, E., and M. Haddad, eds. 1994. *Joint Management of Shared Aquifers: The First Workshop.* Jerusalem: Harry S. Truman Research Institute and the Palestine Consultancy Group.

———. 1995. *Joint Management of Shared Aquifers: Final Report.* Jerusalem: Harry S. Truman Research Institute and the Palestine Consultancy Group.

———. 1998. *Identification of Joint Water Management Structures for Shared Aquifers: A Cooperative Palestinian Israeli Effort.* Washington: World Bank.

Friends of the Earth Middle East. 2009. www.foeme.org.

Greenspan, Itay. 2005. "Reflections from the 2002 Johannesburg Earth Summit." In *Palestinian and Israeli Environmental Narratives: Proceedings of a Conference Held in Association with the Middle East Environmental Futures Project*, edited by S. Schoenfeld, 75–92. Toronto: York University Centre for International and Strategic Studies.

Guha, R. 2000. *Environmentalism: A Global History.* White Plains: Longmans.

Haddad, M., and E. Feitelson, eds. 1995. *Joint Management of Shared Aquifers: The Second Workshop.* Jerusalem: Harry S. Truman Research Institute and the Palestine Consultancy Group.

———. 1996. *Joint Management of Shared Aquifers: The Third Workshop.* Jerusalem: Harry S. Truman Research Institute and the Palestine Consultancy Group.

Haddadin, M. J. 2000. "Negotiated Resolution of the Jordan-Israel Water Conflict." *International Negotiation* 5: 263–88.

Herzog, S., and A. Hai. 2005. *The Power of Possibility.* Berlin: Friedrich Eburt Stiftung.

International Institute for Sustainable Development. 2009. *The Sustainable Development Timeline–2009.* http://www.iisd.org/publications/pub.aspx?pno=894.

Israel Ministry of Foreign Affairs. 1993. "The Declaration of Principles." http://www.mfa.gov.il/MFA/Peace+Process/Guide+to+the+Peace+Process/Declaration+of+Principles.htm.

———. 1994. "Israel Jordan Peace Treaty." http://www.mfa.gov.il/MFA/Peace%20Process/Guide%20to%20the%20Peace%20Process/Israel-Jordan%20Peace%20Treaty.

———. 1995. "The Israeli-Palestinian Interim Agreement." http://www.mfa.gov.il/MFA/Peace+Process/Guide+to+the+Peace+Process/The+Israeli-Palestinian+Interim+Agreement+-+Main+P.htm.

———. 2007. "The Multilateral Negotiations." http://www.mfa.gov.il/MFA/Peace Process/Guide to the Peace Process/The Multilateral Negotiations.

Jayous, A. 2010. "The Oslo II Accords in Retrospect: Implementation of the Water Provisions in the Israeli and Palestinian Interim Peace Agreements." In *Water Wisdom: Preparing the Groundwork for Cooperative and Sustainable Water Management in the Middle East,* edited by A. Tal and A. Abed Rabbo, 43–48. Rutgers: Rutgers University Press.

Jones, A. 2006. "Narrative-Based Production of State Spaces for International Region Building: Europeanization and the Mediterranean." *Annals of the Association of American Geographers* 96 (2):415–31.

Kerret, Dt. 2010. "Article 40: An Israeli Retrospective." In *Water Wisdom: Preparing the Groundwork for Cooperative and Sustainable Water Management in the Middle East,* edited by A. Tal and A. Abed Rabbo, 49–61. Rutgers: Rutgers University Press.

Lesser, P. 2009. "Greening the Mediterranean: Europe's Environmental Policy toward Mediterranean Neighbors." *Mediterranean Quarterly* 20 (2) (Spring): 26–39.

Pace, M. 2006. *The Politics of Regional Identity: Meddling with the Mediterranean.* London and New York: Routledge.

Palestine Environmental NGO Network. 2004. http://www.pengon.org.

Peres Center for Peace. 2009. www.peres-center.org.

Regional Bureau for Arab States. 2009. *Arab Human Development Report 2009: Human Security in the Arab Countries.* New York: United Nations Development Program.

Schoenfeld, S. 2005. "Types of Environmental Narratives and Their Utility for Understanding Israeli and Palestinian Environmentalism." In *Palestinian and Israeli Environmental Narratives: Proceedings of a Conference Held in Association with the Middle East Environmental Futures Project,* edited by S. Schoenfeld, 93–113. Toronto: York University Centre for International and Security Studies.

———. 2010. "Environment and Human Security in the Eastern Mediterranean: Regional Environmentalism in the Reframing of Palestinian-Israeli-Jordanian Relations." In *Achieving Environmental Security: Ecosystem Services and Human Welfare*, edited by P. H. Liotta, D. Mouat, J. Lancaster, B. Kepner, and D. Smith, 113–31. Amsterdam: IOS Press.

Schoenfeld, S., E. Abitbol, and F. De Chatel. 2007. "Retelling the Story of Water in the Middle East." In *Integrated Water Management and Security in the Middle East*, edited by C. Lipchin, E. Pallant, D. Saranga, and A. Amster, 1–29. Berlin: Springer.

Schoenfeld, S., and J. Rubin. 2011. "Contrasting Regional Environmentalisms in the Eastern Mediterranean: A Social Constructionist Perspective." *L'Espace Politique* 14.

Schoenfeld, S., and A. Zohar. 2009. "Two Peoples in a Shared Ecology: Framing Strategies and Outcomes of a Middle East Environmentalist Initiative." Paper presented at the European Sociology Association, Lisbon, September.

Shuval, H., and H. Dwick. 2006. *Water for Life in the Middle East: Proceedings of the 2nd Israeli-Palestinian International Conference on Water for Life in the Middle East*. 2 vols. Jerusalem: IPCRI.

Tal, A., and A. Abed Rabbo. 2010. *Water Wisdom: Preparing the Groundwork for Cooperative and Sustainable Water Management in the Middle East*. Rutgers: Rutgers University Press.

Tolba, M. K., and N. W. Saab, eds. 2008. *Arab Environment: Future Challenges*. Beirut: Arab Forum for Environment and Development.

———. 2009. *The Impact of Climate Change on Arab Countries*. Beirut: Arab Forum for Environment and Development.

Twite, R. 2005. "The Role of NGOs in Promoting Regional Cooperation over Environmental and Water Issues in Israel and Palestine—Successes and Limitations." In *Palestinian and Israeli Environmental Narratives: Proceedings of a Conference Held in Association with the Middle East Environmental Futures Project*, edited by S. Schoenfeld, 247–55. Toronto: York University Centre for International and Security Studies.

Twite, R., and J. Isaac, eds. 1994. *Our Shared Environment*. Jerusalem: IPCRI.

Twite, R., and R. Menczel, eds. 1995. *Our Shared Environment—The Conference 1994*. Jerusalem: IPCRI.

———. 1996. *Our Shared Environment—The Conference 1995*. Jerusalem: IPCRI.

United Nations Environment Programme. 2003. *Desk Study on the Environment in the Occupied Palestinian Territories*. Nairobi: UNEP.

Wapner, P. 1995. "Politics Beyond the State: Environmental Activism and World Civic Politics." *World Politics* 47: 311–40.

Zak, M. 1995 "Thirty Years of Clandestine Meetings: The Jordan-Israel Peace Treaty." *Middle East Quarterly* 2: 1. http://www.meforum.org/article/241.

Zohar, A., S. Schoenfeld, and I. Alleson. 2008. "Nurturing Leaders in Peacebuilding and Coexistence: The Case of the Arava Institute for Environmental Studies." Paper presented at Eighth International Conference of the International Society for Third Sector Research (ISTR), Universtat de Barcelona, Barcelona, Spain, July.

Zwirn, M. J. 2001. "Promise and Failure: Environmental NGOs and Palestinian-Israeli Cooperation." *Middle East Review of International Affairs* 5 (4) (December): 116–26.

CHAPTER SEVENTEEN

THE FUTURE OF THE ISRAELI ENVIRONMENTAL MOVEMENT
Is a Major Paradigm Shift Under Way?

Daniel E. Orenstein and Emily Silverman

THE GOALS AND METHODS OF the environmental organizations in Israel have changed profoundly over the sixty years since the founding of the state. Israeli scholars have pointed to a broad paradigm shift from an early romantic, nature-centered approach to a more pragmatic, public-health emphasis, relying on tools of science, law, and land-use planning (de-Shalit 1995; Tal 2002; Schwartz 2009). At a global scale, paradigm shifts within the environmental movement have also been suggested, representing periods of extreme change with regard to priority environmental issues and policy prescriptions (Carter 2007). Citing the continuing global environmental crisis, some advocate for a new paradigm shift in Israel (Schwartz 2009) and similarly in the United States (Shellenberger and Nordhaus 2005) that would integrate social issues into the environmental agenda. In this chapter, we examine whether the environmental movement in Israel is on the cusp of a paradigm shift toward convergence with a broader social justice agenda. We use case studies of three relatively recent campaigns to ponder the current and future trajectory of the environmental movement in Israel.

An important contextual note: the history of the young Israeli environmental movement is being written by active participants who are creating that same history (look no further than this very edited volume, as its authors all have been intimately involved in the same environmental history that they are writing), rather than by more sober and detached historical analysts. In this chapter, we quote widely from the writings of these participants. Further, we—the authors of this chapter—are not only participants in the same environmental movement, but also colleagues and friends of many of the primary actors.

PARADIGM SHIFTS IN THE ENVIRONMENTAL MOVEMENT: A HISTORICAL OVERVIEW

Scholars of environmental studies describe broad paradigm shifts in the development of the environmental movement in the developed world (e.g., Europe, the United States, and Japan). Carter (2007), for example, describes three "generations" of environmental issues (table 17.1). Prior to the 1960s, the first generation focused on preservation of wildlife and habitats and was represented by economic elite and middle-class interest in aesthetics, hiking, hunting, and other forms of nature recreation. Other prominent issues on the environmental agenda were soil conservation and dealing with localized environmental problems, which were generally by-products of a century of industrialization. The second generation of issues, emerging during the 1960s, has been termed "modern environmentalism." Among the main issues confronted by this generation were population growth, the environmental impact of technology, air pollution, safe drinking water, hazardous waste management, and pesticide use.

Notably, it was during this period that environmentalism evolved into a broader ideology and political movement framed around questions of values and behaviors. Accordingly, the environmental movement became a mass movement drawing from all sectors of society, as exemplified by society-wide participation in the first Earth Day in 1970 (Carter 2007). Beginning in the mid-1970s, Carter suggests, a new, third generation began to think about global issues such as acid rain, ozone depletion, climate change, and loss of global biodiversity. These activists and professionals pushed for and responded to the proliferation of environmental policies and regulatory bureaucracies to promote and enforce new environmental laws and agreements at the national and international levels.

Conco and Debelko (1998) suggest a similar transition is witnessed in the differences between the 1972 United Nations Conference on the Environment in Stockholm, which is symbolic of Carter's second generation, and the 1992 United Nations Conference on Environment and Development in Rio, which is more reminiscent of the third generation (or even the fourth, as we will describe below). The Stockholm Conference was characterized by narrow representation of government representatives focusing on air and water pollution. The latter, by contrast, was attended by a broad range of government representatives, nongovernmental organizations, and grassroots activists and was centered on large-scale and integrated global ecology issues. Further, Conco

TABLE 17.1. Phases of development of the global and Israeli environmental movement

Carter (2007) *Phases of development in the global environmental movement*	de-Shalit (1995) *Predominant Zionist and Israeli attitudes to the environment*	Schwartz (2009) *Paradigms within the Israeli environmental movement*
PRESERVATION AND CONSERVATION MOVEMENTS *Pre-1960s* -"Middle class interest in the protection of wildlife, wilderness and natural resources"	ROMANTIC RURALISM *Early twentieth century* -Infusing nature with quasi-religious meaning, reconnecting Jews with the physical land -Latent anxiety plants seeds of desire to transform landscape -Instrumental and romantic	NATURE PRESERVATION *Prior to 1980s* -Goal of protecting nature from development -Deep roots in the Zionist movement -Nature education for strengthening attachment to the land
	THE ETHOS OF DEVELOPMENT *1930s to late 1980s* -Conquest of nature -Civilizing the environment -Afforestation -Swamp drainage -Urban development -Instrumental and rational	
MODERN ENVIRONMENTALISM *1960s to 1970s* -Popular concern about the environment; proliferation of environmental discourse -Global ecological crisis threatens humanity -Political and activist mass movement demanding radical transformation in values and societal structure	MODERN ENVIRONMENTALISM *Late 1980s through mid-1990s* -Scientifically based philosophy derived from ecology and environmental sciences -Decline in anxiety about the landscape -Rational and noninstrumental	PUBLIC HEALTH *1980s to the present* -Refocus on individual well-being -Humans as part of the environment rather than separate from nature -Values subservient to "objective" science
GLOBAL ISSUES *1970s to present* -Institutionalization of environmentalism, with national ministries, organizations, and policy at the national and global level		PLACE-BASED ENVIRONMENTALISM *The present* -Creating a vision of a good society and a healthy environment -Synthesis of lessons of previous phases, addressing deficiencies, but emphasizing advantages -Humans as integral part of natural world who must define how to best integrate -Public health is an extension of good environmental planning and management (e.g., what is good for nature is good for people and vice versa)

and Debelko note that, in 1972 not all governments had national-level environmental bureaucracies, while twenty years later virtually all nations represented at the Rio conference did. A final important difference was the internationalization of environmental problems. In Stockholm, the agenda was set largely by the industrialized nations, while at Rio the developing world had much greater influence on setting the conference agenda.

A fourth generation of environmentalism began to emerge around the time of the Rio Conference, and ever since has evolved into a broader-based political movement that emphasizes environmental problems as a symptom of more fundamental societal problems of poverty, economic and social inequality, and the loss of communal identity. The Global Greens, a coordinating body of national Green Parties around the world, provides a telling example. Its charter, approved by members from seventy-two countries, elevates to the forefront of Green politics the following six principles: ecological wisdom, social justice ("equitable distribution of social and natural resources"), participatory democracy, nonviolence, sustainability ("provide for the needs of the present and future generations within the finite resources of the earth"), and respect for diversity (Global Greens 2001).

An evolution toward linking environmental to socioeconomic and political issues seems to comply with the theme of Shellenberger and Nordhaus' controversial tome, "The Death of Environmentalism" (2005). This analysis of the American environmental dynamics advocates for a broad-based coalition to combat climate change while simultaneously addressing socioeconomic issues. It recommends bringing together labor groups and environmental groups, as well as private- and public-sector investment, in common cause. Because of their emphasis on markets, these authors' worldview seems to diverge from the Global Greens in economic terms, and Shellenberger and Nordhaus oppose the use of "environmental justice" as a distraction; it is, they claim, ineffectual in addressing the needs of weaker segments of society (Nordhaus and Shellenberger 2007). Both they and the Greens, however, seek to broaden the base of environmental thinking to incorporate social and economic well-being.

The Israeli environmental movement has undergone similar paradigm shifts (de-Shalit 1995; Tal 2002; Schwartz 2009). Similar to the early stages of the American environmental movement, it began with a romantic emphasis on nature preservation. The first Zionist settlers (at least those who represented the Labor Zionist stream of the movement) attached mythical qualities to land and the nature within, as a crucial component of their national redemption. Yet, de-Shalit describes a collective anxiety about the natural environment in Palestine and the beginnings of settlers' strong desire to transform the landscape to something more familiar. From the 1930s this anxiety would lead to a development paradigm that eclipsed sympathies for nature preservation. Those individuals who clung to nature preservation in the face of this push for economic growth and development found themselves relegated to the margins of Israeli society. Yet this cohort would nonetheless form the core of the new Israeli environmental movement that emerged in the early 1950s.

That was when protectors of nature in Israel came together in opposition to the draining of the Hula wetlands as proposed by the Jewish National Fund. The opposition consisted of academics from the biological sciences (ecologists, zoologists, botanists), alongside kibbutz members and young activists. They founded a new organization, the Society for Protection of Nature in Israel (SPNI), whose name reflected their preservationist ambitions (Tal 2002). The emphasis in Israel on establishing nature reserves and protecting attractive, charismatic species is similar to the early years of the American environmental movement, which was symbolized by such figures as John Muir in the early years and later by the Sierra Club's David Brower.

The nature preservation focus was a direct result of the cultural context in which the movement founders lived—like their fellow pro-development citizens, they were infused with Zionist ideology. These "pioneer" environmentalists believed that Jews were returning to Israel to redeem themselves and the Jewish nation by reconnecting to the historic, physical, and biological land of Israel (Tal 2002, 2006). Israeli author and Knesset member Yizhar Smilanski's 1962 speech to the Knesset, a plea to protect open spaces, is exemplary in this regard: "A land where the breeze blows without wildflowers is a place of suffocation. A land where winds cannot blow uninterrupted will be a hotel, not a homeland. A land that is all roads and sidewalks and a sense of ultimate construction will devour all good portions in the hearts of its young people."

Smilanski concludes with a rhetorical, Zionist question: "What should the leaders of the nation do if they want the people of this land to love their land?" (quoted in Tal 2006, 21–24). The answer for Smilanski was to preserve open space and the nature within.

Israeli scholars and activists emphasize the close links between early Israeli environmentalism and the political ideology of Zionism (de-Shalit 1995). There was a synergy, which continues to this day, between activists' desire to protect landscapes that they considered part of their cultural identity and the use of national parks and reserves for the purposes of emphasizing Jewish and Israeli culture and history. For Eilon Schwartz, director of the Heschel Center for Environmental Learning and Leadership, this particular focus for the environmental movement was a unique feature of the first paradigm of Israeli environmental thinking (Schwartz 2009). He recalls how Jewish youth would be "consecrated" through national hikes (Ben-David 1997) and by acquiring encyclopedic knowledge of the trees, flowers, birds, and mammals of the Land of Israel. The formal and informal educational system was co-opted to instill in the youth an appreciation of the natural history of Israel (also see Gordon in this volume). The SPNI, as the first Israeli environmental organization and a major educational body, was founded within this social-cultural milieu and became instrumental in perpetuating it.

The second environmental paradigm in Israel began in the 1980s, toward what de-Shalit calls a scientifically based environmental philosophy, focusing primarily on public health (Tal 2002; Schwartz 2009). These dates follow closely after Carter's "second generation" of global environmental issues (1960s–1970s), catalyzed by the discovery of mercury poisoning in Minamata Bay, Japan (1959), and the publication of Rachel Carson's *Silent Spring* (1962), among other events. New environmental organizations began to focus on public-health issues, the most prominent of those in the initial wave was "Malraz—The Public Council against Noise and Air Pollution" (Tal 2002). Though Malraz was responsible for dozens of grassroots anti-nuisance campaigns, the organization's stature was nonetheless eclipsed by SPNI's public profile during these years (Tal 2002).

Israel's transition from the romantic to the scientific paradigm of environmentalism is captured in the Voice of America (VOA) controversy. In the mid-1980s, the American administration proposed to build a VOA radio transmission station in Israel's northern Arava Valley (Ministry of Environment 1993). Environmentalists opposed the project on nature-driven grounds: the radio towers and the radiation that they would emit would have disrupted bird migration patterns over the Arava, and relatively pristine areas of the Negev desert would be violated by the relocation of Air Force training activities. Local residents added a new type of opposition, arguing from a public-health perspective that the electromagnetic radiation from the proposed towers would constitute a potential health risk.

There is some dispute over which argument was more significant in the decision to cancel the project: de-Shalit asserts that the public-health emphasis had the most significant effect on delaying the station construction (de-Shalit and Talias 1994; de-Shalit 2001); Tal gives much of the credit to the environmental movement, and the SPNI in particular, for bringing the concern for the Arava landscape and the migrating bird populations to public awareness and actively delaying the project until it was eventually cancelled by a new American administration (Tal 2002). Perhaps more attention should be given to the synergistic overlap between the two agendas of nature preservation and public-health concerns. Each agenda resonated with some of the public, or both together influenced individuals, and the combination of agendas and their public impact created enough opposition to delay the project until it was ultimately canceled, albeit for unrelated reasons.

By the early 1990s, the SPNI had become more diversified in its national agenda and increasingly grassroots in its orientation—also a reflection of the larger transformation occurring in Europe and the United States. Local SPNI chapters began to set their agendas in response to issues of environmental importance close to home. They were joined by a proliferation of new environmental organizations with unique, often site-specific, agendas (Tal 2002; Schwartz 2009). Many issues of concern for the SPNI chapters and for many of the new environmental organizations in the 1990s had a public-health focus. Further, major environmental organizations put public health in the center of their activities, including *Adam Teva V'Din*—the Israeli Union of Environmental Defense (IUED; air quality, waste, water quality, and quantity), the Coalition for Public Health (environmental health risks), and Green Course (air quality, waste, water, public transportation).

In the first decade of the twenty-first century, environmental values have proliferated into every aspect of Israeli life. From a mere handful of environmental organizations in the 1950s and '60s, Life and Environment, the umbrella organization of many of Israel's environmental organizations, now claims well over one hundred members. These operate on the local, regional, and national scene and are widely diverse in their issues of concern and target constituencies. All media outlets regularly cover environmental issues. Environmental representatives sit on the national planning board. Representatives of the Israel Green Party have been elected to municipal government, and are, in several cases, an integral part of governing coalitions in municipalities. Environmental organizations have advocated successfully to enact a broad range of environmental laws and environmental concerns that are prominent in Israel's long-term national development plan (National Outline Plan 35).

Despite these gains in activism, media coverage, public support, and electoral presence, many argue that the environmental agenda in Israel is still too limited to bring about lasting change. In 2010, for example, the Green Environment Fund, a consortium of funders of environmental organizations in Israel, launched a process to identify means to expand the agenda of the environmental movement, catalyzing a broader debate among the leadership.

Also in response to the belief that movement gains have not been enough to create an environmentally sustainable society, Schwartz (2009) suggests the need for a new "place-based" paradigm, combining the advantages of the nature preservation and the public-health approaches with a community-based component. In such a paradigm, humans would increasingly see themselves as part of natural systems, and nature would be seen as an intricate part of the human day-to-day living experience, rather than something separate, removed, and untouched. Schwartz calls for the environmental movement to develop a more pluralistic and inclusive agenda, including such pressing issues as rapid population growth, increased material consumption, militarism, and the inequitable distribution of wealth.

A CONVERGENCE OF ENVIRONMENTAL AND SOCIAL AGENDAS?

Has the environmental movement in Israel embraced the notion that environmental challenges are driven by particular social and economic factors that need to be addressed? We use three environmental campaign case studies to assess whether the environmental movement's agenda has been converging with that of the social justice movement, or whether social and environmental movements work together primarily for convenience. Did the environmental groups, on the one hand, and social justice groups, on the other, arrive at similar conclusions regarding the root causes of problems and the ways to address them, revealing a convergence of views and values? Or did they come together for tactical reasons to jointly attack the same problem from different perspectives, suggesting a merger of convenience? Or has an overlap emerged because the leadership of environmental and social justice groups is drawn from the same social milieu or activist pool, whether or not the movement as a whole supports the joint message (fig. 17.1)?

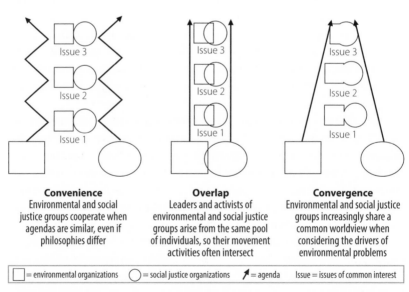

Convenience
Environmental and social justice groups cooperate when agendas are similar, even if philosophies differ

Overlap
Leaders and activists of environmental and social justice groups arise from the same pool of individuals, so their movement activities often intersect

Convergence
Environmental and social justice groups increasingly share a common worldview when considering the drivers of environmental problems

☐ = environmental organizations   ◯ = social justice organizations   ➤ = agenda   Issue = issues of common interest

FIGURE 17.1. Possible trajectories of collaboration between the environmental and social justice movements.

For each case, we look at the goals and the people involved, probing whether the campaign transcended traditional "green goals" (e.g., clean air and water, open space) to include a social agenda (e.g., employment opportunities in low-income areas, access to affordable housing and to transport, and spatial integration). We consider whether the leaders and activists were drawn from the social justice movement alongside the environmental movement, and whether the campaign integrated the needs of low-income or marginal groups in society. We also seek to understand how the combination of social and environmental agendas influenced the outcome of the campaign.

CAMPAIGN ONE: THE TRANS-ISRAEL HIGHWAY

The fight against the Trans-Israel Highway (Route 6) was one of the paramount priorities of the national Israeli environmental movement throughout much of the 1990s—and is usually considered one of its more conspicuous failures (Tal 2002; Garb 2004; Maizlish 2005). Despite the failure at blocking the grandiose North–South toll highway, the campaign is credited with changing the image and style of the environmental movement in Israel (see Maizlish 2005 for a detailed description of the campaign activities and an analysis of the lessons to be learned for organizers). During the course of the campaign, the message changed from aesthetic concerns to protection of open space, and then to the problems of car dependency and the need for investment in public transit, particularly rail. Here, we look at the extent to which the campaign evolved to include a social justice message, alongside the more traditional environmental concerns.

The initial opposition to the highway was late in coming. Its route was first approved in 1976, as part of the National Outline Plan for Roads (NOP 3 1976). In 1993 the Society for Protection of Nature in Israel initially suggested minor changes in the route to reduce the roadway's aesthetic impact and to protect sites of particular natural beauty or interest.

The IUED was then asked to take a stronger stance and petitioned the Supreme Court, in their first major case concerning planning and open space (Maizlish 2005). The legal argument was largely procedural, objecting to the lack of an *integrated* Environmental Impact Statement, in contrast to the analysis of each discrete segment of the road. The Supreme Court rejected the legal petition, and the Highway Company marketed the rejection as a triumph for the highway, a nail in the coffin of the environmentalists' objections.

Environmentalists continued to oppose the highway's construction. By 1995, the SPNI was running full-page newspaper advertisements charging that the road would cut through open landscape on the eastern border with the Palestinian-administered territories, irreparably damaging favorite hiking grounds, wildflowers, and wildlife habitats.

But this limited, first-generation paradigm message seemed particularly weak when contrasted to the arguments marshaled in favor of the highway: it would bring economic prosperity by improving access to the geographic periphery; enable young families to build single-family homes in previously remote areas; and would be built at nearly no cost to the taxpayer, through a "Build-Operate-and-Transfer" mechanism (Garb 2004). The star-studded leadership of the highway company, headed by a popular former IDF chief of staff with the founding general director of the Ministry of Environment and highly respected landscape architects, used clever military tactics to establish the highway as part of the national ethos. They named the road "The Way of the Land," erected signposts declaring "This Way to Highway 6" at major road intersections years before any construction had begun, and distributed hundreds of thousands of free maps of Israel marking the highway as fact (Garb 2004). A few years later, after the assassination of the Yitzhak Rabin, highway planners declared that the future highway would be named after, and thus immortalize, the prime minister. By contrast environmentalists' arguments of the high-speed roadway's damage to wildflowers may have seemed petty, elitist, or anti-progress.

The campaign message and tactics began to change as the opposition's leadership spread from the SPNI old guard to younger activists from the newly formed Green Course and the radical Green Action. Camping in tents on construction sites and confronting bulldozers while riding bicycles (and wearing superhero capes), they argued that mass highways were old-style economic development, and that true economic progress involved freedom from car-dependency and increased investment in public transit.

The SPNI listened, and, along with a new professional transit advocacy organization, Transport Today and Tomorrow, began to include new messages and new partners: the highway would swallow vast tracts of public land and bring low-density urban sprawl; the costs of the highway to the taxpayer would be high, since the Build-Operate-Transfer (BOT) funding mechanism required the government to guarantee revenues up to a high threshold (Garb 1999), and this money should be spent on rail not roads. They also argued that the highway was not fairly compensating Arab towns and Jewish rural communities whose lands would be confiscated for road construction and whose quality of life would be compromised through proximity to the highway.

There were other groups opposed to the road. Landowners, including Jewish collective communities and Arab villages, along the proposed highway route opposed the confiscation of their land for road construction and the potential noise nuisance that would come from the road (Maranz 1993). There was also a potential for opposition to the road on economic grounds, as the road would draw away funding from public transportation and discriminate against citizens who were dependent on those modes of transportation (Fletcher 1999).

While there was some degree of collaboration between landowners and environmentalists, in retrospect, it appears that the alliances across these partners were mostly tactical, and not really a convergence of environmental, social, and economic concerns. The landowners were motivated by "how" questions, rather than "why," and their claims were resolved with adjustments to the road's route and compensation (Garb 2004). The environmentalists, meanwhile, never reached out for a broad-based coalition with the economically disadvantaged, never tried to find common ground that the highway discriminated against those with less access to private automobiles and thus dependent on public transportation (Fletcher 1999), and didn't manage to enlist the mayors and populations in the urban centers in support of funding for public transit. The environmentalists also remained largely agnostic to the geopolitical implications of the highway route, which created a de facto border for the many Arab Israeli towns that now found themselves to the east of the major highway.

With the wisdom of hindsight, the anti-highway campaign may have failed (the highway has long since been paved and even lengthened and widened), but the new alliances formed in the campaign against the Trans-Israel Highway signals a transition within the widening environmental movement to broaden its messages and membership. The struggle may also have contributed to the major increase in budget for rail—from 90 million NIS in 1995 to 1 billion in 2003 (Maizlish 2005). Yet the campaign did not promote a full-fledged third-paradigm approach to public transportation as the economically, socially, and environmentally preferred alternative to road construction.

CAMPAIGN TWO: PRESERVATION OF OPEN SPACES IN THE NEGEV

The social and environmental challenges posed by residential development in the Negev provide excellent case studies of how the social and environmental movements interact over an issue of potentially shared interest. Bedouin and various Jewish communities desire to expand residential settlement, while environmental groups have sought to preserve open spaces and prevent urban and exurban sprawl and social justice groups seek equitable settlement policies for all Negev residents. To understand the perspective of the environmental movement on this heated topic, a short background on open-space preservation as an environmental issue is required.

Open-space preservation has been a perennial high-priority issue of the Israeli environmental movement since the 1950s, although the goals and foci have changed. In early open-space preservation campaigns that sought to save landscapes in their perceived pristine condition, agricultural development was seen as threat. Today, with urbanization and transportation-infrastruc-ture development seen as much greater threats to open space, agriculture has increasingly been viewed as another form of open space worthy of protection. Environmentalists increasingly speak in terms of cultural landscapes and ad-vocate for farmland preservation relying on historic, aesthetic, and cultural values (Egoz 1996; Feitelson 1999), not unlike modern farmland-preservation discourse in North America and Europe.

The diversified approach to open spaces, not only as natural areas, but as areas for human use, often appears in government and environmental NGO discourse at the beginning of the twenty-first century. The comprehensive na-tional outline plan (NOP 35) for urban development and open-space preser-vation embodies this approach in its definition of various types of landscape templates to protect, ranging from agricultural to natural (Assif and Shachar 2005; Han in this volume).

The Open Landscape Institute (DESHE) is explicit in its vision statement: "Open spaces are the basis of life for people and natural phenomena alike. The unique natural and cultural heritage found in Israel, so meaningful to Jews, Muslims and Christians here and around the world, is found in [Israel's] open landscapes. Safeguarding our open landscapes is essential for the supply of vital environmental and social services that will ensure the quality of life for Israel's ever-growing population" (DESHE 2010).

The DESHE statement suggests that a third-paradigm merger of social and environmental concerns is under way. Environmentalists, the statement sug-gests, should prioritize quality of life and access to all scales of public space—from the neighborhood and regional parks to wilderness preservation—for all of Israel's diverse citizens.

Such a paradigm shift is not without its problems. One difficult dilemma still challenging the convergence of the social and environmental paradigms concerns the conflict between preservation of open space and the develop-ment needs of the large Arab-Israeli minority (see Tarabeih in this volume). These citizens live in separate towns with a far less developed urban infra-structure. While Jewish Israeli environmentalists tend to perceive the pres-ervation of open space as a common good, Israel's Arab citizens frequently experience efforts to preserve open space as merely another restriction placed upon Arab towns and villages to prevent their development (Khamaisi 2006).

This feeling is exacerbated when considering a culturally different per-ception of "open spaces" (Benstein 2003) and the long history in Israel of dis-crimination with regard to access to land reserves for development (Yiftachel and Meir 1998; Tarabeih in this volume). We can learn about whether a sec-ond to third paradigm shift is occurring by observing the response of the environmental movement to this quandary: does the environmental movement consider the social impacts of open-space preservation and if so, for whom? The case study of Negev residential development may provide some answers.

Approximately half of the Negev's 160,000 Bedouin live in villages whose legal status on the land the state does not recognize. Further, rapid population growth in this community has led to residential development on open-space reserves not designated for such uses in statutory master plans (Yahel 2006; Tal 2008). The phenomenon typically is described in politically charged terms, whether as:

- Bedouin expressing their legitimate rights to live in the Negev;
- an inevitable outcome of the inability of the state and the Bedouin to come to a mutually agreeable long-term solution regarding land owner-ship and settlement; or
- general disregard for Israeli law displayed by the Bedouin, at the expense of preservation of ecological integrity or, alternatively, potential future Zionist settlements in the Negev.

Despite broadly accepted planning principles not to establish new residen-tial settlements in Israel as embodied in the legislated National Outline Plan 35 (Assif and Shachar 2005), new Jewish ranches and settlements have been promoted and established in contravention of established planning norms (Yonah and Saporta 2002; Alfasi 2006; Orenstein and Hamburg 2009; also see Han in this volume). These ranches and settlements are often promoted as responses to the "demographic challenge" posed by the Bedouin to the state in the Negev. There are three discourses that characterize the opposition to these new communities:

- *the environmental discourse*—detached, low-density settlements are environmentally harmful;
- *the justice discourse*—we cannot provide residential opportunities to Jewish residents while denying Bedouin the same; and
- *the rule-of-law discourse*—these settlements were established without fol-lowing the proper planning procedures and are often in direct violation of them, a discourse that is also used with regard to the Bedouin (Alfasi 2006; Yahel 2006).[1]

A broad, unofficial coalition of opposition has indeed developed around the establishment of Jewish single-family ranches in the Negev, ranging from Bimkom, an NGO of progressive urban and regional planners, and The Arab Center for Alternative Planning, representing the justice discourse, to IUED and SPNI, representing the environmental discourse. Tal (2008) suggests that environmentalists found it useful to raise the rule-of-law discourse in particular to effectively gain support and garner governmental opposition to the ranches.

A 2003 SPNI position paper on the topic of new settlements and ranches affirmed the social as well as the environmental impact of these controversial new communities. It lists under the anticipated social impact of such new settlement development: (1) drawing higher-income families away from existing cities, thereby leaving the cities with poorer population; (2) introducing competition for new members with existing smaller communities, and (3) drawing public funding away from communities with greater needs. The SPNI concludes its position paper with a lofty statement calling on settlement policy to focus on providing for the residential needs of the entire population and closing the economic and social gaps between all sectors, including between Arabs and Jews (Han et al. 2003).

But while there is an ad hoc coalition of environmental and social justice organizations united in its opposition to single-family farms and a limited cross-fertilization of ideas, there are also crucial differences in their approaches to the issue that do not suggest a true convergence. Alongside that rhetoric of social justice, for example, the SPNI document also continues to employs terminology that refers to the "demographic problem"—a blatant euphemism for describing regions in the country with more Arabs than Jews, used to justify land-use policies that discriminate against Arab citizens of Israel (Orenstein and Hamburg 2009): "Demographic balance is a desirable and important goal, although scattering many small and weak settlements does not contribute significantly to enlarging the Jewish population in the periphery. For the price of new communities, it would be possible to attract a large portion of the public to existing cities and smaller communities. Establishing new points of settlement . . . not only does not help strengthen the periphery, but it also places an economic and social burden on existing communities and in this way saps their strength" (Han et al. 2003, 6).

This statement does not suggest that inequitable access to environmental resources (land) is the problem to be addressed, but rather objects to the inappropriate geographic placement of new Jewish settlements. Their simultaneous condemnation of all forms of illegal settlement (e.g., ranches and unrecognized Bedouin settlement) ignores the very different underlying drivers and significance of each phenomenon, while exposing them to criticism from not only advocates for the Bedouin, but also Jewish-Zionist advocates. For example, at a 2010 meeting of the Israel Union of Ecology and Environmental Sciences, audience members chastised an SPNI speaker who spoke critically about Jewish ranches for ignoring the proliferation of Bedouin settlements in the Negev.

For their part, social justice organizations[2] generally do not include environmental considerations in their discourse on Negev settlement, as reflected in a recent comprehensive report on the situation of the unrecognized Bedouin villages (Yehudkin 2007). In fact, this report attempts to downplay fears of uncontrolled sprawling Bedouin development across the Negev by citing the amount of land claimed by Bedouins as a percentage of total area (640,000 dunam, or less than 5.0 percent of the total area of Beer-Sheva subdistrict). The one exception in this report in which environmental issues are addressed is reference to residents of unrecognized villages living without proper infrastructure (water, sewage, roads). All environmental concerns are shown to be interpreted through the lens of social injustice.

A stronger collaboration between environmental and social justice organizations on the issue of single-family ranches could have yielded mutually desired results but seemed to have lacked true convergence of ideas. The ranches are detrimental to open spaces, disperse road and sewage infrastructure in the Negev inefficiently, and are contrary to the higher-density planning vision set out in NOP 35. They also represent an extreme example of social injustice, in which Jewish families, from anywhere in the country, are authorized to establish superlow-density ranches on large plots, while local Bedouin families are restricted from agricultural practices and land claims. Despite the potential for common action among environmental and social activists, in 2010 the Knesset was able to pass legislation authorizing the ranches and their discriminatory impact. Arguably, a shared vision for equitable and environmentally sound Negev settlement and collaborative campaign might have prevented such a setback. And had the groups so coalesced, they might have served as an example of Schwartz's third paradigm (e.g., Orenstein 2007), which calls for a true integration of social justice and environmental goals.

CAMPAIGN THREE: HIRIYA, FROM LANDFILL TO URBAN PARK

Official approval to transform an enormous garbage dump at Hiriya into one of the country's largest metropolitan national parks is usually considered among the major environmental successes of the decade. *Time* magazine once described the Hiriyah site as "a symbol of national sloppiness and ecological neglect" (Beyer 1998), but a major environmental campaign led to a dramatic reversal of its condition, leading to plans to establish there an innovative 700-hectare urban park. As the Israel Union for Environmental Defense writes on its website: "The park will, in the future, serve two million residents in the Gush Dan area and in the whole country, and will be a symbol of environmental and social justice across the generations. Although the process has gone on for many years, the strength and dedication to purpose has paid off."[3]

The plans for the park and the campaign to receive governmental planning permission have been documented from numerous angles, including the environmental benefits of the park (Ministry of Environment 2005), the park design and landscaping (Alon-Mozes 2011), the peculiar role of philanthropy in influencing planning (Ronen-Rotem 2011), and the "privatization of planning" (Arad-Tzvi 2010). Here we focus on a key conflict in the campaign that elucidates the tensions between environmental and social approaches: should the park be used to help regenerate adjacent dilapidated neighborhoods, or should its purpose be to preserve open space? At the heart of the conflict was a controversial proposal to develop housing on some of the park land.

The first vision for the park was launched by the Israel Lands Authority (ILA) in 1995, two years after the decision to close the waste-disposal site. The ILA plan, drawn up by architects Shamai Assif and Na'ama Maizels, emphasized the social transformation of the nearby run-down neighborhoods as well as urban needs for recreation and green open space (Assif 1996). The plans included a significant component of real-estate activity: about two thousand homes, some public buildings, and office structures were to be located adjacent to new "gates" into the park.

The rationale for including these homes and workspaces was in accordance with the prevailing concept that real-estate revenues could be used to leverage park funding. A second rationale was more explicitly rooted in urban design: to frame the area around the park, provide attractive new entrance points, and change the image of the surrounding neighborhoods "from the backyard of Tel Aviv to the front court of the metropolitan area." A change was indeed in order—two of the neighborhoods bordering the park were home to hundreds of illegally constructed tin shanties, possibly the highest concentration of poverty in the entire metropolitan region (fig. 17.2).

During the second stage of planning, responsibility for master-planning the park was transferred from the ILA to the Ministry of Interior's district planning office in Tel Aviv. The district plans were strongly influenced by an unanticipated player—Martin Weill, the charismatic former chief curator of the Israel Museum and newly appointed head of the philanthropic Bracha Foundation. Weill saw the landfill as "a sore in the very belly of the country," and proposed funding to transform the landfill into a park, including an international architectural competition that would ensure high standards of design (Y. Farhi, pers. comm., April 16, 2009; M. Weill, pers. comm., June 21, 2009).

FIGURE 17.2. (*Opposite*) From Landfill to Central Park. A vision for the Ayalon Park (*above*) and an adjacent neighborhood of Argazim (*below*). Environmental activists wanted to assure no building in the park boundaries, while some social activists suggested that a limited amount of construction could have provided a lift to nearby impoverished communities. Photograph above reprinted with permission of Park Ayalon. Photograph below by E. Silverman.

373

The new district plan reenvisioned the park, from an urban park with uses aimed at local residents, to a metropolitan-level park serving the entire Gush Dan region. It downplayed the original social objectives and aspects of neighborhood planning, and focused exclusively on the design and management of open spaces. Among the environmental challenges addressed were solving hydrological problems of drainage, methane capture, and utilization in the former landfill; flood containment and sewage runoff; the hazards of landfill closure; and waste treatment and recycling (Plessner, Guggenheim, and Kaplan 1997; Ministry of Interior 2003).

The district plans initially incorporated the previous proposals for residential and office construction (Plessner et al. 1997) in discrete areas of the park. Mayors of the adjacent towns also supported including an aspect of real-estate development in the plan, vying among themselves for development and assessment rights (D. Sapir, pers. comm., May 20, 2009; D. Sternberg, pers. comm., April 16, 2009; A. Tzach, pers. comm., June 21, 2009). In 2003 the National Planning and Building Commission submitted the plans for formal statutory approval, including limited residential development (Ministry of Interior 2003).

The modest proportions of development were challenged by private landholders within the park territory, who requested substantial additional development rights, proposing ten thousand units of housing and high-rise office buildings on lands earmarked for recreation. The landholders and their representatives were well known in Israel as "real estate sharks" with a history of shrewdly reaping massive profits by rezoning agricultural land as commercial real estate. The landholders were also notorious for their ability to enlist politicians and planning officials in support of profitable development plans (Lichtman 2004; Rinat 2004).

It was at this point that the environmental organizations got involved. In an unusual move, the district planners and the philanthropic funder decided to work together to launch an all-out campaign to preserve the entire area as open space for future generations, with no development whatsoever (N. Angel, pers. comm., April 16, 2009; Y. Farhi, pers. comm. April 16, 2009). This coalition reached out to recruit environmental NGOs, which had tacitly supported the plans, but had not yet been actively involved (Arad-Tzvi 2010). The IUED then challenged the legal rights of the landholders (in this case, the HaZera Company, who had leased the land for agricultural purposes from the Israel Lands Authority), while the Tel Aviv branch of the SPNI headed up the public campaign to keep the future park free of development. SPNI reasoned that parks, like hospitals and trains, could and should be funded by the state, without reliance on the private sector (M. Mahadav, pers. comm., May 20, 2009). The foundation also hired a lobbyist, who worked hard to enlist local mayors in a joint agreement to renounce all development claims within the park. Facing an election year in 2003, the mayors may have wanted to distance themselves from any taint of corruption and agreed to drop all claims to development (D. Sapir, pers. comm., May 20, 2009; A. Tzach, pers. comm., June 21, 2009).

The landholders responded by hiring their own lobbyist—a former staffer at the IUED—who used a surprising tactic. On November 16, 2004, they published ads in national newspapers crudely headlined "The Greens Are Screwing the Blacks," claiming that environmentalists were killing the park at the expense of the poor families of Sephardic (locally known as Oriental or "Mizrachi") origins in the area, by pursuing long-range fantasies of open space that would never be funded (Rinat 2004). The ad, which generated much media buzz, was published in the name of six Mizrachi neighborhood leaders from the area.

The environmental organizations struck back, arguing that local residents would benefit the most from the park-as-green-space. They enlisted a network of local activists and an environmentalist active in the Mizrachi Rainbow Forum (a social justice organization). Together, they managed to convince the signatories to publicly retract and announce their support for a development-free park (S. Avidan, pers. comm., April 16, 2009; R. Hananel, pers. comm., May 7, 2009). Leading environmental activists later acknowledged that they never held discussions among themselves or with local residents about the potential benefits of moderate development, since the pressing campaign required uncompromising opposition to the plans of the specific landholders, and therefore to any development at all (M. Mahadav, pers. comm., May 20, 2009). At least two of the environmentalists in retrospect acknowledged that some degree of development in the park might indeed be beneficial for local residents, the surrounding cities, and the park itself (I. Han, pers. comm., April 16, 2009; M. Mahadav, pers. comm., May 20, 2009). It could also be argued that the low-income local residents would have benefited more directly through gaining immediate access to the extensive adjacent botanic gardens at Mikveh Yisrael, currently lacking funding and closed to the public. On November 11, 2004, a subcommittee of the National Planning and Building Committee unanimously approved the plans for the park with no development rights (see Arad-Tzvi 2010 for a nuanced description of the unprecedented intervention by the prime minister, who personally instructed government representatives to vote against development in the park). As of the summer of 2010, the park is still largely unfunded, and the adjacent areas have become ever-more run down.

Does this case represent a third paradigm convergence of the environmental and the social agendas? After all, the SPNI was able to draw on a net-

work of activists from the low-income neighborhoods and to argue that preservation of the park without any new building would be in their long-term
interests. Its actions, however, were tactical and its position ran counter to the
best interests of the area's local low-income population, representing then a
narrow first- and second-paradigm approach. The environmental movement
led a hard-nosed, top-down public campaign to prohibit all real-estate development in the park, choosing the long-term benefit of open space over the
immediate needs of the local population for developed park land and decent
affordable housing. The environmentalist response to this conflict is indicative of the still persistent rift between the environmental and the social justice
movements.

LEARNING TO WORK TOGETHER

The case studies of the Trans-Israel Highway, Open Space and the Bedouin
settlement in the Negev, and the Hiriya Metropolitan Park provide evidence
for the potential convergence between the social and environmental movements in Israel. In each case, the leadership and activists were drawn from
both environmental and social organizations and the campaign rhetoric included joint messages. The collaboration of diverse organizations and a synthesis of their messages can be seen as strengthening their advocacy positions
and expanding their influence, contributing toward their shared success.

However, a closer look at the case studies indicates that convenience has
been the primary driver for collaborative work, and not a convergence of
worldviews. Each campaign involved a conflict or potential trade-off between
the environmental agenda—primarily open-space protection—and the social agendas of a more equitable distribution of resources and improved standard of living for minority and low-income groups. This includes funding for
public transit, adequate settlement standards for Bedouin, affordable housing for low-income Jewish residents in the center of the country, equal rights
for Israeli-Arab citizens and resolution of the broader geopolitical struggle.
Most of these conflicts went unaddressed or ignored by the campaigns' leadership. Perhaps not surprisingly, these episodes were marked by the formation of ad hoc (and ephemeral) collaborations, creating often-amicable human
ties across the leadership, but failing to create an operational relationship that
continued beyond the given campaign.

Yet there are at least three new directions within the environmental
movement that support the move toward a real convergence. A first important voice is from the philanthropic funders, including Shatil and New Israel
Fund, which includes social equity and environmental sustainability within
its funding purview, and which has been a consistent advocate of framing
environmental issues in terms of justice and equity. Shatil's current funding

initiatives include empowering environmental leaders in Israel's geographic peripheries to confront local environmental problems. The Green Environmental Fund, a collaboration of funders, is also actively seeking methods to incorporate a more explicit social message into the agenda of the environmental movement.

The second significant new voice for convergence is in the political realm. Until 2008, the only explicitly environmental party in Israel was the Israel Green Party, which had a strikingly narrow, second-paradigm agenda. In 2008 the Green Movement was established by many of the most prominent people within the environmental movement and has been noteworthy in its attempts to integrate social, economic, and environmental issues into a single political vision. While the leadership were predominantly prominent environmental activists (including Green Course founding director Eran Ben Yemini, planner and open-space advocate Iris Han, and Professor Alon Tal, who had started and directed a number of Israeli environmental organizations), the ideologues behind the party's platform (Dr. Eilon Schwartz, cofounder of the Heschel Center, and Bar Ilan University professor Noah Efron) were strong advocates of a social-environmental platform that expanded well beyond the traditional issues typical of environmental politics. They integrated topics such as education, the status of women, privatization, and Arab-Jewish relations into the party platform. The participation of Israel-Palestine Center for Research and Information codirector Dr. Gershon Baskin strengthened the pro-peace component of the party's agenda.

Prior to the 2008 national elections, pragmatic considerations and converging ideological concerns led the party to merge with the liberal-religious party Meimad led by Rabbi Michael Melchior, whose primary issues were education, peace, and religious pluralism. The match between Meimad and the Green Movement further exemplifies the identity that this "third paradigm" environmental party was trying to establish for itself.

Although receiving close to 1 percent of the votes, the Green Movement failed to garner enough popular support in the 2008 elections to elect any members of Knesset (see Karassin in this volume), and its future direction remains unclear. Some of the members still see its best chances in a purely environmental party, and further debate continues around the left-right orientation of the party with regard to relations with the Palestinians and the occupied territories. Accordingly, whether the Green Movement will be a second- or third-paradigm environmental party remains, in 2010, an open question.

A third indication of a possible convergence is found in the coalition opposing new legislation for reforms in land-use policy and planning. In early 2009, the newly elected Netanyahu government drafted legislation that would fundamentally restructure the system of land ownership and management in Israel, in particular privatizing public lands. Some six months later, the government released proposals to streamline the planning process, including a significant reduction in public and civil society involvement.

Social and environmental organizations worked together closely to oppose first the land-reform law and then the planning reform law. Coordinated through Shatil and dominated by the environmental organizations, the coalition featured strong participation by social organizations including the Organization for Distributive Justice, the Movement for Quality in Government in Israel, Bimkom—Planners for Planning Rights, and the Association for Civil Rights in Israel (Chudy 2009). The names of the coalition are indicative of the significance accorded to the collaboration: the Social-Environmental Coalition against Land Privatization, and then the Coalition for Responsible Planning. Learning from their environmental colleagues, social justice groups aimed to insert a new agenda into the proposed amendment to the planning law. This agenda includes a call for a social impact assessment alongside environmental impact statements, an expanded role for social advisers similar to environmental advisers, representation for the Ministry of Social Affairs as well as the Ministry of Environmental Protection, and new participation in planning by social justice organizations alongside their environmental counterparts.

One additional indicator of a possible transition to a third-paradigm approach may be seen in the creation of new staff positions at SPNI, IUED and Shatil (the technical assistance arm of the New Israel Fund). These new positions are dedicated to assisting community-based groups to mobilize around issues of open-space protection and abating public-health hazards, alongside advocacy for more equitable distribution of resources and greater commitment to environmental issues among local elected leadership.

Although these trends are inchoate, there is compelling evidence of increasing patterns of collaboration between the social and environmental movements in Israel, although a true convergence is not strong enough to warrant announcing the transition to a new paradigm. This qualification is manifested in Israel's 2009 election results. Although The Green Movement Party ran as a political expression of Israel's progressive civil society, in fact it was dominated by environmentalists and did not succeed in attracting leading figures from Israel's social movements. Perhaps one of the most significant factors in the increased collaboration is the "overlap" among the leadership (fig. 17.1), as key figures study together in programs such as the Heschel Center's leadership program and Shatil workshops, joining together on campaigns and in committees.

For a true third-paradigm convergence to emerge, however, the organizations and their leadership will most likely need to engage directly with thorny conflicts across their agendas, including issues such as urban densities and building heights (high-rise buildings may allow for more "open space" but are typically more expensive than mid-rise buildings), job opportunities in polluting industries, and the distribution of water resources across different population groups. Further down the line, the organizations will need to address nuclear power and weapons capabilities, poverty, population growth, minority rights, and the impact of war and occupation—difficult issues anywhere, and perhaps particularly so in Israel.

NOTES

1. As of July 2010, some Jewish farm settlements whose legality were in question were retroactively sanctioned with the passing of the Negev Development Authority Law (Amendment #4, agricultural/tourism integrated projects, http://www.knesset. gov.il/committees/heb/material/data/kalkala2010-05-03-01.pdf), which gave legal support to existing and future farms and thus weakened the rule-of-law discourse. Nonetheless, it is reasonable to assume that this discourse will now be wrapped into the justice discourse as this law may likely work in favor Jewish residents over Bedouins (see, e.g., Tzfadia 2010). Not without irony, an unrecognized Bedouin village of al-Arakib in the northern Negev was destroyed during the same month as the passing of the Negev Development Authority Law.

2. For example in this case, the Regional Council for the Unrecognized Villages in the Negev, Bimkom—Planners for Planning Rights, and the Arab Center for Alternative Planning.

3. Tzippi Isserov, CEO of IUED. IUED website 2010, http://www.adamteva.org.il/ ?CategoryID=159&ArticleID=937.

REFERENCES

Alfasi, N. 2006. Planning Policy? Between Long-Term Planning and Zoning Amendments in the Israeli Planning System. *Environment and Planning A* 38: 553–68.

Alon-Mozes, T. 2011, "Ariel Sharon Park and the Emergence of Israel's Environmentalism." Paper delivered at SPSD2011, International Conference on Spatial Planning and Sustainable Development, Kanazawa, Japan.

Arad-Tzvi, H. 2010. "Park Ayalon: A 'Green' Campaign'?" Extended seminar paper following Planning with Community course, Technion City, Haifa, Technion–Israel Institute of Technology, October 4.

Assif, S. 1996. *Report on Park Ayalon—The Planning Background*. Jerusalem: Israel Lands Authority. In Hebrew.

Assif, S., and A. Shachar. 2005. TAMA 35—Ikarei H'Tokhnit (NOP 35—Plan Highlights). Jerusalem: National Council for Planning and Building, Israel Ministry of Interior—Planning Authority.

Ben-David, O. 1997. "Tiyul (Hike) 'As an Act of Consecration of Space.'" In *Grasping Land: Space and Place in Contemporary Israeli Discourse and Experience,* edited by E. Ben-Ari and Y. Bilu, 129–46. Albany: State University of New York Press.

Benstein, J. 2003. *Between Earth Day and Land Day: New Directions for Environmental Activism among Palestinians and Jews in Israel*. Tel Aviv: Abraham Joshua Heschel Center for Environmental Learning and Leadership.

Beyer, L. 1998. "Trashing the Holy Land." *Time,* September 7, 54.

Carter, N. 2007. *The Politics of the Environment*. 2nd ed. Cambridge: Cambridge University Press.

Chudy, O. 2009. "Coalitziat Irgunim neged Reformat HaKarkaot: Im Tushar rak Ashirim Yukhlu Lirkhosh Dirot B'Arim HaGdolot" [The Coalition of Organizations against Land Reform: If Approved, Only the Rich Will Be Able to Acquire Apartments in the Big Cities]. *Calcalist,* July 12. http://www.calcalist.co.il/rea_estate/article/0,7340,L-3324862,00.html. In Hebrew.

Conco, K., and G. D. Debelko. 1998. "Introduction." In *Green Planet Blues*, edited by K. Conca and G. D. Debelko, 3–15. Boulder: Westview Press.

de-Shalit, A. 1995. "From the Political to the Objective: The Dialectics of Zionism and the Environment." *Environmental Politics* 4: 70–87.

———. 2001. "Ten Commandments of How to Fail in an Environmental Campaign." *Environmental Politics* 10: 111–37.

de-Shalit, A., and M. Talias. 1994. "Green or Blue and White? Environmental Controversies in Israel." *Environmental Politics* 3: 273–94.

DESHE. 2010. SPNI's Open Landscape Institute—About Us. http://www.deshe.org.il/?CategoryID=289.

Egoz, S. 1996. "Israel's Citrus Grove Landscape—An Opportunity to Balance Urbanization with Cultural Values." *Landscape and Urban Planning* 36: 183–96.

Feitelson, E. 1999. "Social Norms, Rationales and Policies: Reframing Farmland Protection in Israel." *Journal of Rural Studies* 15: 431–46.

Fletcher, E. 1999. "Road Transport, Environment and Social Equity in Israel in the New Millenium." *World Transport Policy and Practice* 5: 8–17.

Garb, Y. 1999. *The Trans-Israel Highway: Do We Know Enough to Proceed?* Jerusalem: Floersheimer Institute for Policy Studies. In Hebrew.

———. 2004. "Constructing the Trans-Israel Highway's Inevitability." *Israel Studies* 9:180–217.

Global Greens. 2001. The Charter of the Global Greens. http://www.global.greens.org.au/charter.htm.

Han, I., Y. Sagi, R. Boral, and Y. Darom. 2003. "New Settlement, New Communities, and New Homesteads." Position paper. Tel Aviv: Society for the Protection of Nature. Department for Protection of Environment and Nature and the Deshe Institute for the Protection of Open Space, the Society for the Protection of Nature. In Hebrew.

Khamaisi, R. 2006. "Environmental Policies and Spatial Control: The Case of the Arab Localities Development in Israel." *Arab Studies Quarterly* 28: 33–54.

Lichtman, M. 2004. "Park Avalon—Makhir HaPakhad" [Park Ayalon—The Price of Fear]. *Globes,* November 28. http://www.globes.co.il/news/article.aspx?did=858412.

Maizlish, M. 2005. *The Struggle against the Trans Israel Highway: Documenting an Environmental Struggle*. Jerusalem: Jerusalem Institute for Israel Studies. In Hebrew.

Maranz, F. 1993. "Damage Control," *Jerusalem Report,* February 25.

Ministry of Environment. 1993. "Voice of America—End of a Struggle." *Israel Environment Bulletin* 16. Jerusalem: Ministry of Environment.

———. 2005. "Parks and Metropolitan Leisure Areas. Report One." Jerusalem: Ministry of Environment. In Hebrew.

Ministry of Interior. 1976. National Outline Plan (NOP) 3: Roads. Ministry of Interior: Planning Authority. Jerusalem: Ministry of Interior.

———. 2003. TAMAM 3/5 2003, Tel Aviv District Outline Plan, Park Ayalon.

Nordhaus, T., and M. Shellenberger. 2007. *Breakthrough: From the Death of Environmentalism to the Politics of Possibility.* New York: Houghton Mifflin Harcourt.

Orenstein, D. 2007. "When an 'Ecological' Community Is Not." *Haaretz,* March 25. http://www.haaretz.com/print-edition/opinion/when-an-ecological-community -is-not-1.216603.

Orenstein, D. E., and S. D. Hamburg. 2009. "To Populate or Preserve? Evolving Political-Demographic and Environmental Paradigms in Israeli Land-Use Policy." *Land Use Policy* 26: 984–1000.

Plessner, U., D. Guggenheim, and M. Kaplan. 1997. *Park Ayalon Reports 1 and 2, Planning Alternatives and Analyses.* Tel Aviv: Israel Ministry of Environment. In Hebrew.

Rinat, Z. 2004. "Zorim Heskemim, Kotzrim Nadlan" [Sowing Agreements, Reaping Real Estate]. *Haartetz,* September 19. http://www.haaretz.co.il/misc/a.000024.

Ronen-Rotem, O. 2011. "The Influence of International Philanthropic Foundations on Urban Environmental Policy in Jerusalem and Tel Aviv." PhD thesis (partial fulfillment), Tel Aviv University.

Schwartz, E. 2009. "Paradigmot Mishtanot B'Tfisa Svivatit" [Shifting Paradigms of Environmental Approaches]. http://heschel.org.il/text_files/paradigms_heb.html.

Shellenberger, M., and T. Nordhaus. 2005. *The Death of Environmentalism.* Environmental Grantmakers Association.

Tal, A. 2002. *Pollution in a Promised Land.* Berkeley: University of California Press.

———. 2006. *Speaking of Earth: Environmental Speeches that Moved the World.* New Brunswick: Rutgers University Press.

———. 2008. "Space Matters: Historic Drivers and Turning Points in Israel's Open Space Protection Policy." *Israel Studies* 13: 119–51.

Tzfadia, E. 2010. "HaHevdel ben Khavat Bodedim L'Kfar Lo Mukar" [The Difference between Homesteads and the Unrecognized Village]. *YNet,* July 18. http://www. ynet.co.il/articles/0,7340,L-3920404,00.html. In Hebrew.

Yahel, H. 2006. "Land Disputes between the Negev Bedouin and Israel." *Israel Studies* 11: 1–22.

Yehudkin, C. 2007. "HaKfarim HaLo Mukarim BaNegev: HaKara V'Shivyon Zkhuyot" [The Unrecognized Villages in the Negev: Recognition and Equal Rights]. Jerusalem: Bimkom–Planners for Planning Rights. In Hebrew.

Yiftachel, O., and A. Meir, eds. 1998. *Ethnic Frontiers and Peripheries: Landscapes of Development and Inequality in Israel.* Boulder: Westview Press.

Yonah, Y., and I. Saporta. 2002. "The Politics of Lands and Housing in Israel: A Wayward Republican Discourse." *Social Identities* 8: 91–117.

EPILOGUE

Daniel E. Orenstein, Alon Tal, and Char Miller

Two contrasting symbols are offered in the title of this edited volume, which was conceived only after we finished reading all of the chapters: ruin and restoration. Taken as a whole, the book indeed displays a somewhat split personality, with several chapters painting a rather optimistic picture of Israel's environmental state and others describing quite the opposite. Note, for example, the development of an environmental bureaucracy that has continued to evolve and improve in its ability to implement effective environmental management and policy, details of which emerge in Tal's chapter on desertification, in Brachya's on government planning, and Kerret's on the marine environment. A particularly compelling instance of this, Kerret observes, is revealed in the improving quality of Israel's coastline environment; this progress is a result of sophisticated and persistent government intervention. Adams, meanwhile, argues convincingly that Israel has produced a cadre of skilled professionals who, through their work in international organizations, manage some of the world's most complicated environmental challenges. No doubt, navigating the intricacies of Israeli environmental reality has prepared these professionals for the challenges of the global environmental agenda.

Yet if measured in terms of carbon emissions (Michaels and Alpert), biodiversity (Yom-Tov), and open space (Han), environmental quality in Israel continues to be degraded, and will continue to be so as long as politics and policies do not confront underlying causal factors, including intense economic development, unchecked population growth (Orenstein), militarized terrain (Gordon), inequalities in Arab-Jewish relations within Israel (Tarabeih), and the tangled relationship between Israel and its neighbors (Schoenfeld).

Environmental quality—whether measured in soil erosion, air quality, public access to beaches, or species diversity—is a function not of isolated problems, but of broader economic, demographic, political, and social processes. Karassin is explicit regarding what is needed to improve the stature of environmental issues in Israel: "future developments in Israeli environmental party politics will greatly depend on a whether there is a solution to the geopolitical conflicts that have characterized the region for over a century." Gordon concurs: "Perhaps it is only with a final-status agreement with the Palestinians and the resolution of the Israeli-Arab conflict as a whole that we may hope for a true normalization of Israeli society; only then might environmental concerns finally receive the paramount place they deserve in Israeli public attention and policymaking." By extension, Orenstein and Sliverman argue, the emergence of a "third paradigm" within environmentalist thought means that peace (like social and economic justice) must be considered a prerequisite for environmental sustainability, as suggested by the Heschel Center (Schwartz 2009) or in the objectives of regional environmental organizations (Schoenfeld).

What this book's historical analyses suggests is that Israel's contemporary environmental movement may not yet be ready to grapple with the pressing questions of war, occupation, poverty, and equitable distribution of resources, despite the realization that these unaddressed drivers underlie much environmental degradation. These searching analyses of Israel's environmental history help us understand, too, that the need for a more robust and inclusive approach to environmental pressures and problems may be the key to the society's capacity to sustain itself across time. Whether Israeli politics and polity can adopt this more holistic perspective remains an open, and urgent, question, and one which may ultimately determine whether the road will lead to ruin or restoration.

REFERENCE

Schwartz, Eilon. 2002. "Appendix I: Three Paradigms of Environmental Education." In *Paths to Sustainability, Shadow Report to the Government of Israel's Assessment of Progress in Implementing Agenda 21.* Paper presented at the World Summit for Sustainable Development, Johannesburg. Tel Aviv: Heschel Center for Environmental Learning and Leadership, 38.

CONTRIBUTORS

Rachelle Adam worked for many years as deputy legal adviser in Israel's Ministry of the Environment, where she was involved in Israel's ratification and implementation of international environmental agreements. Today she is a doctoral candidate at Hebrew University's Law Faculty, researching international biodiversity agreements. She also helps run an NGO dedicated to saving Jerusalem's forestland.

Pinhas Alpert is head of the Porter School of Environmental Studies, professor in dynamic meteorology and climate, Faculty of Exact Sciences, Tel Aviv University, and coauthor of *Factor Separation in the Atmosphere, Applications and Future Prospects*. His research focuses on atmospheric dynamics, climatology, numerical methods, limited area modeling, and climate change.

Valerie Brachya is director of the Environmental Policy Center at the Jerusalem Institute for Israel Studies. She retired from her previous position as senior deputy director general for Policy and Planning in the Ministry of Environmental Protection, where she had been responsible for five departments: environmental planning, environmental economics, landscape and biodiversity, international relations, and environmental policy. During thirty-five years in government service, Ms. Brachya was a founding member of the environmental protection service and a central figure in establishing environment as an integral part of decision making in Israel.

Uri Gordon, PhD in philosophy, Oxford, is a lecturer in environmental politics and ethics at the Arava Institute for Environmental Studies. His research interests include environmental peacemaking, grassroots sustainability, and anarchist political theory.

Iris Han is head of the Research and Planning Department in the Open Landscape Institute (OLI). She has been a member, since 2000, of the National Council for Planning and Building as a public representative for environmental nongovernmental organizations. She holds a master of science degree in urban and regional planning, law studies (LLB).

Orr Karassin is a lecturer and head of the Environmental Law and Policy Program at the Sapir College School of Law. She was a visiting researcher at the London School of Economics Grantham Research Institute on Climate Change and the Environment. Her research interests include environmental law and policy, climate change regulation, private law and environmental liability, natural disaster law, and vulnerability and institutional responses.

Ruth Kark is professor of geography at the Hebrew University of Jerusalem. She has written and edited twenty books and 150 articles on the history and historical geography of Palestine and Israel. Her research interests include the study of land-use patterns in the Middle East and Palestine and Israel in the nineteenth and twentieth centuries; urban and rural settlement processes; and Western nations' and civilizations' ideologies, interests, and activities in the Holy Land.

Dorit Kerret is an assistant professor in the Department of Public Policy, Tel Aviv University. Her research in marine pollution started when she served in JAG as a legal adviser of the Israeli Navy. Her main research interests involve international and comparative aspects of environmental policy, focusing on promoting environmental enforcement and compliance in Israel.

Noam Levin is a senior lecturer at the Hebrew University of Jerusalem. He uses remote sensing and geographic information systems to study terrestrial ecosystems and the interactions between people and their environment.

Lucy Michaels is a British-Israeli environmental activist and researcher. She is currently studying for a doctorate in environmental studies at the Blaustein Institutes for Desert Research, Ben-Gurion University, Israel. She lives in Midreshet Ben Gurion with her husband, Uri Gordon, and daughter.

Char Miller is W. M. Keck Professor of Environmental Analysis at Pomona College (U.S.), has served as associate editor of the *Journal of Forestry and Environmental History*, and is author of *Gifford Pinchot and the Making of Modern Environmentalism* and *Public Lands/Public Debates: A Century of Controversy*. He is editor most recently of *Cities and Nature in the American West* and *River Basins of the American West*.

Daniel E. Orenstein is a senior lecturer in the Faculty of Architecture and Town Planning at the Technion–Israel Institute of Technology. His research focuses on population growth and land-use change, land-use policy, ecosystem service assessment, and population-environment discourse.

Stuart Schoenfeld is associate professor and chair of the Department of Sociology, Glendon College–York University (Toronto). He works on the sociologies of environment and religion, with a continuing interest in transnational networks in both areas and the potential for the emergence of cosmopolitan identities and empathy. His current major research is in the area of environmentalism in the Middle East, using social-constructionist and social-movement perspectives on the development of transnational Middle East environmentalism.

David Schorr is a senior lecturer in the Faculty of Law at Tel Aviv University, where he teaches environmental law and legal history. He is also co-leader of a group working on environmental history at the Van Leer Jerusalem Institute.

No'am G. Seligman was head of the range management section of the soil conservation unit of the Israel Ministry of Agriculture and subsequently head of the Natural Resources Department of the Agricultural Research Organization and taught pastoral systems at the Agricultural Faculty of the Hebrew University in Rehovot.

Hillel Shuval is Lunenfeld-Kunen Emeritus Professor of Environmental Science at the Hebrew University of Jerusalem and head of the Department of Environmental Health Sciences, the Hadassah Academic College-Jerusalem. In 2008 he was presented with the Award for Lifetime Service in Promoting the Environment of Israel and was awarded an honorary doctor of science degree from the University of Michigan for his contributions to environmental science research and for his efforts in furthering peace in the Middle East.

Emily Silverman heads the Community Planning Network at Hebrew University, and the focus of her work is on housing, the social aspects of planning, and urban regeneration. She holds a PhD from the London School of Economics in social policy, an MA from Tel Aviv University in public policy, and a BA from Swarthmore College in sociology.

Alon Tal is an associate professor in the Department of Desert Ecology in the Blaustein Institutes for Desert Studies at Ben-Gurion University. His research focuses on environmental policy and management. Professor Tal has founded and directed several Israeli environmental organizations and presently is chairman of the Green Movement, Israel's Green Party.

Hussein Tarabeih is executive director and cofounder of Towns Association for Environmental Quality (TAEQ) in his native town of Sakhnin. His PhD from the University of Haifa was in the field of environmental conflict resolution in divided societies. He is also adjunct professor with the Institute for Conflict Analysis and Resolution, George Mason University. He has published numerous articles on environmental issues, coexistence, managing environmental conflicts, and the urbanization of Israel's Arab sector.

Yoram Yom-Tov is emeritus professor of zoology at Tel Aviv University, where he worked for more than four decades. He is interested in zoogeography, behavioral ecology of birds and mammals, and bird migration and in factors that determine geographical and temporal changes in body size.

INDEX

Note: Page numbers in italic type indicate illustrations.